ENGLISH LEGAL SYSTEM AND CONSTITUTIONAL LAW

CW01646242

The
University of
Law

ENGLISH LEGAL SYSTEM AND CONSTITUTIONAL LAW
THIRD EDITION

Trevor Tayleur

The University of Law
2 Bunhill Row
London EC1Y 8HQ

© The University of Law 2025

All rights reserved. No part of this publication may be reproduced, stored in a retrieval system, or transmitted, in any form or by any means, without the prior written permission of the copyright holder, application for which should be addressed to the publisher.

Contains public sector information licensed under the Open Government Licence v3.0

British Library Cataloguing in Publication Data

A catalogue record for this book is available from the British Library

ISBN 978 1 80502 211 4

Preface

This book is part of the 'Foundations of Law' series of textbooks, designed to support postgraduates in their study of the core subjects of English law.

It is anticipated that the reader can then move on to studies for their professional examinations (eg the SQE and BSB assessments) comfortable that they have an understanding of foundational legal principles.

Each textbook aims to provide the reader with a solid knowledge and understanding of fundamental legal principles and rules. The series aims to give the reader the opportunity to identify and explore areas of critical interest whilst also identifying practice-based context.

For those readers who are students at The University of Law, the textbooks are used alongside other learning resources to best prepare students to meet outcomes of the Postgraduate Diploma in Law and related programmes.

We wish you every success as you learn about English Law and in your future career.

The legal principles and rules contained within this textbook are stated as at 1 May 2025.

Contents

Table of Cases

Table of Legislation

Primary Legislation

Statutes

R

S

T

EU

International

Secondary Legislation

SIs

1 The English Legal System

Learning outcomes

By the end of this chapter, you should be able to:

- identify and discuss critically some of the ethical issues involved in formulating and enforcing legal rules;
- explain the key features of the historical background of the English legal system;
- distinguish between public and private laws, and criminal and civil laws;
- demonstrate an understanding of the sources of law – case law, legislation, EU law, retained EU law/assimilated law and the European Convention on Human Rights.

1.1 Introduction

The legal system in England and Wales goes back over 1,000 years, and in this chapter you will discover the key features of our rich and colourful legal history. You may be wondering what relevance this has to the present day. However, some aspects of our legal system have remained unchanged for hundreds of years. The position of Lord Chancellor is an ancient judicial role which remains in existence today, and some judgments are still enforced by writs, which have a long, although at times rather less than distinguished, career. More importantly, it is impossible to have a true understanding of our legal system without knowing something of its background.

Although strands of our history remain visible today, the legal system is constantly evolving to take account of the ever-increasing demands of our society. There have been fundamental and far-reaching changes both in the substance of the laws themselves and in the nature of our constitution. Attitudes change and the legal system must reflect this if it is to remain credible. In this chapter, you will develop an appreciation of the difficulty of distinguishing between law and morality, and the impact of moral and social issues upon the laws which bind us. You will identify and critically discuss some of the ethical issues involved in formulating and enforcing legal rules. You may already be aware of some of these, due to the controversy surrounding assisted dying and the question of whether life should mean life for murderers, as these are highlighted by the media. You will be required to keep abreast of these and to ensure that you can distinguish between public and private laws and criminal and civil laws.

1.2 The meaning of 'law'

One starting point for a course on law is to ask the question: 'What is law?' In fact, law is difficult to define because there are so many different types of law. In addition, the law constantly develops to take account of changes in our society. A law which would have been acceptable 200 years ago, for example capital punishment for the offence of stealing a sheep, would be totally unacceptable now. The impact of changing attitudes is particularly evident in the law relating to sexual offences. It may surprise many of you to learn that homosexual behaviour was a criminal offence until 1967, and indeed the age of consent for homosexuals was equalised with that for heterosexuals only in 2003.

The law must also set out a standard of acceptable behaviour, a benchmark against which people are judged. This standard must reflect the views of the majority of the population to ensure it can be enforced. As a result, the law incorporates moral issues as well. Accordingly, to answer the question 'What is law?', we will need to distinguish between the different types of legal rules and purely moral rules.

In the paragraph below, we will consider what makes legal rules.

1.3 Legal rules and social rules

Law is a system of rules. The way we go about our day-to-day life, for example our activities at home, at work, in shops, on the road and aspects of our personal relationships, can all be governed by these legal rules. However, these are not the only rules which govern our lives. There are also social conventions which influence our social conduct.

The different mechanisms used to enforce legal and social rules reflect different social values regarding the behaviour in question. If you steal something, you would expect to be punished under the criminal law. However, you would be surprised to see someone in court if, for instance, they walked in front of you when you were queuing at the Post Office. You would no doubt be annoyed about this happening, but you would probably realise that queuing is not so important to our society that it needs protecting by a legal rule. Of course, if you were to fight someone in the queue to get ahead, then you would expect punishment.

1.4 Law and morality

Underpinning our law are principles of morality. The fact that both rape and murder are criminal offences reflects the understanding that society as a whole considers these activities abhorrent and wishes to punish those who undertake them.

One difficulty with having a legal system entirely based on morality is that this would pose the question as to whose moral standards should be adopted. Indeed, the more diverse and developed our society becomes, the less likely it is that citizens will share an identical moral code. For example, whilst murder and rape are universally condemned, there are other, more controversial areas where there is not such a clear consensus within our society as to whether an act is immoral or not. One such area is euthanasia.

It is currently against the law to help someone to commit suicide, which arguably reflects the supreme moral value that society places on the preservation of life. However, there are many, possibly including you, who believe that this is wrong that it should be left to the individual to decide whether they wish to live or not.

Other areas where there is a moral debate concerning the law include whether the death penalty should be reintroduced for certain types of offence, whether prostitution should be fully legalised, and whether cannabis should have been reinstated as a Class B drug.

There is clearly a divergence between law and morality, and there are some matters which you might well consider immoral but which are not illegal.

The following activity is designed to help you to think about these areas.

Activity 1 Immoral versus illegal

Give at least two examples of behaviour which is considered immoral but not illegal, and behaviour which is illegal but not considered immoral.

Comment

There is potentially a large number of answers which you may have considered, but to choose just a few areas, neither adultery nor making use of legal loopholes to pay less tax are illegal, although many people would consider both to be immoral. Conversely, as discussed above, the use of soft drugs (including cannabis) and soliciting for prostitution are illegal, although many people would consider them not to be immoral. Similarly, driving at a speed just above the legal limit.

As we have seen from the above, why some rules are given the force of law, and others are not, is a difficult question. Law is certainly not the same everywhere; it will reflect different values in different cultures and at different times.

Whichever laws a particular society adopts, every society in every age has found it essential to work out a set of rules to which its members must conform. If we did not have this set of rules there would be no society at all. In every society, individuals have both rights and obligations. By restricting the freedom of each individual, the law protects everyone else from that person's recklessness, violence or dishonesty. The law takes away some of our personal freedoms, but in return it should give us protection.

1.5 Different types of legal rules

Now that we have looked briefly at the difference between legal rules and social rules and law and morality, let us see if we can identify some of the different types of legal rules. One method of classification is between private and public law. Private law is concerned with the private relationship between individuals (including companies) and it is enforced by individuals taking actions against one another in the courts. A claim by a customer against a manufacturer under a guarantee is an example of a private law matter. Public law on the other hand is concerned with both relationships between individuals and the State, and with the State enforcing certain standards of behaviour. A criminal prosecution is an example of public law, as is a local authority issuing a 'stop' notice in respect of a home extension for which planning permission was not obtained.

Another division in addition to public/private, and one which we will study in more detail below, is between civil and criminal law. Laws that concern the relationship between an individual and the rest of the community as a whole are classified as criminal law; laws that concern the relationship between individuals in that community and do not involve or concern the community as a whole are classified as civil law.

1.5.1 Civil and criminal law

It is unlikely that you had any difficulty in distinguishing between legal rules and social rules (ie understanding what a law is). What you may find more difficult is to distinguish between the two types of law – criminal law and civil law. This is perhaps unsurprising given the degree of overlap between the two jurisdictions which exists in a modern society. There is a tendency to believe that most laws are criminal in scope, probably because much media coverage of law concerns the criminal law. However, the majority of laws are actually civil laws and concern the relationship between individuals in the community. Civil laws do not involve the community as a whole.

The following examples help to illustrate the distinction between criminal and civil law:

Example 1

Kevin is driving a car carelessly and knocks Beth over, breaking Beth's leg. This event is governed by both criminal and civil law, as Kevin is liable in both. Beth has been injured and so she can claim compensation for her broken leg, ie damages from Kevin, the driver (civil law – in particular the area of law known as the law of tort). However, you might be trying to cross the road in the future when the same driver comes along and knocks you down. Society as a whole has an interest in making sure that this driver either drives properly or keeps off the roads. This is why our society, represented by the criminal law system, will probably punish the driver by fining him for the inconsiderate, careless or even dangerous way in which he drove (criminal law).

Example 2

Sachin is in the habit of having noisy parties at his house at which loud music is often played late at night, much to the annoyance of his neighbours. Playing excessively loud music at night is not in itself a criminal offence. This does not mean, however, that Sachin's behaviour has no legal consequences. If the noise is sufficiently loud, Sachin's neighbours can bring a private nuisance claim against him in a civil court, asking the court to grant an injunction (a type of court order) telling Sachin to stop playing excessively loud music and to award them damages. The area of civil law involved is known as the law of tort.

Alternatively, the loud noise may constitute a 'statutory nuisance' under the Environmental Protection Act 1990. Sachin's neighbours could complain to the local council which will investigate the matter. If the noise is sufficiently loud to be a statutory nuisance, the council must serve an abatement notice, requiring Sachin to stop or restrict the noise. If Sachin ignores the notice, he will be committing a criminal offence and so could face a criminal prosecution.

Example 3

Toby orders a new toaster online, but when it arrives it does not work.

This is a matter of civil law, in particular the law of contract. Under the Consumer Rights Act 2015, the goods that the seller provides must be of satisfactory quality. If they are not, the seller is in breach of contract, so Toby is entitled to reject the toaster and receive a refund of the price paid, including postage costs

1.5.2 Differences between civil and criminal law

Civil law involves agreements and mainly private resolutions. Criminal law involves punishment. Here is a brief and somewhat global list of the differences between the two areas.

- Civil law deals with contracts, disputes and differences where the outcome is measured in remedies or the payment of monies. In the event of the courts having to make a decision on the facts, a matter must be proved on the balance of probabilities.
- Criminal law imposes restrictions and obligations on the population, where the outcome is measured in punishment for transgressions, with the public taking an interest in both the offence and the punishment. The ultimate penalty is the loss of one's freedom through imprisonment. Criminal matters must be proved beyond reasonable doubt, and the 'golden thread' of justice as stated in the case of *Woolmington v DPP* [1935] AC 462 is that the accused is innocent until proven guilty.

1.5.3 Differences between civil and criminal proceedings

The procedures for deciding cases depend very significantly on whether the matter is a civil one or a criminal one. Different courts hear the two types of cases, and the nature of the proceedings also differs.

A criminal case is called a prosecution. It will normally be started by the State in the form of the police arresting and charging someone. The victim cannot prevent a prosecution nor order its discontinuance. However, in practice, the police rarely commence prosecutions where the victim is reluctant to proceed. If the police do start a prosecution, it is then continued or discontinued by the Crown Prosecution Service (lawyers who are civil servants independent of the police).

In order to secure a conviction in a criminal prosecution, the prosecution must prove its case beyond reasonable doubt. The prosecution will do this by providing evidence of each of the necessary elements of the offence. If the prosecution fails to do this, then the defendant must be acquitted.

The objective of a prosecution is primarily to punish; a defendant who is found guilty will be sentenced to (for example) imprisonment, a fine or a community sentence (eg a community order with a requirement to do unpaid work). In our car accident example, the driver, Kevin, may have to pay a fine and incur penalty points on his licence (which may lead to him being banned from driving). Punishment gives no direct benefit to the victim of the crime; Beth will not receive the fine payable.

Civil proceedings are referred to as actions or claims, not prosecutions. They are commenced by the person who has suffered damage, but could also involve disputes about wills or family matters. In order to succeed in a civil claim, a party must prove their case on the balance of probabilities only, and not beyond reasonable doubt. The objective of suing the driver is that Beth, the claimant, is seeking compensation for the losses she has suffered. If damages are awarded to Beth as a result of the successful civil claim, they are payable to her and are generally assessed on the basis that they should compensate her and not punish the defendant (the driver).

Note that prior to the Civil Procedure Rules 1998 the 'claimant' was called the 'plaintiff', and you may come across this term in some cases.

1.6 Sources of law

At the beginning of this chapter, we discussed the difficulties in answering the question: 'What is law?' because there are different types of law. Thus far, we have made the distinction between criminal and civil law.

However, another way of answering the same question is by identifying the sources of the law. The law of England and Wales has evolved very gradually over many centuries, in a number of different ways. These methods of developing law are usually referred to as sources. Historically, local customs and judges' decisions had most influence, but since the eighteenth century, Parliament has taken over this role. After 1973, European Union (EU) law became increasingly important as yet another source of law, whilst as a result of the Human Rights Act 1998 the European Convention on Human Rights (Convention for the Protection of Human Rights and Fundamental Freedoms, Rome, 4 November 1950) has become enforceable in UK courts. The UK's exit from the EU is clearly another evolution in the character of law in England and Wales.

To understand how and from where our laws have developed, it is useful to have an insight into the history of the English legal system. Note that when we refer to 'English' case law, we actually mean the law of England and Wales, although rather unfairly no reference is usually made to Wales. Scotland and Northern Ireland have their own separate legal systems.

1.7 The history of the English legal system

This section is intended to give you an overview of the historical background to the modern English legal system. The law as we know it today is the product of 1,000 years of history, and some knowledge of this will assist you in your understanding of the current system.

1.7.1 Customs

Although some legislation can be traced back as far as AD600, before the Norman Conquest there was no single system of law common to the whole country. At that time, England was a tribal country, and instead each region had different customs, which were administered by local courts.

After William the Conqueror invaded England in 1066, he realised that it would be easier to control the country if he also controlled the legal system. He imposed his authority by travelling around the country accompanied by his court, listening to and then ruling upon his subjects' grievances. The King would literally sit on a bench to hear these cases. This is why the most important court became known as the Court of King's Bench, the name which is still used today, although during Queen Elizabeth II's reign it was known as the Queen's Bench.

1.7.2 Common or case law

1.7.2.1 The development of the common law

Not all monarchs were interested in hearing cases personally and so, in the years following the Norman invasion, this role was gradually delegated to commissioners, who were known as 'itinerants' as they travelled around the country. Each county would be visited three or four times a year and the justices (as they became known) could hold 'Assizes', or 'sittings', of the royal courts. The justices would hear and decide serious crimes in the Assize Court of the county town, whilst the local sheriff (and later justices of the peace) would deal with less serious offences. During the reign of Henry II (1154–1189), this system became more formal and the tours became more regular as Henry divided up the country into 'circuits' or areas for the judges to visit. For hundreds of years, the laws were enforced by this system of circuit judges from the King's Bench, and the Assizes were not actually abolished until 1971.

However, Henry may have regretted his significant contributions to the development of the English legal system after he was accused of ordering the death of his Archbishop of Canterbury, Thomas Becket. The murder of Becket in Canterbury Cathedral by four of Henry's knights made the King very unpopular and, to avoid a rebellion, Henry accepted the punishment of a public whipping, thus demonstrating that even Kings are not above the law!

Initially, when the judges travelled the country, they would use local customs to decide cases. However, over time, as the judges returned to Westminster and discussed the cases they had considered, they began to use the best customary rulings. These were applied universally, thus leading to the development of a law 'common' to the whole country. As time went by, the King's courts achieved ascendancy over local courts.

Originally, there was no separation of the powers of the State in the way with which we are familiar today. The King exercised judicial as well as executive and legislative powers. However, as the amount of judicial business increased, the common law courts became separated from the other machinery of central government.

Over time, the common law gradually emerged as a system because of the doctrine of *stare decisis* (or standing by previous decisions). When a judge decided a new problem in a case before them, that decision would be followed in subsequent cases by judges as a legal rule. In time, judicial precedent became binding on the courts rather than simply helpful guidance. You will study the doctrine of judicial precedent in greater detail in **Chapter 4**.

1.7.2.2 Problems with the common law

In order to bring an action in the King's courts, a person had to buy a writ from the Chancellor's office. The writ was a sealed letter which was issued in the name of the King and which ordered an individual, such as the sheriff, the lord of the manor, or the defendant, to do something. The basic principle was that a common law right existed only if there was a procedure for enforcing it. An action could be started in the courts only if there was already an appropriate writ in existence which covered the facts of the case. An early example of 'bureaucracy gone mad': no writ, no right!

This meant that although various writs developed over six centuries, the growth in the number of writs, and therefore in the cases which could be brought at common law, was slow. By the thirteenth century there were about 50 existing writs, but many of these were minor factual variations of the basic ones. There was an attempt to mitigate the problems caused by such restrictions, with the passing of the Statute of Westminster in 1285, but this was of limited effect.

Even if a writ was available which met the facts of the case, so that an action could be brought before the courts, the procedure was too inflexible and formal. The plaintiff (today called the 'claimant') who brought the action could plead only one cause of action, and even a trivial error in a writ would lead to the collapse of a case and the plaintiff would have to start all over again (with all the consequent expense and delay).

A further problem with the common law lay in the remedies a successful plaintiff could be awarded. Apart from actions for the recovery of land, the remedy granted to a plaintiff for a civil wrong was damages or payment of a sum of money. The payment of money in this way was not always an adequate remedy; for example, it did not compel someone to cease wrongful actions or fulfil obligations.

In addition, the common law was also limited, because it recognised only certain rights. For instance, it did not recognise the concept of a trust. There were particular problems with mortgages: under the common law, once the date for repayment of a loan had passed, the land became the property of the lender and the borrower was unable to get the land back, even if the borrower could repay the outstanding loan. It was not unknown for lenders to be deliberately absent, so that the money could not be tendered in time for it to be counted by sunset on the repayment day. This meant that the borrower lost the land.

1.7.3 Equity

1.7.3.1 The development of equity

By the fourteenth century, the common law had lost much of its flexibility as the judges felt that they had to apply the law in the way their predecessors had done. Quite apart from abuses of the common law, expense and delay, the law itself was narrow, rigid and dogged by technicalities. There was a growing number of dissatisfied litigants, and the practice grew of petitioning the King direct to ask him to exercise his royal prerogative as the 'fountain of justice'. At first, the King heard the petitions; later, this function was delegated to the Lord Chancellor, the King's principal minister, who became known as the 'Keeper of the King's Conscience'. By 1474, the Chancellor was issuing decrees in his own name and the Court of Chancery was created, separate from the King and the common law courts. The Court of Chancery developed the body of law we know as equity.

Proceedings in the Court of Chancery were started by a petition or bill filed by the plaintiff. There did not have to be a writ and, at first, cases were adjudicated simply on what the Chancellor considered was fair. It was not that equity in the sense of natural justice was totally absent from the common law system, but rigid rules of procedure often prevented justice being done. The Chancellor could develop new rights and remedies as individual cases demanded and justice could be quick and (relatively) cheap. The Chancellor was not bound by the rigid procedures of the common law, but, for instance, could inquire into the facts of a case, or order documents to be produced to enforce legal rights.

Gradually, principles of equity emerged, and eventually equity was to become a separate branch of the law with its own rules and procedure, rather than simply being the application of natural justice to a case.

1.7.3.2 Equitable principles

Initially, there were few guidelines for the Chancellors to use but, as time passed, the judges developed a set of equitable principles or maxims. These were applied by the Court of Chancery and are still relevant today. Set out below are some examples:

(a) Equity looks on that as done which ought to be done: in other words, equity will enforce the intention of the parties, rather than allowing something to founder because of a failure to conform to rigid procedure.

(b) He who comes to equity must come with clean hands: accordingly, an equitable remedy will not be granted to a claimant who has not acted fairly.

(c) Delay defeats equity: as a consequence, a claimant cannot wait too long before making a claim as this may prejudice the other party.

(d) Equity will not suffer a wrong to be without a remedy: this is addressed further at **1.7.3.4**.

1.7.3.3 Equitable rights

Equity came to recognise new rights which were unknown to the common law. For example, the law of trusts originated in the thirteenth century, in the arrangements made by the crusaders for their land whilst they were away at the crusades. A custom developed whereby such landowners would transfer their property to a trusted friend, on the understanding it would be used for the crusader's family, if he did not return. However, because the family did not have a legal interest in the property, the common law courts would not remedy any abuses by the transferee. The Court of Equity intervened to remedy this wrong.

The trust is still relevant today for individuals in ordering their private lives, for instance in taxation matters, in the shared ownership of property or in making provision for dependants. It is also important in matters of corporate or public interest, such as pension funds and charities.

1.7.3.4 Equitable remedies

As the King, and then the Chancellor, was petitioned for justice, new remedies were developed which still exist. An equitable remedy is in the discretion of the court, and this is why the equitable principles referred to at **1.7.3.2** are used. By contrast, a common law remedy is a matter of right: if a claimant proves their case at common law, they are entitled to damages. Two of the equitable remedies which are still important today are:

(a) an injunction, which is an order of the court compelling a person to perform an action or to refrain from an action, for example to demolish a building which has been erected in breach of a promise not to build on land; and

(b) a decree of specific performance, which is an order compelling someone to perform their obligations under a contract or trust.

1.8 Conflict between common law and equity

As equity began to develop into a system of rules, conflicts arose between it and the common law. In some instances, equity did not merely supplement the common law but directly challenged it. In 1615, these disputes came to a head. In the *Earl of Oxford's Case* (1615) 21 ER 485, James I decided that, in cases of conflict, equity should prevail over common law.

1.8.1 The need for reform

Equity was not without its disadvantages. These became apparent as equity hardened into a system of law with rules which became as inflexible as those of the common law. By the nineteenth century, there was an urgent need for reform of the whole legal system. There were too many courts with overlapping jurisdictions, it was expensive and slow to obtain justice and there was an inadequate appeals system.

1.8.2 The fusion of the administration of law and equity

The Supreme Court of Judicature Acts of 1873 and 1875 created a single court structure and merged the separate court systems of equity and the common law. For the first time, court procedure as a whole became regulated by the rules of the Supreme Court rather than being left to individual courts.

As a consequence, all the civil courts can now grant both common law and equitable remedies in the same proceedings. For example, an injunction to stop continuing unlawful behaviour can be ordered in addition to damages for losses accrued to date.

1.8.3 Common law today

We have considered the development of English law and the different meanings which have been attributed to the phrase 'common law'. These are summarised in **Figure 1.1** below. The only distinction which you have not yet covered is in relation to civil law, which is discussed in more detail at **4.13**. However, it has been included here for completeness.

Figure 1.1 The meaning of the common law today

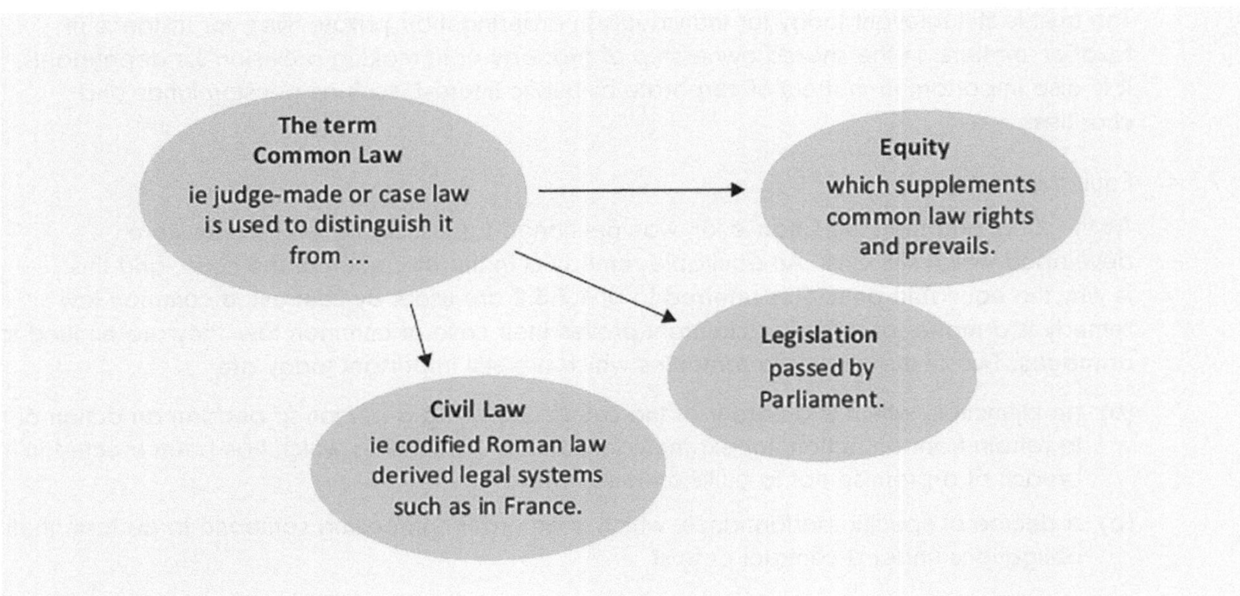

The meaning which has most relevance today is that which distinguishes the law made by judges (case law) from that passed by Parliament. Case law is one of the main sources of English law today, in addition to legislation.

When we refer to case law, what we mean are the decisions in actual cases which have been considered by the courts. These cases are summarised by specialist journalists called court reporters in journals known as law reports.

In **Chapter 3**, you will learn that law reports are available both as bound volumes and online.

1.9 Case law

The traditional view was that the role of the judge was not to make law, but merely to decide what the law was and to apply it to the case in hand. This is known as the declaratory theory of law, namely that judges do not make or create the law; they merely declare what the law is and what it has always been. In other words, law should not originate from judges, but from

Parliament. Despite this, case law remains a major source of law because much of modern English law has never been put into statutory form, and is still to be found in cases, some of which were decided centuries ago. In addition, although legislation does not originate from judges, it has to be interpreted by the courts, and the interpretation they put upon it becomes part of the law (see **Chapter 3** on Statutory Interpretation).

In more recent times, it has become accepted that judges, particularly in the Court of Appeal and the Supreme Court, do make new law. Indeed, Lord Browne-Wilkinson in *Kleinwort Benson Ltd v Lincoln City Council* [1999] 2 AC 349 made this explicit when he stated that: 'The whole of the common law is judge made and only by judicial change in the law is common law kept relevant in a changing world.' This approach was demonstrated by the case of *Re A (Children)* [2001] Fam 147 in which the Court of Appeal had to decide the legality of an operation to separate conjoined twins, Jodie and Mary; the operation would inevitably lead to the death of the weaker twin. As there were no cases which could act as a precedent or legislation on this particular issue, the judges had to decide whether the doctors would be guilty of murder and the weight to be given to the parents' wishes. In the event, the judges ruled that the operation should go ahead.

Accordingly, although the judges' role as law-makers has now diminished, they do retain an influence over certain developments of the law. The next activity is designed to test your ability to think around this concept.

Activity 2 Judges and the law

What do you suppose would be the political objection if judges did make law?

Comment

Judges, unlike Members of Parliament, are not democratically elected. (Senior judges in England and Wales are in fact appointed by the Lord Chancellor on the recommendation of the Judicial Appointments Commission, while Supreme Court justices are appointed by the Prime Minister based on a recommendation of a special appointments commission.) Arguably, it is contrary to basic principles of democracy if the legal rules which hold society together are made by persons who have no democratic mandate and are therefore not accountable to the electorate. Inevitably, though, judges are confronted by novel situations and do need to make law at times. Moreover, judges accept that they are ought not to develop the law in a direction contrary to the expressed will of Parliament *(R (Miller) v Secretary of State for Exiting the European Union* [2017] UKSC 5, [2018] AC 61, para 42).

1.10 Legislation

The most important source of English law is now legislation. The monarch, and subsequently Parliament, has passed laws since before the Norman times. The oldest statute still in force is the Statute of Marlborough of 1267. However, in more recent times the amount of legislation has increased significantly. In 1921, Parliament passed 220 pages of legislation, according to statistics from the House of Commons library (Briefing Paper No CBP 7438, House of Commons Library 4 November 2019, *Acts and Statutory Instruments: the volume of UK legislation 1850 to 2019*, Chris Watson). In contrast, in 2006, 4,911 pages were added to the statute book; the figure for 2006 does appear to be the highest ever. These statutes range in severity, from the Nuclear Explosions (Prohibition and Inspections) Act 1998, which makes it an offence to cause a nuclear explosion, to the Clean Neighbourhoods and Environment Act 2005, which introduces on-the-spot fines of £110 for people who put rubbish out on the wrong day. The world has indeed changed significantly from the times of the Icelandic law-making process, over 1,000 years ago, when a wise man, known as the Lawspeaker, was required to memorise all laws when deciding disputes.

Unlike case law, which applies only to England and Wales, in the absence of specific provisions to the contrary, statutes apply to England, Wales, Scotland and Northern Ireland (the United Kingdom). 'Legislation' is often used as a synonym for 'statute'. However, strictly speaking, a statute is an Act of Parliament, whereas 'legislation' is a generic term which includes other types of legislation such as delegated legislation (see **1.12.3** below) and legislation originating from the EU (see **1.13**).

The Scottish Parliament, Senedd Cymru (or Welsh Parliament) and Northern Ireland Assembly also have significant legislative powers. These are covered in **Chapter 8** on devolution.

The functions of legislation are making, changing and repealing the law, but before we consider these further, we will look at how legislation is made.

1.10.1 Creation of Acts of Parliament

Parliament consists of the Monarch, the House of Commons (which is democratically elected) and the House of Lords (which is not). Both Houses are involved in the process of creating Acts of Parliament. However, before this occurs, the Government will often publish a Green Paper, which is a consultation document on possible new law, and a White Paper, which incorporates the Government's firm proposals for the new law.

An Act will then begin its life as a document known as a Bill. Only when it has passed through all the required stages will it eventually become an Act of Parliament. Debate is an essential aspect of democracy, and indeed the word 'Parliament' comes from the Norman French term meaning 'talking shop'. However, on occasion, controversial laws can take a disproportionate amount of time to complete this procedure. For example, the Hunting Act 2004 took seven years and 700 hours of Parliamentary time before it reached the statute books.

Except in exceptional circumstances, both Houses of Parliament must vote in favour of a Bill. Once both Houses have approved it, the monarch will grant formal approval known as royal assent upon which the Bill will become an Act of Parliament. The stages through which a Bill passes will be considered in more depth in **Chapter 6**.

1.11 The doctrine of parliamentary sovereignty

Parliament is the supreme law-making body in the country. Statute can amend case law, but not vice versa. The principle that only Parliament can make or unmake a law is known as the doctrine of parliamentary sovereignty or the legislative supremacy of Parliament. The doctrine may be explained as follows:

(a) Parliament has the freedom to make laws of any kind. It does not matter if the law is unfair, unjust or practically impossible to enforce.

(b) Statute cannot be overridden by any body outside Parliament. This means that:

  (i) UK courts and international courts have no power under English law to declare an Act of Parliament invalid. (Note, however, judges' powers to make declarations of incompatibility under the Human Rights Act 1998; see **1.15** below.)

  (ii) In the event of conflict between a statute and some other kind of law, statute prevails.

  (iii) Parliament cannot bind its successors. A statute cannot be protected from repeal, and a later Parliament can always change the Acts of its predecessor, whatever words the previous Act may contain to prevent its own repeal. Otherwise, if a Parliament could bind its successors, the doctrine of parliamentary sovereignty would disappear.

There are a number of types of legislation which we will discuss below.

1.12 Different types of legislation

Figure 1.2 Types of legislation

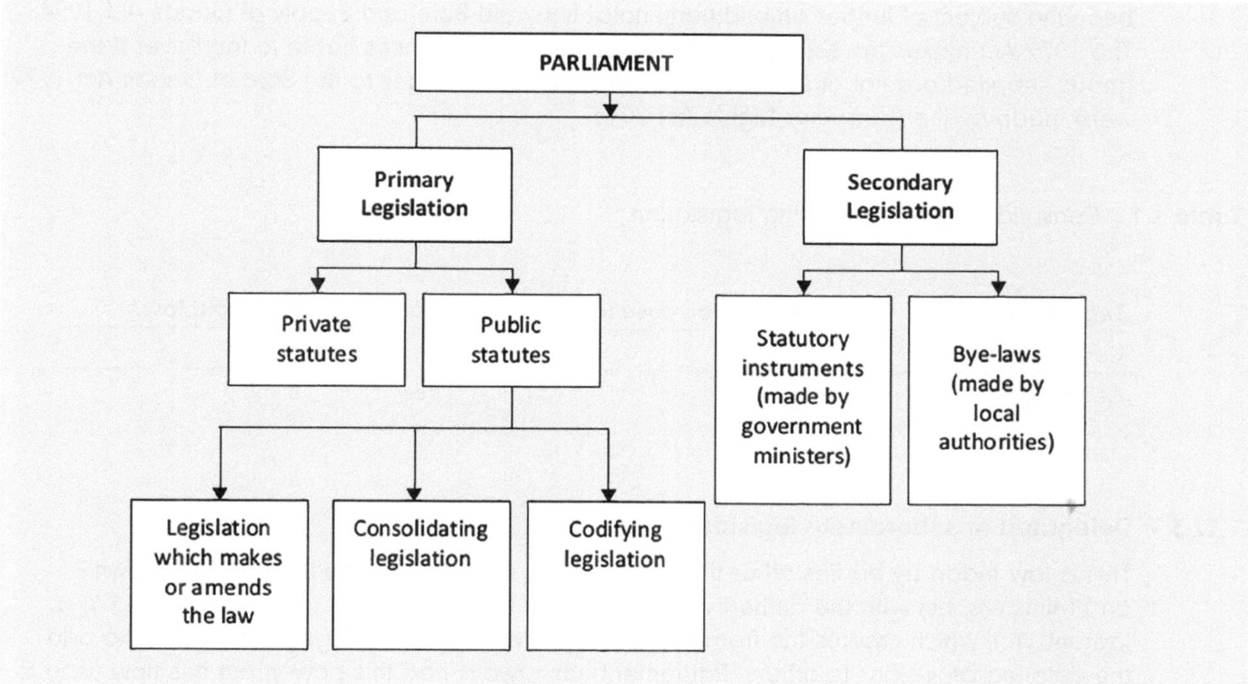

1.12.1 Public and private Bills

Public Bills concern matters affecting the public as a whole. An example of a Public Bill would be the Stalking Protection Act 2019, which dealt with the issue of stalking. They are either government Bills, introduced by a minister as part of the Government's legislative programme, or Private Member's Bills, which are non-government sponsored Bills introduced by backbench MPs.

Private Bills affect particular persons or a particular locality, for example a Bill to build a new section of railway line or reservoir. Bills, whether public or private, are known as primary legislation to distinguish them from secondary or delegated legislation which is addressed below. As mentioned above, it is a presumption that all Acts of Parliament will apply throughout England, Wales, Scotland and Northern Ireland, unless the statute specifically states that it does not apply in any of these jurisdictions.

1.12.2 Consolidating and codifying legislation

Legislation may also be consolidating or codifying, in which case it does not necessarily make or change law.

Consolidation is where one statute re-enacts law which was previously contained in several different statutes (for example, the Insolvency Act 1986). There is a (rebuttable) presumption that consolidation does not materially change earlier legislation. Effectively, consolidating Acts 'tidy up' the law.

Codification is where all the law on some topic, which may previously have been covered by common law, custom and even statute(s), is brought together in one new statute. The codifying statute may, if necessary, change the pre-existing law (for example, the Theft Act 1968).

The law relating to the sale of goods is an interesting example. The law originated in medieval mercantile custom, much of it was then embodied in case law and then the law was codified by the Sale of Goods Act 1893. Over the course of nearly a century, this Act was the subject of a number of statutory amendments, which changed and repealed parts of it. These statutes were then consolidated into the Sale of Goods Act 1979. However, that Act has since been the subject of further amendment, notably by the Sale and Supply of Goods Act 1994. The 1979 Act makes the seller of goods in certain circumstances liable to the buyer if the goods supplied are not of satisfactory quality. Further changes to the Sale of Goods Act 1979 were made by the Consumer Rights Act 2015.

Table 1.1 Consolidating and codifying legislation

Legislation	Can it include case law?	Can it change the old law?
Consolidating	No	Usually not
Codifying	Yes	Yes

1.12.3 Delegated or subordinate legislation

This is law made by bodies other than Parliament, such as local authorities, the Crown and Ministers, but with the authority of Parliament. That authority is usually contained in a 'parent' Act, which creates the framework of the law, but then delegates the power to add the detailed provisions to others. Parliament has always had this power, but it is now used to such an extent that the amount of subordinate legislation far exceeds Acts of Parliament. In 2023, 57 general public Acts were passed; in contrast between 1,500 and 3,500 UK statutory instruments are typically passed each year. Additionally, the devolved governments in Scotland, Wales and Northern Ireland generate a substantial volume of delegated legislation.

Often delegated legislation is technical, eg it updates in line with inflation the allowance paid to a guardian of a minor child who has died. Some is more wide-ranging and fills out the detail of a broad provision in an Act. For example, the Education Reform Act 1988 specifies that there will be a National Curriculum that state schools in England should follow and sets out general principles for the curriculum. Delegated legislation provides full details of the National Curriculum.

1.12.3.1 Statutory instruments

The most common form of delegated legislation is a statutory instrument. Statutory instruments may come into force following either affirmative or negative procedure, reflecting the nature of scrutiny they receive from Parliament. Under the affirmative procedure, a statutory instrument must be actively approved by both Houses of Parliament. In contrast, under the negative procedure, statutory instruments will come into force unless either House votes to annul it within 40 days.

1.12.3.2 Byelaws

Byelaws are local laws made by local authorities and bodies with public functions such as Transport for London to deal with issues affecting their locality or area of activity. These powers are granted by an enabling Act of Parliament. For example, byelaws govern the use of parks, open spaces and burial grounds under local authority control. They have also been used to ban the drinking of alcohol in designated public places. In 1988 Coventry City Council was one of the first local authorities to introduce such a byelaw and many others have followed suit. As byelaws create criminal offences, they cannot take effect until the appropriate Minister has confirmed them.

1.12.3.3 Advantages and disadvantages of delegated legislation

There are several advantages of delegated legislation. The most obvious one is in saving time. Because of the increasing volume of legislation, it would be impractical for Parliament to be expected to consider and debate every detail of each piece of legislation. To overcome this, Ministers and their departments are given authority to make regulations for areas for which they are specifically responsible. The example regarding the Education Act 1996 and the National Curriculum at **1.12.3** above illustrates this. While Parliament approved the concept of the National Curriculum and the general principles governing it, the Secretary of State for Education has the authority under the 1996 Act to introduce statutory instruments setting out the detail of the National Curriculum. It is also much simpler to be able to adopt a statutory instrument to amend the National Curriculum when the need arises rather than going through the process required to pass an amending Act.

Delegated legislation also enables Parliament to call upon technical expertise to assist in drafting regulations such as those relating to health and safety or road traffic matters. Delegation can be extremely useful in dealing quickly with emergencies, such as the outbreak of foot and mouth disease in 2001 or the Covid-19 pandemic between 2020 and 2022, or with rather less weighty matters, eg prohibiting cars from driving along a major road such as the A40 while road works are being carried out.

Delegated legislation is a much faster way of introducing new legislation as it is essentially an administrative act which does not necessarily involve the legislation being debated in the Commons and the Lords. Governments therefore like to make use of it as much as possible.

However, there are a number of disadvantages to the current volume of delegated legislation. It may be difficult for individuals to keep track of what the law is and to comply with it. In addition, Parliamentary control is reduced, particularly as statutory instruments most commonly come into force under the negative procedure explained at **1.12.3.1** above. This means that they automatically become law after 40 days, unless either House passes a resolution to annul them. As a consequence, the constitutional role of Parliament as the scrutiniser of legislation is diminished. The Government used a substantial volume of secondary legislation to combat the Covid-19 pandemic, and concerns have been expressed that this legislation, which imposed unprecedented restrictions on individuals, received inadequate parliamentary scrutiny. Although initially the Government needed to respond very rapidly to the pandemic, in the later stages of the pandemic the Government appeared reluctant to relinquish its law-making powers in favour of Parliament.

Controversy has also arisen in relation to so-called 'Henry VIII' powers, ie powers given to ministers by a parent Act to amend the parent Act itself and other Acts. Critics of Henry VIII powers argue that they are unconstitutional, as only Parliament itself should amend primary legislation; when exercising Henry VIII powers ministers are usurping the role of Parliament. An example is the Legislative and Regulatory Reform Act 2006, which gave so many powers to ministers before it was amended that it was referred to as the 'Abolition of Parliament Bill'. However, even the amended version gives ministers the power to amend primary legislation to promote regulatory reform and to reduce administrative burdens on businesses. The legislation relating to the UK's exit from the EU also grants ministers significant Henry VIII powers.

1.13 European Union legislation

The UK became a member of the European Economic Community (EEC) on 1 January 1973 (having signed the Treaty of Rome 1957 in the previous year). The European Union (EU) is the body which has superseded first the EEC and then the European Community (EC). Following the UK's exit, there are now 27 Member States of the EU.

During the UK's membership of the EU, it followed that EU law applied throughout the UK. Because international law is not regarded as part of our legal system, in order to incorporate

EU legislation into our law without Parliament having to legislate on each separate occasion, it was necessary to enact the European Communities Act 1972.

Much of our national law was affected by membership of the EU, but certain highly significant areas (for example, in relation to commercial and consumer law, employment law, the environment and immigration) were significantly affected.

The UK's exit from the EU has clearly had a profound impact on the relationship between the UK and the EU. The UK left the EU on 31 January 2020 and following an 11-month transition period that ended at 11.00pm on 31 December 2020, EU law ceased to apply in the UK. However, this does not mean that EU law has become irrelevant in the UK. Due to the sheer volume of EU law applying in the UK, it would have been impossible for the Government to have gone through every piece of EU legislation to decide whether to keep, amend or repeal it. Accordingly, a huge legal and regulatory vacuum would have arisen if EU law in its entirety had ceased to apply in the UK at the end of the transition period. Therefore, pursuant to the European Union (Withdrawal) Act 2018, EU law applicable in the UK at the end of the transition period was retained as a novel category of UK law, 'retained EU law', with its own distinct characteristics. The Retained EU Law (Revocation and Reform) Act 2023 has changed the status of retained EU law, and has renamed it 'assimilated law'. For further information, see **Chapter 9** on Retained EU Law/Assimilated Law.

Thus, although much EU law has been repealed (eg in relation to free movement of goods and people), retained EU law/assimilated law is now a significant category of UK law. Lawyers in the UK therefore still need to have a grasp of the essential elements of EU law and how it is made. A key aspect of this is understanding the EU institutions and how they function.

1.13.1 The EU institutions

The institutions are as follows:

(a) The Council of the European Union, consisting of a government representative from each Member State; this is the decision-making body of the Union.

(b) The European Commission, which develops policy. It consists of independent Commissioners appointed by national governments, but who must work independently of national loyalties, and who make proposals for legislation and oversee implementation of legislation.

(c) The European Parliament, which is made up of elected members. Its role was originally consultative, but its powers have increased as a result of more recent Treaties and it is now a significant actor in the EU's legislative process.

(d) The Court of Justice of the European Union ('CJEU'). This refers collectively to two different courts, the General Court and the EU's highest court, the Court of Justice – often referred to as the European Court of Justice. For ease of reference, the Court of Justice will henceforth be abbreviated to the 'ECJ'. The ECJ consists of judges nominated by each of the Member States. Its role is to ensure that EU law is observed throughout the Union.

Be careful not to confuse the ECJ with the European Court of Human Rights, which we will discuss in more detail in **Chapter 2**.

1.13.2 Types of EU legislation

EU legislation can be split between primary and secondary legislation. The primary legislation is in the major treaties, such as the Treaty on European Union (often known as the Maastricht Treaty) ([2008] OJ C115/13) (TEU) and the Treaty on the Functioning of the European Union ([2012] OJ C326/01) (TFEU). This primary legislation is binding on Member States and EU institutions, and its validity cannot be challenged in national courts or the ECJ.

The secondary legislation, which emanates from the institutions, takes the form of Regulations, Directives and Decisions.

1.13.2.1 Treaty articles

The TFEU is divided into short sections known as articles. These articles form part of the legal systems of all the Member States. They may also be directly effective, which means an individual can rely upon rights granted by Treaty articles and enforce them, if necessary, in the national courts. For example, in *Defrenne v SABENA (No 2)* (case 43/75) [1976] ECR 455, the Belgian airline SABENA paid its female flight attendants less than comparable male flight attendants. Ms Defrenne was able to use what is now Article 157 of the TFEU (then Article 119 of the EEC Treaty) to claim equal pay from her employer in the Belgian courts.

1.13.2.2 Regulations

Once a Regulation has been passed, it automatically becomes part of the legal systems of all the Member States. Like Treaty articles, Regulations may also be directly effective. One example of an important Regulation is Regulation (EC) 261/2004 ([2004] OJ L46/1) which requires airlines to compensate passengers in the event of cancellation of flights or significant delays. Many passengers based in the UK have used this Regulation to claim compensation.

1.13.2.3 Directives

Directives are binding as to the result to be achieved on each Member State but leave the choice of form and methods to the national authority. The UK usually implemented a Directive into national law by passing delegated legislation containing provisions aimed at meeting the objectives specified in the Directive. However, if a Member State does not implement a Directive, or implements it incorrectly, it may then have direct effect, and an individual can rely on it in the national courts, but only against the State or a State body.

1.13.2.4 Decisions

Decisions are binding in their entirety upon those to whom they are addressed, ie Member States or individuals. An example occurred when the Commission issued a series of decisions relating to the export of British beef during the foot and mouth crisis of 2001.

1.14 The EU and the legislative supremacy of Parliament

Sections 2(1) and 3 of the now repealed European Communities Act 1972 obliged all UK courts to give effect to any EU law which was directly effective and to follow decisions of the CJEU, ie judgments of both the General Court and the ECJ, although in practice judgments of the ECJ (the higher of the two courts) were more likely to be significant. During the UK's EU membership, UK courts were required to apply a directly effective EU law in preference to domestic law and to interpret all domestic law to comply with EU law, as far as possible.

As a consequence, it was increasingly recognised in the English legal system that directly effective EU law had supremacy over Parliament and was therefore a limitation of parliamentary sovereignty. An example of the way in which the UK courts acknowledged the supremacy of EU law was provided by the case of *R v Secretary of State for Transport, ex p Factortame (No 2)* [1991] 1 AC 603.

In *Factortame*, a number of Spanish fishermen set up a UK company to operate trawlers with the intention of exploiting the UK fishing quota in the North Sea. The Merchant Shipping Act 1988 was enacted to prevent this practice. The Spanish fishermen who found themselves excluded by this rule successfully argued that the Act was contrary to the EC Treaty (now the TFEU). This case was significant because the ECJ stated that national courts were to ignore any national law which ran contrary to directly effective EU law.

The supremacy of EU law no longer applies following the UK's exit from the EU. However, it remains necessary to understand the concept to grasp the nature of retained EU law/assimilated law and the arrangements that now apply between the UK and EU.

1.15 The European Convention on Human Rights and the Human Rights Act 1998

The Human Rights Act (HRA) 1998 requires UK courts to read and give effect to primary and secondary legislation in a way which is compatible with the protection of human rights as defined by the European Convention on Human Rights.

We will address the significance of the Human Rights Act 1998 in more detail in **Chapters 3** and **4**, where we consider the impact it has had on the interpretation of statutes and the doctrine of judicial precedent.

As the Act has a pervasive effect on the drafting of new legislation and the interpretation of existing legislation, set out below is a brief synopsis of its background and importance.

1.15.1 The European Convention on Human Rights

In order to appreciate the impact of the HRA 1998, it is necessary to have some understanding of how human rights were protected prior to the Act coming into force. The European Convention on Human Rights was adopted in 1950. It was drafted by the Council of Europe, an international organisation which was formed after the Second World War, in an attempt to unify Europe. The idea was that the Convention would be a statement of Western Europe's principles (eg opposing Communism) and would prevent large-scale violations of human rights. The rights specifically defined in the Convention include the right to life, freedom from torture or inhuman or degrading treatment or punishment; and the right to a fair trial by an impartial tribunal. A fuller list is set out at **1.15.3** below.

In fact, the Convention has been used primarily to raise questions of violations of human rights in Member States. It has been referred to as a European Bill of Rights.

1.15.2 The Human Rights Act 1998

The HRA 1998 is the statute which incorporates the European Convention on Human Rights into UK law. The Act gives judges at the level of the High Court and above the power to make a declaration of incompatibility, if it is found that an Act of Parliament is at variance with the protection of one or more Convention rights. Prior to making such a declaration, judges will attempt to read the relevant Act in a manner which is compatible with the protection of the Convention right(s).

In order to prevent declarations of incompatibility being made with regard to new legislation, as opposed to legislation already on the statute book, the HRA 1998 requires the Minister who introduces the draft legislation into Parliament to certify either that the Bill is compliant with the Convention rights or that they are unable to certify the Bill's compliance.

The previous Conservative Government established the Independent Human Rights Act Review in December 2020 to examine the framework of the HRA 1998, how it was operating in practice and whether any change was required.

The Panel submitted its report to the Deputy Prime Minister in October 2021, and in response the Government set out proposals to reform the HRA 1998 and submitted the British Bill of Rights Bill to Parliament. The British Bill of Rights would have replaced the HRA 1998, but in June 2023 the Government announced that it had decided not to proceed with the Bill. Unlike the previous Conservative Government, the Labour Government elected in July 2024 generally supports the HRA 1998, so is unlikely to make any significant changes.

1.15.3 Key provisions of the European Convention on Human Rights

These are the main rights protected by the Convention:

(a) right to life (Article 2)

(b) prohibition of torture (Article 3)

(c) prohibition of slavery and forced labour (Article 4)

(d) right to liberty and security (Article 5)

(e) right to a fair trial (Article 6)

(f) no punishment without lawful authority (Article 7)

(g) right to respect for family and private life (Article 8)

(h) right to freedom of thought, conscience and religion (Article 9)

(i) right to freedom of expression (Article 10)

(j) right to freedom of assembly and association (Article 11)

(k) right to marry (Article 12)

(l) prohibition of discrimination in enjoyment of rights granted by the Convention (Article 14)

(m) right to peaceful enjoyment of possessions (First Protocol, Article 1)

(n) right to education and right of parents to educate children in accordance with religious and philosophical convictions (First Protocol, Article 2).

1.15.4 Absolute, limited and qualified rights

Some of the Convention rights are absolute, eg the right to freedom from torture: the Convention allows no circumstances in which torture could be legitimate. But most of the rights are subject to limitations or qualifications. Accordingly, the right to freedom of expression may be interfered with where the matters being expressed are defamatory or harmful to national security. Much of the argument in Convention cases turns not on whether there has been an interference with Convention rights, but on whether that interference is justifiable.

1.16 Summary of the sources of law

Figure 1.3 Sources of law

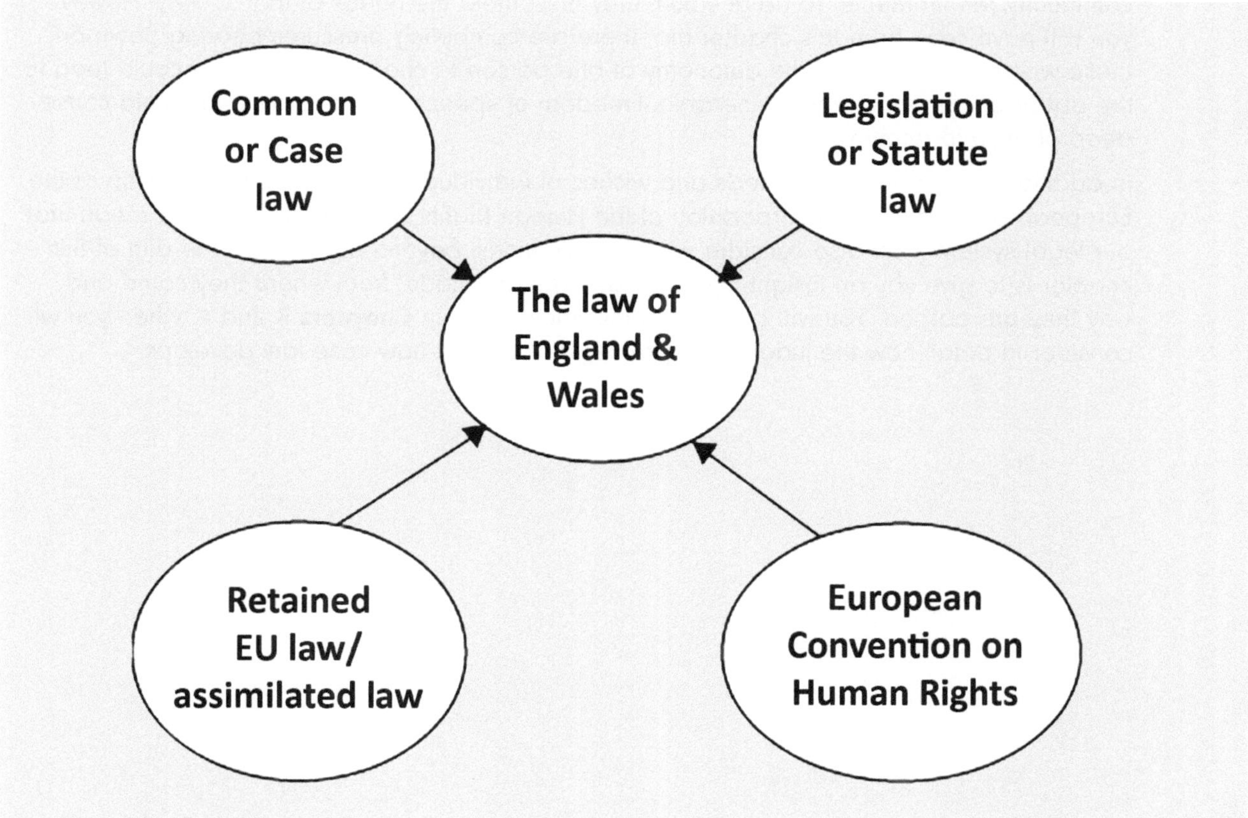

1.17 The chronological development of the sources of law

As you are aware from your consideration of the history of the English legal system, the sources of law change over time. The table below summarises of the main sources of law over the centuries.

Table 1.2 Chronology of the sources of law

Time	Main source of law (Note: there may be more than one.)
Before 1066	Custom
1066 to around the 15th century	common law
15th century to 19th century	common law and equity
20th century up until 1973	UK legislation
1973 to 1998	UK legislation and EU law
1998 to 2021	UK legislation, EU law and the HRA 1998
2021 to date	UK legislation, retained EU law/assimilated law and the HRA 1998

Summary

It is important for you, as a lawyer, to have an understanding of the bigger picture. Laws are not isolated objects - they develop from our complex society, with its moral, social and community requirements. To be of value, they must meet the needs of that society. However, you will have seen from this chapter that there are competing pressures bearing down on those who make the laws. The autonomy of one person to choose when to die could lead to the abuse of someone more vulnerable. Freedom of speech for one individual could cause deep offence to another.

In addition to balancing the needs and wishes of individuals, our former membership of the European Union and the incorporation of the Human Rights Act 1998 into our law mean that our legal system must also consider wider implications, beyond our shores. The aim of this chapter is to give you an insight into the way laws are made, from where they come and why they are passed. You will build upon this knowledge in **Chapters 3** and **4**, when you will consider in detail how the judges interpret legislation and how case law develops.

2 The Court System

Learning outcomes

By the end of this chapter, you should be able to:

- explain the structure of the civil and criminal court system;
- ascertain the relevant court jurisdiction in straightforward cases;
- explain the basic steps involved in civil and criminal cases at first instance;
- explain in outline the circumstances in which it is possible to appeal in civil and criminal cases, and the routes of appeal;
- explain the role of personnel within the court system, including the judiciary, the legal profession and juries.

2.1 The modern court system

Have you ever been in a court? For what types of cases are the different courts responsible? Do you know how legal disputes are resolved and rights enforced? Why is there a need for litigation procedures? Can anyone appeal? In this chapter, we will be discussing these issues and others which arise in relation to the modern court system.

Each year well over a million defendants are proceeded against in magistrates' courts. In addition, there are many civil cases commenced in the courts, and thousands of others dealt with by tribunals, such as employment tribunals, which play an ever-increasing part in the litigation process. Every year, a significant percentage of the population will have been touched by the court system in some way, whether it be as a defendant prosecuted for speeding, a creditor owed money, a member of a jury or as an employee, such as a police officer, bailiff or even an administrator.

In the course of this chapter, we will outline the basic structure of the court system, together with the operation of civil and criminal procedure, including the appeals process. In addition, we will consider the role of juries and other personnel involved in the legal system, including solicitors, barristers and judges. Finally, there will be a discussion of the advantages and disadvantages of tribunals and inquiries.

Courts operate throughout the whole of England and Wales to ensure that justice can be administered locally and that there is access to all. You may well have been into a court, either as a spectator or as a participant in the legal process - willingly or not! Most people do not choose to issue proceedings, but if a dispute cannot be resolved, there needs to be a system in place that can determine a fair outcome.

2.2 The structure of the court system in England and Wales

The Ministry of Justice (formerly the Department for Constitutional Affairs) is responsible for the organisation and smooth operation of the courts. In April 2011 Her Majesty's Courts and Tribunals Service was created to provide support for the administration of justice in both courts and tribunals.

Table 2.1 below sets out the modern court structure, which developed from the Supreme Court of Judicature. You will recall from **1.8.2** that this court was created by the Supreme Court of Judicature Acts 1873 and 1875, in order to replace the separate court systems of equity and common law which had existed up until that point.

Table 2.1 The modern court structure

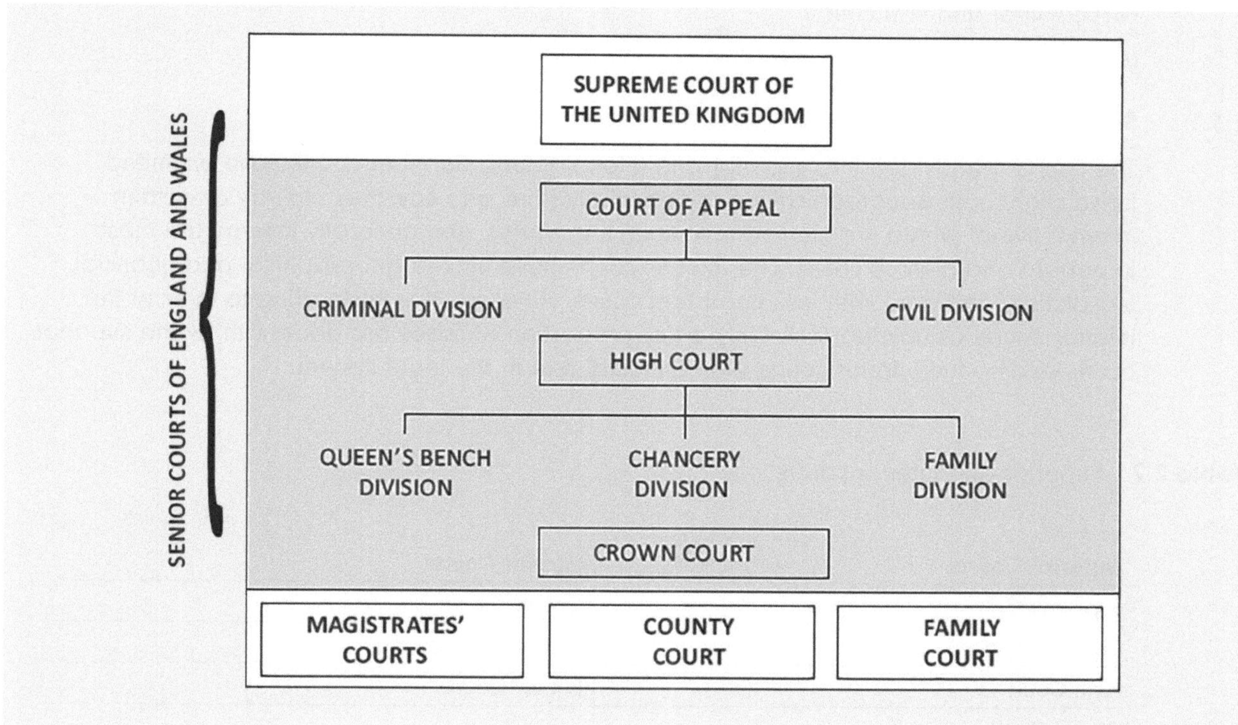

In October 2009, the judicial functions of the House of Lords were taken over by the Supreme Court as a consequence of the implementation of the Constitutional Reform Act 2005. The reason behind the legislation was to establish a complete separation between the United Kingdom's senior judges and the Upper House of Parliament, emphasising the independence of the Law Lords (now the Justices of the Supreme Court) and increasing the transparency between Parliament and the courts. The Justices moved into their own building on the opposite side of Parliament Square, where they continue to operate as the final court of appeal in the United Kingdom. Throughout this book, references will thus be made to the Supreme Court rather than to the House of Lords, unless the latter is correct for historical reasons.

In addition, the title of the Court of Appeal, the High Court and the Crown Court, which were previously known collectively as the Supreme Court of England and Wales, also changed. With effect from October 2009, these courts were renamed the 'Senior Courts of England and Wales'. Accordingly, you will need to look carefully at the context in which the words 'Supreme Court' are being used to understand to which courts reference is being made.

Finally, in 2013, the Crime and Courts Act 2013 established a single County Court, and the actual court houses in which it convenes are now referred to as hearing centres. This statute also created the Family Court, bringing together the family jurisdiction of the County Court, magistrates' courts and the High Court (except certain matters where the High Court has retained jurisdiction).

2.3 The classification of the courts

It will aid your understanding of the court system if you appreciate that the above courts can be classified in three different ways:

(a) superior and inferior courts;

(b) criminal and civil courts;

(c) trial and appellate courts.

2.3.1 Superior and inferior courts

The courts are divided into superior and inferior courts. Superior courts have unlimited jurisdiction, both geographically and financially (that is to say, they may try any claim irrespective of where it arises or how much it is worth), and generally they try the most important and difficult cases. The inferior courts have limited geographical and financial jurisdiction, and deal with less important cases. However, it is misleading to think of the inferior courts as unimportant. Only a tiny proportion of cases are dealt with by the superior courts and so the inferior courts play a crucial role in the legal system.

Table 2.2 Superior and inferior courts

Superior Courts	Inferior Courts
Supreme Court	County Court
Court of Appeal	magistrates' courts
High Court	Family Court
Crown Court	

2.3.2 Criminal and civil courts

The distinction between criminal and civil law has been discussed before in **Chapter 1**, and is fundamental, as their objectives are different. As you have already seen, the principal objectives of the criminal courts are to decide guilt or innocence according to criteria laid down by the criminal law, and to punish the wrong-doer. The principal objectives of the civil courts are to decide disputes between members of society, or between the State and individuals, and to grant an appropriate remedy (usually compensation) to the victim. So the same set of facts, such as a road accident, may lead to proceedings both in the criminal courts (for example, to punish the careless motorist) and in the civil courts (to compensate the injured pedestrian).

Apart from the Crown Court (which deals almost exclusively with criminal matters) and the County Court (which deals only with civil matters), the other courts (Supreme Court, Court of Appeal, High Court, Family Court and magistrates' courts) all have civil and criminal jurisdiction. Later in this chapter we will look at the various courts in more detail.

2.3.3 Trial and appellate courts

The function of trial courts, such as the County Court, is to hear cases at first instance, ie for the first time. They make a ruling on the issues of fact and law which arise in the case.

In contrast, the function of the appellate courts is to reconsider the application of legal principles to a case that has already been heard by a lower court. Some appeal courts also have jurisdiction to reconsider disputed issues of fact, ie disputes about the events leading to the legal action. One particular case may be heard by more than one court before the issues are finally resolved. It is possible for a case to begin in the County Court at first instance and to conclude in the Supreme Court on appeal. The appeals process allows errors of fact, law or procedure to be corrected, and can also assist the sensible development of the law.

As a general rule, it is the superior courts such as the High Court, the Court of Appeal and the Supreme Court which are the appellate courts. However, the High Court does have a dual role of being both a trial and an appellate court, and the Crown Court, although not classified as an appellate court, hears appeals from magistrates' courts.

Table 2.3 Trial and appellate courts

	Supreme Court	
Appeal Courts	Court of Appeal (Civil Division) High Court (all 3 Divisions) Family Court	Court of Appeal (Criminal Division) High Court (QBD)
Courts of First Instance	High Court, Family Court or County Court	Crown Court or magistrates' court
	CIVIL	**CRIMINAL**

The next activity is designed for you to check that you are comfortable with the basic structure of the court system and the classification of the courts.

Activity 1 Structure of the court system

Please review **2.3.1** to **2.3.3** above and answer the following questions:

1. What is the most inferior exclusively civil court?
2. Is it correct to say that the Senior Courts deal exclusively either with civil or with criminal matters but not with both? Give some examples to illustrate your answer.
3. What do you understand by the term appellate court?
4. List two appellate courts.

Comment

1. The County Court. Please note that magistrates' courts, whilst principally criminal in their jurisdiction, do have a limited civil jurisdiction, for example family and licensing matters.

2. All the courts consider both types of cases, although the Crown Court does deal almost exclusively with criminal matters. For example, the Court of Appeal has a civil and criminal division. Also, although the High Court generally deals with civil matters, the High Court of Justice (King's Bench Division) deals with appeals on criminal matters from magistrates' courts.
3. An appellate court is a court to which a decision of a court of first instance is appealed, so that the appellate court may reconsider the application of legal principles to the case.
4. The High Court, the Family Court, the Court of Appeal and the Supreme Court are all appellate courts.

2.4 The civil courts of first instance: the County Court, the Family Court and the High Court

You will have noted from **Table 2.3** above that the civil courts of first instance are the County Court, the Family Court and the High Court. County courts were introduced in 1846 so that claims could be heard more quickly and cheaply.

The hearing centres of the County Court deal with the vast majority of civil claims. Although there are some two million claims issued each year (though this number fell to around 1.3 million in 2020 due to the Covid-19 pandemic and only partially recovered to 1.58 million in 2021), most civil disputes do not end up in court, and those that do often do not go to a full trial.

The County Court deals with a range of cases. Generally, disputes involving amounts of up to £100,000 must be commenced in the County Court. In relation to personal injury claims, though, they must not be started in the High Court unless the value of claim is £50,000 or more. Above these thresholds, claimants can start claims in the County Court and may well prefer to do so as County Court costs are likely to be lower than High Court costs. Indeed, where a claimant has the choice of issuing in the High Court or County Court, then a claim should only be started in the High Court if by reason of:

(1) the financial value of the claim and the amount in dispute, and/or

(2) the complexity of the facts, legal issues, remedies or procedures involved, and/or

(3) the importance of the outcome of the claim to the public in general,

the claimant believes that the claim ought to be dealt with by a High Court judge. A claim should therefore be started in the High Court only if that is where the case should be tried.

Where a claimant chooses to start proceedings in the High Court, the High Court may order the transfer of the proceedings to the County Court if appropriate. Likewise, where a claimant chooses to start proceedings in the County Court, either the County Court or the High Court may order the transfer of the proceedings to the High Court.

The Crime and Courts Act 2013 and the Children and Families Act 2014 transferred family litigation – the protection of children, divorce petitions, violence remedies and adoption – out of the mainstream civil courts (and magistrates' courts) to a Family Court, so that litigants could be subject to a more open and comprehensible forum for settling disputes. Applications are now made to the appropriate regional Family Court, which will then determine the appropriate seniority of judge and location of proceedings. This is a procedure known as 'gatekeeping'. In keeping with changes in the court system as a whole, the aim is to make proceedings cheaper, quicker and less daunting. The Family Court usually sits in buildings shared with other courts around the country. The seniority of judges largely reflects that in other civil courts. Appeals will be either within the Family Court or to the Court of Appeal.

Set out below are tables which summarise the type of work each court deals with, their location and the level of judiciary who sit in each court. These are provided for you to use as reference. Because of the continuing reform to the court system and the complexity of some of the information, the figures used in this chapter in relation to courts and their workload are approximate where necessary.

Table 2.4 County Court

1. WHERE LOCATED?	Currently 199 County Court hearing centres located all over the country.
2. WHO SITS?	Circuit Judges; and District Judges (a junior appointment but candidates must have been legally qualified for five years, eg barristers and solicitors).
3. CIVIL JURISDICTION	(a) General types of work
	(i) contract or tort actions
	(ii) equity jurisdiction, eg mortgages
	(iii) probate claims, eg disputes over wills
	(iv) recovery of land
	(v) some family proceedings
	(vi) disputes under the Consumer Credit Act 1974.
	(b) Some hearing centres have additional jurisdiction to deal with more specialised work, eg divorce and bankruptcy.

Note 1: While there are no jurisdictional limits regarding tort, contract or recovery of land actions in the County Court, there are jurisdictional limits for some other types of claim; eg equity claims above £350,000 and probate claims above £30,000 must be brought in the High Court.

Note 2: Where a claim is only for an amount of money, whether specified or unspecified, and no special procedures are required by any legal requirement, the claim form must be sent to the County Court Money Claims Centre, a centre of the County Court that was created to deal with claims online. Unlike other County Court centres, the Money Claims Centre does not hear cases. If a case needs a hearing, it will be transferred to another centre.

Note 3: Individuals, businesses and government departments claiming a fixed amount of money of less than £100,000 may be able to issue proceedings via the website Money Claim Online (MCOL).

Note 4: The County Court does not have any criminal jurisdiction.

Note 5: The Crime and Courts Act 2013 also established the single Family Court, and so there is no longer a separate family jurisdiction in magistrates' courts and the County Court. In practice, however, the Family Court sits at the hearing centres of the County Court and the magistrates' courts where family cases were already held. (See Table 5.)

Table 2.5 Family Court

1. WHERE LOCATED?	The Family Court is a national court. There is at least one Family Court centre in each Designated Family Judge area, but the business of the court will be conducted at a variety of places within each area. Cases are described as being, eg, 'in the Family Court sitting at Croydon'.
2. WHO SITS?	The list of those who, as a result of their office, are judges of the Family Court extends to 25 categories of judge and magistrate, including:

Table 2.5 (*continued*)

	• circuit judges
	• district judges, and
	• magistrates.
	Judges are allocated according to difficulty and complexity so higher levels of judge sitting within the Family Court include:
	• the Lord Chief Justice
	• the Master of the Rolls
	• the President of the Family Division
	• Judges of the Court of Appeal, and
	• High Court judges.
3. CIVIL JURISDICTION	All family cases must be commenced in the Family Court. The only exceptions are cases invoking the inherent jurisdiction (eg wardship) and certain international cases which are reserved to the Family Division of the High Court. Family Court jurisdiction includes:
	• parental disputes over the upbringing of children
	• local authority intervention to protect children
	• decrees relating to divorce
	• financial support for children after divorce or relationship breakdown
	• some aspects of domestic violence, and
	• adoption.
	Because of this, Family Courts handle both public law and private law matters.
4. CRIMINAL JURISDICTION	Family Courts have a very limited criminal jurisdiction.

Table 2.6 The High Court

(part of the Senior Court from October 2009)	
1. WHERE LOCATED?	The court sits at the Royal Courts of Justice, Strand, London ('The Law Courts') and also at district registries around the country (eg Birmingham, Cardiff, Manchester). District registries are often co-located with County Courts at regional centres.
2. WHO SITS?	Usually one High Court judge will sit alone.
	If necessary, a circuit judge, senior QC, Lord Justice, or a retired judge, may sit instead.
3. THE THREE DIVISIONS	The High Court is one court, but it is divided into three divisions (King's Bench, Chancery and Family).
	Each division has a President (the most senior judge) who is responsible for the administration of the division.
4. KING'S BENCH DIVISION	Main type of work allocated: • contract and tort actions • criminal appeals
	Various specialised courts within KBD, including the Technology and Construction Court and the Administrative Court (which deals with cases of judicial review).
	The KBD also has some appellate jurisdiction, as the Divisional Court hears appeals by way of case stated from a magistrates' court.

Table 2.6 (*continued*)

5. CHANCERY DIVISION	Main type of work allocated:
	• disputes over wills and the administration of estates
	• trusts
	• land and mortgage actions
	• company law
	• bankruptcy
	Three specialised courts within Chancery Division, including the Court of Protection (persons under disability).
	The Chancery Division also has an appellate function dealing with, eg, land registration appeals from the County Court.
6. FAMILY DIVISION	The Family Division has a reduced workload since the creation of the Family Court. It deals with matters such as wardship and international child abduction.

2.5 An overview of civil procedure

The aim of this section is to give you a guide to how civil procedure works. Whilst the detail of issuing and pursuing legal proceedings is beyond the scope of this chapter, some knowledge of the steps you would take if you were representing a client in a civil claim will assist your understanding of how the court system operates. In particular, it highlights the role of the courts as a vehicle to resolving disputes, rather than as separate bodies, distant from the general public. **Table 2.7** below sets out an overview of the basic procedure for a money claim, which is very similar irrespective of whether proceedings take place in the High Court or the County Court. (It is not the aim of this chapter to outline procedure within the Family Court, so this is omitted.)

HM Courts & Tribunals Service (HMCTS) has also introduced an 'online court' for claims of up to £10,000, designed to give litigants effective access to justice without having to incur the disproportionate cost of using lawyers. The Online Civil Money Claims is a digital service provided by HMCTS that enables members of the public to issue claims online for up to £10,000. Parties can also make and accept offers to settle disputes online.

Table 2.7 An overview of civil procedure

Stage 1 **Pre-commencement**	Claimant takes pre-action steps, eg by attempting to reach agreement and settle the dispute without using the courts.
	↓
Stage 2 **Commencement of the proceedings**	Claimant issues proceedings using a claim form. Which court? • Up to £100,000 unless personal injury where claim is for more than £50,000 – County Court. • Above £100,000 (or £50,000 or above if personal injury) – County Court or High Court (see **2.4** above). See **Table 2.6** for further details of the type of work for which each of the three divisions of the High Court is responsible. The King's Bench Division deals with contract and tort claims and is the busiest.
	↓
	Defendant files defence.
	↓
Stage 3 **Interim matters**	The court gives directions on how the case is to proceed: disclosure of documents, exchange of witness statements and experts' reports.
	↓

Table 2.7 (*continued*)

Stage 4 Trial	Some 90% of civil cases do settle, but those which do not will be decided by a single judge at trial who will: • listen to the evidence and to any legal arguments; • apply the law to the facts; and • decide whether or not the claimant has proved their claim on the balance of probabilities. A successful claimant will usually receive damages and costs. If unsuccessful, the claimant will usually be ordered to pay the defendant's costs.
	↓
Stage 5 Post-trial	• Enforcement of judgment, ie the steps taken by the winner to obtain their money, such as obtaining a court order to allow court bailiffs to seize and sell the unsuccessful party's property. *or* • Appeal (see **2.7.2** below).

Set out below is an activity which is designed to test your understanding of whether to issue a claim in the High Court or the County Court.

Activity 2 Issuing proceedings in the civil courts

You must decide whether the following claims should be issued in the High Court or the County Court:

1. A professional negligence claim for damages exceeding £100,000.
2. A simple debt claim for £30,000.
3. A simple debt claim for £250,000.
4. A claim for £25,000 in a technical case involving a considerable amount of expert evidence.
5. A consumer claim for £2,000.

Comment

1. The negligence claim for over £100,000 should be issued in the High Court due to the amount involved (over £100,000) and the nature of the claim (professional negligence – likely to involve some complexity).

3. The simple debt claim for £250,000 could be issued in either the County Court or High Court but, assuming the claim is indeed simple and does not raise any questions of legal complexity, the County Court should be the preferred option.

2., 4. & 5. The simple debt claim for £30,000, the claim for £25,000 in the technical case and the consumer claim for £2,000 would all have to be issued in the County Court.

2.6 Legal costs

The cost of bringing legal proceedings can be very high, and costs can be a significant deterrent to pursuing a legitimate claim. The costs of high value claims which raise complex issues and which are appealed all the way to the Supreme Court can run into many millions of pounds. In straightforward low value claims before the County Court, there are limits on the costs payable; however, the detail is outside the scope of this chapter, as are the various methods for funding legal proceedings. Nonetheless, it is important to know the basic principles.

The general rule is that costs 'follow the event', ie the losing party pays the winning party's legal costs. So if the claimant succeeds in their claim, the defendant will pay the claimant's costs. On the other hand, if the defendant successfully defends the claim, they will be able to recover their costs from the claimant. Even when a party obtains an order for costs against their opponent, they may nevertheless still have to pay their lawyers the difference between the costs payable from the opponent and the total actually charged by their lawyers, as there are limits on the amount of costs that can be recovered.

2.7 The civil appeals system

2.7.1 Introduction

Following the recommendations of Lord Woolf's report 'Access to Justice', a new system of civil appeals was introduced on 2 May 2000. The aim of the new system was to provide a uniform and rationalised system for civil appeals.

The general principles governing civil appeals are set out at **2.7.2** below. The detailed information concerning the rules and time limits associated with appeals are beyond the scope of this chapter. We will then discuss the question of to which particular court a party must appeal.

2.7.2 General principles

2.7.2.1 Permission to appeal

The party who wishes to appeal, who is referred to as the appellant, requires the permission of the court to appeal.

The appellant should first apply for permission to the court which gave the decision being appealed against. In practice, this will be done by making an oral request to the judge after the judge has delivered judgment. If the judge refuses permission then the appellant must make a written request for permission to appeal which will be considered by the appellate court.

The Civil Procedure Rules make it clear that permission to appeal will only be given either if the court considers that the appeal has a real prospect of success, or if there is some other compelling reason why the appeal should be heard. This is in order to prevent the system from becoming inundated with spurious appeals. As a consequence, appeals are generally on points of law and not fact. This is because a judge may justifiably reach a number of conclusions based on the factual evidence, depending upon the credibility of the witnesses and other matters. An appeal on the facts will succeed only if the decision is beyond this range of reasonable conclusions. In contrast, an appeal on a point of law is tantamount to saying that the court got the law wrong, and this is a more straightforward point to argue.

The following example explains the difference between a point of fact and a point of law, and therefore what is and is not a valid basis of appeal.

Example

Suppose that the claimant is suing the defendant, the driver of a car, for injuries caused by the defendant's negligent driving. The judge gives judgment in favour of the defendant driver, on the basis that the accident was caused by the claimant carelessly running out in front of the driver. The claimant considers that the judgment is wrong for two reasons. First, because the judge was wrong to accept the defendant's version of events and not their own, which showed that it was perfectly safe for them to walk out when they did. Secondly, that the judge was wrong because they misstated the law of negligence in their judgment and, had they stated it correctly, they would have given judgment for the claimant.

That the judge accepted the defendant's version of events is a point of fact and is not a valid basis for an appeal, as it is not an unreasonable conclusion for the judge to reach. Misstating the law is a point of law and could form the basis of an appeal.

2.7.2.2 How is an appeal argued?

Because a party is appealing on a point of law and not a point of fact, it follows that the appellant will present legal argument to the appellate court to try to persuade the higher court that the court at first instance got the law wrong. Unlike at first instance, the appellant is not generally permitted to call any witnesses to give evidence before the appellate court.

2.8 The appeal courts

2.8.1 The High Court and the Family Court

Although the High Court is a court of first instance, it is also an appeal court. Most appeals from the County Court will be heard in the High Court, and the details of the High Court's appellate functions are set out in **Table 2.6**, to which you have already referred.

The majority of appeals relating to decisions of the Family Court are to judges of higher seniority within the Family Court.

2.8.2 The Court of Appeal and the Supreme Court (formerly the House of Lords)

Set out in the tables below are the most important aspects of the Court of Appeal and the Supreme Court which you may find useful for reference purposes. The Court of Appeal is divided into two Divisions, one of which deals with civil matters and the other with criminal cases. Both are included in the table for ease of reference, but you will need to refer to **Table 2.15** below as well when considering criminal appeals. The Court of Appeal (Civil Division) typically deals with around 1,300 cases a year.

Very few cases go on to the Supreme Court, which is the highest appeal court in the land. It only deals with cases of real public importance, and in a typical year some 60 appeals would be considered in England and Wales, from the Civil Division of the Court of Appeal. In addition, the Supreme Court would consider a handful of appeals from the High Court – 'leapfrog appeals'.

2.8.2.1 The Court of Appeal

Table 2.8 Court of Appeal

(part of the Senior Court from October 2009)

1. WHERE LOCATED?	The Court of Appeal usually sits at the Royal Courts of Justice, Strand, London.
2. WHO SITS?	Usually three judges, but sometimes five. One judge usually hears applications for leave to appeal.
	Amongst those entitled to sit are:

Table 2.8 *(continued)*

	• Lord and Lady Justices of Appeal (currently 37) • Justices of the Supreme Court;
	• the Lord Chief Justice;
	• the Master of the Rolls; and
	• High Court judges as requested.
3. JURISDICTION	Jurisdiction is entirely appellate. It is one court but divided into two divisions: the Civil Division and the Criminal Division. Both are set out below for ease of reference.
4. CIVIL DIVISION	Appeals in civil cases from:
	(i) High Court;
	(ii) County Court;
	(iii) Family Court; and
	(iv) certain tribunals, eg Competition Appeal Tribunal, Employment Appeal Tribunal, Upper Tribunal (Immigration and Asylum Chamber)
5. CRIMINAL DIVISION	Appeals in criminal cases from:
	(i) Crown Court by the defendant (convictions and sentences);
	(ii) references by Attorney-General on a point of law or against an unduly lenient sentence;
	(iii) confiscation orders imposed by the Crown Court;
	(iv) cases referred by the Criminal Cases Review Commission; and
	(iv) applications for leave to appeal to the Supreme Court.
6. PROCEDURE	The Court of Appeal does not receive evidence from witnesses, but reads documents and hears argument. The majority decision prevails (so an odd number of judges will normally sit).

2.8.2.2 The Supreme Court

Table 2.9 Supreme Court

(The House of Lords until October 2009)	
1. WHERE LOCATED?	Parliament Square, Westminster (though very occasionally it sits elsewhere, eg Belfast, Cardiff, Edinburgh, Manchester).
2. WHO SITS?	3–11 (but usually five) Justices of the Supreme Court.
3. JURISDICTION	Jurisdiction is almost entirely appellate. It is the final court of appeal not only for England and Wales, but also for Scotland (in civil cases) and Northern Ireland. It also has jurisdiction to hear and determine devolution matters under the Scotland Act 1998, the Northern Ireland Act 1998 and the Government of Wales Act 2006.
4. CIVIL APPEALS	Appeals in civil cases from:
	• Court of Appeal (Civil Division);
	• High Court ('leapfrog' procedure – see **Table 10** below); and
	• Scotland and Northern Ireland.
5. CRIMINAL APPEALS	Appeals in criminal cases from:
	• Court of Appeal (Criminal Division);
	• QBD (Divisional Court); and
	• Northern Ireland (not Scotland).
6. PROCEDURE	The Supreme Court does not receive evidence from witnesses, but reads documents and hears argument.

2.9 To which court should a civil appeal be made?

The route which a civil case will take on appeal will depend upon whether proceedings were commenced by the claimant in the High Court or the County Court, and also upon the level of judge who made the decision being appealed against. This is best represented in diagrammatic form.

Table 2.10 Civil appeals system

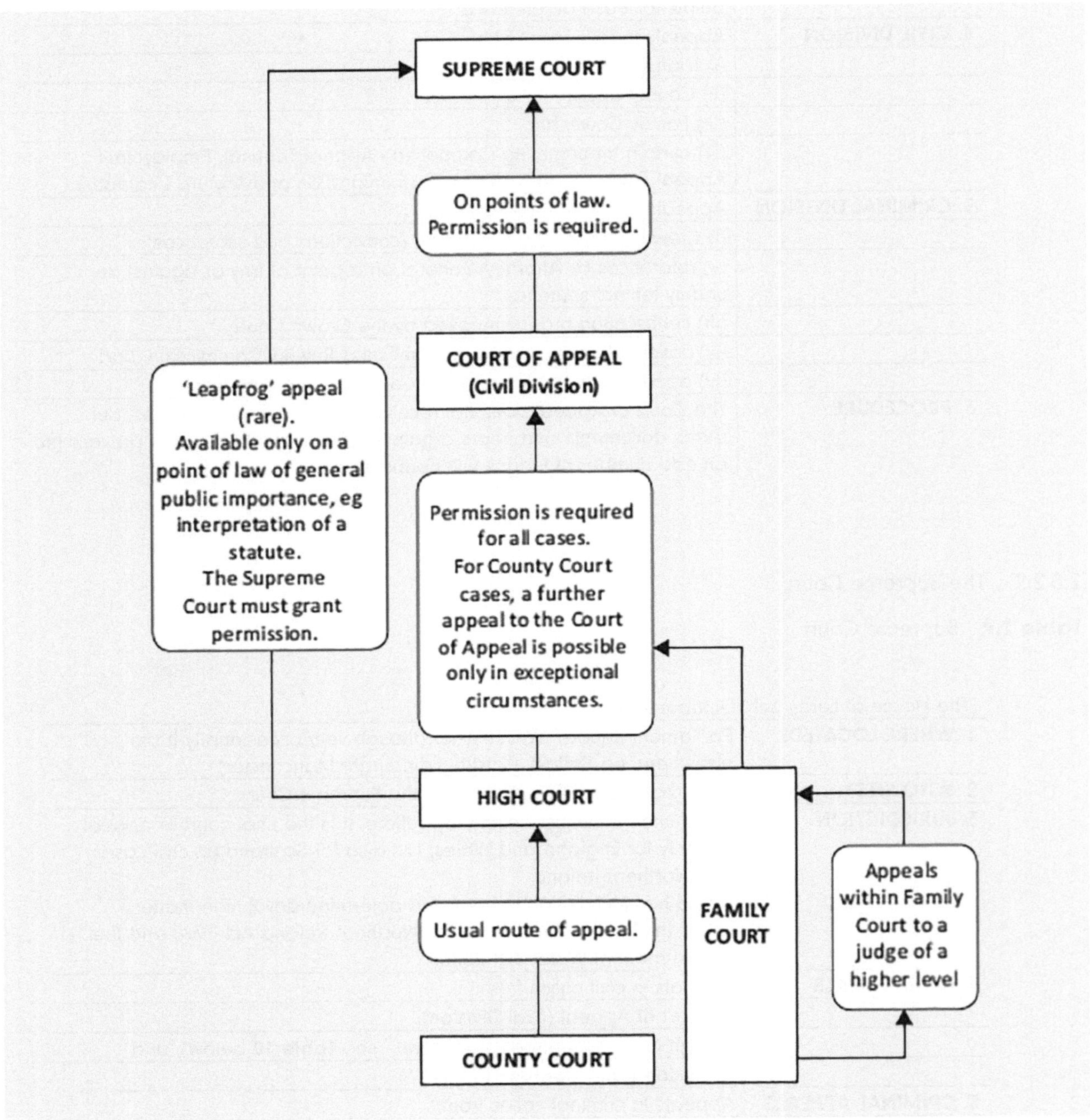

2.10 The criminal courts: courts of first instance

You will recall from **Table 2.3** above that the criminal courts of first instance are magistrates' courts and the Crown Court. In normal times, approximately 95% of all criminal trials are dealt with entirely by magistrates' courts each year; in 2023 magistrates' courts received 1.37

million cases and disposed of 1.34 million. In addition, there are over 70 Crown Court centres in England and Wales, which in 2023 received about 105,000 cases and disposed of 99,000. There is also currently a significant backlog of cases resulting from the Covid-19 pandemic and the closure of a number of Crown Court centres and magistrates' courts, causing considerable concern about the efficacy of the criminal justice system notwithstanding efforts to reduce the backlog.

We have already indicated that most civil cases do not proceed to a full trial. Similarly, some 66% of defendants who appear in the Crown Court plead guilty. Summarised below are the main features of these courts.

2.10.1 Magistrates' courts

Table 2.11 Magistrates' courts

1. WHERE LOCATED?	151, all over the country. Lay magistrates (usually three) who are not legally qualified, or a sole district judge who is.
2. WHO SITS?	Lay magistrates are assisted by the clerk to the justices to advise them on questions of law, practice and procedure.
3. CRIMINAL JURISDICTION	(a) Issue of summonses and warrants for search or arrest.
	(b) Hearing bail applications.
	(c) Trial of summary offences.
	(d) Mode of trial procedure to decide whether a case should be tried summarily in magistrates' court or on indictment in Crown Court.
	(e) Youth Courts.

Note: The magistrates also have a limited civil jurisdiction, for example, licensing and certain types of family proceedings, the latter under the auspices of the single Family Court.

2.10.2 The Crown Court

Table 2.12 Crown Court

(part of the Senior Court from October 2009)

1. WHERE LOCATED?	The Crown Court is one court, but the country is divided into six circuits for administrative convenience, eg Midland and Oxford, Northern, South-Eastern. The Crown Court sits at over 70 centres.
	The Crown Court for the City of London is called the Central Criminal Court – better known as the 'Old Bailey'.
2. WHO SITS?	Depends on the gravity and/or nature of work:
	High Court Judge (mainly QBD) or Circuit Judge or Recorder (part-time appointment, eg solicitor or barrister of 10 years' standing). Magistrates may sit with judges on appeals.
	AND jury for trial.
3. CRIMINAL JURISDICTION	(a) Trials on indictment (with jury).
	(b) Committals for sentence from magistrates' courts where the magistrates' sentencing powers are inadequate. (Maximum of 12 months' imprisonment (increased from six months from 18 November 2024) and/or an unlimited fine.)
	(c) Appeals by defendants convicted summarily in magistrates' courts.

Note: The Crown Court has a very limited civil jurisdiction, eg appeals on licensing from magistrates' courts.

2.11 An overview of criminal procedure

It is important to appreciate that criminal procedure is very different from civil procedure, although the Criminal Procedure Rules, which are similar in style to those used in civil litigation, were introduced in 2005 and are now set out in SI 2015/1490 (as amended). In order to understand the process, it is essential to comprehend the classification of criminal offences. This is because the procedure differs depending upon the type of offence involved.

There are numerous criminal offences which vary in importance and severity. Indeed, over 3,000 new criminal offences were created in the 10 years following 1997 – almost one a day. Although official statistics are no longer readily available, the rate at which new criminal offences are created has generally slowed down, though the Covid-19 pandemic did result in a significant increase.

Criminal offences can be divided into three categories:

(a) Summary only offences, such as driving without insurance or common assault. These are minor offences and must be dealt with in magistrates' courts.

(b) Indictable only offences, for example murder or robbery. These are the most serious offences and can be tried only in the Crown Court.

(c) Either way offences may be dealt with in either court. These are typically offences which are capable of being more or less serious depending upon the way in which they were committed. For example, theft may involve taking a chocolate bar from the local shop, or a sophisticated fraud involving millions of pounds.

2.11.1 Summary offences: role of the magistrates at summary trial

If the offence before the court is a summary only offence, such as careless driving, it must be dealt with by a magistrates' court.

There are about 14,500 magistrates in England and Wales and they hear over 95% of criminal cases. The number has fallen from around 25,000 in 2012, despite a recent increase. At trial, it is the role of the magistrates to adjudicate on matters both of fact and law. The vast majority of magistrates are lay people who are not qualified lawyers, although there are a few exceptions, these being professional magistrates who are known as district judges.

Lay magistrates are advised on the law by a legally qualified clerk. They hear cases as a panel of three, whereas district judges will hear cases on their own. In order to convict a defendant, the magistrates must be satisfied that the prosecution has proved beyond all reasonable doubt that the defendant committed the offence.

2.11.2 Offences triable only on indictment: roles of the judge and jury at trial

Indictable only offences must be dealt with by the Crown Court. If the defendant pleads not guilty, they will be tried by a judge and jury. However, if convicted, they will be sentenced by the judge.

The jury system has been an important aspect of our legal system for hundreds of years. Before juries were introduced, 'trial by ordeal' was common – usually by water. The accused person would be thrown into the water; if they were innocent, they would sink, but if they floated, they were declared to be guilty and despatched in another way. Not an approach which would be sanctioned under the Human Rights Act!

Henry II introduced juries so that local people would be involved in the administration of justice. However, in the early days, jurors did not have an easy time, and those who could not agree would be refused food or water until they did. So, a defendant's guilt could depend upon how hungry the jurors were.

Table 2.13 An overview of criminal procedure

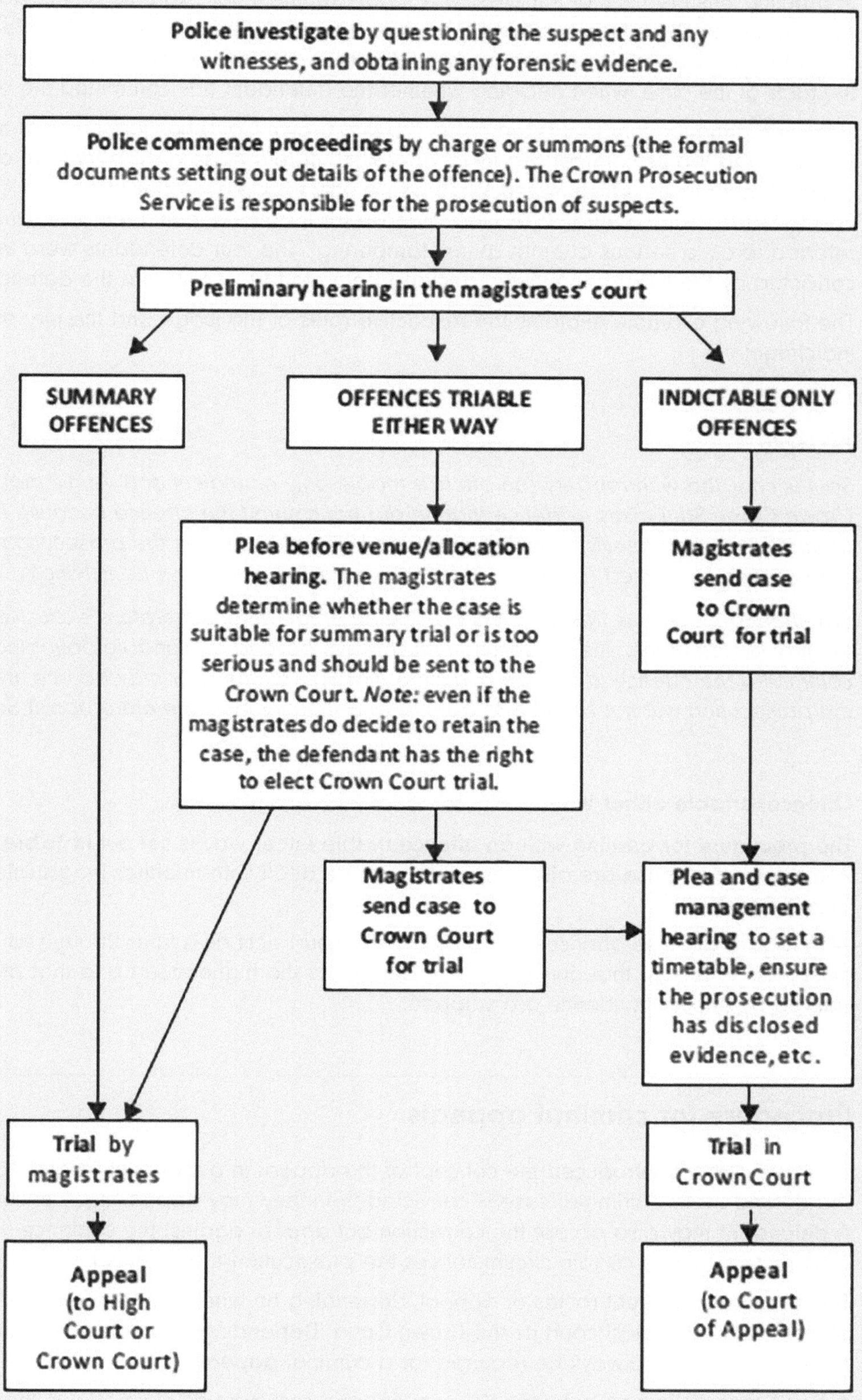

Nowadays, the jury system provides a safeguard against the abuse of judicial power. At trial on indictment, it is for the jury to judge the facts and for the judge to direct the jury on the law. In practice, this means that if there is any legal argument, for example on the admissibility of evidence, this will be heard in the absence of the jury. At the conclusion of the legal argument, the judge will then explain to the jury what the relevant law is and instruct it to apply this law to the facts of the case, when deciding whether the defendant has committed the offence or not.

However, although jury trial is the norm, the first Crown Court non-jury criminal trial in England and Wales commenced in January 2010. It related to a robbery from a warehouse at Heathrow airport which netted £1.75m and only took place after three previous jury trials had failed to reach a verdict. The last of these trials collapsed in 2008 after what the judge referred to as 'a serious attempt at jury tampering'. The four defendants were tried and convicted by the judge alone, who decided both matters of law and the defendants' guilt.

The following example explains the respective roles of the judge and the jury at trial on indictment.

Example

Saul is charged with robbery (an offence triable only on indictment). At his trial in the Crown Court, Saul gives evidence that he did not commit the offence because he was at home watching television with his girlfriend at the time when the prosecution say the offence was committed (an 'alibi' defence). The prosecution says he is lying.

Whether Saul's alibi is true or not is a question of fact and is therefore exclusively for the jury to determine. The prosecution must prove beyond reasonable doubt that Saul committed the offence. If the jury conclude that Saul's alibi is or may be true, it follows that the prosecution will not be able to do this, and the jury must therefore acquit Saul.

2.11.3 Offences triable either way

The procedure for dealing with an offence triable either way is set out in **Table 2.13** above. Remember that these are offences which may be dealt with in either magistrates' courts or the Crown Court.

With regard to these offences, the magistrates' court acts as a filter through which such cases must pass to ensure that only genuine cases get to the higher court and that prosecutions not backed by enough evidence are stopped.

2.12 Procedure for criminal appeals

We have already introduced the concept of the appeal in a civil context at **2.7.2** above. If a defendant in a criminal case is convicted then they may appeal against conviction. A defendant may also accept the conviction but appeal against the sentence. If a defendant is acquitted, then in certain circumstances the prosecution may appeal against this decision.

There are two different routes of appeal, depending on whether the defendant's trial took place in a magistrates' court or the Crown Court. Depending upon the circumstances, permission will not always be required for a criminal appeal.

A significant distinction between the criminal and civil systems of appeal is that the right to appeal is more readily available in a criminal than a civil context. Public policy dictates that there should be a greater freedom to appeal because of the serious damage to an individual's reputation if they are convicted of a criminal offence, plus the fact that they may also be deprived of their liberty.

2.13 Appeal after summary trial in a magistrates' court

Most criminal cases are dealt with in a magistrates' court. The defendant has the right to appeal to the Crown Court against sentence if they pleaded guilty, and against conviction and/or sentence if they pleaded not guilty. Most criminal appeals will go no further than the Crown Court.

Either the prosecution or the defence may appeal to the High Court, but only on points of law. This is comparatively rare as the magistrates tend to deal with the less serious offences, but previous examples have included a challenge to the accuracy of the equipment used by the police to record speeding motorists.

Table 2.14 Summary trials: appeals

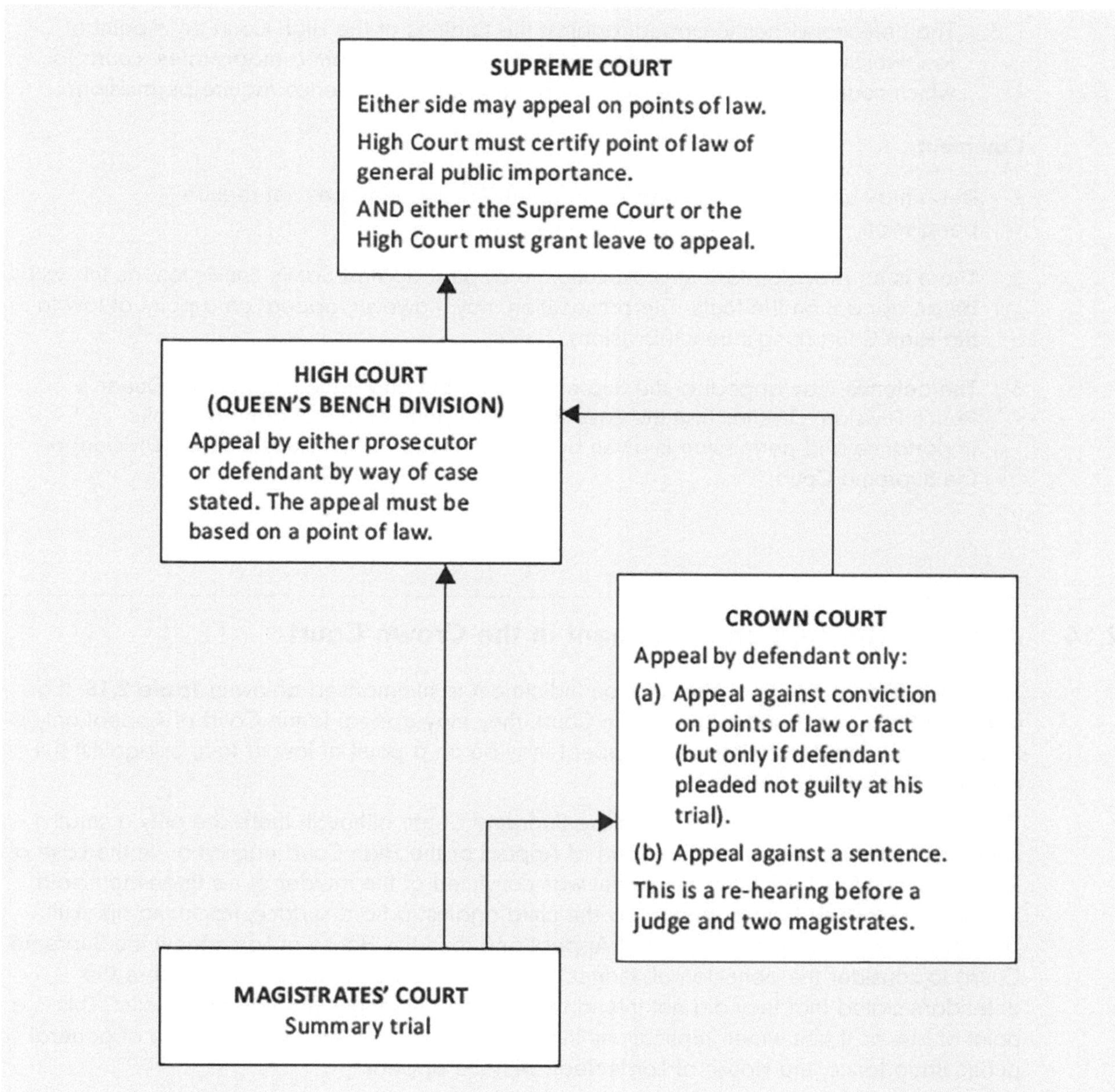

The aim of the next activity is to ensure you have understood the various methods of appealing against a decision of the magistrates.

Activity 3 Appeal from magistrates

Please review **2.13** above and answer the following questions using **Table 2.14**, 'Summary Trials: Appeals' above:

1. Dean pleads not guilty to common assault, a summary offence, and is convicted by the magistrates, as the magistrates accept the evidence of the victim. Dean wishes to appeal against his conviction. To which court should he appeal and does he require permission?
2. Sam pleads not guilty to a summary offence and is acquitted by the magistrates. Can the prosecution appeal on the basis that Sam should have been convicted on the evidence presented to the court? Would your answer be different if the prosecution wished to argue that the magistrates misstated the law?
3. The defence wishes to appeal against the findings of the High Court on a point of law, which was previously appealed to the High Court from a magistrates' court. To which court should the defence appeal and does the defence require permission?

Comment

1. Dean may appeal to the Crown Court (on the facts) and does not require permission.
2. There is no provision for the prosecution to appeal against Sam's conviction, as this will be an appeal on the facts. The prosecution may, however, appeal on a point of law to the High Court (King's Bench Division).
3. The defence may appeal to the Supreme Court, but only if the High Court (Queen's Bench Division) certifies that the case involves a point of law of general public importance and permission is given by either the High Court (King's Bench Division) or the Supreme Court.

2.14 Appeal after trial on indictment in the Crown Court

The procedure for appeals after trial on indictment is summarised below in **Table 2.15**. If a defendant has been tried in the Crown Court, they may appeal to the Court of Appeal only if they have obtained permission. An appeal may be on a point of law or fact, or against the sentence imposed.

Thereafter, the route of appeal lies to the Supreme Court, although there are only a small number of such appeals from the Court of Appeal or the High Court each year. In the case of *R v Woollin* [1999] 1 AC 82 a defendant was convicted of the murder of his three-month-old son. Woollin lost his temper and threw the child against a hard surface, fracturing his skull. The case was referred to the Court of Appeal and then the House of Lords (now the Supreme Court) to consider the definition of 'indirect intent' for murder, in those cases where the defendant stated that they did not intend to kill or cause serious harm to their victim. This is a point of law as it has wider implications than simply this case. As it was an issue of general public importance, the House of Lords dealt with the appeal.

The appeal route for trials on indictment from the Crown Court is set out in **Table 2.15** below.

Table 2.15 Trial on indictment: appeals

SUPREME COURT
Appeal on points of law only. Court of Appeal must certify point of law of general public importance; AND Court of Appeal or Supreme Court must grant leave to appeal. Either side may appeal.
↑
COURT OF APPEAL (CRIMINAL DIVISION)
Appeal by defendant only with leave May be against conviction or sentence; on a point of law or fact. **Attorney-General's reference procedure** Following an acquittal in the Crown Court, the Attorney-General may refer a point of law for clarification to the Court of Appeal - but this does not affect the acquittal (Criminal Justice Act 1972, s 36). Where the Attorney-General believes that the trial judge has imposed a sentence which is unduly lenient (in certain serious offences), they may refer the case to the Court of Appeal where the sentence can be replaced by one the Court of Appeal considers to be more appropriate (Criminal Justice Act 1988, ss 35, 36).
↑
CROWN COURT
Trial on indictment before judge and jury.

The aim of this next activity is to ensure you have understood the various methods of appealing against a decision of the Crown Court.

Activity 4 Appeal from the Crown Court

Please review **2.14** above and answer the following questions. You may find it helpful to look at **Table 2.15**.

1. Howard is convicted of murder after a Crown Court trial. Is Howard able to appeal against conviction and, if so, to which court should he appeal?
2. Jemma is convicted of robbery after a Crown Court trial. The prosecution considers the sentence imposed by the trial judge to be unduly lenient and wishes to appeal it. Can the prosecution do this and, if so, what is the procedure?
3. Sergei is convicted of robbery after a Crown Court trial and appeals against conviction to the Court of Appeal (Criminal Division) on the basis that he was mistakenly identified. However, his appeal is dismissed. Can he appeal this decision of the Court of Appeal (Criminal Division) and, if so, what is the procedure?

Comment

1. Howard may appeal to the Court of Appeal (Criminal Division), but only if the trial judge issues a certificate that the case is fit for appeal or if the Court of Appeal (Criminal Division) gives permission.
2. The prosecution may appeal Jemma's sentence as of right. The procedure is that the Attorney-General will refer the sentence to the Court of Appeal (Criminal Division).
3. Sergei cannot appeal. An appeal from the Court of Appeal (Criminal Division) to the Supreme Court is possible only on a point of law and not against conviction.

2.15 Other courts

In addition to the courts outlined above, the law of England and Wales is also affected by the Privy Council, the Court of Justice of the European Union and the European Court of Human Rights. The main features of these courts are summarised below.

2.15.1 The Judicial Committee of the Privy Council

Table 2.16 The Judicial Committee of the Privy Council (PC)

1. WHERE LOCATED?	Parliament Square, Westminster.
2. WHO SITS?	At least three (and usually five) of the following:
	• Justices of the Supreme Court • Former Justices of the Supreme Court
	• Judges of the Court of Appeal of England and Wales, the Inner House of the Court of Session in Scotland, or of the Court of Appeal in Northern Ireland who are members of the Privy Council
	• Commonwealth judges who are members of the Privy Council.
3. JURISDICTION	(a) Appeals from UK overseas territories, Crown dependencies and certain Commonwealth countries.
	These decisions are not binding on English courts. However, they are highly persuasive, because of the seniority of the Judicial Committee's personnel
	(b) Domestic jurisdiction: It has jurisdiction to hear appeals on certain matters, including • from the Disciplinary Committee of the Royal College of Veterinary Surgeons; and • against certain Schemes of the Church Commissioners under the Mission and Pastoral Measure 2011
4. PROCEDURE	The judges read documents and hear argument, and then give 'advice' (not a judgment) to the King. The advice takes the form of one opinion.
	Dissenting opinions are allowed.

The Privy Council dealt with 39 appeals between 1 April 2023 and 31 March 2024. Amongst the civil matters previously considered was a challenge on environmental grounds to the construction of a dam in Belize and an appeal from New Zealand on the extent to which the law of defamation applies to Members of Parliament. Criminal appeals, mainly from Trinidad and Tobago, have related to the mandatory death penalty.

However, the role of the Privy Council has declined since New Zealand abolished this route of appeal and the Caribbean Court of Justice was established in 2005.

2.15.2 The Court of Justice of the European Union

The 'Court of Justice of the European Union' (CJEU) refers collectively to the Court of Justice and the General Court. The highest court in the EU's judicial hierarchy is the Court of Justice (referred to in **Table 2.17** below as the ECJ). Originally the ECJ was the only court, but as explained below the General Court was subsequently created.

Table 2.17 Court of Justice of the European Union

1. WHERE LOCATED?	Luxembourg.
2. ECJ: WHO SITS?	Judges are appointed by agreement among the governments of the Member States (at least one judge from each). The judges are assisted by Advocates-General.
3. ECJ: JURISDICTION	The principal jurisdiction of the ECJ includes:
	(a) ensuring European law is applied uniformly in all Member States. It does this by giving preliminary rulings on the interpretation of the Treaties, the interpretation or validity of acts of EU institutions, and the interpretation of the statutes of certain other EU bodies;
	(b) actions against Member States to determine whether they have failed to fulfil their obligations under the Treaties. These may be brought either by the Commission or by one Member State against another for failure to fulfil its Treaty obligations.
	The ECJ has limited power to deal with actions brought by individuals: most actions are brought by Member States or the EU institutions, or are referred by national courts.
4. ECJ: PROCEDURE	Only one collegiate judgment is delivered. The Advocate-General assigned to the case assists the court by presenting an opinion (a detailed analysis of all the relevant issues of fact and law) together with their recommendations to the court (which may or may not be followed).
5. THE GENERAL COURT	The General Court (originally the Court of First Instance) was created by the Single European Act 1986, in order to help with the increasing workload of the ECJ. Its jurisdiction includes: (a) judicial review against the institutions of the EU brought by natural or legal persons (many of these involve competition law); (b) actions brought by Member States against the Commission; (c) actions for damages against institutions of the EU; (d) actions relating to Community (EU) trademarks. There is a right of appeal on matters of law to the ECJ.

Note 1: Although EU law has ceased to apply in the UK following the UK's exit from the EU, judgments of the CJEU in respect of retained EU law/assimilated law handed down before the end of the transition period remain authoritative. Judgments following the end of the transition period remain persuasive. See **Chapter 9**.

Note 2: The ECJ retains jurisdiction to hear references from UK courts relating to the citizens' rights provisions in the Withdrawal Agreement between the UK and EU governing the UK's exit from the EU. See **Chapter 9**. The citizens' rights provisions concern the rights of EU citizens resident in the UK or UK citizens resident in the EU at the end of the transition period. UK courts can make references to the ECJ regarding citizens' rights for a period of eight years from the end of the transition period.

2.15.3 The European Court of Human Rights

The Council of Europe, an international organisation, was set up in 1949 following the end of World War II to uphold human rights, democracy and the rule of law in Europe. It has 46 member states; the only two European countries that are not members are Belarus and Russia. Russia withdrew from the Council of Europe on 16 March 2022 following its invasion of Ukraine.

The European Court of Human Rights functions under the auspices of the Council of Europe.

Table 2.18 European Court of Human Rights (ECtHR)

1. WHERE LOCATED?	Strasbourg.
2. WHO SITS?	Judges are appointed from each State which is a party to the European Convention on Human Rights of 1950 (ECHR).
	A noteworthy example of an inter-state claim is *Cyprus v Turkey* (App 25781/94), 10 May 2001 [GC], (2002) 35 EHRR 731, in which the ECtHR found that Turkey had committed numerous violations of the ECHR arising from the invasion of northern Cyprus in 1974. These violations related, amongst other things, to Turkey's continual and severe failure to carry out an effective investigation into the disappearance of Greek-Cypriots, and depriving Greek Cypriot owners of their property rights. Ukraine has brought several inter-state cases against Russia arising from Russia's occupation of Crimea in 2014, the situation in eastern Ukraine and the shooting down of Malaysian Airlines Flight MH17. As the events giving rise to these cases occurred before Russia's withdrawal from the Council of Europe, in theory the claims can proceed but in practice this is likely to prove very difficult. A notable ruling against the UK arising from an individual petition occurred in October 2005, as the ECtHR ruled that the UK's blanket ban on prisoners' voting rights violated the ECHR (*Hirst v United Kingdom (No 2)* [2005] ECHR 681). Ultimately, the UK satisfied the Council of Europe that its rules were compatible with the ECHR.

2.16 Tribunals and inquiries

So far in this chapter we have considered the court system. However, there is also a system of tribunals and inquiries, which operates in parallel to the courts but is an increasingly important part of the legal system.

2.16.1 Tribunals

Whilst not strictly courts, tribunals have a quasi-judicial role, largely mirroring the lower courts in the court system in specific fields.

Tribunals are established by statute to deal with certain types of claim only. Most were created in the second half of the twentieth century. A significant difference between tribunals and courts is that members of tribunals, unlike judges, will usually have extensive practical knowledge of the types of cases which come before them.

The most common examples are employment tribunals, which have jurisdiction to hear complaints from ex-employees who believe that they have been unfairly or wrongfully dismissed from their jobs. They also hear complaints of sex and race discrimination, as well as claims for redundancy payments and parental leave.

In 2007, most tribunals were organised into a unified structure. First-tier tribunals are equivalent to trial courts (such as the County Court), and appeals on questions of law are heard by Upper Tier tribunals. Further appeals beyond the tribunal system are to the Court of Appeal.

2.16.2 Advantages of tribunals over courts

Tribunals may provide a quicker, cheaper and more convenient system of settlement than courts. However, due to the complexity of the issues involved, some tribunals such as employment tribunals have seen an increased involvement of lawyers and greater procedural formality. Another advantage is that tribunals are staffed by people who have expert knowledge about the complex questions raised in the particular disputes and who often have extensive practical experience.

2.16.3 Control of tribunals by the courts

The regular courts are able to interfere whenever the legality of the tribunal's action has been called into question. There may be an appeal on a point of law, or the judicial review procedure may be used.

2.16.4 Inquiries

Statutes will sometimes provide for the holding of statutory inquiries to examine common specific situations where courts may not necessarily have the expertise or appropriate procedures. An example of such an inquiry is when the Charity Commission investigates misconduct in the management of a charity. Planning inquiries are a common means of hearing appeals from interested parties in relation to decisions allowing or disallowing the development of land. An Act of Parliament or rules or regulations made under that Act will usually set out the procedure that a statutory inquiry should follow.

The Government may under the Inquiries Act 2005 set up a statutory public inquiry on an ad hoc basis to deal with specific issues of public concern, and these sometimes resemble a court case. The Government will often appoint a senior member of the judiciary to chair an inquiry as this adds a sense of authority and impartiality, but it is not a legal requirement. The 2005 Act gives statutory public inquiries powers to call and question witnesses. However, these inquiries do not necessarily reach a 'decision' in the judicial sense – instead they investigate facts and reach conclusions.

There have been a number of very significant and sometimes controversial public inquires. For example, the Bloody Sunday Inquiry was established in 1998 (under the predecessor to the 2005 Act) and reported in 2010. This inquiry involved an international panel of judges chaired by Lord Saville, a Law Lord and Supreme Court Justice, and concluded that in January 1972 the British Army in Northern Ireland had shot dead 13 and wounded 15 unarmed civil rights demonstrators without any justification.

Another noteworthy inquiry was the Leveson Inquiry which reported in 2012 on the role of the press and police in phone-hacking.

Following the fire at Grenfell Tower on the night of 14 June 2017, the Government set up the Grenfell Tower Inquiry chaired by retired judge Sir Martin Moore-Bick to examine the circumstances around the fire. There were two phases to the inquiry: Phase 1 addressed the events on the night of the fire, while Phase 2 investigated the causes of these events, with the Phase 2 report being published on 4 September 2024.

On occasion the Government will set up a non-statutory public inquiry. While holding a non-statutory inquiry allows for greater freedom regarding procedure, such inquiries cannot compel witnesses to give evidence.

A notable example was the Chilcott Inquiry, established to examine how and why the UK's involvement in Iraq started and what lessons can be learned. It began its work in 2009 and published its report in July 2016.

Since the 2005 Act, non-statutory inquires have become less frequent, but a recent exception is the inquiry into matters related to Sarah Everard's kidnapping and murder in 2021 by a serving police officer.

2.16.5 How tribunals differ from inquiries

The essential difference between tribunals and inquiries is that the former, like the courts, reach their own independent decision by applying established principles of the law.

An inquiry, on the other hand, is designed to obtain facts and opinions from all parties concerned. After the inquiry, it will then be for some other person, such as the Minister for State, to reach a decision, but from a fully informed standpoint. In other words, inquiries form part of the process by which government Ministers exercise their discretion.

2.17 Personnel within the legal system

2.17.1 Lord Chancellor and the Secretary of State for Justice

The role of the Lord Chancellor changed on 3 April 2006, as a result of the Constitutional Reform Act 2005, which shifted the roles and responsibilities associated with this position and that of the Lord Chief Justice. The Lord Chancellor, currently Shabana Mahmood, continues to be the government Minister responsible for the judiciary and the courts' system, but they are no longer a judge or head of the judiciary. This role has been taken over by the Lord Chief Justice, who now has responsibility for many of the judicial functions formerly undertaken by the Lord Chancellor. The effect of the Act is to separate and clarify the duties which each position has.

In addition, with effect from May 2007, the Lord Chancellor took up responsibility for the new Ministry of Justice formed as a consequence of the division of the Home Office. Their remit as Secretary of State for Justice also includes responsibility for prisons, probation and sentencing.

There have been claims that the creation of the role of Secretary of State for Justice has diminished the role of the Lord Chancellor. Traditionally, the Lord Chancellor was a senior lawyer near the end of their political career. As such, they would act in Government as protector of the constitution and remind their fellow Ministers of the importance of adhering to the rule of law and the importance of judicial independence. Now, the Lord Chancellor is a political appointee, often with political ambitions of their own. Recent Lord Chancellors have been criticised for failing to stand up for the justice system and the constitution. For example, during controversial litigation regarding the UK's exit from the EU, the *Daily Mail* published the headline 'Enemies of the People', with photographs of three High Court judges who had ruled that Parliament must pass legislation triggering the Article 50 process to leave the EU. It has been argued that the headline, combined with the lack of sufficient action from the then Lord Chancellor, Liz Truss, resulted in judges fearing for their safety and recruitment and retention in the judiciary becoming much more difficult.

2.17.2 The judiciary

In the discussion of the courts, we referred to various judges. It can be difficult to understand who the various judges are, their roles and how they 'fit' into the court system. **Table 2.19** below gives you some guidance in this regard and you may find it useful for reference purposes, particularly when considering judgments in a case and determining the hierarchy of the courts, as required in **Chapter 4**.

2.17.3 The Attorney-General and Solicitor-General

The Attorney-General and the Solicitor-General (who acts as the Attorney-General's deputy) are the legal advisers to the Crown, and are assisted by junior counsel to the Treasury (who are practising barristers).

Both the Attorney-General and the Solicitor-General are normally barristers and are usually members of the House of Commons, though the current Attorney-General, Lord Hermer, is a member of the Lords. The Attorney-General is a political appointee (ie they are a member of the Government of the day). The Attorney-General's role is to advise government departments and answer questions in Parliament; to represent the Crown in some civil proceedings and those criminal trials where important constitutional or political issues arise (eg treason); and also to bring actions on behalf of the public, for instance to restrain a public nuisance.

Although a member of the Government, the Attorney-General has a duty to represent the public interest in criminal matters.

The law officer for Scotland at the Westminster Parliament is now called the Advocate-General for Scotland.

Table 2.19 Who's who in the judiciary?

President of the Supreme Court
Lord Reed of Allermuir

↓

Justices of the Supreme Court
e.g. Lord Briggs of Westbourne, Lady Rose of Colmworth

↓

Lady Chief Justice
Baroness Carr of Walton-on-the-Hill
President of the Courts of England and Wales* and Head of the Judiciary of England and Wales (a role previously held by the Lord Chancellor). Head of Criminal Justice (unless he appoints another person)
*The LCJ is President of the Court of Appeal, the High Court, the Crown Court, the County Court and the magistrates' court

↓

Master of the Rolls
Sir Geoffrey Vos
President of the Civil Division of the Court of Appeal

Other Heads of Division

President of the KBD (High Court)	**President of the Family Division** (High Court)	**Chancellor of the High Court** (Chancery Division)
Dame Victoria Sharp	Sir Andrew McFarlane	Sir Julian Flaux

↓

Lord and Lady Justices of Appeal
These judges sit in the Court of Appeal

↓

High Court Judges

↓

Circuit Judges and Recorders
Usually sit in the Country Court of Crown Court in a particular region

↓ ↓

District Judges and Deputy District Judges	**District Judges and Deputy District Judges (Magistrates' Courts)**
Usually sit in the County Court	Deal with the more complex cases in the magistrates' courts

↓

Magistrates
Not legally qualified

Note 1: Correct as at April 2025.

2.18 The legal profession

The legal profession is divided into two main branches, barristers and solicitors, although in recent years the distinctions between them have become blurred. There is also recognition and encouragement (for instance in the Courts and Legal Services Act 1990) of the part to be played by others in the provision of legal services, eg legal executives and licensed conveyancers.

Traditionally, the Bar has been viewed as the senior branch of the profession, both for its long historic roots and because the more senior judges (and until relatively recently all judges) have been appointed from amongst barristers. The Bar is, however, comparatively small; in 2024 there were approximately 18,700 practising barristers, employed and self-employed, in England and Wales, compared to over 170,000 practising solicitors.

The two professions are organised separately. Historically, the Law Society and the General Council of the Bar (Bar Council) had both represented and regulated solicitors and barristers respectively. However, at the request of the Government, Sir David Clementi (Chairman of Prudential plc and former Deputy Governor of the Bank of England) conducted a wide-ranging review of the regulation of legal services in England and Wales. The Clementi Review reported in December 2004, identifying many areas where restructuring was considered necessary, and concluding that the current regulatory arrangements were 'inflexible, outdated and over-complex'. This led ultimately to the enactment of the Legal Services Act 2007 which received Royal Assent on 30 October 2007.

The Act established the Legal Services Board, independent of the Government, to be the oversight regulator of legal services, and the 2007 Act also designated the Law Society and Bar Council as approved regulators of their respective professions. However, as a result of the regulatory system introduced pursuant to the Act, they now discharge their regulatory functions via their regulatory arms, the Solicitors Regulation Authority (SRA) and the Bar Standards Board (BSB), which effectively function as independent bodies.

Both the SRA and BSB have Codes of Conduct, which set out in some detail requirements of conduct and form the basis on which disciplinary action can be taken against members of the profession who do not comply. Both barristers and solicitors owe a duty to the court, as well as to the client they represent, or for whom they act.

2.18.1 Barristers

The work of a practising barrister is essentially as a consultant offering specialised services as an advocate and in giving opinions, ie advice on specific areas of law. Until 1990, only barristers were entitled to appear in the High Court, the Court of Appeal and the Supreme Court, and for most purposes in the Crown Court. The Courts and Legal Services Act 1990 extended rights of audience in all courts to include, for example, solicitors who have qualified for rights of audience. The Access to Justice Act 1999 makes it clear that rights of audience will depend in future on fitness and qualification, not on whether one is a barrister or solicitor, or practising in the High Court or the County Court.

Practising barristers are not permitted to enter into a professional partnership with other barristers, though they may be partners in a firm of solicitors, or own or manage alternative business structures discussed at **2.18.3** below. Instead, barristers are members of Chambers, a form of association which is less than a partnership and which provides, amongst other things, for the sharing of office expenses and staff with other barristers. Practising barristers have to be members of one of the four Inns of Court: each Inn's main function is to maintain a collegiate framework for the Bar and promote legal education and professional conduct. In order to qualify, a barrister still has to be 'called to the Bar' by one of the Inns.

2.18.2 Solicitors

The work of many solicitors is more general than that of a barrister. A solicitor is the first point of contact for most individuals or organisations seeking legal advice, and a solicitor may have to deal with a wide variety of problems.

However, solicitors do frequently specialise in particular areas of legal work, and the distinction between solicitors and barristers is not so clear-cut as it used to be. Although it is usually the solicitor who instructs counsel, barristers may also be directly hired by certain professionals, eg accountants. Furthermore, the Bar Council has launched Public Access, a scheme which allows anyone to go directly to a barrister, without having first to instruct a solicitor.

Solicitors are entitled to practise in partnership with other solicitors, and most of them do this, although there are currently approximately 1,460 sole practitioners (ie solicitors who practise on their own), compared to approximately 4,000 in July 2010.

2.18.3 Alternative business structures

The Legal Services Act 2007 provided for significant changes in how barristers and solicitors practise with the introduction of alternative business structures (ABSs). In practice, the SRA is the main regulator of ABSs, though other legal regulators such as the BSB and the Council of Licensed Conveyancers can license ABSs.

ABSs are a distinct type of law firm. Examples include firms with more than 25% non-lawyer managers, firms taken over by non-lawyer businesses and firms providing both legal and non-legal services; however, they must have at least one lawyer-manager as well as non-lawyer involvement to meet the criteria for becoming an ABS.

As indicated above, an ABS will have to be licensed by a licensing authority such as the SRA as a licensed body. However, the introduction of ABSs does not allow non-lawyers to carry out activities that are reserved by statute to lawyers, eg the conduct of litigation, appearing as an advocate before a court, conveyancing and probate work.

The Co-operative Society was one of the first ABSs to be authorised following the grant of a licence by the SRA in March 2013. The first ABSs also included small existing solicitors' firms who have brought in non-lawyer partners as practice managers. It should be clear from this that ABSs will not follow one single model. Some may be very similar to traditional law firms but owned at least in part by non-lawyers. An alternative model is that of a 'one-stop-shop' where a well-known company provides a whole range of services (legal and non-legal) such as estate agency, conveyancing, mortgages, will-writing and insurance under one brand. The introduction of ABSs has had a significant impact on the legal profession.

2.18.4 Other roles for barristers and solicitors

By no means all solicitors and barristers work in private practice. Many are employed, for example, in business and industry. Many solicitors, in particular, are involved in local government or in the administration of the courts, for example as magistrates' court clerks.

2.19 The jury

At **2.11.2** above we briefly discussed the role of the jury in a Crown Court trial. Here, we will consider the purpose of the jury in greater detail, and additionally describe who can and cannot sit on a jury, outline the role of a jury in a criminal trial, and discuss the advantages and disadvantages of a jury system and possible alternatives.

2.19.1 Purpose of the jury trial

Juries are used in both civil and criminal actions to weigh up the evidence and decide what are the true facts of the case. The judge directs them as to what is the relevant law, and the jury applies the facts to the law and reaches a verdict.

In a criminal case, the jury merely states that the accused is either guilty or not guilty, and gives no reasons. The decision cannot be disputed, as the jury deliberates in secret, and is arrived at on the basis the jury chooses, according to the evidence and the jurors' conscience. The judge then decides on the appropriate sentence. In civil cases (see **2.19.3**), a jury will decide on the facts of the case (ie in favour of the claimant or defendant) and the amount of damages.

2.19.2 The criminal jury

Juries are most often found in the Crown Court. Only approximately 3% of all criminal cases reach the Crown Court. Of these, less than a third are jury trials, as there are many pleas of guilty without a trial taking place.

2.19.3 The civil jury

It is rare to have a jury in a civil action in the UK. Juries are allowed, at the discretion of the court, only in cases involving:

(a) fraud;

(b) libel and slander (ie defamation actions);

(c) malicious prosecution;

(d) false imprisonment.

Of these situations, juries are most frequently used in defamation cases. The right to a jury is qualified, even in the above cases, if the judge considers that the case requires investigation of documents, etc which cannot conveniently be made with a jury.

2.19.4 People who can sit on a jury

Anyone who is on the electoral register and aged between 18 and 70 is qualified to serve on a jury. Jurors are randomly selected by computer from the electoral register. Some people never get called, whilst others are called more than once. Certain people are disqualified from jury service, eg anyone who has been sentenced to a term of imprisonment of five years or more.

Historically, those who were concerned with the administration of justice, such as judges, magistrates and police officers, were ineligible for jury service. This provision was removed by the Criminal Justice Act 2003. However, anyone may apply for discretionary excusal, perhaps because of work or family commitments.

2.20 The common law versus the civil system

You are aware from reading both this chapter and **Chapter 1** that our legal system is a common law one. Elsewhere, many countries adopt a different approach to dispensing justice, and this is known as the 'civil law system'.

In a common law system, the courts decide cases using an adversarial approach; whereas in a civil law system, an inquisitorial method is used. **Table 2.20** below summarises some of the key differences.

Table 2.20 Common law/civil law systems

The Common Law System: an adversarial approach to justice	The Civil Law System: an inquisitorial approach to justice
Used in England and Wales.	Used in much of continental Europe.
Has been described as a 'contest'.	Has been described as a 'search for the truth'.
Lawyers play a central role in presenting the case.	Lawyers play a secondary role to the judge.
The judge acts as an 'umpire' and takes a fairly passive role.	Judges have a more active role in running the case and even investigating it.

You will re-visit the two systems again at **4.13.1**. Although **Table 2.20** implies that the two systems are entirely distinct, this is not always the case. For example, the Coroners' Courts use an inquisitorial approach, and the growing tendency in the courts to use written evidence and summaries of legal arguments is also a step in this direction. There are, of course, advantages and disadvantages to each approach.

Summary

It is vital for a lawyer to have an understanding of the court system in England and Wales, as this provides the machinery by which disputes are resolved. Knowledge of the law alone is not sufficient as, in practice, the client will require information not only on the merits of their case, but also on what further steps can be taken to enforce their rights.

As a lawyer, you will need to be able to identify the correct court in which a claim should be issued, know how to progress the case to its conclusion and when, and if, your client can appeal. This chapter provides you with the relevant knowledge to do this. You will build on your knowledge of the courts structure when you look (in **Chapter 4**) at how precedents in one court can bind another.

3 Statutory Interpretation

Learning outcomes

When you have completed this chapter, you should be able to:

- understand and explain the principles of statutory interpretation, in particular rules of construction and rules of language;
- evaluate and apply the principles of statutory interpretation;
- use your knowledge of the principles of statutory interpretation to find solutions to legal problems.

3.1 Introduction

In **Chapter 1**, you discovered that there are four main sources of English law - case law, UK legislation, retained EU law/assimilated law and the European Convention on Human Rights. However, although case law retains its importance, its dominance as a source of law has, in the last 150 years, been overtaken by legislation. This is due to the rise of democracy in this country. The judges' historical role as law-makers is arguably contrary to the basic principles of democracy, as judges are appointed rather than being elected by the populace.

Despite this, the judges' influence remains, as they are frequently called upon to interpret statutes. However conscientious the parliamentary counsel (the people who draft statutes), the language used is not always as clear as it could be. Alternatively, changes in our society mean that statutes are being applied to issues which even the most far-sighted drafter could not have foreseen. Who could have predicted the prevalence of Internet shopping when the Sale of Goods Act was passed in 1979; or contemplated jet skis when defining a ship for the purposes of the Merchant Shipping Act 1995?

This chapter explains and analyses the approaches used by practitioners and the courts in seeking to resolve these problems. You will see that the choice of which of the various approaches, rules and principles of statutory interpretation are applied can affect the outcome of the case. Accordingly, knowledge of these principles and the ability to use them effectively are essential tools in a lawyer's armoury.

3.2 Why is statutory interpretation necessary?

Statute is the primary source of law in England and Wales. Parliamentary counsel often have to turn complex rules and subtle nuances into reliable and unambiguous language. Often, statutes need to be applied in a world beyond the imagination of even the most forward-thinking drafter. Some statutes can then become at best ambiguous and, at worst, lead to absurd consequences.

So, the simple answer as to why we need to interpret legislation is to resolve ambiguities in order to find its true meaning. Even straightforward words can have more than one meaning. Consider this example:

(a) A woman without her man is nothing.

(b) A woman; without her, man is nothing.

You can probably guess the problems caused by the conflicting interpretations here. All that is required, to alter the meaning of these words, is to add punctuation.

3.3 Meaning of words

Despite the best endeavours of parliamentary counsel, the meaning of words is not always clear. Sometimes it is the drafting which is at fault, using a vague or general word rather than a specific word, but often it is because a word has more than one meaning. This arises because the tradition in English legal drafting (unlike the continental system) is to be all-embracing, that is, attempting to cover every eventuality. Therefore the statute or document must be general, and yet detailed and precise.

You may think the solution is to choose words which have only one meaning. However, as you have seen above, this is easier said than done. Many words have more than one meaning. In many cases this does not matter; it may be that the word can have only one meaning in a particular context, or that the other meanings are so obscure that they are for lexicologists (those who study the history and meaning of words) only. In some cases, however, the meaning may not be clear from the context, in which case there is scope for ambiguity.

The case of *Corkery v Carpenter* [1951] 1 KB 102 illustrates how ambiguities may arise. Under s 12 of the Licensing Act 1872, someone found drunk in charge of a 'carriage' on the highway is guilty of an offence. The issue of statutory interpretation which arose in the case related to the word 'carriage', specifically whether the reference to 'carriage' in the 1872 Act could include a bicycle. The court held that a bicycle was a 'carriage' for the purposes of the 1872 Act. This shows how the meaning of a particular word in a statute can be crucial, as it can determine whether a defendant is guilty of a criminal offence or not, or whether someone can claim damages in a civil action.

In this chapter we will look at the 'tools' which lawyers use to assist them in reaching a conclusion as to the meaning of particular words.

3.4 Interpretation

Lawyers and judges spend a great deal of time interpreting legal documents. These include statutes and statutory instruments; contracts and wills. Some of the problems of interpretation are common to all kinds of document and others are not. Statutes and statutory instruments are always drafted by lawyers. However, contracts and wills are sometimes drafted by non-lawyers, and in practice this is bound to affect the approach of judges to their interpretation. In particular, it is important to consider what the parties are saying to each other and what meaning each of them might reasonably attach to what the other says.

3.4.1 Problems of interpretation

There is another reason why we need to interpret legislation, this being to decide whether it applies to a particular set of facts. We will look at these difficulties of interpretation in the next activity.

Activity 1 Interpretation

This activity is divided into two parts and is included entirely for illustrative purposes, to demonstrate how even simple words can have more than one meaning. However, the same problems of interpretation arise in more complex and realistic statutes. Please read the comment on Part 1 before moving on to Part 2.

Assume there is a statute which makes it a criminal offence to wear red socks in a public place.

What problems could possibly arise when the wording is as straightforward as that?

Part 1

The wording of the statute is: 'It is a criminal offence to wear red socks in a public place.'

Consider how the word 'red' might give rise to problems of interpretation.

To get you started, by way of an example, imagine that Albert was found wearing maroon socks in a public place.

In deciding whether Albert has committed the offence, you might suggest that it is debatable whether the problem is with the meaning of 'red' as such, or as to whether those particular socks are red.

Comment

You might have thought that the word 'red' is clear enough and would not cover maroon. However, the problem is neatly illustrated by the definition of 'red' from *Chambers' 21st Century Dictionary*: 'referring to the colour of blood, or a colour similar to it' and 'said of hair, fur, etc: of a colour which varies between a golden brown and a deep reddish-brown'.

Part 2

Now consider the other words in the criminal offence, and identify any problems with the words. Use the grid below for this exercise.

Word(s)	Problem	Example

Comment

In fact, every part of this offence gives rise to the problem: what does each word mean?

1. 'wear': What if Albert was using a red sock as a hat and therefore wearing it on his head?
2. 'socks': What if he was wearing only one sock?
3. 'public place': What if Albert was on his university premises? Is that a public place?

Having identified the problem, the next stage is to determine how to solve it. To assist in this regard, judges have formulated various rules. Effectively, these are judicial 'tools'.

3.4.2 The modern approach to statutory interpretation

Traditionally, books on statutory interpretation stated that there were rules of construction and interpretation that guided the way that courts should interpret legislation. While judges did not normally regard these rules as strict instructions as to how they should interpret statutes and employed them flexibly, they did set out the parameters within which judges were expected to operate. Accordingly, students have historically studied the literal, golden and mischief rules of statutory construction.

However, the courts have moved away from this approach, as illustrated by the House of Lords' judgment in *R (Quintavalle) v Secretary of State for Health* [2003] UKHL 13. In his speech, Lord Bingham summarised the modern approach as follows:

> The court's task, within the permissible bounds of interpretation, is to give effect to Parliament's purpose. So the controversial provisions should be read in the context of the statute as a whole, and the statute as a whole should be read in the historical context of the situation which led to its enactment.

Quintavalle concerned the interpretation of the definition of 'embryo' in the Human Fertilisation and Embryology Act 1990. The Act defined embryos as meaning 'a live human embryo where fertilisation is complete' (s 1(1)(a)), and it empowered the Human Fertilisation and Embryology Authority (HFEA) to grant licences to use embryos outside the human body. The issue was whether the HFEA had the power to license the use of human embryos produced by cell nuclear replacement (CNR – commonly known as cloning), as embryos produced by CNR are not fertilised.

The claimant, acting on behalf of the Pro-Life Alliance, argued that that the HFEA could not license embryos produced by CNR, as its powers to grant licences only extended to those produced by fertilisation. The definition of embryos in s 1(1)(a) specifically referred to fertilisation, so could not extend to CNR. If the claimant's argument had succeeded, the cloning of human embryos would have been left in legal limbo and not subject to regulation. However, CNR did not exist when Parliament enacted the Act, so the Act could not have referred to it.

The House of Lords adopted a purposive interpretation of the definition of embryo in s 1(1)(a). Essentially, in adopting a purposive approach, the courts look at the aim of the statute and interpret it in such a way as to achieve that aim; see further the discussion at **3.10** below.

The aim of the Act was to protect embryos created outside of the human body. It created a comprehensive system of regulation for such embryos, permitting certain practices while banning others. Parliament did not intend any activity in this field to be outside the scope of regulation. As CNR did not exist at the time the Act was passed, it would have been impossible for the Act to refer to it. However, Parliament could not have intended to distinguish between an embryo created by CNR and one produced by fertilisation; accordingly, the reference in s 1(1)(a) to fertilisation was not integral to the definition of embryo.

It was also appropriate to construe the Act in the light of the new scientific knowledge and to apply it to current conditions. Under the 'always speaking' principle, a statute may be applied in circumstances which the legislature did not envisage at the time of its enactment because the statute as properly construed does apply to new or changed circumstances. Therefore, embryos created by CNR were subject to regulation by the HFEA under the Act. However, under the 'always speaking' principle, it is only possible to apply an updating interpretation where the new situation falls with the legislative intention. Courts cannot use the principle to fill a gap in an Act unless it is clear from the terms of the Act itself that it should apply to the gap.

Quintavalle is now one of the leading cases on the modern approach to statutory interpretation. Nonetheless, it is appropriate to analyse and critically evaluate the traditional approaches as the literature on statutory interpretation still frequently refers to them; moreover, you will find references to them in case law.

3.5 Rules of construction

The rules of construction were the traditional starting point for students of statutory interpretation. This expression is used to distinguish the 'rules' of statutory interpretation from any other rules or aids. Although they are commonly referred to as 'rules', the use of quotation marks indicates that they have more in common with general principles. Note the use of the word 'construction', which in a legal context means the same as 'interpretation'. It is important to realise that these 'rules' are not binding, and in reality they are different methods of approaching the interpretation of statutes and are therefore not rules in the strict sense of the word. Moreover, the House of Lords' judgment in *Quintavalle* shows that these 'rules' are often now of historical interest, albeit judges still on occasion refer to them.

Students of the traditional approach often reached two conclusions: some judges had their own 'favourite' rule; and different outcomes might result from the use of different rules. Indeed, some commentators took the view that a judge first decided what the outcome of the case should be, and then chose whichever rule gave that result. There was no obligation on judges to state which rule they were using, and therefore it may not always be easy to work this out from the judgment. It was also permissible and possible to interpret legislation without using any particular rule.

There are three rules of construction, which we will discuss in more detail below. While courts now generally use the modern approach set out in *Quintavalle*, these rules played an important part in the development of statutory interpretation and so it is still essential to study them.

3.6 The literal rule

3.6.1 Meaning of the rule

This rule stipulates that words must be given their plain, ordinary and literal meaning. If the words are clear, they must be applied, even though the intention of the legislator may have been different, or the result is harsh or undesirable.

An explanation of the rule was given in the *Sussex Peerage Case* (1844) 1 Cl & Fin 85:

> If the words of the statute are in themselves precise and unambiguous, then no more can be necessary than to expound those words in that natural and ordinary sense. The words themselves alone do, in such a case, best declare the intention of the law giver.

This is the oldest of the rules, and judges often adopt a literal interpretation of statutes today. Even without the instructions for **Activity 1**, it is likely that your first instinct would have been to look up any doubtful words in a dictionary. This is perfectly logical because we start from the assumption that the words have been carefully chosen in order to carry out the intention of Parliament, or that of the person on whose behalf the document has been drafted. The grammatical meaning of a statute carries great weight. However, there is no strict literal rule that courts must always follow the grammatical meaning of a statute. Nevertheless, there must be strong reasons for a court to depart from the grammatical meaning.

3.6.2 Problems with the rule

Another reason for the popularity of this rule is that, as you will remember from your study of the sources of law, Parliament is the UK's main law-maker, and judges should take care not to make decisions that thwart Parliament's will. There is always the danger that a particular interpretation may be contrary to the will of Parliament, and therefore some judges prefer to stick to a literal approach so as to avoid this.

However, the irony of this rule is that its very use may defeat the intention of Parliament and lead to absurd results, as a critical evaluation of case law will show.

For instance, in the case of *Whiteley v Chappell* (1868) LR 4 QB 147, the defendant pretended to be someone who was on the voters' list but who had died. He was charged with impersonating 'a person entitled to vote', but was found not guilty. The reluctant conclusion drawn by the court was that the defendant could not be convicted of the statutory offence because the person he impersonated was dead, and on a literal construction of the relevant statutory provision, the deceased was not 'a person entitled to vote'.

Using the literal rule can also lead to injustice. For example, in the case of *London & North Eastern Railway Co v Berriman* [1946] AC 278, a railway worker's widow was denied compensation because her husband was killed when oiling points and this was 'maintaining' the line not 're-laying or repairing it', as required by the relevant statute.

These decisions surely cannot have been the intention of Parliament. However, the literal rule does not take into account the consequences of a literal interpretation, only whether words have a clear meaning which makes sense in that context. As Lord Esher stated in 1892: 'If the words of an Act are clear, then you must follow them even though they lead to a manifest absurdity' (*R v City of London Court Judge* [1892] 1 QB 273, 290). If Parliament does not like the literal interpretation, then it can always amend the legislation. However, modern case law shows that Lord Esher's views are now outmoded.

3.7 The golden rule

3.7.1 Meaning of the rule

The golden rule is an adaptation of the literal rule. It provides that where there are two meanings to a word or words, they should be given their ordinary meaning as far as possible, but only to the extent that they do not produce an absurd or totally obnoxious result:

> ... the grammatical and ordinary sense of the words is to be adhered to, unless that would lead to some absurdity or inconsistency with the rest of the instrument, in which case the grammatical and ordinary sense of the words may be modified, so as to avoid that absurdity or inconsistency, but not farther. (Lord Wensleydale in *Grey v Pearson* (1857) 10 ER 1216, 1234)

The case of *Adler v George* [1964] 2 QB 7 provides an effective example of the application of the golden rule. The defendant was convicted by the magistrates of an offence under s 3 of the Official Secrets Act 1920, because he had obstructed a member of Her Majesty's forces whilst 'in the vicinity of any prohibited place'. In this instance, the defendant was inside Marham Royal Air Force station, and he argued that he could not therefore have been 'in the vicinity' of the station as he was actually on the base itself.

However, it would have led to an absurd result if the defendant had been found not guilty. Such an outcome would have meant that the offence could only be committed if the obstruction occurred outside the base and not within its grounds. Clearly, this would not serve the purpose of the Act, which was to protect such military bases.

3.7.2 Use of the rule

This rule may be used in two ways. Here we look at the narrow sense; in **3.7.3** we examine the wider sense.

The golden rule is applied most frequently in a narrow sense where there is some ambiguity or absurdity in the words themselves. As Lord Reid stated in 1962, if a word is capable of more than one meaning, you can choose between those meanings, 'but beyond that you must not go' (*Jones v DPP* [1962] AC 635, 662).

The next case illustrates the sort of absurdity which the golden rule aims to counter. The case of *R v Allen* (1872) LR 1 CCR 367 required an interpretation of s 57 of the Offences Against the Person Act 1861. This section provided that: 'Whosoever, being married, shall marry another person during the life of the former husband or wife ...' shall commit the offence of bigamy.

If the word 'marry' had been given a literal interpretation it would be impossible for anyone ever to commit this offence as one cannot marry another person if one is already married. The purported second marriage would not be a valid marriage, so anyone going through the ceremony would not legally be marrying another person. The court therefore interpreted the word as meaning 'going through the ceremony' of marriage to avoid an absurd result.

A comparison of *Whiteley v Chappell* analysed at **3.6.2** above with *R v Allen* above does raise the question why the court used the literal rule for one and the golden rule for the other. In both instances, the court was required to decide between two different meanings of a word. Whilst the result of the *Allen* case is logical, as the effect of a literal interpretation would have made it impossible for anyone to commit bigamy, there is no obvious reason why the judges did not use the golden rule in the *Whiteley* case. The justification was that, under the statute, it would still have been an offence to impersonate a living person. Nevertheless, it would have been perfectly possible for the judges to have used the golden rule, and it is arguable that it would have led to a more sensible outcome. Indeed, were a *Whiteley*-style situation to arise again, it is very likely that modern-day judges would depart from the literal rule.

3.7.3 Other use of the golden rule

The second use of the golden rule is in a wider sense to avoid a result which is obnoxious to principles of public policy, even where words have only one meaning.

In *Re Sigsworth* [1935] Ch 89, the court had to consider the meaning of s 46 of the Administration of Estates Act 1925, in a case where the son had murdered his mother. Because there was no will, under the intestacy rules as set out in the Act, the son would have inherited his mother's residuary estate as her 'issue' (child). There was no ambiguity in the Act, but the court held that the son, as issue, could not inherit because this would produce an obnoxious result, contrary to the general principle of public policy that a murderer should not reap the fruits of his crime. As a consequence, the judges effectively wrote into the Act that the 'issue' would not be entitled to inherit where he had killed the deceased.

The golden rule plays little, if any, part in modern statutory interpretation. While occasionally a judge may make passing reference to it, the modern approach of interpreting a statute within its overall context will enable judges to depart from an absurd or literal constriction where necessary.

3.8 The mischief rule

The mischief rule requires the interpreter of the statute to ascertain the legislator's intention.

'Mischief' is itself a good example of a word having more than one meaning. The original meaning, which is the one intended here, was 'harm or wrong'. The court considers what 'mischief' or defect in the existing law the statute was intended to remedy using a four-stage test:

(a) What was the law before the statute was passed (ie the common law)?

(b) What was the 'mischief and defect' which was not remedied by the existing law?

(c) What remedy did Parliament propose to put it right?

(d) What is the true reason for the remedy?

You will recall from our discussion of *Corkery v Carpenter* [1951] 1 KB 102 at **3.3** above that under s 12 of the Licensing Act 1872, a person found drunk in charge of a 'carriage' on the highway is guilty of an offence. In that case the court took the view that the word 'carriage' could include a bicycle for the purpose of construing the Act. The judge based his reasoning on the mischief the Act intended to remedy. The Act was aimed at drunken persons in charge of some form of transportation and the exact nature of that transportation was interpreted widely. The mischief the statute intended to remedy was injury to the public from drunken drivers in order to preserve public order.

There are some relatively modern cases which according to a number of commentators apply the mischief rule. The case of *Royal College of Nursing v DHSS* [1981] AC 800 is one such case. The Royal College of Nursing challenged the legality of a statement issued by the Department of Health and Social Security that it was lawful for nurses to carry out abortions. Subject to certain conditions, s 1(1) of the Abortion Act 1967 provided that it would be not an offence 'if a pregnancy is terminated by a registered medical practitioner [ie a doctor]'. Advances in medical science resulted in many cases in the replacement of surgical abortions by hormonal abortions, and nurses commonly administered the requisite drugs. Applying the literal approach, the Court of Appeal held that the Department's guidance was unlawful and doctors had to perform the whole process personally ([1980] 11 WLUK 69).

On appeal, the House of Lords by a 3:2 majority reversed the Court of Appeal's judgment, based on an analysis of the mischief that the 1967 Act intended to remedy. Parliament had passed the

1967 Act to remedy the unsatisfactory and uncertain state of the law, to broaden the grounds on which it was legal to perform abortions, and to ensure that abortions were performed with proper skill in hygienic conditions. Accordingly, the majority held that that Parliament in making abortion lawful had contemplated a team effort, and the DHSS's guidance had been correct. An abortion is lawful where the termination is prescribed and initiated by a medical practitioner who remains in charge of it, and is carried out pursuant to their instructions by qualified nursing staff.

The literal rule would have meant that many doctors and nurses had unknowingly performed illegal abortions since the Act came into force. Notwithstanding this, the minority in the House of Lords still preferred the literal approach, stating it was up to Parliament to change the law to allow nurses to complete terminations.

Another interesting example of this approach is the judgment of the Supreme Court in *R (Electoral Commission) v Westminster Magistrates' Court* [2011] 1 AC 496. The United Kingdom Independence Party (UKIP) had received substantial donations from one of its supporters, Alan Bown. Unfortunately for UKIP, Mr Bown's name was not on the electoral register, although he was entitled to be registered. Political parties are not allowed to receive donations from individuals whose names are not on the electoral register. The Electoral Commission therefore applied for a forfeiture order under s 58(2) of the Political Parties, Elections and Referendums Act 2000 in respect of the impermissible donations. Section 58(2) provides: 'The court may, on an application made by the Commission, order the forfeiture by the party of an amount equal to the value of the donation.'

The Court of Appeal adopted a literal interpretation of s 58(2) ([2010] 2 WLR 873). Although the court had a discretion whether or not to order forfeiture, this discretion was very limited and, in the absence of special circumstances, forfeiture should follow as a matter of course. Moreover, the wording in s 58(2), 'an amount equal to the value of the donation', meant that an order for forfeiture had to be for the full amount of the donation; there was no power to order forfeiture of a lesser amount. The wording of the statute was clear; it was 'all or nothing'.

UKIP appealed to the Supreme Court where the majority held that s 58(2) permitted the forfeiture of a sum less than the total impermissible donations. In coming to this conclusion, the Supreme Court analysed the mischief the legislation was designed to prevent, namely the receipt by a political party of funding from foreign sources. Proof of acceptance of a donation from an impermissible source raised a presumption that the donation was foreign. If the party was unable to rebut that presumption, forfeiture of the whole amount should follow. If, on the other hand, the party succeeded in showing that the mischief against which the Act was directed had not occurred – that the donation in question was not a foreign donation – then it would be able to rebut the presumption. UKIP had accordingly rebutted the presumption by showing that the donor was entitled to be placed on the electoral register. The amount forfeited should therefore reflect the fault of the party in accepting the donations. Therefore the Supreme Court ordered that UKIP should forfeit only those donations made after the party had learned that Mr Bown was not on the electoral register. Accordingly, the amount UKIP forfeited was £14,481, rather than the full amount of the impermissible donations, £349,216.

Some commentators consider that the *RCN* and *Bown* cases are examples of the application of the mischief rule. While this is a plausible argument, other recent case law such as *Quintavalle* suggests that the courts were probably applying the purposive approach (see **3.10** below), namely that the purpose of each of the statutes in question was to remedy a particular mischief or problem.

3.9 Engineering the result?

A cynical view of the judiciary's approach to statutory interpretation is that judges decide what outcome they want to reach and then choose which rule or method justifies that interpretation. The effect of the three traditional rules of construction is that different decisions could be reached, depending upon which was used on the given facts. For example, in the *Whiteley v Chappell* case above, you will recall that the defendant was found not guilty of the offence of impersonating 'a person entitled to vote', because the person had died and therefore was not entitled to vote in the literal meaning of the words.

The result would have been different if the court had used the mischief rule instead. The aim of the legislation was clearly to prevent people from voting when they were not entitled to vote or had already voted, and so it would have been an offence to impersonate someone who was dead.

The case of *Smith v Hughes* [1960] 2 All ER 859 also demonstrates the interaction between the rules. The court considered the meaning of s 1(1) of the Street Offences Act 1959 pursuant to which it is an offence for a prostitute to solicit in a 'street or public place'. The women prosecuted under s 1(1) were not actually in the street, but were inside their homes, tapping on their windows and calling to attract the attention of men.

If the court had applied the literal rule, the women would have been acquitted. The reason is that they were in their own homes and, using the plain, ordinary or literal meaning, 'a street or public place' does not include private residences. However, the women were found guilty. Lord Parker used the mischief rule and stated that the aim of the Act was 'to clean up the streets, to enable people to walk along the streets without being molested or solicited by common prostitutes'.

Questions of statutory interpretation usually only reach the courts because there is at least some doubt about the interpretation of the statutory provisions in question. Sometimes the choice lies between two reasonable interpretations, as the differing views of the Court of Appeal and House of Lords/Supreme Court in the *RCN* and *Bown* cases show. Statutory interpretation involves far more than applying a set of rules; in complex cases it involves analysing the language used, looking at the context and attempting to discern the aim of the legislation.

3.10 The purposive approach

The purposive approach is a more modern style of interpreting statutes, and it has become increasingly influential. The judges look at the reasons why the statute was passed and its purpose, even if it means distorting the ordinary meaning of the words. This approach was influenced by our membership of the European Union as it is widely used in EU law, which is drafted with the expectation that judges will consider the policy behind the words. However, the principle is not confined to EU law, and judges regularly adopt a purposive approach when considering all types of statute. Indeed, the mischief rule, although historically distinct from the purposive approach, has effectively been subsumed into the purposive approach.

In *Quintavalle* (above), Lord Steyn clearly demonstrated a shift from a literal approach to a purposive one:

> The pendulum has swung towards purposive methods of construction. This change ... has been accelerated by European ideas ... [N]owadays the shift towards purposive interpretation is not in doubt.

Lords Reed and Hodge, giving the leading judgment in *Test Claimants in the FII Group Litigation v HMRC* [2020] UKSC 47, further demonstrated the purposive approach's significance by stating:

> It is the duty of the court, in accordance with ordinary principles of statutory interpretation, to favour an interpretation of legislation which gives effect to its purpose rather than defeating it.

Figure 3.1 below summarises the traditional rules of construction and also takes into account the development of the purposive approach.

Figure 3.1 Rules of construction

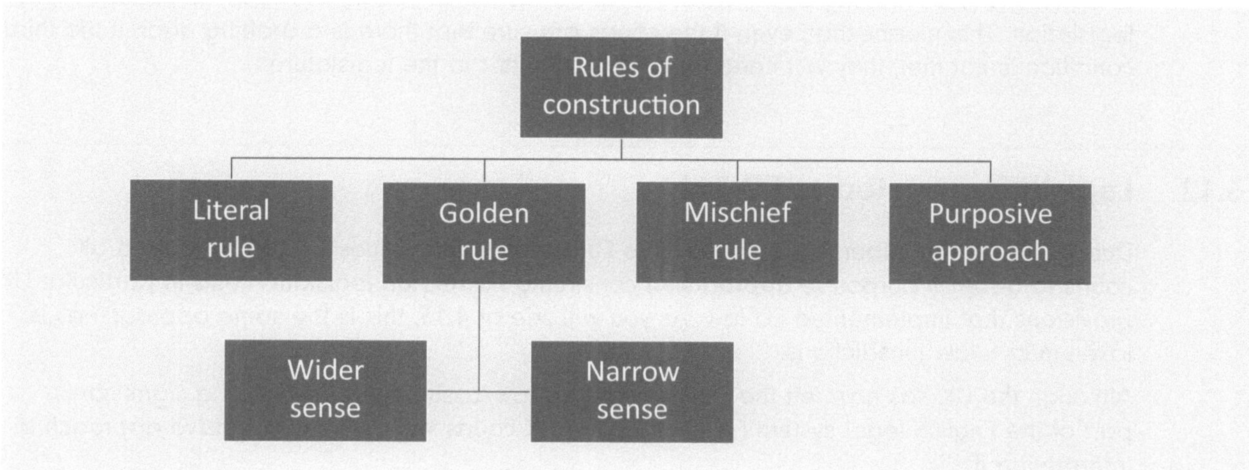

3.11 Rectification of a statute

In the case of *Inco Europe Ltd v First Choice Distribution* [2000] 1 WLR 586, the House of Lords stated that words could be added to a statute to resolve an obvious drafting error. This case concerned complex arbitration issues, and the appellant wanted to appeal from the High Court to the Court of Appeal. The relevant legislation, the Supreme Court Act 1981 (as amended), only permitted a right of appeal in limited circumstances. Those circumstances included those provided for by Part I of the Arbitration Act 1996. However, Part I of the 1996 Act did not actually set out any circumstances in which an appeal would be permitted. In this instance, the House of Lords added a right of appeal from the High Court to the Court of Appeal, despite the absence of any such appeal in the statute.

Lord Nicholls acknowledged in his speech that if the legislation were to be read literally, no appeal would lie to the Court of Appeal. However, several features make it plain that something went awry in the drafting. The Supreme Court Act 1981 had been amended when the Arbitration Act 1996 had been enacted, and the aim of those amendments had been to retain the situation under the previous arbitration legislation under which a right of appeal had existed. However, on a literal meaning of the language, the amendments to the 1981 Act did not retain the right of appeal.

In coming to their conclusion, the House of Lords did have regard to the purposive approach (see **3.10** above). Lord Nicholls stated that the starting point was to consider what was the purpose of the Act, and bearing that in mind he continued, 'I am left in no doubt that, for once, the draftsman slipped up ... Given the intended object of the section is plain, it should be read in a manner which gives effect to Parliamentary intention.'

Lord Nicholls concluded by stating that: 'I freely acknowledge that this interpretation [that a right of appeal does lie to the Court of Appeal] involves reading words into the paragraph.' However, he went on to state that: 'The court must be able to correct obvious drafting errors.' Nonetheless, he acknowledged that before rectifying a statute in this way, the court must be sure:

(1) of the intended purpose of the statute or provision;

(2) that inadvertently the drafter and Parliament failed to give effect to that purpose in the provision in question; and

(3) of the substance of the provision Parliament would have made, although not necessarily the precise words that Parliament would have used, had the error in the bill been noticed.

Lord Nicholls emphasised the crucial nature of the third condition as otherwise any attempt to determine the meaning of the statute would cross the boundary between construction and legislation. This means that, even if the courts are sure that there is a drafting error, if the third condition is not met, they will need to leave the matter to the legislature.

3.12 Legislation related to EU law

During the UK's membership of the EU, the European Communities Act 1972 required UK courts to adopt a purposive approach in construing EU related legislation and in particular UK provisions that implemented EU law. As you will see at **4.13**, this is the same approach as is taken in civil law jurisdictions.

Although the UK has now left the EU, retained EU law/assimilated law forms a significant part of the English legal system (see **1.13**), and UK courts will apply a purposive approach to interpreting it.

European Union legislation is drafted in a very different way from English statutes. It follows the civil law tradition, which favours simplicity of drafting and a high degree of abstraction, rather than the exhaustive approach adopted in the UK. This means that a purposive approach is vital when interpreting legislation, so that questions of wide economic or social aims are often considered by the courts. The same principles will apply to interpreting retained EU law/assimilated law.

The case of *Litster v Forth Dry Dock and Engineering Co Ltd* [1990] 1 AC 546 provides a good illustration of the purposive approach. In that case, employees were dismissed one hour before a business was transferred to a new owner. The employees claimed they were unfairly dismissed. Regulation 5 of the Transfer of Undertakings (Protection of Employment) Regulations 1981 (SI 1981/1794) (a statutory instrument which implemented an EU Directive) provided that a transfer shall not terminate the contract of any person employed 'immediately before the transfer'. The House of Lords read in the additional words 'or would have been so employed if he had not been unfairly dismissed before the transfer' for a reason connected with the transfer. This was necessary to achieve the purpose of the EU Directive, which was to protect the employees on the transfer of a business.

Notwithstanding the UK's exit from the EU, UK courts would probably still adopt a very similar approach should a comparable situation now arise. There are also specialised rules for interpreting retained EU law/assimilated law, which are covered in **Chapter 9**.

We shall again analyse the interaction of the different rules by examining the facts of *Litster v Forth Dry Dock and Engineering Co Ltd* (above). Apart from adopting a purposive approach, as discussed above, we shall consider whether the judges could have used the traditional rules of construction to interpret the statutory instrument, in order to reach the same conclusion.

The literal rule would not have achieved the same result, as the employees were not employed 'immediately' before the transfer. They had been dismissed. However, a similar result could have been achieved using the mischief rule, because the mischief the Act intended to prevent was the dismissal of workers at or about the time of the transfer. Accordingly, one hour could still have been interpreted as 'immediately' before the transfer. Arguably the golden rule would also have protected the employees, as it would be absurd to allow employers to evade liability under the law, simply by dismissing their workers minutes before the transfer took place. However, would these two rules have worked if it had been a day or a week before the transfer? This is less clear.

As decisions of the CJEU handed down before the end of the transition period (31 December 2020) relating to retained EU law/assimilated law remain binding on all UK courts apart from the Supreme Court and Court of Appeal (and courts of equivalent status), its rules of legal reasoning remain important in our legal system and have an indirect influence on interpretation.

3.13 The impact of the Human Rights Act 1998 on principles of statutory interpretation

Section 3 of the Human Rights Act 1998 provides that 'so far as it is possible to do so, primary and subordinate legislation must be read and given effect in a way which is compatible with the Convention rights'. As we have seen at **1.15.2**, if the court cannot achieve this, it may make a declaration of incompatibility pursuant to s 4 of the 1998 Act in respect of the relevant piece of legislation.

The practical effect of s 3 was considered by the House of Lords in the case of *R v A (No 2)* [2002] 1 AC 45. The House of Lords had to decide whether s 41 of the Youth Justice and Criminal Evidence Act 1999, which sets out the circumstances in which a defendant on trial for rape may question his victim in the witness box, was compatible with a defendant's right to a fair trial under Article 6 of the European Convention on Human Rights.

The specific issue of statutory interpretation concerned s 41(3)(b), which prohibited a defendant from questioning the complainant/victim about her sexual behaviour unless the issue in question was that the victim consented to sex and the 'sexual behaviour of the complainant to which the evidence or question relates is alleged to have taken place at or about the same time as the event which is the subject matter of the charge against the accused'.

It was the defendant's case that the complainant consented to sex as he and the complainant had been conducting a continuing sexual relationship. At the first instance, the trial judge refused to allow the defendant to question the complainant about their continuing relationship on the basis that to do so was prohibited by s 41(3)(b). The defendant appealed against this preliminary finding on the basis that not allowing him to question the complainant in the above fashion deprived him of a fair trial under Article 6.

The majority of the House (Lord Hope dissenting) held that whilst it was quite clear that the literal interpretation of s 41 was that the evidence could only relate to acts which were contemporaneous to the incident charged, which was not the case with the defendant, it was necessary to apply the interpretative obligation under s 3 of the Human Rights Act 1998. Accordingly, the appropriate test for whether the defendant could question the victim would be whether the evidence to be obtained by the questioning was so relevant to the issue of consent that to exclude it would endanger the fairness of the trial under Article 6.

On the facts of this case, the defendant failed. However, *R v A* provides an interesting illustration of the thin line between judges interpreting and making law, as it seems clear that they have given s 41(3)(b) a very different meaning from the one intended by Parliament when it was drafted. Some critics have argued that the House of Lords should have issued a declaration of incompatibility rather than effectively rewriting s 41.

Chapter 6 analyses the Human Rights Act 1998 in more depth.

Figure 3.2 How the mischief rule differs from the purposive approach

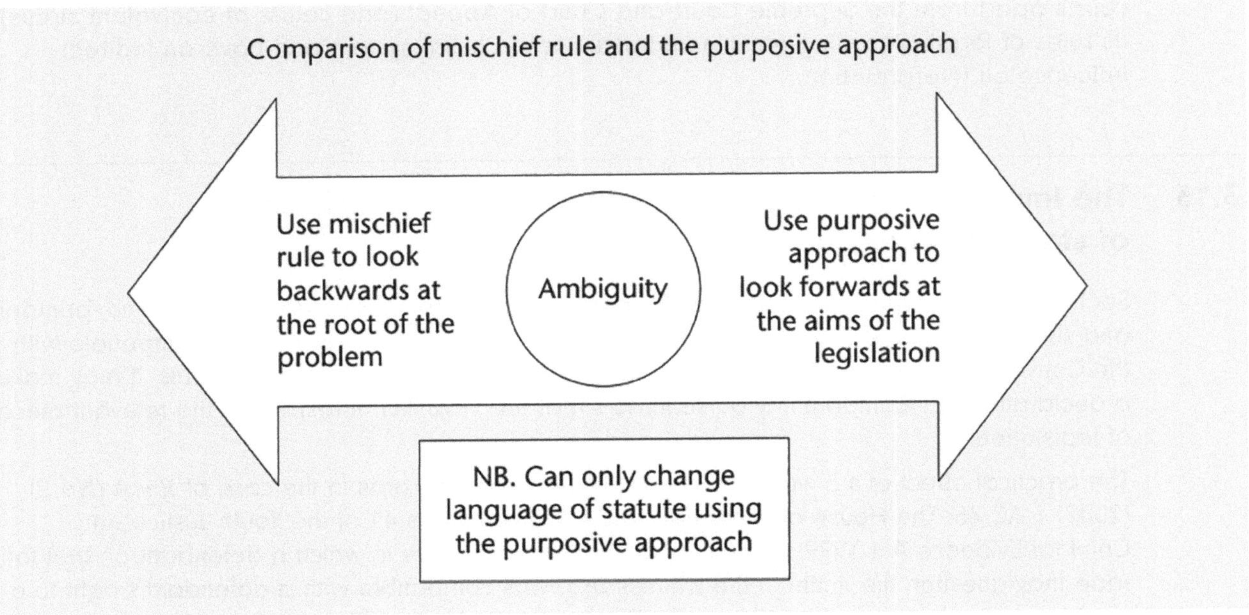

(The modern approach exemplified by *Quintavalle* suggests the courts now pay little regard to this distinction.)

3.14 Rules of language

3.14.1 Introduction

The rules of language are similar to the rules of construction in that they are not rules in the strict sense of the word but general principles that judges may apply when they read a statute. Judges will not always make it clear in their judgment which, if any, of the rules of language they may have utilised; however, unlike the traditional rules of construction, judges still make frequent use of the rules of language.

There are three separate rules of language, which we shall discuss below. Note that judges can use both rules of language and rules of construction alongside each other.

3.14.2 *Noscitur a sociis* (recognition by associated words)

Noscitur a sociis literally means 'known by the company it keeps'. That is to say that a word derives meaning from surrounding words. Have a look at the following activity and decide how you would resolve the ambiguity.

Activity 2 Applying the rule of *noscitur a sociis*

A clause in a lease agreement states: 'Only the following animals are permitted in this block of flats – dogs, cats, hamsters and gerbils'. Would this include a leopard?

Comment

Common sense would suggest that leopards would not be included. However, lawyers must be able to justify this conclusion, and to enable them to do this they use rules of language. The rule which assists here is that of *noscitur a sociis,* because the clause contains an exhaustive list of animals. Looking at the type of the other animals in the list, a leopard would not be included because 'cats' in this context means 'domestic cats'.

Noscitur a sociis was used to assist in the interpretation of the Factories Act 1961, which required that all 'floors, steps, stairs, passageways and gangways' had to be kept free from obstruction. The question which the court had to decide in *Pengelly v Bell Punch Co Ltd* [1964] 1 WLR 1055 was whether a floor used for storage came under the provisions of the Act. The court held that as all the other words were used to indicate passage, a floor used exclusively for storage did not fall within the Act.

3.14.3 *Eiusdem generis* (of the same kind or nature)

If a general word follows two or more specific words, that general word will only apply to items of the same type as the specific words. *Eiusdem* (or *ejusdem*) *generis* means 'of the same type'.

3.14.3.1 Applying the rule of *eiusdem generis*

To determine whether this rule applies, it is helpful to use the structured approach set out below:

(1) Are there *general* words following a list of *specific* words?

(2) If so, what *type* are the specific words?

(3) Interpretation: any new item will be included in the statute only if it is of the same type as the specific words.

The case of *Wood v Commissioner of Police of the Metropolis* [1986] 1 WLR 796 illustrates the use of the *eiusdem generis* rule. The defendant was charged with committing an offence under s 4 of the Vagrancy Act 1824 after using a piece of broken glass, which had fallen out of his front door. Section 4 of the 1824 Act made it an offence to be armed with 'any gun, pistol, hanger, cutlass, bludgeon or other offensive weapon' with intent to commit a serious offence. The issue therefore was whether a piece of broken glass fell within the scope of 'other offensive weapon'.

A comparison of the wording of s 4 with the definition used in the *Pengelly* case above shows a difference in format. In the *Pengelly* case, the Act provided a closed list of the types of floors, etc which had to be kept free from obstruction. However, the list of weapons in s 4 of the Vagrancy Act 1824 is not exhaustive, as it includes 'other' offensive weapons. The court used the *eiusdem generis* test to decide if the piece of broken glass was an 'other offensive weapon'.

If a general word follows two or more specific words, that general word will only apply to items of the same type as the specific words, as *eiusdem generis* means 'of the same type'. Applying the structured approach set out earlier in this paragraph leads to the following conclusion:

(1) There are general words ('or other offensive weapon') following a list of specific words.

(2) The specific words are all of the same type in that they are items made or adapted as weapons. Because they have been designed as weapons, they have a common feature.

(3) Interpretation: broken glass is not of the same type as it was neither made nor adapted for causing injury to a person. It is not enough that an item has the potential for such use.

Accordingly, the broken glass was not an 'other offensive weapon'.

It would have been different if the wording of s 4 of the Vagrancy Act 1824 had ended with the words '... any other offensive weapon whatsoever'. The addition of the word 'whatsoever' would indicate that the legislature had intended all offensive weapons of whatever nature to be covered.

The case of *Powell v Kempton Park Racecourse Co* [1899] AC 143 provides another example of the use of the rule of *eiusdem generis*. Here, the House of Lords had to decide whether s 1 of the Betting Act 1853, which prohibited the keeping of a 'house, office, room or other place' for the purpose of betting, applied to Tattersall's Ring, which was an outdoor area at the racecourse. The court said it did not, as the specific places were all indoors.

In terms of the distinction between the two above rules, the *eiusdem generis* rule is used for a list containing general words, whereas *noscitur a sociis* is used for specific words and comparing the placing of words in legislation.

3.14.4 *Expressio unius est exclusio alterius* (expressing one thing excludes another)

This means 'to express one is to exclude others'; therefore mention of one or more specific things may be taken to exclude others of the same type.

In *R v Inhabitants of Sedgley* (1831) 2 B & Ald 65, the court held that the poor rate levied on occupiers of 'lands, houses and coal mines' under the Poor Relief Act 1601 could not be levied on owners of other types of mine.

This case is perfectly clear, as otherwise there was no explanation for the insertion of the word 'coal'. However, care must be taken when using this particular rule, as the omission may be inadvertent.

A more recent example of the use of this rule can be found in the case of *R v Secretary of State for the Home Department, ex parte Crew* [1982] Imm AR 94. Here, it was used to exclude the father of an illegitimate child from rights under the immigration law at the time, because the definitions section specifically mentioned the mother alone.

Note that the most commonly used rule of language is the *eiusdem generis* rule.

In the next activity you have an opportunity to apply these rules of language.

Activity 3 Rules of language

Consider the following examples, which are taken from two decided cases. If you were the judge hearing the case, which of the above three rules would you apply and why? What would be the result?

1. A statute requires an employer to protect employees from 'danger from shock, burn or other injury'. Does this include tripping?
2. The statutory definition of '... "equipment" includes any plant and machinery, vehicle, aircraft, and clothing'. Does it include a ship?

Comment

1. The *eiusdem generis* rule was applied in this case (*Lane v London Electricity Board* [1955] 1 WLR 106), as there are specific words which are followed by the general words 'or other injury'. However, as shock and burn were both dangers from electricity, they were regarded as a different type from tripping over the cables, so tripping was excluded.
2. The Court of Appeal applied the *expressio unius est exclusio alterius* rule in this case (*Coltman v Bibby Tankers Ltd* [1987] 2 WLR 1098); in its view Parliament had, by expressly including in the definition of 'equipment' means of conveyance on land and in the air, specifically excluded means of conveyance on the sea. (The specific reference to 'aircraft' meant that the word 'vehicle' was limited to conveyance on land.) However, the House of Lords reversed this judgment and took a different approach ([1988] AC 276). The word 'includes' before the start of the list was an indication that the list was not closed, so the House of Lords interpreted 'equipment' widely to include a ship.

It is also important to understand that often the use of the word 'include' indicates that what is being offered is not a standard definition as, for instance, in the definition of a business in the Unfair Contract Terms Act 1977, which is stated to include the activities of a profession. This definition does not define the core meaning of business at all, but simply indicates that certain things which are not normally regarded as businesses should be treated so for the purpose of the statute; see further **3.15.2** below. Note that, although when there is a list of words, the inclination is to use one of these rules of language, the purposive approach could also have been used. Indeed, in *Coltman v Bibby Tankers Ltd*, one of the reasons the House of Lords interpreted 'equipment' widely was to give effect to the aim of the statute.

3.15 Aids to interpretation

3.15.1 Introduction

In addition to using the rules of construction and language we have discussed above, it is open for the courts to use the following aids to interpreting a statute in the event that its meaning is not clear.

3.15.2 Intrinsic aids (the use of the statute itself)

The statute must be read as a whole, and the words read in context (note the overlap with 'rules of language').

Any words which have been debated by Parliament and are thus part of the statute are legitimate aids. Therefore, the long and short titles, preamble (not commonly found in modern statutes), punctuation and headings may be used.

Marginal notes are not debated in Parliament and therefore are not normally used. For example, in *Chandler v DPP* [1964] AC 763, the court decided that in s 1 of the Official Secrets Act 1911, 'espionage' included sabotage, and declined to use the marginal note which read 'spying' as an aid.

An interpretation section in an Act may be used, but is subject to contrary intention in the text. Many Acts now contain a section which defines the key words used. For example, s 33 of the Offensive Weapons Act 2019 states that in the Act '"applicant" means an applicant for a knife crime prevention order', while '"harm" includes physical and psychological harm'. The definition of 'applicant' uses the word 'means'; this indicates that it is an exhaustive definition of the defined term and displaces its natural meaning. The definition of 'harm' uses the word 'includes' and, as indicated in **Activity 3** above, this means that it is an inclusive definition and modifies the natural meaning of the defined term by extending it or clarifying possible doubt about what it covers. Occasionally, a definition will be 'exclusive' and narrow the meaning of a word by excluding something which would normally be within its scope.

3.16 Extrinsic aids (aids outside the statute itself)

3.16.1 Interpretation Acts

The Interpretation Acts give definitions of words commonly found in legislation. For instance, s 6 of the Interpretation Act 1978 states that, in all legislation, the masculine includes the feminine, and the singular includes the plural unless indicated otherwise. It is now modern practice to use inclusive language in drafting statutes; however, there are numerous older statutes in force where it is still necessary to rely on s 6 as such statutes will often refer to the masculine when they mean both masculine and feminine.

3.16.2 Dictionaries

Dictionaries can be referred to when a word has no specific legal meaning. Dictionaries are of particular value where judges are using the literal approach (see **3.6** above).

3.16.3 Other statutes

The court may look at other statutes. These could either be earlier statutes replaced by the current statute, or any other statute. However, just because a word has been interpreted in one statute does not mean it will be interpreted the same way in another.

3.16.4 *Hansard*

Traditionally, because the court was allowed to interpret only the words used, it was not usually permissible for courts to refer to the preparatory work. Therefore, although all Parliamentary debates about the statute in the House of Commons and the House of Lords are recorded in *Hansard*, generally a court cannot refer to this explicitly as an aid to interpretation.

However, over time there was some relaxation of this strict rule, particularly in order to identify the 'mischief' which an Act is intended to remedy. This culminated in *Pepper v Hart* [1993] AC 593, when the House of Lords (now the Supreme Court) decided that the courts could refer to Parliamentary material recorded in *Hansard* if:

(a) the statute is ambiguous or obscure, or its literal meaning leads to an absurdity; and

(b) the material consists of clear statements by a Minister or other promoter of the Bill.

This case concerned teachers at an independent school whose children could be educated for one-fifth of the school's normal fee. The question was whether reduced school fees were to be treated as a taxable benefit under s 63 of the Finance Act 1976. There was an ambiguity in the statute, and the issue arose as to whether the court could take account of statements made by the Financial Secretary to the Treasury during the report stage of the Bill. The House of Lords decided that it could.

3.17 Presumptions

3.17.1 Introduction

In addition to the above rules and aids, the courts apply certain presumptions in interpreting legislation which we shall discuss below.

3.17.2 When do presumptions apply?

Certain presumptions are applied in interpreting legislation. It is always possible to rebut any presumption, ie to bring strong evidence to prove that Parliament had a contrary intention. Note the use of the word 'strong'. If it was only necessary to bring 'evidence', there would be no presumption at all.

Imagine an old-fashioned pair of scales (like those held by the Statue of Justice): if they are evenly balanced, then it is only necessary for one party to bring *some* evidence to tilt the scales either way. However, if they are already tilted in favour of one party, the other must bring enough evidence not only to even things out, but to go further and tilt them in their favour. Therefore, this evidence must be strong.

You will find presumptions in various areas of the law, but for statutory interpretation here are some examples:

(a) *Against alteration of the common law.* Unless the statute expressly states an intention to alter the common law, the interpretation which does not alter the existing law will be preferred.

(b) *Against the retrospective operation of statutes.* Where an Act of Parliament becomes law, a presumption arises that it will apply only to future actions. This is particularly important in relation to taxation and criminal law cases. However, some legislation is specifically stated to have retrospective effect; an example is the War Crimes Act 1991, which allows the prosecution of those suspected of committing acts of atrocity during World War II.

(c) *Against criminal liability without guilty intention (mens rea).* There is a presumption in favour of *mens rea* or guilty mind in criminal matters. When creating new criminal offences, Parliament does not always define the *mens rea* required. In these cases, the presumption will be applied. In *Sweet v Parsley* [1970] AC 132, a school teacher was convicted of drugs offences after her tenants were discovered growing cannabis in her rented house. She was found guilty, despite her lack of knowledge of the situation, but the decision was later overturned by the House of Lords (now the Supreme Court) using this presumption.

(d) *Against deprivation of the liberty of the individual.* Accordingly, any ambiguity in a penal or criminal statute will be interpreted in favour of the citizen.

(e) *Against deprivation of property or interference with private rights.*

(f) *Against binding the Crown.* Unless there is a clear statement to the contrary, legislation is presumed not to apply to the Crown.

(g) *Against ousting the jurisdiction of the courts.*

In the next activity you have an opportunity to use the 'rules' and aids studied above.

Activity 4 Problems of interpretation

Let us assume, for the purposes of this activity, that the legislation banning smoking has been extended so that it is an offence for a man to smoke a cigarette in any public place.

Which of all the above 'rules' and aids are likely to be the most helpful in each of cases 1. to 3. below? Do not try to reach a conclusion as to whether each person has committed the offence.

1. Jack is arrested for sitting in a public house with an unlit cigarette in his mouth.
2. Mandy is arrested while smoking a cigarette in the street.
3. Anwar is found smoking in his local park. Is this a public place?

Comment

1. The mischief rule or the purposive approach. We would need to consider why it was an offence to smoke in order to determine whether having an unlit cigarette in Jack's mouth was included. The mischief or purpose of the Act is to prevent people from inhaling the smoke from others' cigarettes. There are health and safety issues which apply. An unlit cigarette would not be included on this basis. However, if the purpose of the Act was to prevent the public being 'offended' by the sight or use of cigarettes, Jack is guilty. This interpretation is, however, unlikely.

We could also use the literal rule. This would also result in Jack being found not guilty, as he is not 'smoking' a cigarette in the accepted sense.

2. Section 6 of the Interpretation Act 1978 (an extrinsic aid) states that the masculine includes the feminine and vice versa, therefore Mandy would be guilty.

3. We may be able to find another statute in which 'public place' is defined (another extrinsic aid) (in fact, there is such a definition in s 16 of the Public Order Act 1986). However, we would also have to look at the purposive approach again to determine whether there is any similarity of purpose between the two statutes in order to decide whether it should be interpreted in the same way.

Figure 3.3 Principles of interpretation

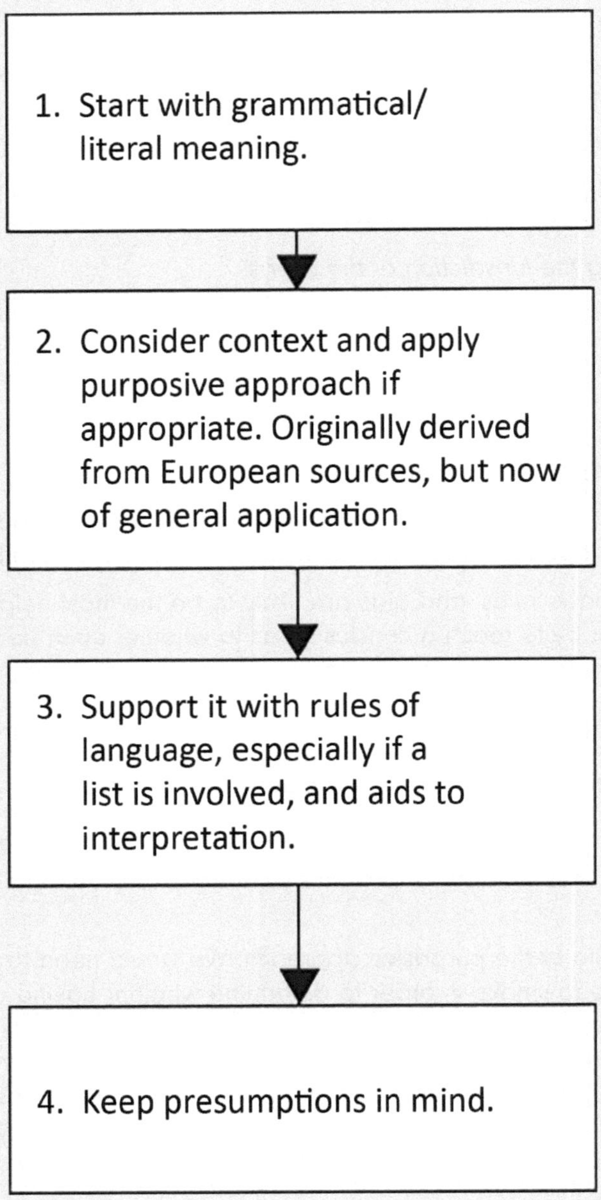

Summary

In conclusion:

(a) Traditionally there were three basic rules of construction, but the courts now prefer a purposive approach to interpret disputed provisions.

(b) While the grammatical meaning of the words in a statute provides a useful starting point, in cases of dispute the courts will apply the purposive approach and take into account the wider context.

(c) There are other rules of language, aids and presumptions which judges may use to interpret disputed provisions.

(d) The role of the courts is to implement the legislative intention and not to decide what the law should be.

(e) Sometimes the various rules, approaches and principles interact with each other. For example, intrinsic aids to support the purposive approach; or the purposive approach to rebut the presumption of *mens rea* being required.

You may find it helpful to adopt the approach set out in **Figure 3.3** above when considering which principles of interpretation to use.

The law is not static - it is constantly evolving to meet the needs of an ever-changing society. Its ability to adapt to new situations is a strength of our legal system. The principles of statutory interpretation are the key to this flexibility, as well as providing an essential tool in remedying obvious absurdities in statutes.

In this chapter, you have studied the way in which statutes are interpreted and the means by which this is done. You have considered the long-established literal, golden and mischief rules, and their more recent companion, the purposive approach, which is now the predominant method used to resolve disputes in interpretation. We have also discussed the rules of language, the aids to interpretation and the presumptions. Most importantly, you have begun to develop your ability to interpret legislation, to understand its effect and to use this knowledge to solve legal problems. You have also looked at the role of courts in interpreting legislation, but what happens if two courts come to different conclusions? The doctrine of precedent, which you will study in **Chapter 4**, identifies which decision should be followed.

4 The Doctrine of Precedent

Learning outcomes

When you have completed this chapter, you should be able to:

- read cases, identifying the *ratio* and examples of *obiter dicta*;
- explain and evaluate the role and relevance of the doctrine of precedent to the English legal system, and compare it with civil law jurisdictions;
- understand and analyse whether a precedent is binding or not;
- apply and distinguish cases when looking at a fact pattern.

4.1 Introduction

You will recall from **Chapter 1** that there are four main sources of English law - case law, UK legislation, retained EU law/assimilated law and the European Convention on Human Rights. However, for much of the last 1,000 years, case law and, as a consequence, the judges have been the key players in the development of the English legal system. Indeed, it is only in the last 150 years that this dominant position has given way to the increasing influence of legislation. However, case law continues to play a vital role in all areas of the law, particularly contract and tort.

In this chapter, you will develop your understanding of how case law continues to be used. Obviously, every case is important to the parties concerned, but not every case is of value to the public as a whole. We will identify how and why some cases are elevated to a position of influence, whereas others are not. This will build on your understanding of the courts, from **Chapter 2**. In addition, it will involve the study of the principles of law, known as the *ratio decidendi*, which can be found within the judgment and how these can be distinguished from the less important aspects of the judges' comments - the *obiter dicta*. In addition, we will look at which courts' decisions are binding on others, the hierarchy of the courts, and how judges can avoid awkward precedents should they wish to do so.

The ability to select and use appropriate cases to support a legal argument is a key skill for all lawyers. Barristers in particular must research and cite relevant cases when drafting legal opinions or making legal submissions, and all lawyers must be able to apply appropriate legal principles to the facts of the case they are advising upon. Of more immediate concern to you in your study of the law is that this same skill is an essential requirement when you are carrying out legal research.

England and Wales is a common law jurisdiction. Law is developed and interpreted by judges. There are very clear rules which judges must abide by when formulating their decisions. This chapter sets out these rules and some of the methods used by practitioners and the courts to ensure they operate within those rules.

Although on occasion judges have to engage in judicial law-making, as a general rule they seek to decide cases in accordance with existing rules. We have already encountered (at **1.7.2.1**) the doctrine of precedent, which is sometimes referred to by its Latin name of *stare decisis* ('let the decision stand'). It developed slowly over several centuries and requires that, in certain circumstances, English courts (unlike courts in civil law jurisdictions) are bound to follow decisions which have been reached in previous cases. This is important not only to common law, where the law comes from cases, but also to the interpretation of legislation by the judges.

4.1.1 When does the doctrine apply?

A proposition stated in one case is binding in a later case if it is:

(a) a proposition of law;

(b) part of the *ratio decidendi* of a case;

(c) decided in a court whose decisions are binding on the present court; and

(d) there are no relevant distinctions between the two cases.

A case must be decided in the same way as an earlier one if its material facts (ie those which are legally relevant) are the same. The part of the earlier case which is potentially binding is called the *ratio decidendi*, usually shortened to *ratio*, the 'reason for the decision'. Accordingly, the later court does not have to accept and follow everything the previous court said, only the principle going to the heart of the decision. Whether the *ratio* is binding depends upon both the hierarchy of the courts and the isolating of the *ratio decidendi* of the previous case. It requires efficient law reporting, so that previous decisions can be considered in detail.

4.1.2 Why do we have this doctrine?

This is the question you will consider in the next activity.

Activity 1 Consistency and certainty

This activity will enable you to think about the reasons for having a doctrine of precedent. It is divided into two parts. Please read the comment to Part 1 before moving on to Part 2.

Part 1

Imagine you are watching a soccer match (or any game that has a referee, rules and a concept of 'foul play').

In the first minute, a player from Team A commits what you regard as a foul by a reckless challenge on a player from Team B. Despite this, the referee allows play to continue and Team A scores. Team B protests and the referee has to separate players who are arguing heatedly. No one is sent off.

Five minutes later a player from Team B (which you support) commits what you think is a similar challenge on a player from Team A. The referee awards a free kick and sends off the Team B player for his first foul in the game.

Team B loses the match.

1. What principles of fairness do you think have been violated here?
2. Looking at it from the referee's point of view, why might they think they have acted properly?

Comment

1. It is a basic principle of justice that 'like cases should be treated in like ways' (the consistency principle). The two players apparently committing fouls should have been treated in the same way.

   It is also a basic principle of justice that people should be able to assume that rules will be applied to them in a predictable way (the certainty principle). Here you might say that the rules were not correctly applied to the player from Team B.

   The punishment should fit the crime (the proportionality principle). Here you may think it is excessive for the player from Team B to be sent off for a first offence.

   These principles of justice apply to law as they do to refereeing a soccer match, with the possible difference that, at least in common law cases, courts formulate the 'rules' as they decide cases, rather than having a rigid set of rules already in place. There is also an important practical consideration in adopting such a system, in that it is more efficient to apply past precedents rather than 'reinvent the wheel' by arguing a case from the beginning again.

   It also ensures that the public know what the law is; as we have discussed in **Chapter 1**, the law must be respected by the majority of the population if it is to remain credible. It has been suggested that the only winners, if the law is uncertain, are the lawyers. This point is illustrated by a well-known cartoon in which two farmers are arguing over the ownership of a cow. One farmer is pulling at the head and the other at the tail, whilst the lawyer is sitting happily in the middle milking the cow!

2. The referee may have seen the two incidents differently from you, and may have thought the first incident involving Team A was not a foul.

   The referee may have believed it proper to send off the player from Team B for the first foul because referees have an overriding duty to control the game. The previous protests showed that Team B were not accepting the referee's authority, or the game was slipping out of control.

These considerations also apply in the legal system.

Different people may see facts differently, so the results of cases may be difficult to predict, even if laws are certain and consistently applied. No two cases are ever exactly the same.

Like referees, courts may have an element of discretion, particularly when sentencing or granting remedies. A court might, for instance, impose harsher penalties as an example or a deterrent in a situation where there is a serious threat to public order.

The doctrine of precedent therefore aims to ensure that the law is certain, and applied consistently, with due regard for differences between cases and the context in which decisions are taken.

Part 2

What do you consider to be the disadvantages of certainty?

Comment

Nevertheless, certainty has its disadvantages. What if everyone, public and lawyers alike, think the first decision was wrong? Even if it was the correct decision at the time, times change. For example, society's attitude towards cohabitation has changed. In previous centuries, contracts between cohabitees were often held to be void on public policy grounds. The simple answer to these problems, remembering that judges exercise self-restraint in making law, is for Parliament to legislate to change the law. Unfortunately this takes time, and so at the end of this chapter, we will look at how judges can 'get around' the doctrine of precedent.

4.1.3 What is a 'proposition of law'?

The proposition must be one of law not fact. You will recall this distinction from your consideration of the civil and criminal appeal process in **Chapter 2**. One way of deciding whether something is a fact is to consider whether it can be proved, or at least inferred, from the evidence. However, it is not always easy to separate fact from law. In *Qualcast Ltd v Haynes* [1959] AC 743, the employer provided protective clothing and informed the workers that it was available, but did not ensure that they wore it. A worker was injured while working and sued the employer for negligence.

At first instance, the judge said that he was bound by a previous decision to hold that the employer was negligent. However, the House of Lords held that whether an employer who did not ensure that workers used protective clothing was negligent was a question of fact in each case, and not a proposition of law. That it was fact, not law, becomes clearer when we look at the decision in this case: the employer was not negligent as the risk was obvious, the injury unlikely to be serious, and the worker experienced. However, on a different set of facts, an employer could be negligent.

The distinction between fact and law is not one which one can intuitively perceive on some kind of self-evident basis, but is itself historically derived. It is related to the division of function between judge and jury, so that at one level questions of law are issues which were decided by the judges and questions of fact were decided by juries. However, many questions involve mixed questions of fact and law. The question of whether someone (for example a car driver who injures a pedestrian) is negligent is a classic example of a mixed question of fact and law.

4.1.4 Matters of law and fact

We shall use the case of *DPP v Johnson* [1995] 1 WLR 728 to illustrate the distinction between matters of law and fact. Section 5(1) of the Road Traffic Act 1988 provides that 'if a person drives ... a motor vehicle on a road ... after consuming so much alcohol that the proportion of it in his breath ... exceeds the prescribed limit he is guilty of an offence'. Mr Johnson was stopped by the police, breathalysed and charged under s 5(1) as the breathalyser showed that he was above the limit.

A month previously, Mr Johnson's doctor had injected him with a pain-relieving drug containing a preservative, benzyl alcohol, which was released intermittently and unevenly directly into the lungs, and which could have affected the breathalyser reading. Neither Mr Johnson nor his doctor knew of the presence of alcohol in his body emanating from the injection. In effect it was the injection that had caused him to be over the limit.

For the prosecution to succeed, it would be necessary for the court to make the following findings:

(1) That the proportion of alcohol in Mr Johnson's breath exceeded the prescribed limit contrary to s 5(1)(a) of the Road Traffic Act 1988

(2) That the injection of alcohol into the body is a mode of consumption of alcohol within the definition of s 5 above.

Proposition (1) is a matter of fact and depends upon the reading given by the intoximeter when Mr Johnson's breath was tested. A fact is, therefore, a statement which depends on the evidence.

Proposition (2) is a point of law, as it determines what constitutes a mode of consumption for the purposes of the Act. While you might consider whether someone has consumed alcohol is a point of fact, here it involved a point of law - whether injecting alcohol into a person's body constitutes consumption regardless of that person's knowledge. This was a matter of statutory interpretation - the meaning of consumption. The High Court held that, although the primary meaning of 'consuming' was consuming by mouth, it was capable of a variety of meanings depending on its context and included the introduction of alcohol into the body by injection or other means.

4.2 The concept of *ratio decidendi*

Now that we have introduced the doctrine of precedent we will move on to consider *ratio decidendi.*

The *ratio decidendi* (often shortened to *ratio*) forms part of the judgment of a case, and we will therefore consider it in context by first looking at judgment.

4.2.1 The judgment

Precedent can operate only if the legal reasons for past decisions are known and so, at the end of a case, the judge gives judgment. Everything a judge says is part of the judgment, but you need to be able to distinguish between the *ratio*, a proposition of law which is binding, and any *obiter dictum* (plural *obiter dicta*), which is a proposition of law stated by a judge that is not necessary for their conclusion. The decision is the result of the case (for example, that the defendant committed an offence) and is of legal and practical interest only to the parties, and binding only on them.

To summarise, although who wins is the most important aspect for the parties, for lawyers the vital part is where the judges set out the reasons for that decision. It is this legal principle which becomes the binding part of the judgment and the precedent for future cases. We shall illustrate this point by analysing the case of *Corkery v Carpenter* [1951] 1 KB 102, which you have already considered in **Chapter 3** in the context of statutory interpretation. Very briefly, the facts are that the defendant, who had been pushing his bicycle home along the street while drunk, was convicted of the offence of being drunk in charge of a carriage on the public highway pursuant to s 12 of the Licensing Act 1872.

It is generally necessary for a judge to do three things:

(a) Decide what the legally relevant or material facts are; for example, that the defendant was drunk while in charge of a bicycle on a public highway.

(b) State the relevant law; for example, that s 12 of the Licensing Act 1872 makes it an offence to be drunk while in charge of any 'carriage' on a public highway.

(c) Apply the law to the facts in order to decide the outcome of the case; for example, that the defendant was drunk while in charge of a carriage, so had committed an offence.

The legal principle in this case that became binding is that a bicycle is a 'carriage' for the purposes of the Licensing Act 1872, and, accordingly, a person who is in charge of a bicycle, while drunk, is guilty of an offence. In subsequent prosecutions based on s 12 of persons in charge of bicycles, the guilt or otherwise of the defendant in *Corkery v Carpenter* would not be a significant consideration; in contrast, the meaning of 'carriage' to include bicycles would be highly significant.

4.3 How to find the *ratio* of a case

4.3.1 Introduction

Sir Rupert Cross said:

> The *ratio decidendi* of a case is any rule of law expressly or impliedly treated by the judge as a necessary step in reaching his conclusion, having regard to the line of reasoning adopted by him ... (*Precedent in English Law*)

Note that the requirement that it be a proposition of law does not mean that the facts are irrelevant: the proposition of law is the application of the law to the material facts. Although 'material' or 'relevant' are the terms commonly used, you can start by thinking of them as the essential facts.

We shall again analyse the case of *Corkery v Carpenter* to illustrate the concept of material facts. Which of the following were material facts?

(a) the defendant's drunkenness;

(b) the fact that the defendant was a man as opposed to a woman;

(c) the colour or make of the bicycle;

(d) the fact that the defendant was on a public road; and

(e) the fact that the defendant was in charge of a bicycle.

Neither the fact that the defendant in *Corkery v Carpenter* was a man nor the colour or make of the bicycle was material. This is because it was not necessary for the court to take any of these facts into account when determining the *ratio* of the case, ie the court would have reached exactly the same decision if a woman and not a man had been in charge of a different model of bicycle or one of a different colour.

Obviously, it is material that the defendant was drunk and on the public highway, otherwise he could not have been guilty of the offence. It was material that he was in charge of a bicycle, but does this mean that this case would be binding on a later case where the defendant was, for example, on a skateboard? We will consider this point further when looking at narrow and wide *ratios*.

Finding the *ratio* of a case is a skill which you will develop gradually. It is arguably one of the more difficult legal skills to acquire, and will come only with practice: there are no real shortcuts. You can start to practise in the next activity. You are looking for the legal reasoning in the case which is essential for the decision. The *ratio* must involve the facts which are essential for that decision, as they are the basis on which the legal principle operates. The problem is that, often, judgments are lengthy; judges say many things and the *ratio* may be buried amongst a mass of other statements. Unfortunately, the *ratio* is not highlighted or labelled in any way. In addition, judges frequently have more than one reason for their decision; and there may be more than one judge, not necessarily giving the same reasons.

4.3.2 Step-by-step guide

As far as multiple judge courts are concerned, one needs to distinguish between the *ratio* of the individual judge and the *ratio* of the court as a whole. Each judge must have a reason for their decision, but it does not follow that there is any single reason for the decision of the court as a whole, since each of the judges may give different reasons which may be inconsistent.

When is the *ratio* of a case determined? You cannot simply say that the *ratio* of case A is not known until we have case B. Legal discussion about the *ratio* of case A will be ongoing while waiting for the later case to turn up. However, it needs to be recognised that, sometimes, deciding what the *ratio* is can be a difficult matter about which there may be strongly held but differing views. In time, the analysis of case A will undoubtedly be affected by the later decision in case B of what is the *ratio* of case A. This will not necessarily prevent the court in case C from saying that the court in case B got it wrong and that the *ratio* in case A is something else.

As mentioned above, judges do not label any particular part of their judgment as the *ratio,* and the *ratio* is not simply to be found in the most quotable sentences in the judgment. Nevertheless, the structure of the judgment will be an important factor in deciding what is the *ratio*. Quite often, judges have alternative lines of argument, and the ones which they decide to adopt will be an important factor in deciding the *ratio*.

The next activity is designed to introduce you to how to find the *ratio* of a case.

Activity 2 Finding the *ratio*

In the case of *Donoghue v Stevenson* [1932] AC 562, the claimant and her friend went to a café, where the friend bought ginger beer which was in an opaque bottle. The claimant drank some of the beer, but when the friend poured out some more it contained a decomposing snail. The claimant suffered shock and was later ill. The claimant could not sue for breach of contract, because her friend had purchased the beer and so the claimant had no contract with the café.

However, the House of Lords decided that the claimant was entitled to damages from the manufacturer.

Consider each of the following, stating whether or not you think it is the *ratio* of this case, and give reasons for your answer:

1. The manufacturer owes a duty to take reasonable care that the consumer is not injured by a snail in a bottle of ginger beer.

2. The manufacturer owes a duty to take reasonable care that the consumer is not injured by a foreign body in a container.
3. The manufacturer owes a duty to take reasonable care that the consumer is not injured by defective products.
4. A person owes a duty to take reasonable care that they do not commit any act which they could reasonably foresee as injuring another person.

Comment

It is likely that you disregarded 1. It was not material that it was a snail or that it was a bottle of ginger beer. It is more difficult to decide between 2 and 3. However, consider whether it would have made any difference if the snail had been in a slice of cake, rather than in a container such as a bottle? Obviously, it would not and so we can eliminate 2.

You may have disregarded 4 as being too wide. However, this is the 'wide *ratio*' which was actually followed in later cases and formed the basis of the law of negligence as we know it today. An alternative view is that 3 was actually the *ratio* at the time, and although 4 was later adopted, it was originally regarded as being too general. You can now see why finding what you believe to be the essential facts is only the start of learning how to find the *ratio*.

4.3.3 Narrow and wide *ratios*

As you will have discovered in **Activity 2** above, there may be an almost infinite number of possible *ratios*. Some are intolerably narrow and some are impossibly wide. It is the number of facts considered to be material which will make the *ratio* either narrower or broader. The more general the statement of facts, the greater the number of subsequent cases which will be 'caught' by the principle and therefore the wider the *ratio*. The more specific the facts considered relevant, the narrower the *ratio*. The formulation of the judgment will be an important factor. It would be unlikely in many cases that the narrowest and widest statements would actually be a *ratio*. The example of *Donoghue v Stevenson* brings this out well in eliminating 1 and 4, but it does not tell you whether the *ratio* is 2 or 3. To do this, you would need to read the judgments.

We shall now analyse the facts of the case of *Rylands v Fletcher* (1868) LR 3 HL 330 to illustrate the concepts of material facts and narrow and wide *ratios* further. The facts were:

(1) The defendant had a reservoir built on his land.

(2) A contractor who carried out the work was negligent.

(3) Water escaped and flooded the claimant's mine.

The outcome of the case was that the defendant was liable to the claimant for damages.

The facts considered to be material by the court were (1) that the defendant had a reservoir on his land and (3) that water escaped and flooded the claimant's mine. Fact (2) was found to be immaterial and, by discounting it, the House of Lords formulated a wide *ratio* based on strict liability for the escape of water. This means that it is irrelevant that the defendant was not at fault in any way and that the damage was due to the negligence of the contractor (a third party).

You may have thought that negligence would be required for liability. This is perfectly sensible, but the outcome can be justified on public policy grounds, on the basis that the claimant, who had suffered considerable damage to his land, was not at fault at all. Also, although not relevant to the decision, many landowners would be insured against such claims.

A narrow *ratio* would limit the effect to the building of reservoirs and the escape of water. In fact, the House of Lords formulated a *wide ratio*: 'The person who for his own purposes brings on his land and collects and keeps there anything likely to do mischief if it escapes, must keep it at his peril, and, if he does not do so, is prima facie answerable for all the damage which is the natural consequence of its escape.'

4.4 Difficulties in finding the *ratio*

What are the difficulties in finding the *ratio*?

(a) Very old cases may state no reason for their decision, and their authority is then weak.

(b) Not all the reasons given for a decision are essential. Subsequent cases may help clarify what is considered to be essential for the decision.

(c) A subsequent case may decide that there was more than one *ratio*. This may occur for one of two reasons:

   (i) A judge may give more than one reason for their decision because there are a number of points of law at issue. For example, imagine that Manuel was arrested after being found in his university halls of residence with an unlit cigarette in his mouth. He is being tried under the Health Act 2006 for the criminal offence of smoking a cigarette in a public place. You will recall that we considered this offence in **Activity 4** in **Chapter 3**.

   The judge may reach a decision in two ways. The judge may decide that 'smoking' includes only the smoking of a lighted cigarette. Alternatively, the judge may decide that a university hall of residence is not a public place. If the judge gives reasons regarding both of these, then a later court could decide either that there are two *ratios* or, alternatively, that the one regarding the place is not essential. This is because if 'smoking' only includes cigarettes which have been lit then it is not necessary to decide whether a university hall of residence is a public place or not, as Manuel would be not guilty in any event. However, if the judge decided only that a hall of residence is not a public place, there is no *ratio* binding on future courts as to whether a cigarette needs to be lit to constitute an offence. (Note: in fact the legislation is drafted in such a way that a university hall of residence would be included.)

   (ii) The court is an appellate court with more than one judge. You will recall from **Chapter 1** that appellate courts such as the Supreme Court, the Court of Appeal and the appellate section of the High Court (the Divisional Court) contain more than one judge.

Another reason why a case may have more than one *ratio* is that the judges may have reached the same decision (which may be a majority decision) but for different reasons. An extreme example of this is the case of *Esso v Commissioners for Customs & Excise* [1976] 1 WLR 1, where the issue was whether Esso had to pay purchase tax (the forerunner to VAT) on the World Cup coins which it gave away with petrol. Of the five judges in the House of Lords, one dissented from the final judgment (which was therefore a majority decision of 4:1) and no more than two of the other judges delivered similar *ratios* on any point. And even when two of the judges in the majority gave similar *ratios*, the two other judges in the majority gave contradictory *ratios*.

In such a situation, a later court is permitted to decide that there is no discernible *ratio* and therefore it will not be binding on future courts. You may be interested to know that the authors of the two leading textbooks on the law of contract are divided on this case.

4.5 What is the *obiter dictum*?

Once the *ratio* has been identified, the legal reasoning in the remainder of the judgment forms the so-called *'obiter dicta'* ('other things said'). Accordingly, a proposition of law, stated by a judge, which is not necessary for their conclusion is called an *obiter dictum* - *'dicta'* being the plural equivalent. Effectively, the concept is negatively defined, as it is anything which does not form part of the *ratio*. *Obiter dicta* are not binding on future courts, although they may be persuasive according to the reputation of the judge in question, the seniority of the court and the circumstances in which they were made.

4.5.1 Types of *obiter dicta*

First, a proposition may be *obiter* if it is wider than necessary to decide the particular case. However, at the other end of the spectrum, there is a very fine dividing line between this type of *obiter dictum* and the concept of the wide and narrow *ratio* discussed in **4.3.3** above. You could take a cynical view that if the later court wants to adopt the wide *ratio*, it is *ratio*; if not, they take a narrow *ratio* and the rest is *obiter*.

Secondly, a proposition may be *obiter* if a judge speculates about the decision they would have made if the facts of the case had been different. This is the easiest type of *obiter dictum* to identify.

We shall use the case of *Crossley v Rawlinson* [1982] 1 WLR 369 to illustrate how to identify *obiter dicta*. The High Court had to decide whether the plaintiff (now claimant) could recover damages for an injury suffered while on the way to a rescue. The defendant was driving his lorry along a road, when, due to his negligence, a tarpaulin covering the lorry caught fire. The defendant then stopped the lorry on the roadside. The plaintiff, a nearby AA patrolman, saw the fire and ran to help to put it out. While running towards the lorry along a path by the road, the plaintiff tripped over a concealed hole and fell, injuring himself. He claimed damages. As the plaintiff's claim was based on the tort of negligence, he had to show that the injuries he suffered were reasonably foreseeable.

Richard Tucker QC, sitting as a judge of the High Court, stated in his judgment:

> Thus if I were answering the question whether in the present case the plaintiff's damage is too remote, my instinctive feeling would be that it is. If I were answering the question, as in my judgment I have to, whether it ought reasonably to have been foreseen that the plaintiff would suffer this or any other injury while running along the path, I would say, and do say, that no reasonable man could reasonably have foreseen it. I reach this conclusion with reluctance because on any view the plaintiff acted with very great presence of mind and with the best possible motives. I think it unfortunate that such a man should not be awarded damages for an injury which was not his fault. I dismiss the allegation that he brought it about by his own carelessness, but it was an accident in the true sense of the word, which neither party could reasonably have foreseen.

The following words in this that are most likely *obiter*.

- 'Thus if I were answering the question whether in the present case the plaintiff's damage is too remote, my instinctive feeling would be that it is.'

  The judge was not answering the question whether the damage was too remote; he had to answer the question whether it was reasonably foreseeable, so this sentence is *obiter*.

- 'I reach this conclusion with reluctance because on any view the plaintiff acted with very great presence of mind and with the best possible motives. I think it unfortunate that such a man should not be awarded damages for an injury which was not his fault.'

  This section is clearly *obiter* as the judge is speculating. His words are 'by the way' and are not relevant to the decision which he reaches on the law.

- 'I dismiss the allegation that he brought it about by his own carelessness, but it was an accident in the true sense of the word.'

  This sentence is also *obiter*, because it is answering a slightly different point of law from the central issue of reasonable foreseeability.

The third reason a proposition may be *obiter* is if the judge says what their decision would have been if they had not been bound by judicial precedent.

Fourthly, a proposition will generally be regarded as *obiter* if it forms part of a dissenting judgment. A dissenting judgment refers to the situation in an appellate court where one judge (in a three-judge Court of Appeal) or one or two judges (in a five-judge Supreme Court) find(s) for the opposite party to the majority of judges. For example, if, in a three-judge Court of Appeal, two judges find in favour of the appellant and allow the appeal, and the third judge finds in favour of the respondent and dismisses the appeal, the majority view will prevail and the third judge will have produced a dissenting judgment.

Figure 4.1 below summarises the principles which you have just been analysing.

Figure 4.1 Summary diagram: *ratio* and *obiter*

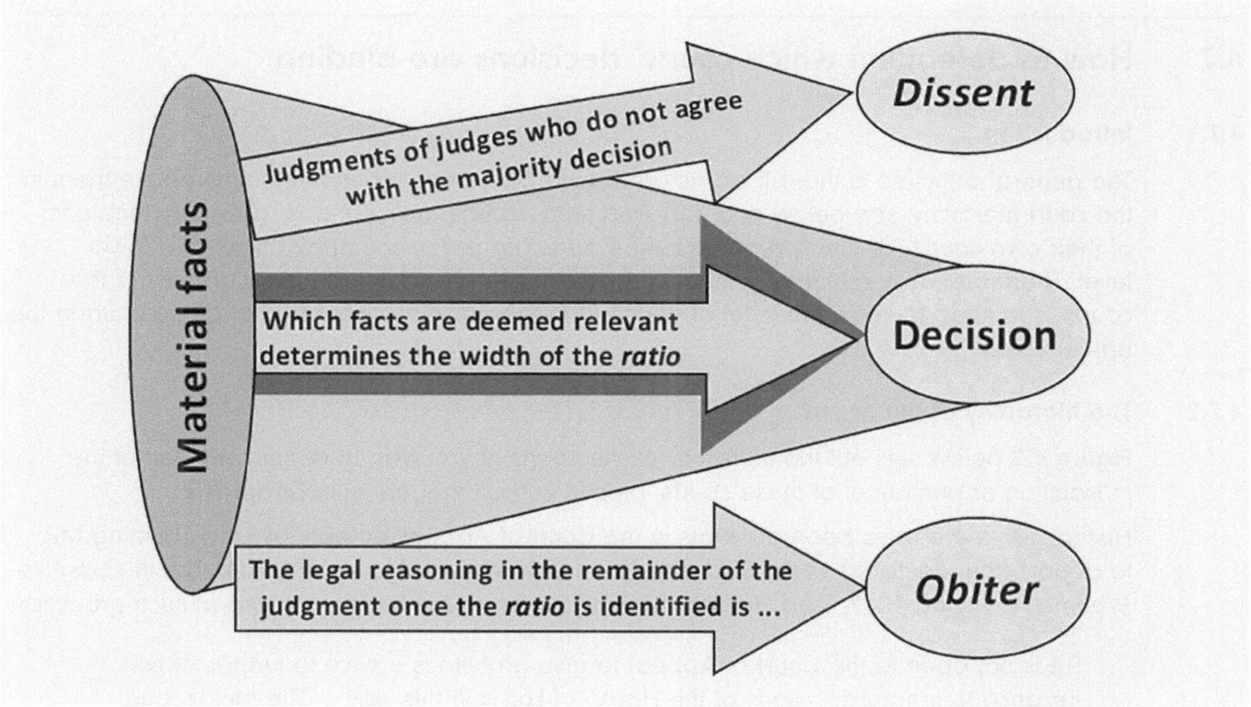

4.6 Finding the *ratio* and *obiter dictum*

The judgments of Schiemann J and Balcombe LJ in *DPP v Johnson* [1995] 1 WLR 728 provide helpful illustrations of the difference between *ratio* and *obiter*. You will remember from **4.1.4** above that the case involved an issue of statutory interpretation of s 5(1) of the Road Traffic Act 1988 – whether 'consuming' included the introduction of alcohol to the body by injection.

The ratio of this case is that on the true construction of s 5(1), 'consuming' is not restricted to drinking but includes the introduction of alcohol into the body by injection. There are also two very interesting *obiter dicta*.

Schiemann J refers to the consumption of alcohol by inhalation. However, this case did not involve the inhalation of alcohol. He goes on to state that the word 'consume' can be construed sufficiently widely to 'embrace ingestion in any form'. Balcombe LJ also concluded that 'consume is wide enough to include other methods of the ingestion of alcohol into the breath, blood or urine of the person concerned'.

Although these comments are, strictly speaking, *obiter*, it is apparent from the comments made by the judges that they favour a wider *ratio*, such that the word 'consuming' includes the introduction of alcohol into the body by any means. Which of the two *ratios* will be adopted will depend upon future cases.

In this section, you have considered what is a *ratio* and how *ratios* evolve over time. Being able to identify *ratios* and *obiter dicta* are skills which will be crucial to your understanding of all areas of the law but particularly the laws of contract and tort, which are still dominated by the common law and therefore evolve by application of the doctrine of precedent.

4.7 How to determine which courts' decisions are binding

4.7.1 Introduction

The general principle is that all courts are bound by superior courts (ie courts above them in the court hierarchy, see below and **2.2**), and some courts are bound by previous decisions of their own courts (or their predecessors). Courts are never bound by courts of a lower level. Therefore, as a preliminary point, it is necessary to understand the hierarchy of the courts. You need to know the level of the court in the present case and that of the court in the earlier case.

4.7.2 The hierarchy of the courts

Figure 4.2 below sets out the hierarchy of the courts. If you wish to remind yourself of the jurisdiction or personnel of these courts, please consult the tables in **Chapter 2**.

Historically, there have been attempts in the Court of Appeal, notably by Lord Denning MR, to depart from decisions of the Supreme Court (formerly the House of Lords), but in *Cassell v Broome* [1971] AC 1027, Lord Hailsham LC made very clear his displeasure at such practices:

> [I]t is not open to the Court of Appeal to give gratuitous advice to judges of first instance to ignore decisions of the House of Lords in this way ... The fact is, and I hope it will never be necessary to say so again, that in the hierarchical system of courts which exists in this country, it is necessary for each lower tier, including the Court of Appeal, to accept loyally the decisions of the higher tiers ...

Figure 4.2 below sets out clearly which courts bind which others, in a vertical hierarchy. The related question of whether a court is bound by its own previous decisions is, however, more complex. We will now look at each court in turn and consider when it is bound by its own previous decisions.

Figure 4.2 Who binds whom?

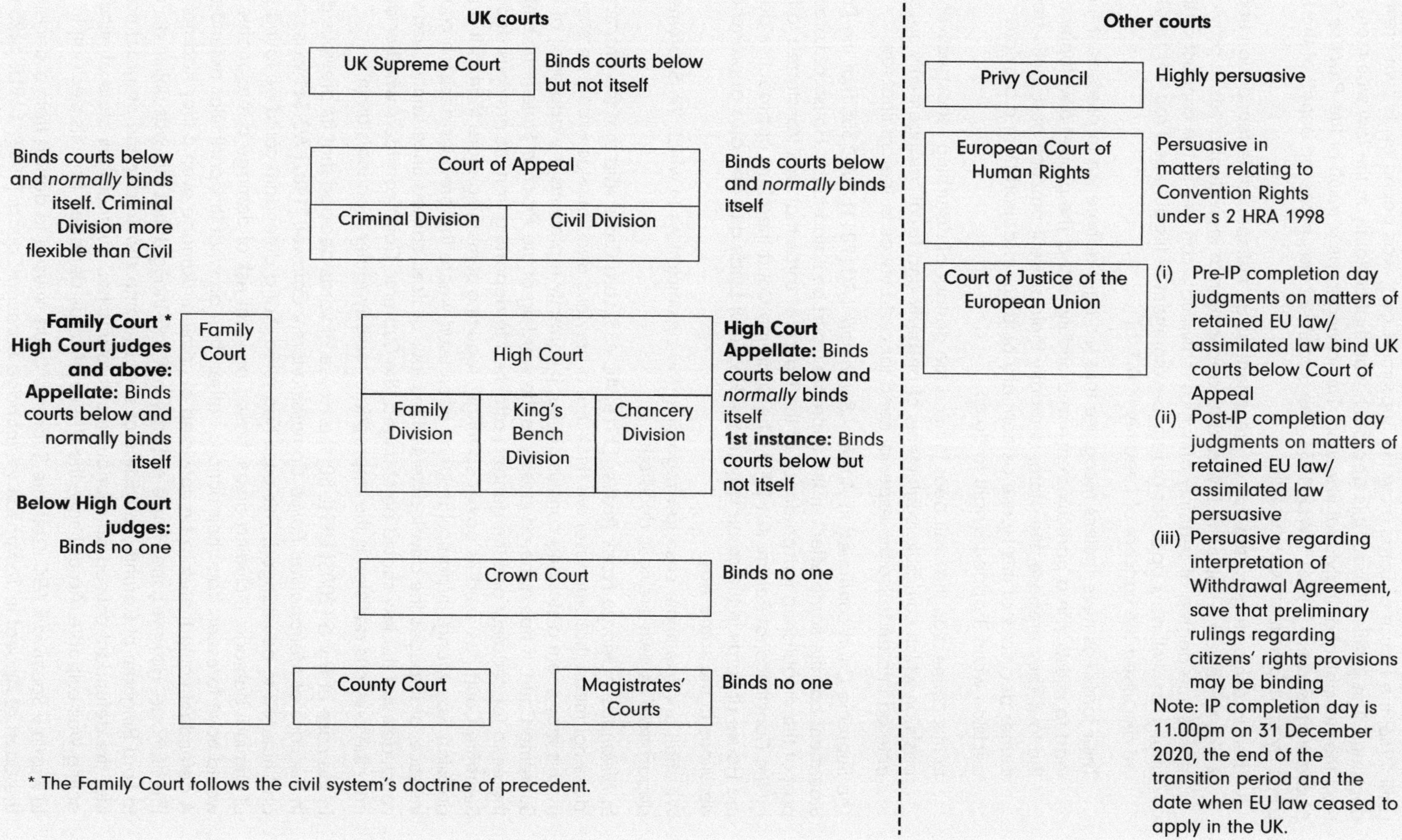

* The Family Court follows the civil system's doctrine of precedent.

4.7.3 The Supreme Court

Until 1966, the House of Lords (now the Supreme Court) was bound by its own previous decisions. The justification for this approach was that certainty in the law was more important than the possibility of individual hardship. This changed as a result of the *Practice Statement (Judicial Precedent)* [1966] 1 WLR 1234. The Statement was made on behalf of the House of Lords by Lord Gardiner LC, who said:

> Their lordships regard the use of precedent as an indispensable foundation upon which to decide what is the law and its application to individual cases. It provides at least some degree of certainty on which individuals can rely in the conduct of their affairs, as well as a basis for orderly development of legal rules. [You will recall that we discussed the concept of certainty in **4.1.2.**]
>
> Their lordships nevertheless recognise that too rigid adherence to precedent may lead to injustice in a particular case and unduly restrict the proper development of the law. They propose, therefore, to modify their present practice and, while treating former decisions of this House as normally binding, to depart from a previous decision when it appears right to do so.
>
> In this connection they will bear in mind the danger of disturbing retrospectively the basis on which contracts, settlements of property and fiscal arrangements have been entered into and also the especial need for certainty as to the criminal law.

The Supreme Court confirmed in *Austin v Southwark LBC* [2011] 1 AC 355 that the Practice Statement has the same effect in the Supreme Court as it had in the House of Lords, as it was part of the established jurisprudence of the House of Lords that was transferred to the Court by the Constitutional Reform Act 2005. The Supreme Court therefore approaches decisions of the House of Lords in the same way as the House of Lords did, and also approaches its own decisions in the same way.

We shall analyse some case law regarding the circumstances in which the Supreme Court will depart from its own previous decisions.

In *Miliangos v George Frank Textiles* [1976] AC 433, Lord Cross said that the *Practice Statement* 'does not mean that whenever we think that a previous decision was wrong we should reverse it'. This may seem a startling conclusion, but it correctly represents the approach of the Supreme Court. It has adhered closely to the wording of the *Practice Statement*, emphasising the need for certainty and the dangers attached to departing from its previous decisions. The Supreme Court has used its power sparingly, requiring something more than that a previous decision was wrong. In particular, it has been used where the previous decision causes injustice, or impedes the development of the law, or itself caused uncertainty. Even where it concludes that the law should be changed, the Supreme Court considers whether departure from the previous decision is the appropriate remedy rather than legislation.

In the case of *R v G* [2003] UKHL 50, the House of Lords decided that its previous decision in the case of *Metropolitan Police Commissioners v Caldwell* [1982] AC 341 was unjust and needed to be changed. This case had ruled that a defendant could be found guilty of criminal damage, including arson, based on what risk of damage a reasonable person would have foreseen from their actions, rather than on what this particular defendant foresaw. A defendant could therefore be convicted of criminal damage even if they had not foreseen the damage. However, the House of Lords in *R v G* thought that this was unjust as, according to Lord Bingham of Cornhill, conviction of serious crime should depend on proof not simply that the defendant caused an injurious result to another, but that their state of mind when so acting was culpable. Accordingly, the House of Lords departed from its decision in *Caldwell.*

In *Austin v Southwark LBC* itself, the Supreme Court refused to depart from a decision of the Court of Appeal in *Thompson v Elmbridge Borough Council* [1987] 1 WLR 1425 which the Supreme Court had upheld in *R v Knowsley* [2009] AC 636. The case involved the interpretation of s 82(2) of the Housing Act 1985 and when a secure tenancy (a tenancy where the tenant has statutory protection from eviction) came to an end under that section. There were two possibilities: the first was that it came to an end on the date that a court issued an order for possession; the second was that it only ended when the possession order was actually executed and the tenant evicted from the premises.

In *Thompson* the Court of Appeal had chosen the first interpretation, and the Supreme Court had declined to depart from it in *Knowsley* notwithstanding reservations concerning the merits of the decision. In *Austin* the Supreme Court thought there was much to be said for the second interpretation, but nonetheless declined to overrule *Thompson* and *Knowsley*. There were two reasons for this decision. Firstly, there had been a considerable passage of time since *Thompson* (about 20 years) and a large number of cases had proceeded on the basis that *Thompson* accurately stated the law. Secondly, Parliament had passed an Act in 2008 on the basis that the judgment in *Thompson* had been correct. Accordingly, it would have undermined that Act and Parliament's intention if the Supreme Court had held that *Thompson* was no longer good law.

The Supreme Court is therefore reluctant to depart from its previous decisions where to do so would disturb existing contracts, property rights and tax arrangements. As court judgments apply retrospectively, people who in good faith had entered into arrangements that they thought were lawful could find that their arrangements were in fact unlawful. In criminal law, it would be unfair if a person who believed reasonably they were acting lawfully were penalised because a subsequent Supreme Court had retrospectively ruled that their conduct was in fact unlawful. It is important that people should be able to conduct their affairs and regulate their conduct with certainty.

4.7.4 The Court of Appeal

Civil Division

In *Young v Bristol Aeroplane Co Ltd* [1944] KB 718, a 'full' court of six members was convened to decide whether the Court of Appeal is bound by its own decisions. It decided that it is normally so bound, but subject to three exceptions:

(a) where its own previous decisions conflict; or

(b) where its previous decision has been implicitly overruled by the Supreme Court; or

(c) where its previous decision was made *per incuriam* (as explained below).

Since this decision, two further exceptions have been added:

(d) where it was an interim decision by two judges; or

(e) where one of its previous decisions is inconsistent with a subsequent decision of the European Court of Human Rights.

Let us now consider each of these exceptions in turn:

(a) *Where its own previous decisions conflict.*

Strictly speaking, there should never be two or more previous decisions which conflict because this means that the later decision did not follow the precedent set by the earlier one. However, this can arise in a number of ways. The court in the second case may not have been aware of the first case, either because it was only a few days earlier or because it was never officially reported. The second case may have distinguished the first. One of the cases may have itself been decided *per incuriam* (see below).

Other reasons for the second decision not following the first decision are that the first decision was not cited to the court, or that it was cited but misunderstood by the second court.

(b) *Where its previous decision has been implicitly overruled by the Supreme Court.*

This gives rise to the question: 'How can a decision be implicitly rather than expressly overruled?' This could happen where a case has bypassed the Court of Appeal and gone straight to the Supreme Court (the 'leapfrog' procedure; see **2.8.2.2**); or where another Court of Appeal case has been expressly overruled without the case in question being cited to the Supreme Court. The latter could arise where the Supreme Court case was on rather different facts, or even on a different issue.

(c) *Where its previous decision was made per incuriam.*

Per incuriam means 'through carelessness'. This must be construed narrowly. It is not enough for the previous decision to be wrong. In *Morelle v Wakeling* [1955] 2 QB 379, Lord Evershed MR said it only applied to 'decisions given in ignorance or forgetfulness of some inconsistent statutory provision or of some authority binding on the court concerned'.

According to Lord Donaldson MR in *Duke v Reliance Systems Ltd* [1988] QB 108, a decision is *per incuriam* if the court *must* have reached a different conclusion, not might. In *Williams v Fawcett* [1986] QB 604, the Court of Appeal declared *per incuriam* several of its previous decisions which had held that a person could not be committed to prison for breach of a non-molestation order unless the notice had been signed by the 'proper officer' of the court. This was not a requirement of the statute or the procedural rules.

(d) *Where it was an interim decision by two judges.*

This exception was added by the case of *Boys v Chaplin* [1968] 2 QB 1. It is important to note that it must be an interim decision, not the final one. It therefore does not apply to a final decision, even if there were only two judges.

(e) *Where one of its previous decisions is inconsistent with a subsequent decision of the European Court of Human Rights.*

In this instance, the Court of Appeal is free (but not obliged) to depart from its decision.

Criminal Division

All the exceptions which apply to the Civil Division apply to the Criminal Division. However, in addition, the Court of Appeal has a wider discretion where the liberty of the individual is at stake. In *R v Gould* [1968] 2 QB 65 Diplock LJ said:

> ... if upon due consideration we were to be of the opinion that the law had been either misapplied or misunderstood in an earlier decision ... we should be entitled to depart from the view as to the law expressed in the earlier decision notwithstanding that the case could not be brought within any of the exceptions laid down in *Young v Bristol Aeroplane Co Ltd.*

Where a case does not fall within *Young v Bristol Aeroplane*, a full court (nowadays of five members) may be convened to consider the matter.

Are the Civil and Criminal Divisions bound by each other?

There has been no ruling as to whether the two Divisions are bound by each other, but as their predecessors (the Court of Appeal and the Court of Criminal Appeal) were not bound by each other, it is thought that they are not. You may wonder how there could be conflict between Civil and Criminal Divisions at the Court of Appeal, since one of them is dealing with civil law and the other with criminal law. However, there are, for example, cases you will read about in public law on the right of protest which can be relevant in civil law (trespass) and criminal law (public order offences).

4.7.5 The High Court

The High Court has a dual function both as a court of first instance and as an appellate court. The appellate jurisdiction of the High Court is next in the court hierarchy and is known as the

Divisional Court of the High Court. It deals with appeals such as those by way of case stated from the magistrates' courts and, in addition, it considers applications for judicial review, often immigration and planning cases but also other areas of law. These decisions are binding precedents for magistrates' courts.

The Divisional Court of the High Court is bound by its own decisions, subject to the same exceptions as the Civil Division of the Court of Appeal and, arguably, the Criminal Division (*R v Greater Manchester Coroner, ex p Tal* [1984] 3 All ER 240).

In contrast, decisions of individual High Court judges in first instance cases are binding on the County Court but not on other High Court judges. However, in the interests of certainty, and bearing in mind that many cases may not get beyond the High Court, judges try not to depart from previous decisions.

4.7.6 The Crown Court

The Crown Court, like the High Court, is not bound by its own previous decisions; but in the interests of certainty in criminal matters, it is strongly persuaded by them. Note that for most cases, the judge sits with a jury, and therefore it is only the judge's decision on points of law which is relevant. Decisions in the Crown Court are, in practice, very seldom reported.

4.7.7 The County Court, the Family Court and magistrates' courts

These are 'inferior courts'; they do not bind any other courts and are not bound by their own decisions. The reasons for this include:

(a) Decisions are all first instance.

(b) Only one judge hears a case in the County Court.

(c) In the magistrates' courts, decisions are made either by some 24,000 magistrates who are not legally qualified, or by a District Judge (ie a professional magistrate) sitting alone.

(d) There are hundreds of inferior courts throughout the country.

Cases in these courts are not usually reported, and no record of them is kept at the Public Records Office. Thousands of cases proceed through hundreds of such courts every year, and it would be impossible for each court to keep track of the decisions of others. Each individual court does, however, attempt to follow decisions within its own court or area, in order to provide some measure of consistency, although this often reflects local views or practices.

4.7.8 Court of Justice of the European Union

The Court of Justice of the European Union (CJEU) is not bound by its own previous decisions for the simple reason that it does not have a concept of precedent (*stare decisis*). This is because the system adopted by the court was based on that used in the national courts of all the original Member States of the EU, whose legal systems developed from the civil (Roman) law system.

However, in practice, decisions of the courts of civil law countries do have an important effect in developing the law in those countries, and judges and commentators consider carefully what has been said by previous judges. Indeed, the CJEU recognises the principle of legal certainty and has considered it necessary to 'explain itself' when it has departed from previous cases, for example in a well-known ECJ case *Keck and Mithouard* (cases C-267 and C-268/91) [1993] ECR I-6097. The difference is that courts in civil law countries do not raise single decisions to the theoretically high status which they have in English law.

The following activity is designed to test your knowledge and understanding of the doctrine of precedent.

Activity 3 The hierarchy of the courts

In each of the following questions, please consider if Court B would be bound by the doctrine of precedent to follow a previous decision of Court A on that issue (you should assume for the purposes of this exercise that the two cases are indistinguishable on the facts).

For example, in question 1 you are being asked whether a High Court would be bound by an earlier decision of the County Court.

Questions	Decision in Court A	Is Court B bound by the earlier decision in Court A?	Yes/No?
1.	County Court	High Court	
2.	magistrates' court	Crown Court	
3.	High Court	County Court	
4.	County Court	County Court	
5.	Court of Appeal	High Court	
6.	magistrates' court	County Court	
7.	Crown Court	Crown Court	
8.	Court of Appeal	Crown Court	
9.	Supreme Court	Court of Justice of the European Union	
10.	Court of Appeal	Court of Appeal	
11.	High Court QBD (not Divisional Court)	High Court QBD (not Divisional Court)	
12.	Court of Justice of the European Union	Court of Justice of the European Union	
13.	Supreme Court	Supreme Court	
14.	Supreme Court	Privy Council	

Comment

Please compare your answers with the table below which shows the correct answers. If any were wrong, please review the relevant section above to satisfy yourself that you understand the correct answer.

Questions	Decision in Court A	Is Court B bound by the earlier decision in Court A?	Yes/No?
1.	County Court	High Court	N
2.	magistrates' court	Crown Court	N
3.	High Court	County Court	Y
4.	County Court	County Court	N
5.	Court of Appeal	High Court	Y
6.	magistrates' court	County Court	N
7.	Crown Court	Crown Court	N
8.	Court of Appeal	Crown Court	Y
9.	Supreme Court	Court of Justice of the European Union	N*

Questions	Decision in Court A	Is Court B bound by the earlier decision in Court A?	Yes/No?
10.	Court of Appeal	Court of Appeal	Y**
11.	High Court QBD (not Divisional Court)	High Court QBD (not Divisional Court)	N
12.	European Court of Justice	European Court of Justice	N***
13.	Supreme Court	Supreme Court	N†
14.	Supreme Court	Privy Council	N

*Subject to preliminary rulings on citizens' rights provisions in the Withdrawal Agreement.

**Subject to *Young v Bristol Aeroplane.*

***But does not generally depart from its previous decisions.

†But does not normally depart (see Practice Statement, 1966).

4.8 Distinguishing cases

4.8.1 Introduction

We will now consider the final element of the doctrine of precedent, which is that a proposition stated in one case will be binding in a later case only if there are no relevant distinctions between the two cases.

We have already learned that if the earlier case was decided in, for example, a higher court, its *ratio* is binding on lower courts. However, you will recall that the *ratio* is the application of the law to the material facts, and that it is the later court which determines for itself both what is the *ratio* of the earlier case and what are the material facts of the later case. If a court considers a case before it to be different in some material way from the precedent cited, either on the facts or the law, the earlier case need not be followed. The present case will be distinguished and, as a consequence, the later court could decide not to apply the *ratio* of the earlier case. Indeed, where the court is anxious not to be bound by a particular precedent, some distinctions are drawn which are very fine.

4.8.2 How courts distinguish cases

As we have seen above, a case is binding on a later case if there are no relevant distinctions between the two cases. In *Corkery v Carpenter* [1951] 1 KB 102, which you have already considered, the defendant, who was pushing a bicycle, was convicted of being drunk in charge of a carriage on a highway. The court had to consider the interpretation of the word 'carriage' under the Licensing Act 1872. Lord Goddard CJ referred to two cases in his judgment where the courts concerned had interpreted the word 'carriage' to exclude bicycles, but went on to distinguish them.

Williams v Ellis concerned the Turnpike Act which imposed tolls 'for every horse, mule, or other beast drawing any coach, sociable, chariot, berlin, landau, vis-à-vis, phaeton, curricle ... and ... every carriage of whatever description, and for whatever purpose, which shall be drawn or impelled, or set or kept in motion by steam or other power or agency'. The court held that a bicycle was not caught by those particular words which had to be construed *ejusdem generis* with the carriages previously specified.

Simpson v Teignmouth and Shaldon Bridge Co [1903] 1 KB 405 concerned an Act of 1825 which provided for a toll to be paid by 'every coach, chariot, hearse, chaise, berlin, landau, and phaeton, gig, whiskey, car, chair, or coburg, and ... every other carriage hung on springs' using a particular bridge. The court came to the conclusion that a bicycle did not come within any of the words in that section.

Lord Goddard was able to distinguish both cases by relying on the wording of the statutes, as those cases related to different statutes from the one which he was considering in *Corkery*. Moreover, the words of the Licensing Act were wide enough to embrace a bicycle under the expression 'carriage'. As such, he could distinguish the *Corkery* case from the two earlier cases.

The next activity will help you to analyse whether relevant distinctions exist or not.

Activity 4 Distinguishing cases

Using *Corkery v Carpenter* as summarised in this chapter, and in the absence of any further information, consider whether there are any relevant distinctions between those facts and the facts below. Assume that the facts other than those stated are the same as in *Corkery v Carpenter*. Please bear in mind that there may not necessarily be a clear-cut answer.

Facts	Distinguishable?		
	Yes	No	Maybe
1. Defendant was drugged			
2. Defendant was pushing a scooter (non-motorised)			
3. Defendant was riding a tricycle			
4. Defendant was on roller blades			
5. Defendant was in a car park			
6. Defendant was on his garden path			

Comment

Please compare your answers with the table below together with the accompanying notes.

Facts	Distinguishable?		
	Yes	No	Maybe
1. Defendant was drugged			x
2. Defendant was pushing a scooter (non-motorised)			x
3. Defendant was riding a tricycle		x	
4. Defendant was on roller blades			x
5. Defendant was in a car park			x
6. Defendant was on his garden path	x		

Notes:

1. Defendant was drugged. At first sight this appears to be clearly distinguishable, as drink and drugs are different. However, whether by alcohol or by drugs, the defendant is intoxicated and a person on drugs may lose control of their faculties in the same way as a person who is drunk.

At the time of *Corkery v Carpenter*, the court would have used the mischief rule to determine what 'mischief' the Act was aimed at preventing. In this instance, it is to stop people who are not in control of their faculties from being a danger to other users of the public highway. However, judges today are more likely to refer to the 'purpose' of the legislation, as this approach has become more prevalent in recent times. Whichever is cited, in this example the outcome is the same. It is not clear-cut as to whether the facts are distinguishable or not as, in practice, the point could be argued either way. However, given the attitude of the courts to driving while under the influence, the case is unlikely to be distinguished.

2. Defendant was pushing a scooter. This is more difficult; the *Oxford English Dictionary* defines carriage as 'a wheeled passenger vehicle, especially one with four wheels and pulled by horses'. Clearly, in *Corkery v Carpenter* the court was prepared to consider that a bicycle was a carriage, and it would therefore be only a small incremental step to consider a scooter to be a carriage. However, a scooter could be distinguished on the basis of the mischief rule or (if considered today) a purposive approach. Such a defendant is unlikely to be a danger to the public as they would be travelling slowly, whereas on a bicycle they could travel at a considerable speed, and also because, if they lost control of the scooter, it would immediately fall to the ground.

3. Defendant was riding a tricycle. The argument is very similar to that put forward for the scooter. There is no reason why a tricycle should not be regarded as a 'carriage' if a bicycle is.

4. Defendant was on roller blades. It could be argued that roller blades are used to convey a person, just as a bicycle does. There is, however, an argument that roller blades are not a carriage on the basis that they physically attach to the person and are therefore more analogous to clothing.

5. Defendant was in a car park. This should be distinguishable, as a car park is clearly distinct from the highway. However, a counter-argument is that members of the public are just as much at risk in a car park from a drunken cyclist as if the cyclist were on a public highway.

6. Defendant was on the garden path. This should be distinguished, as a garden path is clearly distinct from the highway, not least because it is private property.

The following example will further develop your understanding of the whole of the doctrine of precedent, including distinguishing cases.

Example

Assume that Emily, who was pushing a skateboard, is being tried in a magistrates' court for the offence of being drunk in charge of a carriage on the public highway. We shall work through how the magistrates might approach the case.

Firstly, they would seek to identify whether there is any binding precedent. Corkery would be binding, as it was in a higher court, namely the High Court King's Bench Division.

Secondly, they would seek to identify possible ratios. They could decide that the ratio is very narrow, ie that a bicycle is a carriage. Alternatively, a wide ratio would be that 'carriage' means any sort of vehicle. It is perhaps more likely that they would opt for a ratio which falls between these two, such as that 'a bicycle is a carriage because it is a type of vehicle'.

Thirdly, they would apply the selected ratio to Emily's case. If they apply the narrow ratio, Emily is not guilty as a skateboard is clearly not a bicycle. However, if they adopt the wide ratio, the opposite result may occur, as a skateboard could constitute a type of vehicle and therefore be a carriage. The magistrates would accordingly have to determine whether a skateboard is a carriage or not. Here are some arguments that they could consider.

Arguments for a skateboard being a 'carriage' include:

(a) Both a bicycle and a skateboard are propelled by the rider's muscle power alone.

(b) Lord Goddard CJ's view was that a bicycle was a carriage because it carries, and the same reasoning would apply to a skateboard.

(c) The aim of the Act is to protect the public and to preserve public order. Lord Goddard stated that a drunken person with a bicycle was dangerous whether they were pushing or riding their bicycle, because they do not have proper control over it. A skateboard would be dangerous on the same basis.

Arguments against a skateboard being a 'carriage' include:

(a) A skateboard does not come within the popular meaning of a 'carriage', and this is endorsed by the dictionary definitions of the word (see analysis below).

(b) A skateboard is purely a leisure item, unlike a bicycle which can be used to travel from A to B. This is supported by the fact that a skateboard can be used on a pavement.

(c) A skateboarder has to keep putting their foot down to propel the board along. If they lose control, they will fall off and the skateboard will quickly stop, so there is no danger to the public.

If the magistrates looked 'vehicle' up in a dictionary (using a literal approach), they would have seen that the most relevant meaning is that it is 'a thing used for transporting people or goods, especially on land, such as a car, lorry or cart' (Oxford Dictionary of English). Going a bit deeper, 'transporting' (a key word used in the definition of vehicle) involves taking or carrying people or things from one place to another. A skateboard obviously is not a car, lorry or cart, but the use of 'such as' shows that the dictionary definition is not exhaustive and Lord Goddard regarded a bicycle as a vehicle. However, it may be stretching the meaning of vehicle too far to include a skateboard, particularly as the aim of using a skateboard is usually for pleasure and not to get from one place to another. While a bicycle does arguably take or carry a person from one place to another, like a car, a skateboard does not. On a literal approach, a skateboard is not a vehicle and hence not a carriage within the meaning of the Licensing Act 1872.

Conversely, if the magistrates return to the purpose of the Act, they will find that it is for the protection of the public and the preservation of public order; they may therefore decide that Emily is guilty.

You will have seen from the activity and example above that, as the facts of any two cases are rarely identical, it is never easy to predict when a court will or will not distinguish. You can also see that the court may reach one conclusion, but a differently-constituted court might have reached the opposite conclusion. If a third case comes to court then, assuming that both earlier cases are at the same level and binding on the third court, that court could decide to follow either or (by distinguishing yet again) neither earlier case. This is how 'conflicting' cases at the same level arise. They are rarely genuinely conflicting. The court in the second case has usually distinguished the first.

4.8.3 Applying and distinguishing a *ratio* in a subsequent case

Society is constantly changing. Forty years ago, who could have foreseen the spectacular rise in the use of computers and the Internet? It is essential for any legal system to be able to develop to meet such changes and the judges have an important role to play in this. Let us consider an example, which involves the doctrine of consideration, which relates to the law of contract.

On a basic level, the doctrine of consideration establishes the principle that a promise will create an enforceable contractual obligation only if something of value is offered in return for that promise. To give a simple example, if I were to promise you £10, this is clearly a gift as you have not promised me anything of value in return and have not therefore provided any consideration in respect of my promise. If, however, I were to promise you £10 if you agree to wash my car, then this would constitute a binding contract, as your promise to wash my car is of value in the eyes of the law.

The case of *Stilk v Myrick* (1809) 2 Camp 317 established the important principle that performance of an existing contractual duty is not good consideration.

The facts of the case were briefly as follows: the plaintiff (now claimant) entered into a contract with the defendant, who was the ship's captain, to sail a ship from London to the Baltic and back. During the voyage two crew members jumped ship. The captain, unable to find additional crew, promised to pay additional wages to the remaining crew members, including the plaintiff, if they would sail the ship back short-handed. On returning to London, the captain refused to pay the plaintiff the additional wages on the basis that the plaintiff had not given any consideration for the promise, because he was only doing what he was already contractually obliged to do.

The plaintiff sued for the extra wages and the court found in the captain's favour on the grounds that performance of an existing contractual duty is not good consideration. This principle was adopted by the courts in numerous subsequent cases as the *ratio* of *Stilk v Myrick*, and indeed is so well-known that it is often referred to as the 'rule in *Stilk v Myrick*'.

However, almost 200 years later, in the case of *Williams v Roffey Brothers* [1991] 1 QB 1, the Court of Appeal had to consider whether to apply or distinguish the earlier case.

Example

The facts of Williams v Roffey Brothers are set out below. When considering whether the Court of Appeal would follow or distinguish Stilk v Myrick, it is essential to think carefully about how times and business practices have evolved since the 1800s.

The defendant building contractors had entered into a contract to refurbish a block of 27 flats -they sub-contracted the carpentry work to the plaintiff company for a price of £20,000. After work had started, the plaintiff got into financial difficulties because it had quoted too low a price for the job and had not supervised its workers properly.

The defendant was concerned that, as a result of these financial difficulties, the plaintiff might not be able to finish the work on time. This would cause the defendant to have to pay financial penalties to the customer for late completion of the work.

In order to ensure that the plaintiff did finish work on time, the defendant agreed to pay the plaintiff an extra £575 per flat. The work was completed on time but then the defendant refused to pay the extra money on the basis the plaintiff had given no consideration for the promise, as it was already contractually bound to complete the work for the initial price. The plaintiff then sued.

The Court of Appeal held that the plaintiff had provided consideration for the promise and the defendant was therefore bound to pay the additional amounts. According to the Court, the consideration provided by the plaintiff was the 'practical benefit' that the defendants received by having the job done on time and not having to pay the penalty to their customer.

You may think it must follow from this that the Court of Appeal distinguished *Stilk v Myrick*. In fact, the Court of Appeal affirmed the earlier case but stated that this decision was a refinement of the principle. Businesses nowadays need to be able to effectively renegotiate terms of a contract. If a party sees a real practical benefit in the other contracting party performing its contractual obligations and is prepared to pay extra for it, why should that agreed variation not be binding?

You will find more detail in contract law textbooks, but you will see that without understanding how the doctrine of precedent works, you would not be able to see how the law evolves.

4.9 Other ways of avoiding awkward precedents

4.9.1 Overruling

This occurs when a principle laid down by a lower court is declared incorrect and not followed by a higher court in a different later case. The higher court will set a new 'correct' precedent.

4.9.2 Departing

A court can depart from an earlier case. This usually occurs where the House of Lords *Practice Statement* is used, or the Court of Appeal applies one of the exceptions set out in *Young v Bristol Aeroplane Co Ltd* (see **4.7.4**).

4.9.3 Reversing

This occurs where the decision of a court in the same case is altered by a higher court on appeal. For example, the Court of Appeal may come to a different conclusion from the High Court on a point of law; in this situation, the Court will reverse the decision made by the High Court. While this is an example of the operation of the doctrine of precedent, in that the statement of law as determined by the higher court becomes the *ratio*, reversing the decision prevents the earlier court decision becoming binding.

4.10 Persuasive decisions

If a court is not bound by any previous decision on a point then it is free to reach its own decision on that point. However, even if a court is not technically bound by an authority, it is nevertheless entitled to consider that authority and may be 'persuaded' by the reasoning. The following authorities are not binding but are persuasive, ie they may assist or influence a court in reaching a decision:

(a) *The decisions of non-binding courts*, for example equivalent or lower courts in the hierarchy.

(b) *Obiter dicta*. An interesting example of this is the statement by Denning J (as he then was) in *Central London Property Trust Ltd v High Trees House Ltd* [1947] KB 130, that a landlord who has agreed to accept half rent for a given period cannot later claim back rent for this period. This was *obiter*, because the landlords were only claiming full rent for the future. It was later considered by the Court of Appeal in *Combe v Combe* [1951] 2 KB 215. It was not binding on this court, not only because it was *obiter*, but also because it was a decision of the High Court. However, the Court of Appeal was 'persuaded' by this judgment and this *dictum* became what is now known as the doctrine of promissory estoppel, a principle of contract law.

(c) *Decisions of the Privy Council* (see **Table 2.16** in **Chapter 2** and below for more on the Privy Council).

    Although the Judicial Committee of the Privy Council hears appeals from Commonwealth countries, and for that purpose, it is a court of the relevant country in which the case was heard at first instance, its judgments can also be highly persuasive. The members of the Council are, for the most part, the same as for the Supreme Court, so it is likely that the Supreme Court would reach the same decision were the case brought in England. Obviously, this depends on a sufficient degree of similarity between the laws of the two countries. For this reason, the foreign decisions which have the greatest influence on English courts are those from countries whose system is based on the English common law (as opposed to those based on the civil law tradition). This includes many Commonwealth countries, Northern Ireland and the USA.

An example of an extremely influential Privy Council decision is that of *Attorney-General for Jersey v Holley* [2005] 3 WLR 29, in which the legal definition of the defence of provocation in homicide was discussed. Although not binding, this case has been followed in England and Wales (*R v James, Karimi* [2006] EWCA Crim 14). Indeed, the Court of Appeal explicitly followed the Privy Council decision as opposed to the earlier House of Lords' (now the Supreme Court) decision in *R v Smith (Morgan)* [2001] 1 AC 46. Although this is very much an exception to the normal rules on precedent, it is a good illustration of just how persuasive a decision of the Privy Council can be in the right circumstances. Here, it was because of the seniority of the judges involved (nine Law Lords considered the issue). Indeed, Lord Nicholls stated quite specifically: 'This appeal is concerned to ... clarify definitively the present state of English law, and hence Jersey law, on this important subject.'

(d) *Decisions of foreign courts.* Although Scots law is based on the civil law system, if a case is on the interpretation of a statute which applies equally to both jurisdictions, such decisions will be strongly persuasive.

On matters of EU law, decisions of courts of other Member States may be of value. In addition, cases from countries which are even further afield may be relevant. One example of a case commonly cited in textbooks and courts as a persuasive authority is the US case of *Shuey v United States* 92 US 73 (1874). This is a case concerning contract law, which deals with the issue of revocation of an offer made to the public at large, as there is no binding authority from a court of England and Wales on this point. Such cases are more likely to be persuasive if they are from similar common law systems.

(e) *Decisions of the European Court of Human Rights.* Under s 2 of the Human Rights Act 1998, a court determining a question which has arisen in connection with a Convention right must take into account any judgment of the European Court of Human Rights. This is tantamount to saying that such decisions are highly persuasive. In the House of Lords decision of *R (Alconbury Developments Ltd) v Secretary of State for the Environment, Transport and Regions* [2003] 2 AC 295, Lord Slynn, whilst specifically acknowledging that decisions of the European Court of Human Rights were not binding on English courts, said that: 'In the absence of any special circumstances it seems to me that the court should follow any clear and constant jurisprudence of the European Court of Human Rights.' See **6.5.5** for further discussion of this point.

(f) *Statements in legal textbooks or periodicals.* In the case of *R v G* [2003] UKHL 50, Lord Bingham referred to the work of seven different academic writers when considering the meaning of recklessness in criminal damage.

Once a court has followed persuasive authority in this way, the decision in the later case then becomes *ratio* and is binding on future courts.

4.11 The Human Rights Act 1998 and precedent

4.11.1 Introduction

Having considered the doctrine of precedent in some detail, we must now examine how the Human Rights Act 1998, to which you were introduced in **Chapter 1**, impacts on the doctrine of precedent.

4.11.2 The impact of the Human Rights Act 1998

The 1998 Act guarantees certain fundamental rights contained in the European Convention on Human Rights ('Convention rights') and allows individuals to enforce these rights before the courts of England and Wales. Section 2(1) of the Act makes it clear that when the courts and tribunals of England and Wales decide questions in connection with Convention rights, they must take into account all relevant judgments, decisions, declarations and opinions of the European Court of Human Rights (ECtHR), the European Commission of Human Rights (now abolished and not to be confused with the EU body) and the Committee of Ministers of the Council of Europe. This is highly significant, as it requires the courts of England and Wales to take into account their decisions when otherwise it would be up to the courts to decide if they should take any such decisions into account.

Note that the obligation imposed on domestic courts is to 'take into account' judgments of the ECtHR; they are not bound to them. However, in practice domestic courts do normally follow them (*R (Alconbury Developments Ltd) v Secretary of State for the Environment, Transport and Regions* (above)). Nonetheless, in 2006, the House of Lords departed from a decision of the ECtHR and instructed the lower courts to follow House of Lords decisions should a conflict occur (*Kay and others v London Borough of Lambeth* [2006] UKHL 10). If the Human Rights Act 1998 is replaced by the proposed British Bill of Rights Bill, it seems that domestic courts will no longer be obliged to take into account judgments of the ECtHR; see further **6.5.6.5** below.

4.12 Do judges make law?

In **Chapter 1** we discussed case law as a source of law, and this can lead to the tensions between the judiciary and the legislature, as discussed below. You will be aware from this chapter of the substantial influence which judges have over the development of the law. Let us re-visit the question of whether judges do make law.

4.12.1 The declaratory theory of the common law

This is the classic theory, as propounded by Brett MR in *Munster v Lamb* (1883) 11 QBD 588, that judges do not make or change the law but merely declare it. This is, of course, consistent with the principle of the legislative supremacy of Parliament as referred to in **Chapter 1**. According to this theory, the most judges will ever do is to apply existing principles of the common law to new sets of facts.

4.12.2 The modern view

There was a growing view in the 1970s and 1980s that the declaratory theory was a practice more observed in the breach. The theory was finally laid to rest by the judgment of Lord Browne-Wilkinson in *Kleinwort Benson Ltd v Lincoln City Council* [1999] 2 AC 349 . He stated: '... the whole of the common law is judge made and only by judicial change in the law is common law kept relevant in a changing world'.

Hence it is now generally accepted that judges, particularly in the Court of Appeal and the Supreme Court, do make new law. This was demonstrated in *Re A (Children)* [2001] Fam 147, where the Court of Appeal had to decide the legality of an operation to separate conjoined twins, Jodie and Mary, which would inevitably lead to the death of the weaker twin. As there were no cases which could act as a precedent, nor legislation on this particular issue, the judges had to decide whether the doctors would be guilty of murder and the weight to be given to the parents' wishes. They ruled that the operation should proceed.

By deciding questions which have not previously been considered, judges break new ground. Their decisions create new law if they are followed as 'precedents' by courts in later cases. This aspect of the role of the judiciary is not usually controversial. However, there are cases where the role of the judiciary has been controversial, for example *R v A (No 2)* [2002] 1 AC 45 (discussed at **3.12**). Section 41(3)(b) of the Youth Justice and Criminal Evidence Act 1999 prohibited a defendant being prosecuted for rape from questioning the complainant/victim about her sexual behaviour. An exception to this rule was that the court could permit such questioning where the issue in question was that the complainant had consented to sex and her alleged sexual behaviour took place at or about the same time as the suspected rape. The defence wanted to question her regarding her previous sexual relationship with the defendant.

On a literal interpretation of s 41, such questioning was not permissible; they could only question her about acts which occurred at about the same time as the incident charged. However, the majority of the House of Lords thought this would contravene the defendant's right to a fair trial under Article 6 of the ECHR. Accordingly, the House of Lords under s 3 of the Human Rights Act 1998 interpreted s 41 as allowing sexual history evidence where such evidence is 'so relevant to the issue of consent that to exclude it would endanger' the defendant's right to a fair trial (Lord Steyn, para 46).

Some critics have argued that the Parliament did not intend the 1999 Act to be construed in this way, and the House of Lords' decision was contrary to the will of Parliament. Parliament clearly intended that victims of rape should be shielded from cross-examination about their past sexual history as that was irrelevant to whether they had consented to sex in relation to the incident charged. The better option would have been for the House of Lords to issue a declaration of incompatibility under s 4 of the Human Rights Act 1998.

Another highly controversial case is the Supreme Court's judgment in *R (Miller) v The Prime Minister; Cherry v Advocate General for Scotland* [2019] UKSC 41. The case concerned whether the advice given by the Prime Minister, Boris Johnson, to the Queen that Parliament should be prorogued for five weeks in the period leading up to the UK's exit from the EU, then due to take place on 31 October 2019, was lawful. (Prorogation brings to an end the current parliamentary session and during prorogation Parliament is unable to meet. Accordingly, at a time of considerable political and constitutional turmoil, Parliament would have been unable to scrutinise the Government's Brexit policies.) The Supreme Court held that the Prime Minister's advice was unlawful and the prorogation was therefore void.

The reason that this judgment is controversial is that critics of it believe that it is a long-established principle of constitutional law that the royal prerogative power to prorogue Parliament is not justiciable, ie cannot be challenged in the courts. The Supreme Court's judgment was therefore a political one that changed the constitutional relationship between the Government and Parliament. On the other hand, the Supreme Court based its judgment on the fundamental constitutional principles of parliamentary sovereignty and executive accountability. The prorogation would have prevented Parliament from exercising its role of holding the Government to account.

The circumstances of this case were highly unusual, and judges usually exercise their law-making functions with caution. Lord Bingham, in 1997, identified five situations where judges would be reluctant to make new law:

(1) Where right-minded citizens have legitimately arranged their affairs on the basis of a certain understanding of the law.

(2) Where a legal rule, which is acknowledged as defective, needs to be replaced by a detailed legislative code with qualifications, exceptions and safeguards, and that code requires research and consultation that judges are not equipped to perform.

(3) Where the question involves an issue of current social policy on which there is no consensus in the community.

(4) Where Parliament is currently addressing the issue.

(5) Where the issue is far removed from ordinary judicial experience.

(Tom Bingham, 'The Judge as Lawmaker: An English Perspective' in Paul Rushworth (ed), *The Struggle for Simplicity in the Law: Essays for Lord Cooke of Thoroton* (Butterworths Wellington, NZ, 1997)

Although Lord Bingham was writing extra-judicially and other judges might approach judicial law-making differently, this does summarise the views of a very eminent British judge and so has considerable weight.

4.13 The advantages and disadvantages of the doctrine of precedent over the civil law system

At **2.20**, you were introduced to the differences between the common law and civil law systems. In particular, you considered features of the adversarial approach adopted in the common law and the inquisitorial method used in civil law systems. In this paragraph, you will find out more about these.

4.13.1 The meaning of the term 'civil law system'

A civil law system is the generic description given to those legal systems which are based on Roman law, in direct contrast to common law systems which, as we have seen in **Chapter 1**, are based on case law and the principle of precedent (*stare decisis*). Broadly speaking, most of the Member States of the European Union have a civil law system whereas most Commonwealth countries have a common law system; South Africa and Sri Lanka are notable exceptions as both have Roman-Dutch civil law-based systems, albeit with common law and customary law influences. Please note that this meaning of the term 'civil law' differs from the way in which we used the term in **Chapter 1**, when distinguishing between civil law and criminal law.

An important feature of most civil law systems is that they are based on a written code, such as the 'Code Napoleon' in France, and the role of the judiciary is essentially to apply that code. By contrast, in common law systems, although, as we have seen in **Chapter 1**, statute is an important source of law, it is by no means the only source of law and there is no all-encompassing code. (South Africa and Sri Lanka are exceptions to codification as Roman-Dutch law remains uncodified.)

4.13.2 The advantages and disadvantages of the two systems

We will consider briefly some of the relative advantages of civil and common law systems. To a great extent, as the two systems are mirror images of one another, any advantage of the civil law system is a disadvantage of the doctrine of precedent and vice versa.

First let us consider the principles of consistency and certainty which we discussed at **4.1.2** above. The doctrine of precedent provides certainty and consistency, and saves having to 'reinvent the wheel'. However, the civil law system allows for change, as the code may be amended (in the same way that statutes are amended) either if a decision is later considered to be wrong, or if attitudes or policy change.

The civil law style of drafting legislation is to state general principles. This means that, inevitably, when judges come to apply the law they tend to look at the purpose behind the law, as very often the law will not cover the specific facts of the case. We have already addressed this principle in the context of statutory interpretation. Therefore, when a case is decided in the light of the purpose behind a general principle, it would be more difficult to apply it as a precedent to future cases.

The Court of Justice of the European Union (CJEU) is an interesting example of a court which, as in civil law jurisdictions, operates without the doctrine of precedent. However, that is not to say that the CJEU does not follow previous cases. In fact, the CJEU usually does follow previous decisions because the purpose behind the legislation remains the same. It could therefore be argued that this system has achieved a balance, in that it provides a large measure of consistency but it is still possible for the CJEU to change its approach if attitudes or policy change. For example, we referred at **4.7.8** to the case of *Keck v Mithouard* (cases C-267 and C-268/91) [1993] ECR I-6097. The ECJ wished to change its approach on the free movement of goods, and therefore explicitly stated and explained why it was not going to follow previous decisions. What this approach does not provide is certainty, but it is impossible to have certainty without losing some of the other advantages. Which system is better therefore depends on how important certainty is to you.

Summary

The role of case law in the English legal system is a vital one. It provides a body of law which can be drawn upon by judges, and indeed other lawyers, to decide or advise upon future cases. The advantages are consistency and certainty in the application of the law.

In this chapter, you have studied the doctrine of precedent and been introduced to the (at times) difficult concepts of *ratio decidendi* and *obiter dicta*. You have also discovered that not all courts are equal and that the hierarchy of the courts affects the value given to a particular case or legal principle. However, despite being the highest court in the land, even the Supreme Court must take account of external influences due to the Human Rights Act 1998, as all UK courts must take into account ECtHR jurisprudence when interpreting Convention rights. Moreover, although the UK's exit from the EU has profoundly reduced the significance of the CJEU within the English legal system, its pre-IP completion day judgments on retained EU law/ assimilated law remain binding on courts below the Court of Appeal.

Identifying the *ratio* of a case is not always straightforward, but it is a vital skill for lawyers. The outcome of a given case will often depend on the judge's determination of the *ratio* of an earlier case.

5 Constitutional Fundamentals and Sources of the Constitution

Learning outcomes

By the end of this chapter you should be able to:

- explain the meaning of the word 'constitution' and understand the ways in which a constitution may be classified or described;
- appreciate the key principles upon which the UK constitution is based;
- explain and analyse the diverse sources of the UK constitution, including constitutional conventions;
- understand the distinctions between the 'legal' and 'non-legal' sources of the UK constitution; and
- understand and analyse the relationship between the royal prerogative and constitutional conventions.

5.1 Introduction

In this chapter you will consider some fundamental constitutional principles and then examine the various sources of the UK constitution.

In outline, a constitution is the set of rules by which a state or country operates – it gives powers to various branches of state and says what rights and freedoms individual citizens of the state are to have. Although every country has a constitution, the format of the constitution may differ greatly from one country to another. You will examine the methods by which constitutions may be classified or described. For example, you will consider the difference between a written constitution and an unwritten constitution.

Once you have considered how a constitution may be classified, you will examine the key features of the UK constitution. Some of these features may already be familiar to you. You will begin to see why some commentators describe the UK constitution as unique.

The UK constitution has a variety of sources. You will consider these in detail, examining the difference between the 'legal' and 'non-legal' sources. You will also think about the degree of flexibility within the UK constitution.

5.2 What is a constitution?

Constitutions are used in many types of organisations (for example political parties, clubs and societies) to establish the fundamental rules and principles by which the organisation is governed. A political constitution deals with the entire organisation of a state and how its legal order is established. It will also give effect to the values that society regards as important.

For our purposes as constitutional lawyers, a constitution will usually define a state's fundamental political principles, establish the framework of the government of the state, and guarantee certain rights and freedoms to the citizens. The fundamental political principles of a state will be the key political ideas or doctrines on which the state is based. The framework of government will set out the powers and duties of the executive, legislative and judicial branches of the state (see **5.4.2** below). The rights and freedoms of citizens will be those basic rights and freedoms which it is agreed all citizens of the state should enjoy (for example, the right to free speech, or the right to vote in free elections).

5.3 Classifying constitutions

Although we can identify what the basic elements of a constitution are, the constitution of a state may be classified or described in a number of different ways. The 'classification' of a constitution means identifying what the most important features of that particular constitution are. The following paragraphs explain how constitutions can be classified and how the UK constitution is usually classified.

5.3.1 Written/unwritten

A state with a written or codified constitution will have its constitution set out in a single document. This document will contain the fundamental laws of the constitution and define the powers of the different branches of state. It may also contain a Bill of Rights setting out the fundamental civil liberties to be enjoyed by citizens of the state.

A state with an unwritten or uncodified constitution will not have its constitution set out in a single authoritative document. Rather the constitution will be made up of a number of different sources, such as statute and case law.

The UK has an unwritten constitution in the sense that there is no single authoritative written document that sets out how the government should operate and what the rights of individual citizens are. Rather, the UK constitution is made up of a variety of different sources, which you will examine in detail later in this chapter.

The UK is highly unusual in having an unwritten constitution; Israel and New Zealand are the only other contemporary examples. The reason usually given for this is that written constitutions are usually drafted following a major historic defining moment, such as independence, revolution or the total collapse of the previous system of government. Thus, the US constitution was drafted following its declaration of independence from Great Britain in 1775, while the current South African constitution came into force in 1994 following the end of *apartheid*. As no such defining moment has occurred in the UK since the drafting of constitutions became politically fashionable, the UK has not had a reason for codifying its constitution.

5.3.2 Republican/monarchical

A state with a republican constitution will usually have a president (often elected directly or indirectly) as its head of state. A state with a monarchical constitution will have an unelected monarch as head of state (although the monarch's role may be largely ceremonial).

The UK has a monarchical constitution. The head of state is the Monarch, who is unelected and head of state by virtue of their position within the royal family. As you will see later, however, in practice the Monarch exercises little real power. Most of their powers are, by convention, exercised by the government on their behalf.

5.3.3 Federal/unitary

A state with a federal constitution will have a division of power between the central government and regional government. Accordingly, the central federal government cannot legislate regarding matters reserved to the states, though defining the boundary between federal and state powers often leads to controversy and legal disputes. A state with a unitary constitution will have a single sovereign legislative body, with power being concentrated at the centre.

The constitution of the UK is unitary. The Parliament at Westminster is the supreme (or sovereign) law-making body, and other law-making bodies within the UK (such as the Scottish Parliament or local authorities) derive their law-making powers from powers they have been given by the Westminster Parliament. However, some commentators argue that, as a result of devolution, the UK constitution now exhibits some quasi-federal characteristics. As further powers are devolved, this argument is likely to take on increasing strength. Nonetheless, in contrast to a federal state, the Westminster Parliament can override devolved law-making bodies even in respect of powers that have been devolved.

5.3.4 Rigid/flexible

A state that has a rigid constitution has a constitution that is said to be 'entrenched'. This means that the constitution may be changed only by following a special procedure. Most states with written constitutions tend to be rigid. A state that has a flexible constitution has a constitution that is comparatively easy to change because no special procedures are necessary for the constitution to be amended.

As a result of being unwritten, the UK constitution is flexible. Although from a political point of view it may often be difficult to amend the constitution as some principles attract widespread adherence across the political spectrum, legally it is possible to change the constitution quite easily because there are no lengthy or complex procedures to follow.

5.3.5 Formal separation of powers/informal separation of powers

A state that has a formal separation of powers has a clear separation both of functions and of personnel between the executive (ie the government), the legislative (ie the parliament) and the judicial (ie the courts) branches of state. A state that has an informal separation of powers is likely to have a significant degree of overlap in terms of functions and personnel between the executive, the legislative and the judicial branches of state.

The UK constitution has a largely informal separation of powers. Although it is possible to identify the executive, legislative and judicial branches of state, no formal mechanism exists to keep them separate, and there is a degree of overlap between them both in terms of function and personnel. There is little formal separation of powers under the UK constitution because there is no written constitution to strictly separate the membership and functions of each branch of state from other branches of state.

5.3.6 Comparison with other constitutions

Employing the classifications used at **5.3.1–5.3.5** is also a useful way of highlighting the differences between the UK constitution and the constitutions of other states. For example, if we were using these classifications to describe the constitution of the United States of America, we would have selected the opposite word or phrase from each pair.

A crucial difference is that the USA has a written constitution which contains rules on how the Government is to operate, together with a Bill of Rights which details the rights which ordinary citizens enjoy. It also has a republican constitution, because there is an elected President as head of state as opposed to an unelected monarch. The USA has a federal system of government, with power split between the national government in Washington and the various individual states. Largely as a result of being written, the US constitution is said to be rigid (or 'entrenched'). In particular, it may be altered only by following a special procedure.

Lastly, the US constitution has enshrined the principle of the formal separation of powers between the three branches of state: there is almost no overlap in functions or personnel between the executive (ie the President), the legislature (ie Congress) and the judiciary (ie the Supreme Court).

5.4 Core constitutional principles

Before you consider the detailed sources of the UK constitution, you need to be familiar with the core principles on which the UK constitution is based. These principles are:

(a) the rule of law;

(b) the separation of powers; and

(c) the sovereignty (or supremacy) of Parliament.

In this section you will briefly consider the rule of law, the separation of powers and the sovereignty of Parliament, but you will study them in more depth in later chapters.

5.4.1 The rule of law

You will study this in more detail in **Chapter 7**. Its key elements, though, can be summarised as follows:

- There should be no arbitrary exercise of power by the state or government – all actions of the state or government must be permitted by the law.
- Laws should be made properly, following a set procedure.
- Laws should be clear – laws should be set out clearly and be accessible, and a citizen should be punished only for a clearly defined breach of the law.
- Laws should be certain – laws should not operate retrospectively and a citizen should not be punished for an act that was not a crime at the time they carried out that act.
- There should be equality before the law – all citizens should have equal access to the legal process for the redress of grievances, and the law should treat all persons in the same way (for example, the law should not provide special exemptions or 'get-outs' for government officials).
- The judiciary should be independent and impartial – the courts should be sufficiently independent from the legislature and the executive so that judges can uphold the law without fear of repercussions from the other branches of state.

5.4.2 The separation of powers

Writing in the 18th century, the French political philosopher Charles de Montesquieu stated:

> When the legislative and executive powers are united in the same person, or in the same body ... there can be no liberty ... Again, there is no liberty if the power of judging is not separated from the legislative and the executive. (*De l'Esprit des Lois,* 1748)

Montesquieu meant that, to prevent arbitrary or oppressive government, the different branches of state had to be kept separate in terms of their functions and personnel. He identified three different branches of state:

(a) the legislature (or parliament) - the body that makes the law. In the UK the legislature (Parliament) comprises the Monarch, the House of Lords and the House of Commons;

(b) the executive (or government) - the body that implements the law. In the UK the executive is made up of the Monarch, the Prime Minister and other government ministers, the civil service, and the members of the police and armed forces; and

(c) the judiciary (or courts) - the body that resolves disputes about the law. The judicial branch of state is made up of the Monarch, all legally qualified judges, and magistrates (non-legally qualified members of the public who deal with some criminal matters).

As a result of the complex way in which modern states work, it is unrealistic for each branch of state to be kept completely separate from the others. Most constitutions have therefore developed the concept of 'checks and balances'. The idea behind this is that each branch of state is kept in check by powers given to the other branches, so that no one branch of state may exert an excessive amount of power or influence.

In **Chapter 7** you will analyse the extent to which the UK constitution is based on the separation of powers.

5.4.3 The sovereignty of Parliament

You saw at **5.3.3** that the UK has a unitary constitution, with the Westminster Parliament being the supreme law-making body. The doctrine of the supremacy (or sovereignty) of Parliament is central to an understanding of how the UK constitution operates.

Parliamentary sovereignty (or supremacy) is a common law doctrine accepted by the judiciary, under which the courts acknowledge that legislation enacted by Parliament takes precedence over the common law. The classic definition of parliamentary supremacy was provided by Professor AV Dicey:

> The principle of parliamentary sovereignty means neither more nor less than this: namely, that Parliament ... has, under the English constitution, the right to make or unmake any law whatever; and, further, that no person or body is recognised by the law ... as having a right to override or set aside the legislation of Parliament. (*An Introduction to the Study of the Law of the Constitution,* 1885)

Dicey's definition of parliamentary sovereignty has two parts.

Firstly, Parliament can pass whatever legislation it likes; thus it can introduce or repeal any law as it sees fit. So, in an often quoted example, Parliament could, if it wished, ban smoking on the streets of Paris.

Secondly, no other person or body can challenge or override legislation which Parliament has enacted. In particular, this means that the courts must uphold legislation passed by Parliament and cannot declare legislation to be unconstitutional. This contrasts with the position in the USA, where the Supreme Court can strike down an Act of Congress as being unconstitutional.

You will consider the principle of parliamentary sovereignty in more detail in **Chapter 6**, which will also analyse the extent to which there may be limitations on Parliament's ability to legislate as it wishes.

5.5 Sources of the UK constitution

The constitution of the UK is not set out in a single written document. Rather, the UK constitution is unwritten or uncodified and has a variety of different sources. It is helpful to think of it as being like a jigsaw - it is made up of a variety of different parts, and only when those parts are pieced together can the constitution as a whole be understood.

In this section, you will consider the different sources of the UK constitution. There are four principal sources:

(a) Acts of Parliament;

(b) case law;

(c) the royal prerogative; and

(d) constitutional conventions.

Each source will be considered in turn.

5.5.1 Acts of Parliament

Although our constitution is said to be unwritten, many important aspects of it are located in various statutes that Parliament has enacted.

Magna Carta 1215: This has symbolic value as the first assertion of the limits on the powers of the Monarch and of the rights of individuals. Magna Carta was extracted from King John by his feudal lords and guaranteed certain rights to 'freemen of the realm', including trial by jury.

Magna Carta embodies the principle that government must be conducted according to the law and with the consent of the governed. It established the principle that no one is above the law and compelled King John to renounce certain rights, respect specified legal procedures and accept that his will could be bound by the law. It also introduced the right to protection from unlawful imprisonment

Bill of Rights 1689: This imposed limitations on the powers of the Crown (ie the Monarch) in its relationship with Parliament. The Bill of Rights removed the power of the Monarch arbitrarily to suspend Acts of Parliament and the power of the Monarch to impose taxation without Parliament's consent.

The Bill of Rights also provided that Parliament should meet on a regular basis, elections to Parliament should be free from interference by the Monarch, and 'freedom of speech and debates in proceedings in Parliament ought not to be impeached or questioned in any court or place out of Parliament' (see **Chapter 6**).

Acts of Union 1706–07: These united England and Scotland under a single Parliament of Great Britain (the Parliament at Westminster). They also contained provisions to preserve the separate Scottish church and legal system (see **Chapter 6**).

Parliament Acts 1911 and 1949: The Parliament Acts altered the relationship between the House of Lords and the House of Commons. These Acts ensured that the will of the elected House of Commons would prevail over that of the unelected House of Lords by enabling legislation to be enacted without the consent of the House of Lords (see **Chapters 6 and 7**).

Police and Criminal Evidence Act 1984: This Act is relevant to civil liberties. It provides the police with extensive powers of arrest, search and detention, but also contains important procedural safeguards to ensure that the police do not abuse such powers.

Public Order Act 1986: This Act is also relevant to civil liberties. It allows limitations to be placed on the rights of citizens to hold marches and meetings in public places.

Human Rights Act 1998: The Human Rights Act 1998 (HRA 1998) incorporates the European Convention on Human Rights (ECHR) into our domestic law. It marks a fundamental change in the protection of human rights by allowing citizens to raise alleged breaches of their human rights before domestic courts (see **Chapter 6**).

Acts of devolution (eg Scotland Act 1998): The Acts of devolution created a devolved system of government in various parts of the UK. Acts establishing the Scottish Parliament, the Senedd Cymru or Welsh Parliament and Northern Ireland Assembly have decentralised the process of government and given greater autonomy to these parts of the UK (see **Chapter 8**).

Constitutional Reform Act 2005: This Act reformed the office of Lord Chancellor, transferring the Lord Chancellor's powers as head of the judiciary to the Lord Chief Justice and permitting the House of Lords to elect its own Speaker. It also provided for the creation of a Supreme Court (to replace the Appellate Committee of the House of Lords) and created a new body (the Judicial Appointments Commission) to oversee the appointment of judges (see **Chapter 7**).

European Union (Withdrawal) Act 2018 and European Union (Withdrawal Agreement) Act 2020: These Acts provided for the UK's departure from the European Union ('Brexit'). The European Union (Withdrawal) Act 2018 repealed the European Communities Act 1972 (ECA 1972), which had paved the way for the UK's membership of the European Union. It also ended the supremacy of EU law and introduced into the UK's legal systems the concept of retained EU law/assimilated law (see **Chapter 9**).

Although the above Acts are of great constitutional importance, each was enacted by Parliament in the same way as any other Act of Parliament. No special procedure or majority was required. Similarly, these Acts are not 'entrenched'. In other words, each Act may be repealed by an ordinary Act of Parliament, just as with any other statute. No special procedure is required for its repeal. However, as you will see later, some recent Acts of Parliament, such as the Scotland Act 2016, contain provisions stating that Parliament will not legislate to achieve certain aims without first holding a referendum on the relevant issue.

As a result of having an unwritten constitution, in strictly legal terms, it is easy for Parliament to make significant changes to the constitution. In the absence of a written constitution setting out a 'higher' form of law against which all other legislation may be judged (and also as a result of the development of the doctrine of parliamentary sovereignty), Parliament may enact such legislation as it wishes and our courts cannot strike down such legislation as being unconstitutional. Factors that limit Parliament's ability to change the constitution tend to be more political, economic or social as opposed to strictly legal. You will consider this further in **Chapter 6**.

5.5.2 Case law

5.5.2.1 The common law

The common law is an important source of some key principles of our constitution.

(a) Residual freedom

The principle of 'residual freedom' (upon which civil liberties in this country are based) developed through the common law. It means that citizens are free to do or say whatever they wish unless the law (primarily expressed through Acts of Parliament) clearly states that such an action or statement is prohibited.

(b) Actions of the state must have legal authority

It has also been established through the common law that actions taken by state officials (such as police officers) must have a legal basis if they are to be lawful. This again links to the principle of the rule of law.

Activity 1 Actions of the state must have legal authority

Assume that state officials break into the house of a well-known political activist to search for evidence of anti-government leaflets. The officials have a search warrant, but there is no statutory or common law authority for the issue of the warrant.

Do the officials have the right to claim that their actions are lawful because such actions are necessary in the interests of the state?

Comment

The answer to the question is 'No'.

The scenario you considered is based on the very significant case of *Entick v Carrington* (1765) 19 St Tr 1030. The Secretary of State issued a general warrant for the arrest and search of Entick, who had allegedly been publishing 'seditious material'. The court found that there was no legal authority that enabled the Secretary of State to issue such general warrants, and so the search was unlawful.

The case established the principle that state officials could not act in an arbitrary manner and that the exercise of power by the state had to have clear legal authority. Further, the law did not provide state officials with any form of exemption or 'get out' from legal accountability for their actions.

At **5.5.2.2** below you will consider in more detail the way in which the judiciary prevents the state (or 'executive') exercising its powers in an unlawful manner.

(c) Legal disputes should be resolved by the judiciary

One of the earliest examples of the common law setting out constitutionally important principles is the *Case of Prohibitions (Prohibitions del Roy) (*1607) 12 Co Rep 63. The case concerned a dispute over land, which the King sought to settle by making a ruling. The court held that the Monarch had no power to decide legal matters by way of arbitrary rulings, and that legal disputes should properly be resolved by the courts. Chief Justice Coke ruled that:

> ... the King in his own person cannot judge any case ... this ought to be determined in some Court of Justice ... so that the Court gives the judgment.

The resolution of legal disputes by the judiciary is another aspect of the rule of law.

(d) Habeas corpus and individual liberty

Although it is now strengthened by statute, the remedy of habeas corpus, whereby an individual who has been detained by the state has the right to have the legality of that detention tested before a court, developed originally through the common law.

(e) Right to a fair hearing

Through the common law, the courts have repeatedly stressed the importance of the right to a fair hearing as a fundamental constitutional principle and an important part of the rule of law. The right to a fair trial is also contained in Article 6 of the ECHR, which now forms part of UK law following the enactment of the HRA 1998.

(f) Parliamentary supremacy

You have already considered this principle briefly at **5.4.3** above. Parliamentary sovereignty (or supremacy) is a common law doctrine accepted by the judiciary. In the cases of *Edinburgh & Dalkeith Railway Co v Wauchope* (1842) 8 Cl & F 710 and *Pickin v British Railways Board* [1974] AC 765, the courts developed and then applied the common law 'Enrolled Act' rule which is at the centre of parliamentary sovereignty. The rule states that once an Act of Parliament has been entered onto the parliamentary roll, the courts will not question the validity of that Act or hold the Act to be void. You will examine these cases in more detail **in Chapter 6**.

5.5.2.2 Judicial review of executive actions

In addition to the common law being the source of several important constitutional principles, the courts have also developed the process of 'judicial review'. This is a mechanism that enables the courts to ensure that the Government and other public bodies exercise the powers that they have been granted in the proper way and so do not breach the rule of law.

The next activity will allow you to consider what is meant by 'judicial review' in more detail.

Activity 2 Judicial review of executive actions

You may have seen or heard references, in newspaper or television reports, to citizens seeking judicial review of a decision made by a government minister or other public body. What do you think is meant by 'judicial review' of the actions of the executive? Why is it constitutionally important that the courts perform this role?

Comment

Judicial review is the role played by the High Court in ensuring that the Government and other public bodies act within the powers they have been granted by Parliament. In *St Helen's Borough Council v Manchester Primary Care Trust* [2008] EWCA Civ 931, May LJ defined the function of the court in judicial review proceedings as being to review decisions of statutory and other public authorities, 'to see that they are lawful, rational and reached by a fair process'.

The UK does not have a written constitution creating a 'higher authority' against which individual pieces of legislation may be measured. As a consequence of this, and also because of the doctrine of parliamentary supremacy, courts in the UK do not have the power to review the constitutionality of legislation. The courts do, however, have the ability to review the way in which public bodies exercise the powers which Parliament has conferred upon them.

Judicial review is constitutionally important because it enables the courts to hold the executive (ie the Government) to account for its actions. This prevents the Government acting in an arbitrary, illegal or irrational manner, and ensures that decisions are taken in a fair and unbiased way.

For more information regarding judicial review, please refer to standard textbooks on administrative law.

5.5.2.3 The interpretation of statute

In addition to developing important constitutional principles through the common law, the judiciary have also made decisions of constitutional significance when interpreting statute law. A noteworthy example of this is *R (Miller) v Secretary of State for Exiting the European Union* [2017] UKSC 5 (*Miller (No 1)*). In this case, the Supreme Court interpreted the ECA 1972 as preventing the Government from using the royal prerogative (see **5.5.3** below) as the legal basis for the notice of withdrawal from the EU.

5.5.3 The royal prerogative

5.5.3.1 Scope of the royal prerogative

The UK Government derives most of its powers from various statutes in which Parliament has given government ministers authority to make decisions or take action in a particular area. In addition, however, some powers that the Government exercises are derived from the royal prerogative.

Dicey defined the royal prerogative as follows:

> the residue of discretionary or arbitrary authority, which at any given time is legally left in the hands of the Crown ... Every act which the government can lawfully do without the authority of an Act of Parliament is done in virtue of this prerogative. (*An Introduction to the Study of the Law of the Constitution*, 1885)

Prerogative powers derive from the common law and are exercised by (or in the name of) the Monarch. The royal prerogative is essentially what remains of the absolute powers that at one time were exercised by the Monarch and that have not been removed by Parliament.

Although there is no definitive list of prerogative powers, the modern extent of the royal prerogative covers the following principal areas:

(a) Foreign affairs:
   (i) declarations of war and the deployment of armed forces overseas;
   (ii) making treaties; and
   (iii) the recognition of foreign states.

(b) Domestic affairs:
   (i) the summoning of Parliament;
   (ii) the appointment and dismissal of the Prime Minister (and other government ministers);
   (iii) the giving of Royal Assent to bills;
   (iv) the dissolution of Parliament;
   (v) defence of the realm (ie the deployment of armed forces within the UK);
   (vi) the exercise of the prerogatives of pardon and mercy;
   (vii) granting public honours; and
   (viii) the setting up of public bodies to disburse funds made available by Parliament.

Although the Monarch is legally responsible for the exercise of the prerogative powers, most of these powers are by convention exercised by the Prime Minister and other government ministers on the Monarch's behalf.

The ability of the Government to spend money to exercise its prerogative powers does however depend on Parliament's willingness to vote to provide the necessary funds.

You will consider the way in which the Government's exercise of royal prerogative powers may be regulated or controlled by Parliament and the judiciary in **Chapter 7**.

5.5.3.2 The royal prerogative and statute

Acts of Parliament can remove prerogative powers, as the Crown Proceedings Act 1947 shows. This Act abolished the immunity that the Crown previously had in respect of claims against it both in tort and contract. Another more recent example of Parliament removing a prerogative power is the Fixed-term Parliaments Act 2011 (though the Dissolution and Calling of Parliament Act 2022 has now repealed the 2011 Act). The 2011 Act provided for fixed days for polls for parliamentary general elections, and it was envisaged that elections would be held every five years; however, early elections took place in 2017 and 2019. While in force, it removed the power that the Monarch had exercised under the royal prerogative to dissolve Parliament at a time of their choosing (by convention, the Monarch would always dissolve Parliament when requested to do so by the Prime Minister).

The position, however, is more complex when an Act does not explicitly override an aspect of the prerogative, but nonetheless covers the same subject matter. In *Attorney General v De Keyser's Royal Hotel* [1920] AC 508, during World War I a hotel was requisitioned by the Government for staff officers. The hotel sought compensation under the Defence Act 1842, which authorised requisitioning and set out a right to compensation. The Government argued it was using the royal prerogative and did not have to pay compensation. The House of Lords stated that the issue depended on the construction of the statute. It might add a statutory power or it might replace (and thus repeal) the prerogative power.

In this case the statute set out limitations and conditions on the exercise of the power of requisitioning. It must have been contrary to the intention of Parliament for a government to avoid these using the royal prerogative. Lord Dunedin stated that 'if the whole ground of something which could be done by the prerogative is covered by the statute, it is the statute that rules'. Lord Atkinson commented that the prerogative had been abridged by statute and so remained in abeyance as long as the statutory power remained in force. This suggests that if the statute were repealed, the prerogative power would revive.

The Court of Appeal reached a contrasting decision in *R v Secretary of State for the Home Department, ex p Northumbria Police Authority* [1989] QB 26. The Home Secretary wanted to supply plastic bullets to local police forces, cutting out the police authorities. He issued circulars to Chief Police Officers inviting them to apply direct for stores if they anticipated any problem with their local police authority. The Northumbria Police Authority argued that, as the Police Act 1964 gave police authorities the power to supply such equipment to police forces, statute conflicted with the prerogative power, so the circulars were unlawful.

The court held that under the royal prerogative the Home Secretary had the power to maintain the Queen's Peace and to keep law and order. The court held that the statutory power could co-exist side by side with the prerogative power, as they were not inconsistent. The prerogative would only be curtailed if inconsistent with the statutory powers.

The House of Lords took a similar approach in *R v Secretary of State for the Home Department, ex p Fire Brigades Union* [1995] 2 AC 513 to the one they had taken in the *De Keyser* case. In 1964 the Government had set up a criminal injury compensation scheme under prerogative powers with compensation being assessed on the basis of common law damages. Parliament then passed the Criminal Justice Act 1988, which provided for a new scheme with compensation payable on the same basis. Instead of bringing the Act into force, the Home Secretary introduced under prerogative powers a new tariff-based system which generally provided less compensation. The claimants challenged the legality of the new scheme.

The House of Lords held that the new tariff scheme was unlawful. It was an abuse of the prerogative power to introduce a tariff scheme inconsistent with the statutory scheme approved by Parliament. Statute had restricted the Home Secretary's ability to introduce a prerogative scheme based on inconsistent criteria.

As explained at **5.5.2.3** above, in *Miller (No 1)* the Supreme Court ruled that the ECA 1972 had curtailed the Government's powers with regards to foreign relations. It could not use the prerogative to change domestic law and to nullify rights that Parliament had created by statute.

The Dissolution and Calling of Parliament Act 2022 is an interesting development as it revives the royal prerogative power to dissolve Parliament. Some doubts have been expressed whether it is possible to 'revive' a prerogative, but Parliament has done so by legislating to make the prerogative power 'exercisable again' (s 2(1) of the 2022 Act). The accepted current position of law is accordingly in line with the principle set out in *De Keyser*. While the prerogative power to dissolve Parliament was 'in abeyance' while the Fixed-term Parliaments Act 2011 was in force, it revived upon the repeal of the 2011 Act.

5.5.4 Constitutional conventions

Constitutional conventions are a non-legal source of the constitution. Accordingly, the courts will not directly enforce them. Nonetheless, they play a crucial role in the UK constitution and the workings of government.

5.5.4.1 Defining a constitutional convention

The sources of the constitution you have considered so far are often said to be its 'legal' sources because they have a clear legal basis. Constitutional conventions are an important 'non-legal' source of the constitution. Marshall and Moodie defined constitutional conventions as:

> rules of constitutional behaviour which are considered to be binding upon those who operate the constitution but which are not enforced by the law courts ... nor by the presiding officers in the House of Commons. (*Some Problems of the Constitution* (Hutchinson, 1971))

This definition may be broken down into three parts:

(a) 'rules of constitutional behaviour' - ie how those who perform a role within the constitution should behave;

(b) 'considered to be binding' - ie there should be no deviation from these rules;

(c) 'not enforced' - ie the rules have no legal basis and so will not be enforced by any judicial body.

Constitutional conventions are flexible. As they are 'non-legal', such conventions do not require any particular step or procedure for their creation. Similarly, if a constitutional convention becomes obsolete, it can be dispensed with without any formal steps being taken.

To gain a proper understanding of how the UK constitution works, you need to appreciate the central role played by constitutional conventions. Set out below is a table with some legal rules of the constitution and how in practice their operation is affected by conventions.

Table 5.1 Legal rules and conventions

Legal rule		Convention
Royal Assent is required for a bill to become a valid Act of Parliament. The Monarch may refuse to give Royal Assent.	→	The Monarch, on the advice of the Prime Minister, always assents to a bill that has passed through Parliament.
The Monarch constitutes part of the executive branch of government.	→	The Monarch acts only on the advice of the Prime Minister and other ministers, and in practice most decisions are taken by the Prime Minister and other ministers themselves. Executive powers are exercised through ministers, who are collectively and individually responsible to Parliament.
The Government is the 'Monarch's government', and the Monarch can therefore appoint and dismiss its members as they choose.	→	The Monarch must appoint as Prime Minister the person who can command the support of the majority of the House of Commons (nowadays usually an elected party leader successful in a general election). The Monarch must appoint and dismiss ministers on the advice of the Prime Minister, all of whom must be members of the House of Commons or Lords. Most will be members of the Commons.

5.5.4.2 Important constitutional conventions

Set out below are the most common constitutional conventions in the UK:

(a) The Monarch plays no active role in matters of government, and the legal powers that are vested in the Monarch are exercised on their behalf by the elected government of the day. For example, the Monarch will appoint and dismiss government ministers on the advice of the Prime Minister.

(b) The Monarch, acting on the advice of the Prime Minister, will not refuse Royal Assent to a bill that has been passed by the House of Commons and the House of Lords. If advised by the Prime Minister to assent to a bill, the Monarch will always do so. (Indeed, the last time a Monarch refused Royal Assent was in 1707.)

(c) The Monarch will appoint as Prime Minister the person who is best able to command the confidence of the House of Commons.

(d) Following the repeal of the Fixed-term Parliaments Act 2011 and the revival of the prerogative power by the Dissolution and Calling of Parliament Act 2022, the Monarch legally can dissolve Parliament at will, but will normally do so on the advice of the Prime Minister.

(e) All government ministers will be members either of the House of Commons or of the House of Lords, and the Prime Minister (and most other senior government ministers) should be a member of the democratically elected House of Commons rather than the unelected House of Lords. It is now rare for a peer (other than the Leader of the House of Lords) to sit in the cabinet, the appointment in November 2023 of former Prime Minister Lord Cameron as Foreign Secretary providing a departure from the norm.

(f) Individual ministerial responsibility. Government ministers are responsible to Parliament both for the running and proper administration of their respective departments, and also for their personal conduct. There must be no conflict of interest between a minister's public duties and their private interests. A minister who breaches this convention should resign. For example, in 1982 the Foreign Secretary, Lord Carrington, resigned following criticism of the administrative failings of his department, which had failed to foresee the Argentine invasion of the Falkland Islands.

Ministerial resignations owing to departmental failings are, however, comparatively rare.

In contrast, resignations relating to a minister's personal conduct are more frequent. For example, in November 2017 Priti Patel resigned as International Development Secretary after conducting unauthorised meetings with Israeli officials, and in June 2021 Matt Hancock resigned as Health Secretary after admitting breaking coronavirus rules by kissing and embracing an aide in his office. There is further analysis of this convention at **7.3.4.2**.

(g) Collective cabinet (or ministerial) responsibility. This constitutional convention has several aspects to it:

    (i) The cabinet is collectively responsible to Parliament for the actions of the Government as a whole, and the Government must retain the confidence of the House of Commons. A government that is defeated on a vote of 'confidence' in the House of Commons must resign (as did the Labour Government when it lost such a vote in 1979).

    (ii) The cabinet must be united in public in support of government policy, and so a cabinet minister must resign if they wish to speak out in public against such policy, as did Robin Cook in 2003, when he wished to voice his opposition to the war in Iraq, and Boris Johnson in July 2018 over Theresa May's Brexit policies.

    (iii) Cabinet discussions must remain secret.

(h) The unelected House of Lords will not reject legislation that gives effect to an important manifesto commitment of the democratically elected Government (the 'Salisbury Convention').

(i) The UK Parliament will normally only legislate on a matter that has been devolved to the Scottish Parliament, Senedd Cymru or Northern Ireland Assembly if the relevant legislature has given its consent (the 'Sewel Convention'). Note that as regards the Scottish Parliament and the Senedd Cymru, this convention has been placed onto a statutory footing. The Scotland Act 2016 added into s 28 of the Scotland Act 1998 a provision stating that it is recognised that the Parliament of the United Kingdom will not normally legislate with regard to devolved matters without the consent of the Scottish Parliament. The Wales Act 2017 added an equivalent provision into s 107 of the Government of Wales of Act 2006 as regards the Senedd Cymru.

(j) Members of the judiciary do not play an active part in political life.

(k) Ministers and Members of Parliament do not criticise in public individual members of the judiciary.

5.5.4.3 Why have constitutional conventions developed?

Reasons why conventions have developed include:

(a) To limit the wide legal powers of the Monarch without the need for major constitutional upheaval.

It would be unacceptable in a modern democracy for an unelected Monarch to have wide powers, so by convention these powers are now exercised by ministers on the Monarch's behalf.

In a similar way, the convention that the House of Lords will not reject legislation giving effect to an important manifesto commitment of the democratically elected Government ensures that the House of Commons takes precedence over the non-elected House of Lords.

(b) To enable the constitution and the Government to operate effectively and flexibly

If the Monarch were to disregard the conventions outlined at **5.5.4.2(a)–(d)** above, serious constitutional difficulties would arise. For example, there would be a constitutional crisis were the Monarch ever to refuse Royal Assent to a bill that had passed the Commons and Lords.

Further, there would be legislative deadlock if the Monarch failed to appoint as Prime Minister someone who could command the confidence of the House of Commons. Likewise there would also be legislative deadlock if the Government failed to resign were it to lose a vote of confidence in the House of Commons

(c) To ensure that the Government is accountable to Parliament for its actions.

Individual ministerial responsibility ensures that government ministers are held to account for their actions and do not abuse their powers (ministers are not legally accountable to Parliament).

Collective cabinet responsibility ensures that the Government as a whole must retain the confidence of Parliament, and can be held to account by Parliament for its actions.

(d) To maintain the separation of powers between the different branches of state.

The convention that members of the judiciary do not play an active role in politics helps to preserve judicial independence. Similarly, the convention that ministers and MPs do not criticise individual members of the judiciary also helps to preserve this (again there is no direct legal accountability to Parliament).

The following example shows the interaction between the royal prerogative and constitutional conventions.

Example

Suppose a bill has passed through all stages in Parliament and has been submitted to the Monarch for Royal Assent. The Leader of the Opposition has called on the Monarch to refuse Royal Assent as the bill, on the Government's own admission, breaches international law, and it is unconstitutional for Parliament to legislate contrary to international law which is also binding on the Monarch.

By convention the Monarch always grants Royal Assent to a bill that has been passed by Parliament. Legally they could refuse, but not in reality. Indeed, the last time the Monarch refused Royal Assent to a bill was in 1707. Parliament is sovereign and can pass Acts that breach international law, and there is no precedent for the Monarch to refuse Royal Assent in those circumstances.

Whilst there might be academic debate whether it is 'unconstitutional' for Parliament to breach international law, that will not affect the granting of Royal Assent.

5.5.4.4 Constitutional conventions and the courts

As you have seen, constitutional conventions differ from laws because they are non-legal rules and so are not enforceable by the courts. The judgment of the Privy Council in *Madzimbamuto v Lardner-Burke* [1969] 1 AC 645 illustrates this.

In 1965 the white minority government of Southern Rhodesia issued a unilateral declaration of independence from Britain. However, the UK Parliament passed the Southern Rhodesia

Act 1965, which declared that Southern Rhodesia remained part of the UK's dominion territories. The validity of the Act was challenged on the basis that there was an established constitutional convention that the UK Parliament would not legislate for Southern Rhodesia (now Zimbabwe) without the consent of the Rhodesian Government.

The Privy Council refused to enforce the convention and held that Parliament could pass legislation which ran contrary to an existing convention. In his judgment, Lord Reid said: 'Their Lordships in declaring the law are not concerned with [conventions] ... They are concerned only with the legal powers of Parliament.'

The Supreme Court reaffirmed that the courts cannot enforce conventions in *Miller (No 1)* (above). The Court emphasised that this was because conventions operated in the political sphere alone. It also stated that including reference to the Sewel Convention in statute had not turned it into a legal rule. Thus, despite the fact that triggering the Article 50 notice of the UK's intention to leave the EU might breach the Sewel Convention, there would be no legal remedy.

This does not mean, however, that constitutional conventions have no legal significance. In *Carltona Ltd v Commissioners of Works* [1943] 2 All ER 560, the Minister of Works had delegated emergency powers to requisition property to a civil servant. Owners of a factory requisitioned in this way applied for judicial review of the decision, arguing that the minister himself should have taken the decision. The Court of Appeal recognised that under the convention of ministerial responsibility the minister was accountable to Parliament for this decision.

The case of *Attorney General v Jonathan Cape* [1976] QB 752 reinforces the *Carltona* judgment. The Attorney General sought an injunction to restrain the publication of Richard Crossman's book, *The Diaries of a Cabinet Minister*. Crossman had been in the Cabinet from 1964 to 1970, but publication did not come within the provisions of the Official Secrets Acts.

The Attorney General sought, therefore, to rely on the constitutional convention of collective cabinet responsibility as one of the principal grounds on which to restrain publication. He argued that Crossman's diaries divulged details of dissent within the Cabinet, thereby breaching the convention. Against this, it was argued that the convention imposed no obligation in law, and the court could not restrain publication as no issues of national security were involved.

The equitable doctrine of breach of confidence that a person should not profit from the wrongful publication of information received in confidence was also a powerful reinforcement of the Attorney General's arguments. The High Court recognised the existence of the convention of collective responsibility which requires Cabinet members to keep Cabinet discussions secret. The court also accepted the possibility that the convention of collective responsibility, along with other factors, could impose on ministers a duty of confidence in respect of Cabinet discussions. While the court would not directly enforce the convention, it could take it into account when deciding whether the information in question was confidential.

However, as the Cabinet meetings concerned had taken place many years previously, it was no longer in the public interest to prevent publication and so the court refused to grant an injunction. Significantly, however, the court indicated that it could have prevented publication had it been in the public interest to do so.

These cases demonstrate that whilst the courts recognise the existence of constitutional conventions, they are not prepared to enforce such conventions directly. Nonetheless, conventions may indirectly give rise to legal obligations which the courts will enforce. However, if Parliament passes an Act which breaches a convention, the Act might be 'unconstitutional', but the courts will not refuse to apply it for that reason.

5.5.4.5 Codification of conventions and the Ministerial Code

Historically, constitutional conventions have tended to be uncodified. However, some commentators have suggested that conventions should be put on a statutory footing and given the same status as laws. It is argued that codifying constitutional conventions would promote certainty and clarity. However, those who oppose this argue that any attempt to give constitutional conventions the same force as laws will erode their flexibility. It is also argued that the use of constitutional conventions is too wide-ranging for them to be codified and that, because conventions are not fixed but rather appear and disappear as circumstance demands, any attempt at codification would require regular amendment.

Perhaps the strongest argument against the codification of constitutional conventions is that they often deal with sensitive political matters, where codification might lead to a constitutional crisis. For example, many constitutional conventions exist to limit the role of the unelected Monarch. However, any attempt to formalise in legal terms the limitations on the powers of the Monarch could be very controversial.

Nonetheless, in December 2010 the Government published for the first time the Ministerial Code, a document setting out the main laws, rules and conventions affecting the conduct and operation of government. Accordingly, many of the conventions described in this chapter have been set out in written form. However, the Ministerial Code is not intended to have any legal effect but instead to provide guidance to ministers and officials.

The Ministerial Code is officially overseen by the adviser on ministerial interests, though the adviser can only investigate alleged breaches of the Code if requested to do so by the Prime Minister. Moreover, the final decision on enforcing the Code is up to the Prime Minister. Thus in November 2020 Boris Johnson, who was Prime Minister at the time, took no action against the Home Secretary, Priti Patel, after the adviser, Sir Alex Allan, found that her conduct towards Home Office staff had amounted to bullying. He concluded she had breached the Code, even if unintentionally. Sir Alex resigned after the Prime Minister took no action. In contrast, in April 2023 Dominic Raab resigned as Deputy Prime Minister and Justice Secretary after an inquiry by Adam Tolley KC into allegations of bullying found that he had acted in an 'intimidating' and 'aggressive' way towards officials.

The Code also provides that ministers who knowingly mislead Parliament will be expected to offer their resignation to the Prime Minister. Whilst this does not explicitly cover the Prime Minister, opposition politicians called on the then Prime Minister, Boris Johnson, to resign over the so-called 'Partygate' affair, arising out of gatherings held at 10 Downing Street, the official residence and the office of the Prime Minister, while Covid-19 lockdown restrictions were in force. They accused Mr Johnson of deliberately misleading Parliament when he assured Parliament that all rules had been followed. After reports emerged that parties had taken place at 10 Downing Street during lockdown, in December 2021 Mr Johnson set up a Cabinet Office inquiry (chaired by Sue Gray, a very senior civil servant) to investigate whether these gatherings breached Covid-19 restrictions.

As the Metropolitan Police started its own investigation in January 2021, Ms Gray delayed releasing her final report until the police had concluded their investigation. Subsequently, the police issued fixed penalty notices for breach of Covid-19 restrictions, including one on Mr Johnson for a gathering taking place on 19 June 2020. Mr Johnson then apologised to Parliament, stating that it had not occurred to him at the time or subsequently that the gathering could amount to a breach of the rules. Ms Gray then issued her report in which she found that whatever 'the initial intent', many of the gatherings breached Covid-19 restrictions and this should not have happened, irrespective of the pressures that existed at the time. She further concluded that there were 'failures of leadership and judgment in No 10 and the Cabinet Office'. Subsequently, Mr Johnson survived a vote of no confidence requisitioned by some Conservative Party MPs by 211 votes to 148. Nonetheless, Mr Johnson resigned as Prime Minister in July 2022 after he had claimed that he was unaware of specific complaints of sexual misconduct made against Chris Pincher MP before appointing him as deputy chief whip of the Conservative Party. However, it then transpired that Mr Johnson had previously been briefed about complaints against Mr Pincher. Mr Johnson tried to stay in office, but mass resignations from the Government forced him to step down.

Additionally, in April 2022 Parliament voted to refer to the Commons Select Committee of Privileges the question of whether Mr Johnson knowingly misled Parliament. The Privileges Committee started its investigation when the police had completed their own inquiries and heard evidence from Mr Johnson himself. In its final report issued in June 2023, the Privileges Committee found that Mr Johnson had committed repeated offences with his Partygate denials and had deliberately misled Parliament. The Committee would have recommended his suspension from Parliament for 90 days if he had not already resigned as an MP. Subsequently MPs voted by 354 votes to 7 to approve the report.

5.5.5 Other sources of the constitution

In addition to the sources of the constitution outlined at **5.5.1** to **5.5.4** above, there are some additional, comparatively minor sources of the UK constitution. Such sources include the laws and customs (ie the internal rules and procedures) of Parliament and various academic writings on the UK constitution.

One of the most significant rules of parliamentary procedure is the 'sub-judice' rule, namely that cases in which proceedings are active in UK courts must not be referred to in any parliamentary motion, debate or question. There is further discussion of this rule at **7.4.2**.

The seminal work on parliamentary rules and procedures is Erskine May, *Parliamentary Practice: A Treatise upon the Law, Privileges, Proceedings and Usage of Parliament* (1844) which in a much updated version is now available online via Parliament's website.

Dicey's historic book, *Introduction to the Study of the Law of the Constitution* (1885) has also been influential in defining the key principles of parliamentary sovereignty and the rule of law.

5.6 A written constitution for the UK?

A frequent topic of debate for constitutional lawyers and commentators is whether the UK should have a written or codified constitution. The constitutional turbulence resulting from Brexit has led in some quarters to increased calls for a codified constitution.

Arguments in favour of a codified constitution include:

(1) It could promote civil cohesion by educating and informing UK citizens about how government operates through an accessible document that reflected shared values and principles. Citizens would have a much clearer understanding of their rights and responsibilities.

(2) It would achieve a proper separation of powers between the legislative, executive and judicial branches of state by defining the roles of each branch of government clearly. In particular, it could provide an effective system of checks and balances which would limit the current executive dominance of Parliament in the UK. The Partygate saga shows that the current informal system which relies on constitutional conventions provides insufficient accountability of the executive.

(3) It would lead to more effective protection of human rights if there were a Bill of Rights that could not be altered at the whim of an individual government. (Such a Bill would be a constitutional document setting out the rights which every citizen can legitimately expect the Government to guarantee and protect. The Bill of Rights enacted by Parliament in 1689 is more a statement of the rights of Parliament against the Monarch than a statement of the rights of individual citizens. Moreover, Parliament can repeal it like any other statute.)

    In the USA, it is only possible to amend the Bill of Rights by following a special procedure for constitutional amendment and, as such, the rights contained in the Bill are 'entrenched'. The US Supreme Court also has the power to strike down legislation that violates the Bill of Rights.

(4) It would help to achieve clarity in other areas, eg by putting prerogative powers on a statutory footing, thereby significantly reducing uncertainty about their scope. Also, it could clarify the role of referendums; referendums have not traditionally formed part of the UK constitution and are difficult to reconcile with parliamentary sovereignty, as the events following the referendum in 2016 on EU membership illustrate.

Arguments against a codified constitution include:

(1) It would be very difficult to determine who should draft the constitution. None of the existing institutions have the political legitimacy to draft it, and creating a constituent or citizens' assembly to do so would prove highly problematic.

(2) An uncodified constitution is flexible and can develop organically in response to events and in fact it dealt well with the aftermath of the 2016 referendum. In any event, there is little evidence that a codified constitution would have avoided the turmoil surrounding Brexit.

(3) A codified constitution would represent the values prevailing at the time at which it was drafted and may soon become out of date, as shown by efforts at gun control in the USA. Legislation to limit guns has often been thwarted by the 'right to bear arms' contained in the Bill of Rights, a document that was created in completely different circumstances.

(4) A codified constitution would give too much power to the judiciary which would consequently become excessively politicised. Events in the USA demonstrate the dangers, as graphically illustrated by the controversy over the case of *Roe v Wade* 410 US 113. In 1973 the US Supreme Court held that women had a constitutional right to an abortion, but in June 2022 the court controversially overruled *Roe v Wade* in *Dobbs v Jackson Women's Health Organization* 142 St C 2228 (2022). Fiercely contested political issues should be decided through the democratic electoral and legislative process, rather than by unelected judges.

(5) Events in the USA following the election in November 2024 of Donald Trump to a second term as President show that codified constitutions are no better than uncodified ones in preventing the executive from abusing its powers. The use by President Trump of executive orders (directives issued by the President without congressional approval) to cut foreign aid and other federal government programmes, impose tariffs, dismiss civil servants, limit rights to USA citizenship and implement many other radical measures have proved particularly controversial.

    Both types of constitution require a sense of restraint on the part of those who wield power to ensure the upholding of constitutional norms.

There is no right or wrong answer regarding whether the UK should have a codified constitution. However, the lack of political consensus in favour of one means that there is little likelihood of codification in the near future. However, as you work through the following chapters of this textbook, you may find it interesting to critically evaluate arguments for and against codification.

Summary

In this chapter you have considered what a constitution consists of and the nature of the UK's unwritten or uncodified constitution. This means that there is no single document that can be labelled 'the Constitution'. Nonetheless, the UK does have a constitution with diverse sources, in particular:

- Statute: These include statutes of constitutional significance such as the Human Rights Act 1998 and the European Union (Withdrawal) Act 2018.
- Case law: Judicial decisions have been responsible for many key constitutional principles, such as the requirement for government actions to have legal authority, and the right to a fair trial.
- Royal prerogative: This comprises what is left of the Monarch's arbitrary powers and has been very substantially curtailed by statute.
- Constitutional conventions: These are a non-legal source of the constitution and aid the operation of the UK constitution.

Figure 5.1 below summarises the sources:

Figure 5.1 Sources of the UK constitution

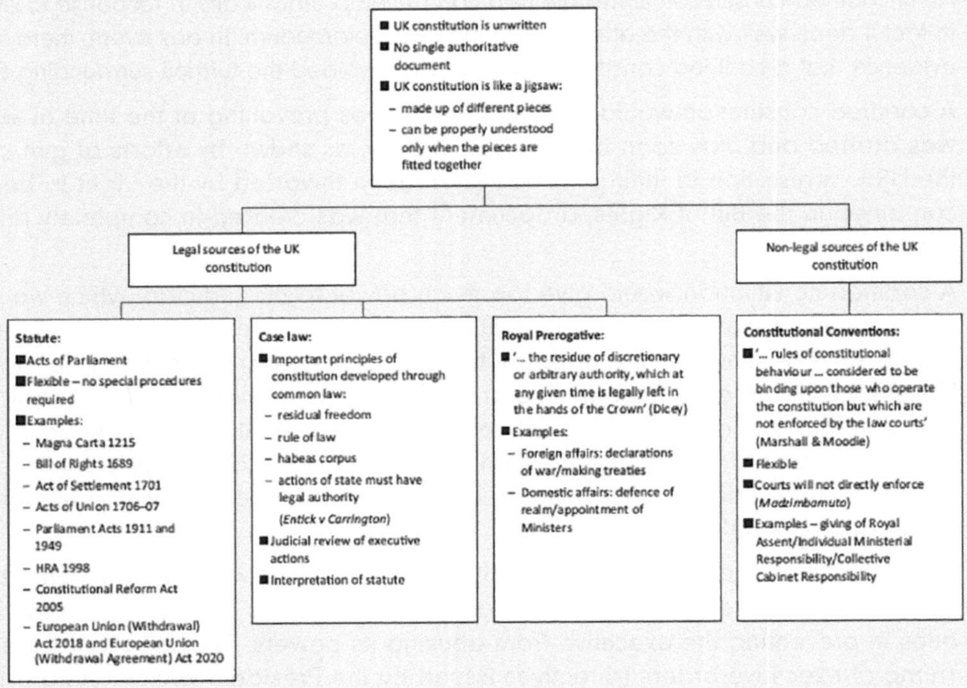

Although it is important to be able to summarise the characteristics of the UK constitution and to be able classify its sources, neither of these is an end in itself. To understand constitutional law, as any other area of law, you need to see it as a system of related principles. To construct a legal argument, defending some point of constitutional law or arguing for change, you need to show how the rule helps to maintain the system, or why a change will advance the purposes of the system. It is important, therefore, that as you progress through the constitutional law chapters of this book, you to try to link particular provisions with general principles of the constitution, such as the rule of law or the separation of powers, or with aspects of legitimacy such as democratic representation.

Finding system in the sources is often a matter of interpretation. What the rule of law, the separation of powers or democratic legitimacy actually require in a system of government is frequently a matter of argument. There is necessarily an element of subjectivity in this, and therefore it is important to develop your own opinions.

Forming an opinion or argument of law is, however, different from forming an opinion as a voter in an election for example. An opinion on the law is in the form 'I think a court is likely to decide that ...', rather than 'I think the law should say that'. The first is an argument about how the law is likely to be interpreted, in the light of the previous practice of the State; the latter is an argument about how the State should change the law. In the context of constitutional law, you must then, in forming your legal opinion, attempt to be objective. You should take account of existing legal principles. You should also face the fact that the shared beliefs of the community may not be your beliefs. But given this necessary attempt at objectivity, you can of course still have your own view on what it would be right for the law to provide.

6 Parliament and Parliamentary Sovereignty

Learning outcomes

By the end of this chapter you should be able to:

- explain the role and functions of the UK Parliament;
- describe the composition of Parliament and the procedure Parliament follows when enacting legislation;
- analyse and evaluate the nature of the relationship between the House of Commons and the House of Lords;
- define the doctrine of parliamentary sovereignty;
- understand the historical development of parliamentary sovereignty and give examples of how parliamentary sovereignty asserts itself;
- analyse the limitations on the operation of parliamentary sovereignty in both a domestic and a European context;
- define the meaning of parliamentary privilege and analyse its scope.

6.1 Introduction

6.1.1 Essential features

In **Chapter 5** you considered some core constitutional principles, including the role of Parliament and the principle of parliamentary sovereignty (or supremacy). In this chapter you will consider the functions and procedures of the UK Parliament and analyse parliamentary sovereignty in more depth.

You will begin by examining the composition of Parliament, and then consider the legislative process in Parliament and the relationship between the House of Commons and the House of Lords.

You will then move on to parliamentary sovereignty, analyse its definition and chart its history and development. You will then analyse the limitations on the doctrine of parliamentary sovereignty, from both a domestic and a European viewpoint.

Finally, you will consider the meaning of parliamentary privilege, and how it enables parliamentarians to speak freely in debates and protects Parliament's internal affairs from interference by the courts.

6.1.2 Parliament: elements and functions

Parliament consists of three central elements: the House of Commons, the House of Lords and the Monarch. Of the three elements the House of Commons is the most important. Parliament's main functions may be summarised as:

- scrutinising the work of the Government
- passing legislation, ie making new laws
- debating the key issues of the day
- approving the funding necessary for the Government to carry out its statutory duties and legislative proposals
- providing the personnel for Government (since all government ministers are drawn from either the House of Commons or the House of Lords).

It is actually the Government that is responsible for drafting most legislation that is placed before Parliament, and so, when it passes legislation, Parliament's role is that of formal enactment of legislation rather than making the law on its own initiative.

6.2 The composition of Parliament

The UK Parliament comprises two separate Houses: the House of Commons, and the House of Lords together with the Monarch. Acts of Parliament must normally be approved by both Houses and also receive Royal Assent.

6.2.1 The House of Commons

The House of Commons is a representative body, the membership of which is elected. There are currently 650 Members of Parliament. Members of Parliament are elected by attaining the most votes at a general election in their respective constituencies (the 'first past the post' system).

The Speaker is the chair of the House of Commons. By convention, they perform their duties impartially (eg ruling on procedural points and controlling debate).

Statute limits the number of holders of ministerial office in the Commons to 95 (House of Commons Disqualification Act 1975, s 2 – see **Chapter 7**).

By convention, the Prime Minister is a member of the House of Commons, as are most other cabinet ministers (see **Chapter 5**).

6.2.2 Recall petitions

The Recall of MPs Act 2015 introduced a process whereby an MP can be removed from their seat and for a by-election to follow.

A recall petition may be opened if any one of the following conditions is met:

(i) The MP is convicted of an offence and receives a custodial sentence.

(ii) Following a report from the Committee on Standards, the MP is suspended from the Commons for at least 10 sitting days.

(iii) The MP is convicted of providing false or misleading information for allowances claims.

Once a recall petition has been triggered, the MP will be removed from their seat and a by-election called if at least 10% of registered voters in their constituency sign the petition within six weeks. The recalled MP can stand as a candidate at the by-election.

So far the recall mechanism has been used successfully four times, twice in 2019 and twice in 2023. The prospect of a recall petition may also have contributed to the resignation of a few MPs.

6.2.3 The House of Lords

The House of Lords is not elected and is not a representative body. Historically the House of Lords was made up largely of hereditary peers (ie peers entitled to sit in the House of Lords by virtue of their birth). However, the House of Lords Act 1999 enacted the first stage of what the then Labour Government intended to be full-scale reform of the upper House by removing the bulk of hereditary peers from the House. Nonetheless, the Act allowed up to 92 hereditary peers to remain.

Most members of the House of Lords are life peers appointed under the Life Peerages Act 1958. Such peers are appointed by the Monarch on the advice of the Prime Minister (although the Prime Minister will in turn have received suggestions as to whom to appoint from a non-political Appointments Commission, which puts forward prospective peers from a range of different professions, interests and political affiliations).

The current membership of the House of Lords is as follows:

- The Lords Temporal – life peers (currently about 700) created under the Life Peerages Act 1958 and up to 92 hereditary peers.
- The Lords Spiritual (26 senior clergy of the Church of England).

In May 2011 the Government published a White Paper (including a draft bill) setting out its proposals for the reform of the House of Lords. The White Paper proposed that the House of Lords be reduced in size (to 300 members), with 80% of members being elected and the remaining 20% appointed. Those members who were to be elected would serve a single 15-year term. Although the House of Lords Reform Bill was a response to manifesto commitments by each of the three main UK parties, it aroused controversy among Conservative backbenchers, some of whom were concerned that a mostly elected House of Lords would challenge the primacy of the Commons, and some of whom felt that reform was not a priority at a time of economic difficulty. Critics in other parties and in the House of Lords also opposed the Bill. As a consequence, the House of Lords Reform Bill was withdrawn by the Government, after receiving its second reading in July 2012.

Nonetheless, there is a widespread view that the unelected House of Lords in its current form is unsuited to a modern constitutional democracy. Accordingly, following its victory in the July 2024 general election, the Labour Government submitted the House of Lords (Hereditary Peers) Bill to Parliament providing for the abolition of the remaining hereditary peers. Parliament is very likely to pass the Bill.

In addition to abolishing the hereditary peers, the Labour Party has also suggested:

- reforms to the appointment process to enhance the national and regional representation in the second chamber;
- introducing a mandatory retirement age;
- implementing a participation requirement;
- replacing the House of Lords with a 'new second chamber that better represents the regions and nations'.

The Labour Government intends to consult on these proposals.

6.2.4 The meeting and duration of Parliament

6.2.4.1 Meeting

Under the Meeting of Parliament Act 1694, Parliament must be summoned every three years. By convention, Parliament meets throughout the year, since taxes require annual renewal and political reality, coupled with the volume of work, means that it is in almost permanent operation.

6.2.4.2 Duration

The Parliament Act 1911 limits the maximum life of a Parliament to five years. Historically, however, most Parliaments have not in fact lasted for the full five-year term. Until recently this was because, acting pursuant to the royal prerogative, the Monarch has dissolved Parliament at the request of the Prime Minister, and successive Prime Ministers have tried to seek dissolution at a time when their political parties were popular with the electorate so as to maximise their chances of success in the subsequent general election.

This was changed by the Fixed-term Parliaments Act (FTPA) 2011. This provided for fixed days for polls for parliamentary general elections, and the election held on 7 May 2015 took place pursuant to its provisions. The FTPA 2011 also made provision for the holding of early parliamentary general elections in the event of a vote of no confidence (unless a new government could be formed) or a vote by at least two-thirds of all MPs in favour of an early election. In April 2017, MPs used this latter provision to vote for a general election which took place on 8 June 2017.

In October 2019, following unsuccessful attempts by the Government to obtain the requisite two-thirds majority to trigger a general election, Parliament enacted the Early Parliamentary General Election Act 2019 to circumvent the FTPA 2011 in order to pave the way for the December 2019 general election. Only a simple majority of MPs was needed for the Act to pass.

In December 2020 the Government submitted a bill to Parliament providing for the repeal of the FTPA 2011 and the revival of the prerogative power to dissolve Parliament. The Dissolution and Calling of Parliament Act 2022 has repealed the FTPA 2011, so dissolution of Parliament is once again a royal prerogative power; see **5.5.3.2** above.

6.2.4.3 'Sessions'

Each Parliament is divided into 'sessions'. Parliamentary sessions now usually start in the spring of one year and end in the spring of the next. Parliamentary sessions generally last for a year, although they can be longer, which most often happens when important constitutional issues are being debated. The issues surrounding Brexit led to the longest session of Parliament since the Civil War, lasting from 13 June 2017 to 8 October 2019.

A session ends when Parliament is 'prorogued' by Royal Decree. Prorogation terminates all business pending at the end of a session. Any public bills that have not passed into law will normally lapse, although it is possible to carry over public bills from one session to the next, subject to agreement.

6.3 The legislative process

The legislative procedure for primary legislation differs according to the type of bill passing through its parliamentary stages. As most legislation is in this category, we will concentrate on 'public bills', ie those that apply to the public in general. ('Private' bills in contrast only change the law for an individual or locality.) Unless the Parliament Acts procedure is used (see **6.3.4** below), a bill must have been approved in the same form by each House before it is presented for Royal Assent.

6.3.1 Public bills

Public bills alter the general law (ie the law that concerns the public as a whole). There are two forms of public bill:

(a) Government bills: These bills are bills submitted to Parliament as part of the Government's legislative programme. They are usually listed in the King's Speech at the start of a parliamentary session and are usually public bills. The relevant government department decides on the detailed contents.

(b) Private members' bills: These are bills introduced by MPs or Lords who are not government ministers. Although only a small minority of these become law due to lack of parliamentary time, they sometimes create significant publicity regarding an issue so may indirectly influence the Government's legislative proposals. For example, a private members' bill criminalising upskirting failed to become law. However, subsequently, a government-backed bill passed through Parliament, culminating in the Voyeurism Act 2019 which made upskirting a specific criminal offence.

Moreover, in most parliamentary sessions, a limited number of private members' bills do become Acts. For example, in the 2022–23 session, 24 such bills received Royal Assent. Often their content is not controversial, eg the British Sign Language Act 2022 recognises British Sign

Language as a language of England, Wales and Scotland and requires the Government to promote and facilitate its use. In contrast, the European Union (Withdrawal) Act 2019 and the European Union (Withdrawal) (No 2) Act 2019 which effectively prevented the UK from leaving the EU were highly controversial. It was government policy at the time to leave open the possibility of leaving the EU without first reaching a deal with the EU, but these Acts prevented this. The Government therefore vehemently opposed the private members' bills that led to these Acts. However, the circumstances surrounding the passage of these bills were unprecedented and are unlikely to occur again.

Notable Acts which started as private members' bills include the Murder (Abolition of Death Penalty) Act 1965, which abolished the death penalty for murder, and the Abortion Act 1967, which provided a clearly prescribed legal route for abortions.

The table below summarises what happens at each stage of the legislative process.

Table 6.1 The legislative process

First reading This stage is purely formal: the title of the bill is read out and it is then printed and published.
↓
Second reading At this stage the main debate takes place in the House of Commons on the general principles of the bill.
↓
Committee stage The bill is usually referred to a general (or public bill) committee, consisting of 16–50 members appointed by the Committee of Selection. There is proportional representation of parties on general committees (ie they reflect the division of the parties within the House). Important bills (for example, bills of constitutional significance or concerned with authorising government expenditure) or bills that require little discussion because they are uncontroversial and unimportant may be referred to the 'Committee of the Whole House'. The purpose of the committee stage is to examine the bill in detail. Amendments may be made to its clauses.
↓
Third reading This stage involves the consideration of the bill as amended – normally the debate is brief and only verbal amendments may be made. This is the final opportunity to vote on the bill; often MPs do not.
↓
Proceedings in the House of Lords These do not begin until after the third reading in the Commons. The procedure in the Lords is similar to that outlined above, except that the Committee of the Whole House almost invariably takes the committee stage. When the bill has received its third reading in the Lords, it must be sent back to the Commons if the Lords have made any amendments. Theoretically, the bill can go backwards and forwards an indefinite number of times until the proceedings on it are terminated by prorogation. In practice, however, if the Commons disagrees with Lords' amendments and restores the original wording, the Lords will usually accept it.
↓
Royal Assent Once Royal Assent is received, a bill becomes law and is referred to as an 'Act of Parliament'. The Act may suspend its 'commencement' until some future date, which may be determined by delegated legislation made under the Act.

Except for financial measures, which must be introduced by a minister in the Commons, a bill can generally be introduced in either House first.

Scottish devolution (**Chapter 8** below) also has an impact on parliamentary procedure. The so-called 'West Lothian Question' attracted increasing attention following the referendum on Scottish independence held in September 2014. If some issues (such as education) are devolved to the Scottish Parliament so that English MPs do not discuss them at Westminster, why should Scottish MPs retain a vote at Westminster on corresponding English issues?

In October 2015 the House of Commons approved a change of parliamentary procedure. This added a new stage to the usual procedure, allowing MPs for English constituencies (or English and Welsh constituencies) to vote on issues deemed to affect only England (or only England and Wales), giving these MPs a veto on legislation at committee stage before all MPs from across the United Kingdom voted in the bill's final readings. Parliament, however, abolished this procedure (known as 'English votes for English laws') in July 2021.

6.3.2 Private bills

Private bills relate to matters of individual, corporate or local interest, and affect particular persons and/or a particular locality (eg a bill authorising the building of a new railway line or tunnel).

6.3.3 The relationship between the House of Commons and the House of Lords

Although a bill must be passed by both Houses of Parliament, the House of Commons is the more important of the two. This is because the members of the House of Commons are directly elected by the people at a general election, and so the House of Commons has more democratic legitimacy than the (currently) unelected House of Lords.

By convention the Prime Minister will sit in the House of Commons. Similarly, most cabinet and junior government ministers will be drawn from the Commons.

The House of Lords is often described as being a 'revising chamber'. There is a constitutional convention, the Salisbury Convention, that the House of Lords will not reject a bill giving effect to a major part of the democratically elected Government's manifesto. Rather, the House of Lords will use its considerable expertise to make small changes to legislation with which it disagrees. Amendments are often proposed during proceedings in the Lords and, in a significant number of cases, the Government accepts amendments after a defeat there. The House of Lords has on occasion opposed controversial bills, but ultimately will usually give way if the Commons persists in overriding the Lords' objections.

If the House of Lords rejects a bill that has passed the House of Commons, the bill may still eventually become law as a consequence of the provisions of the Parliament Acts of 1911 and 1949; see **6.3.4** below.

6.3.4 The Parliament Acts 1911 and 1949

The Lords' role is constrained by the Parliament Acts 1911 and 1949, which ensure that ultimately the will of the Commons may prevail. The passage of both Acts resulted from conflict between the two Houses of Parliament.

Historically, the House of Lords had powers equal to those of the Commons, and the Prime Minister would often be drawn from the Lords. A constitutional convention did come into existence, however, whereby the Lords would not reject the Government's Finance Bill if the Commons had passed it.

In 1909, in breach of this convention, the House of Lords rejected the Finance Bill containing the Liberal Government's budgetary proposals. This provoked outrage in the House of Commons, with MPs angry that unelected peers could effectively scupper the plans of the democratically elected Government. In response, the Government introduced a bill to limit the powers of the House of Lords to reject legislation which had been passed by the Commons. The Prime Minister, Herbert Asquith, forced the House of Lords to agree to this bill by threatening to flood the House of Lords with new peers who would support the bill if the Lords initially rejected it.

The bill was enacted as the Parliament Act 1911. The Act abolished the Lords' right to reject money bills which had been passed by the Commons, and curtailed the power of the Lords to reject non-money bills. Such bills could only be delayed by the Lords for a two-year period. If, after two years had elapsed, the Lords still refused to accept the bill, the Act provided that the bill would nevertheless become a valid Act of Parliament if it had passed the House of Commons and received Royal Assent.

At the end of World War II, a Labour Government was elected with a radical agenda to take into state ownership many industries. Fearing that a Conservative-dominated House of Lords would reject these plans, the Government proposed reducing the power of the Lords to delay the passage of legislation from two years to one year. The bill to achieve this was twice rejected by the Lords, following which the bill took effect under the provisions of the 1911 Act. The bill was eventually enacted as the Parliament Act 1949.

The combined effect of these two Acts is that they permit the Monarch to give Royal Assent to a bill that lacks the consent of the House of Lords, provided that the Speaker has certified that the provisions of the Acts have been complied with. These are as follows:

- 'Money bills' (ie public bills certified by the Speaker as dealing only with national taxation or supply): A money bill passed by the Commons can be presented to the Monarch for assent one month after being sent to the Lords and will become law even though it lacks the consent of the Lords.
- Other public bills: If passed by the Commons and rejected by the Lords in each of two successive sessions, a bill can be sent to the Monarch for their assent. One year must elapse between the second reading in the Commons in the first session, and the third reading there in the second session. Bills seeking to extend the maximum duration of Parliament are excluded.

There had since the passing of the 1949 Act been some academic debate about the validity of that Act and Acts passed under its authority, the Act itself having been passed via the 1911 Act. This debate was settled by the House of Lords (in its judicial capacity prior to the creation of the Supreme Court) in *R (Jackson) v Attorney General* [2005] UKHL 56. It was argued that the 1949 Act was not a valid Act on the grounds that the procedure set out in 1911 Act should not have been used to enact it. The House of Lords rejected this argument and held that the 1949 Act had been properly enacted.

In fact most conflicts between the Lords and Commons are resolved by agreement and application of the usual conventions, rather than by use of the Parliament Acts. They have been used rarely, the only occasions since 1949 being for the War Crimes Act 1991, the European Parliamentary Elections Act 1999, the Sexual Offences (Amendment) Act 2000 and the Hunting Act 2004.

6.3.5 Delegated legislation

The provisions of an Act of Parliament often confer upon ministers a power to make delegated or subordinate legislation. Delegated legislation is every exercise of power to legislate that is conferred by or under an Act of Parliament. Delegated legislation may be made by ministers in the form of rules or regulations (often 'statutory instruments'), which supplement the provisions of an Act of Parliament.

Parliament's role is confined to scrutiny of delegated legislation. This is in fact not too different from Parliament's actual role in relation to primary legislation, but there are important distinctions. Neither House of Parliament can amend delegated legislation, and often it can come into effect without either House voting upon it at all. The 'parent' or 'enabling' Act will stipulate the parliamentary procedure to be followed, but the following are the most commonly used procedures:

- Affirmative resolution procedure: The instrument either cannot come into effect, or ceases to have effect, unless one or both Houses passes a resolution approving the instrument.
- Negative resolution procedure: The Government is required to 'annul' the instrument if either House passes a resolution rejecting the instrument within a specified period (usually 40 days) after it is 'laid before Parliament'.

The House is assisted in scrutiny of delegated legislation by the Joint Select Committee on Statutory Instruments (representing both Lords and Commons). Its job is to draw the attention of Parliament to instruments that for various reasons might need to be debated.

6.4 The sovereignty (or supremacy) of Parliament

6.4.1 Definition of parliamentary sovereignty

You considered the meaning of the doctrine of 'parliamentary sovereignty' (or supremacy) in **Chapter 1**. The classic definition of this term was provided by AV Dicey:

> The principle of parliamentary sovereignty means neither more nor less than this: namely, that Parliament ... has, under the English constitution, the right to make or unmake any law whatever; and, further, that no person or body is recognised by the law ... as having a right to override or set aside the legislation of Parliament.
> (*An Introduction to the Study of the Law of the Constitution*, 1885)

Dicey's description may be broken down into three parts:

(a) Parliament is the supreme law-making body and may enact or repeal laws on any subject.

(b) No Parliament may be bound by a predecessor or bind a successor – a particular Act of Parliament cannot be entrenched, or be given a 'higher' status than any other Act.

(c) No other person or body (but particularly a court of law) may question the validity of an Act of Parliament or declare that Act to be unlawful.

6.4.2 The development of parliamentary sovereignty

Following the English Civil War during the 1640s and Oliver Cromwell's brief republic, the Stuart Monarchy was restored to the throne in 1660 with the accession of Charles II. When Charles died in 1685, his brother, James II, became king. James was a devout Catholic, and tensions developed between James and a staunchly Protestant Parliament. A number of parliamentarians opened secret negotiations with William of Orange, the Protestant husband of James's daughter, Mary, with a view to his taking the throne by force. In 1688 William landed with his army in England, but James had already fled to France (the 'Glorious Revolution').

In 1689 William, who was not yet king, summoned a Convention (or meeting) of peers and commoners. The Convention declared itself to be the Parliament of England (it is now known as the 'Convention Parliament') and passed the Bill of Rights, which set out the terms on which the Crown was offered to William and Mary.

The terms of the Bill of Rights altered the balance of power between the Monarch and Parliament in favour of the latter. It removed the powers of the Monarch arbitrarily to suspend Acts of Parliament and to impose taxation without Parliament's consent. The Bill of Rights also provided that Parliament should meet on a regular basis and that elections to Parliament should be free.

In terms of parliamentary sovereignty, the most significant part of the Bill of Rights is article 9, which provided that 'freedom of speech and debates or proceedings in Parliament ought not to be impeached or questioned in any court or place out of Parliament'.

6.4.3 The 'Enrolled Act' rule

Although article 9 of the Bill of Rights guaranteed free speech in Parliament, the doctrine of parliamentary sovereignty as defined by Dicey has been developed by the judges through the common law.

The courts have consistently rejected challenges to Acts of Parliament based on alleged irregularities in the procedure by which Parliament passed the relevant Acts. In *Edinburgh & Dalkeith Railway Co v Wauchope* (1842) 8 Cl & F 710 it was claimed that the enactment of a private Act was defective as due notice had not been given to a party affected by its passage. The House of Lords dismissed the claim, Lord Campbell observing:

> All that a court of justice can do is to look to the Parliamentary Roll: if from that it should appear that a bill has passed both Houses and received Royal Assent, no court of justice can enquire into the mode in which it was introduced into Parliament, what was done previously to it being introduced ... or what passed ... during its progress ... through Parliament.

This has become known as the 'Enrolled Act' rule – once an Act of Parliament has been entered onto the Parliamentary roll, the courts will not question the validity of that Act or hold the Act to be void.

In the later case of *Pickin v British Railways Board* [1974] AC 765, Lord Reid confirmed that the courts had no power to disregard an Act of Parliament, or to investigate proceedings that had taken place in Parliament to determine whether there had been any irregularity of procedure or fraud.

The more recent case of *R (Jackson and others) v HM Attorney General* [2005] UKHL 56 suggests that the courts may, in certain circumstances, be prepared to consider the validity of an Act of Parliament. The case concerned a challenge to the validity of the Hunting Act 2004, which had been enacted pursuant to the Parliament Acts 1911 and 1949. As explained at **6.3.4** above, it was claimed that the 1911 Act could not be used to enact the 1949 Act. If this argument had succeeded, then the Hunting Act would have been invalid as it had been passed using the procedure set out in the 1949 Act. A strict application of the 'Enrolled Act' rule would have precluded the House of Lords from considering the case. However, the House of Lords held that it did have jurisdiction to consider the validity of the Hunting Act as a question of statutory interpretation of the 1911 Act, namely whether the 1911 Act could be used to enact the 1949 Act. It thus concluded that there was no conflict with the 'Enrolled Act' rule.

6.4.4 The unlimited legislative competence of Parliament

Parliamentary sovereignty asserts itself through Acts of Parliament (ie statutes), rather than through mere parliamentary resolutions. Dicey's definition of parliamentary sovereignty states that there are no limits on Parliament's legislative powers.

Examples of the unlimited legislative competence of Parliament include:

(a) Statute may override international law. *In Cheney v Conn* [1968] 1 All ER 779, a taxpayer challenged an income tax assessment on the ground that part of the tax would be used to finance the manufacture of nuclear weapons, which was contrary to the Geneva Convention, an international treaty to which the UK was a party. The challenge was unsuccessful. The court held that the statute that imposed the tax prevailed over international law.

This aspect of parliamentary sovereignty is of contemporary relevance due to proposals announced in May 2022 by the Government for Parliament to pass legislation overriding certain provisions in the Withdrawal Agreement agreed between the UK and the EU (Agreement on the withdrawal of the United Kingdom of Great Britain and Northern Ireland from the European Union and the European Atomic Energy Community ([2020] OJ L29/7)) (the Withdrawal Agreement) - see also **6.5.3.1** below and **Chapter 9**. The Withdrawal Agreement set out the terms on which the UK left the EU, and includes provisions known as the Northern Ireland Protocol aimed at preventing a hard border on the island of Ireland between Northern Ireland and the Republic of Ireland.

The UK Government wanted Parliament to enact the Northern Ireland Protocol Bill which would have unilaterally overridden certain provisions of the Northern Ireland Protocol, as in its view these provisions were causing instability in Northern Ireland. The Government believed that it was acting within international law as it was taking steps to safeguard the Belfast or Good Friday Agreement of 1998 which ended three decades of sectarian violence known as 'the Troubles'. While much legal opinion took the opposite view, Parliament could still have passed the Bill even if it had breached international law. However, in February 2023, the UK and EU concluded the Windsor Framework, resolving the dispute regarding the Northern Ireland Protocol. The UK Government therefore withdrew the proposed legislation.

(b) Statute may override constitutional conventions. The case of *Madzimbamuto v Lardner-Burke* [1969] 1 AC 645 is the authority for this. In 1965, Southern Rhodesia issued a unilateral declaration of independence from Britain. However, the UK Parliament passed the Southern Rhodesia Act 1965, which declared that Southern Rhodesia remained part of the UK's dominion territories. The validity of the Act was challenged on the basis that there was an established constitutional convention that the UK Parliament would not legislate for Southern Rhodesia without the consent of the Rhodesian Government. The challenge was unsuccessful. The House of Lords held that the convention was overridden by the Southern Rhodesia Act.

The Supreme Court confirmed this in *R (Miller) v Secretary of State for Exiting the European Union* [2017] UKSC 5 (*Miller (No 1)*). The Sewel Convention provides that the UK Parliament will not normally legislate for Scotland without the Scottish Parliament's consent; however, the Supreme Court held that it was not legally binding even though it had been codified; see **5.5.4.4** above.

(c) Statute may alter the constitution. You have already considered statutes that are of constitutional importance in **Chapter 5**. Some examples of statutes that have altered the constitution include the Acts of Union 1706–07 (which united England and Scotland under a single Parliament), the Parliament Acts, the Human Rights Act (HRA) 1998 (which incorporated the Convention for the Protection of Human Rights and Fundamental Freedoms (the ECHR) (Rome, 4 November 1950) into the UK legal system) and the European Union (Withdrawal) Act (EUWA) 2018 (which paved the way for the UK's exit from the EU).

(d) Statute may operate retrospectively. In *Burmah Oil Co v Lord Advocate* [1965] AC 75, Burmah Oil sought compensation from the British for the destruction of oil installations during World War II (to prevent Japanese forces obtaining control of them). The House of Lords found that the Crown was liable to pay compensation. Parliament then enacted the War Damage Act 1965. This Act applied retrospectively and so removed the right to compensation.

A recent example is the Terrorist Offenders (Restriction of Early Release) Act 2020, which increased the time offenders who have been convicted of some terrorist offences must serve in jail before being eligible for parole (released on licence).

(e) Statute may abolish or curtail aspects of the royal prerogative. Some examples of this include:

(i) the Crown Proceedings Act 1947, which abolished the immunity of the Crown in respect of claims made against it in either tort or contract;

(ii) the FTPA 2011 which, until its repeal, removed the power of the Monarch to dissolve Parliament and required Parliament to sit for a fixed period of five years before a general election automatically took place (see **6.2.3.2** above);

(iii) *Attorney-General v De Keyser's Royal Hotel* [1920] AC 508, where a hotel was taken for wartime use by the War Office during World War I. The lessees of the hotel sought compensation under the Defence Act 1842, which authorised requisitioning and provided for compensation. The Government argued that irrespective of the statutory provisions, there was a prerogative power entitling the Crown to requisition the land of a subject in time of emergency and that compensation was not payable as of right. The court held that the terms of the Defence Act, whilst not expressly abolishing this prerogative power, had put the power 'into abeyance';

(iv) *R v Secretary of State for the Home Department, ex p Fire Brigades Union* [1995] 2 WLR 464, where, in 1964, the Government used prerogative powers to introduce a non-statutory scheme to compensate the victims of crime. This scheme was put on a statutory basis by provisions in the Criminal Justice Act 1988, but the Secretary of State had discretion as to when these provisions should be brought into force. In 1993 the provisions had still not been brought into force, and the Secretary of State announced plans to introduce a less generous scheme using prerogative powers. The House of Lords held that he was unable to do this. Although the statutory scheme had not yet been implemented, the fact that Parliament had approved it prevented the prerogative being used to introduce a less generous scheme;

(v) *Miller (No 1)*, where the Government argued that it could trigger Article 50 of the Treaty on European Union giving notice of the UK's withdrawal from the EU using its prerogative powers to make or unmake treaties. The majority of the Supreme Court held that the European Communities Act (ECA) 1972 was inconsistent with the future exercise by government ministers of any prerogative power to withdraw from the EU treaties. The ECA 1972 had given domestic effect to the EU treaties, and EU rights had thereby become enforceable in UK courts. As withdrawal from the EU amounted to a fundamental constitutional change by removing EU law as a source of domestic law, it needed the consent of Parliament. Parliament subsequently passed the European Union (Notification of Withdrawal) Act 2017.

6.4.5 Express and implied repeal of statute

You saw at **6.4.1** above that one aspect of parliamentary sovereignty is that no Parliament may be bound by a predecessor or bind a successor. This is given effect through the doctrines of express and implied repeal.

If a later Parliament expressly repeals the contents of an Act made by an earlier Parliament, that earlier Act will no longer be valid. But what happens if a later Parliament passes an Act that contradicts the contents of an Act made by an earlier Parliament but does not expressly repeal that earlier Act? In these circumstances the doctrine of implied repeal will apply.

In *Ellen Street Estates v Minister of Health* [1934] KB 590, the claimant sought to persuade the court to apply compensation provisions contained in the Acquisition of Land (Assessment of Compensation) Act 1919 rather than those contained in the later Housing Acts of 1925 and 1930. The two sets of statutory provisions were inconsistent, but the earlier ones were more favourable.

The 1919 Act stated that any provisions of any other Act 'so far as inconsistent with this Act shall cease to have or shall not have effect'. The claimant argued that this could be construed so as to govern future Acts, and the later Housing Acts contained no express provisions to repeal the 1919 Act.

The Court of Appeal dismissed the claim because it considered that the later Housing Acts impliedly repealed the 1919 Act to the extent of any inconsistency between them. Maugham LJ said in his judgment:

> The legislature cannot, according to our constitution, bind itself as to the form of subsequent legislation, and it is impossible for Parliament to enact that in a subsequent statute dealing with the same subject matter there can be no implied repeal.

In other words, a later Act of Parliament will impliedly repeal the provisions of an earlier Act to the extent of any inconsistency between the two Acts.

6.5 Limitations on the supremacy of Parliament

6.5.1 Domestic limitations

6.5.1.1 The Acts of Union

The United Kingdom was formed following Acts of Union with Scotland in 1706–07 and Ireland in 1801. Some commentators have argued that, as a consequence, Parliament was born 'unfree', because it is limited by the terms of these Acts and cannot legislate so as to override their provisions.

Of particular importance are the Acts of Union 1706–07. These gave effect to a Treaty of Union by which the English and Scottish Parliaments agreed to vest their authority in a new Parliament of Great Britain. The Acts made explicit provision for the preservation of the separate Scottish legal system and the Church of Scotland. Some have argued that, as a result of these provisions, the Acts of Union are in effect a partial written constitution for the UK, by which subsequent Parliaments are bound. Such arguments have become somewhat academic, however, with the return of devolved legislative power to a Scottish Parliament (see **6.5.1.2** below).

Although the matter has never been directly considered by the courts, *obiter* comments by the Scottish Court of Session in the case of *MacCormick v Lord Advocate* 1953 (Scot) SC 396 suggested that the Westminster Parliament was bound by the terms of the Acts of Union.

6.5.1.2 Devolution

On coming to power in 1997, the Labour Government devolved power to Scotland, Wales and Northern Ireland. You will cover devolution in more depth in **Chapter 8**, so in this chapter we shall simply consider its impact on parliamentary sovereignty.

The Scotland Act 1998 established a Scottish Parliament and Executive. Legislative powers in certain areas (such as health, education and legal affairs) are devolved to the Parliament. Other areas (such as foreign affairs and defence) are reserved to the Westminster Parliament. The Scotland Act 2012 gave additional powers over some aspects of taxation and other areas to the Scottish Parliament. The Scotland Act 2016 amends the Scotland Act 1998 and includes provisions stating that:

(a) the Scottish Parliament and Scottish Government are a permanent part of the constitutional arrangements of the UK;

(b) neither the Scottish Parliament nor Scottish Government may be abolished unless the people of Scotland vote for this in a referendum; and

(c) the UK Parliament will not normally legislate with regard to devolved matters without the consent of the Scottish Parliament (the Sewel Convention).

The Scotland Act 2016 also increased the range of devolved powers, including the power to vary income tax rates and thresholds.

The Government of Wales Act 1998 established a Welsh Assembly, initially without legislative powers. The Wales Act 2017 has now changed this, so that devolution in Wales follows a similar format to that in Scotland. The Wales Act 2017 has now devolved power to the Welsh Parliament (now commonly known as the Senedd Cymru) to legislate in those areas that are not reserved to Westminster. The Wales Act 2017 also mirrors the provisions in the Scotland Act 2016 relating to permanency, the need for a referendum and setting out the Sewel Convention.

The Northern Ireland Act 1998 devolved powers to a Northern Ireland Assembly and created a 'power-sharing executive' (which can be, and indeed on occasions has been, suspended under the Act – following the elections in May 2022, it proved very difficult to form a new executive; eventually a new executive was formed in February 2024 with Sinn Féin's Michelle O'Neill becoming First Minister, the first time that a Nationalist rather than a Unionist has held this post – see further **8.1.3** below). It also contains a provision that Northern Ireland shall not cease to be part of the UK unless the people of Northern Ireland vote for this in a referendum.

The most significant devolution of power has been to Scotland under the terms of the Scotland Act. The Scottish Parliament is not a sovereign legislature in the way that the UK Parliament is as it derives its powers from the Scotland Act, an Act of the UK Parliament. Although its legislation is designated as primary legislation, ie the Scottish Parliament has the power to pass Acts, the Scottish Parliament may legislate only to the extent that it is given power to do so by the UK Parliament under the Scotland Act.

The UK Parliament can also still legislate for Scotland, although the Sewel Convention provides that the UK Parliament 'will not normally legislate with regard to devolved matters without the consent' of the devolved legislatures. As a general rule, in normal circumstances the UK Parliament is unlikely to legislate in devolved areas without the devolved legislature's consent. However, aspects of the European Union (Withdrawal Act) 2018 and the European Union (Withdrawal Agreement) Act 2020 related to devolved matters, even though international relations are reserved to the UK Parliament. The Scottish Parliament, Senedd Cymru and Northern Ireland Assembly all refused their consent to the bill leading up to the 2018 Act, and the Scottish Parliament also refused consent to the 2020 Act. The UK Parliament nevertheless enacted them.

Subsequently, in 2020, both the Scottish Parliament and the Senedd voted to withhold consent to the UK Internal Market Bill governing trade between the nations of the UK post-Brexit. Additionally, in 2020, the Scottish Parliament withheld consent for the European Union (Future Relationship) Bill governing the UK's post-Brexit relationship with the EU.

Whether the UK Parliament can repeal the Scotland Act 1998 is a matter of debate. The Scotland Act 2016 states that the Scottish Parliament and Scottish Government are a permanent part of the constitutional arrangements of the UK, and that neither the Scottish Parliament nor Scottish Government may be abolished unless the people of Scotland vote for this in a referendum. Thus, without such a referendum, it would be difficult for the UK Parliament to do this. Depending on your view of the 'manner and form debate' (which you will consider at **6.5.1.5** below), you may take the view that such difficulties would be political only. Alternatively, you may take the view that the courts would not uphold legislation repealing the Scotland Act 1998 in the absence of a referendum.

6.5.1.3 Acts of independence

During the 20th century, Parliament enacted various Acts granting independence to former colonies of the British Empire. Would it be possible for Parliament to reverse such legislation and resume legislating for former colonies?

In strict legal terms, Parliament could reverse such legislation. But, as with Scottish devolution, both for political and practical reasons it is most unlikely that Parliament would ever consider repealing such legislation. Furthermore, even if Parliament did repeal the Acts of independence and resume legislating for the colonies, such legislation would be unenforceable.

6.5.1.4 Limits on the doctrine of implied repeal

At **6.4.5** above you considered the doctrine of implied repeal. This holds that an Act of Parliament will impliedly repeal the contents of an Act of an earlier Parliament to the extent of any inconsistency between the two Acts.

It has been suggested, however, that the doctrine of implied repeal may not apply to 'constitutional statutes'. In *Thoburn v Sunderland City Council* [2002] EWHC 195 (Admin), the defendants were charged with offences of using weighing machines not calibrated in metric units, or failing to indicate a unit price per kilogram for various foods. This was required by UK regulations made in 1994 under s 2(2) of the European Communities Act (ECA) 1972 to implement a European metrification directive. The defendants relied on s 1 of the Weights and Measures Act 1985 ('s 1 WMA'), which permitted both metric and imperial weights. They argued that, although the 1994 regulations purported to amend s 1 WMA to prefer metric weights, s 1 WMA had already impliedly repealed s 2(2) of the ECA 1972. That meant the 1994 regulations were invalid.

In rejecting their submissions, Laws LJ commented (*obiter*) that the ECA 1972 was a constitutional statute and could not therefore be impliedly repealed. The repeal of such a statute by Parliament had to be express. He suggested that there are two types of statute, 'ordinary' and 'constitutional'. Statutes that are 'constitutional' are of such significance that the courts would require actual intention from Parliament to change them, not an implied intention.

The test for a constitutional statute is:

(a) the statute must condition the legal relationship between citizen and state in some general, overarching manner; or

(b) the statute must change the scope of fundamental constitutional rights.

Laws LJ said that several key statutes satisfied this test:

> We should recognise a hierarchy of Acts of Parliament: as it were 'ordinary' statutes and 'constitutional' statutes... Examples are the Magna Carta, the bill of Rights 1689 ... the Human Rights Act 1998 ... [and] ... the European Communities Act ... Ordinary statutes may be impliedly repealed. Constitutional statutes may not.

For a constitutional statute to be repealed, there had to be 'express words' or 'words so specific that the inference of an actual determination to effect [the repeal of a constitutional statute] ... was irresistible'.

Clearly, Laws LJ had in mind only a very limited number of statutes as being of sufficient importance to satisfy this test.

Laws LJ's views have subsequently found support in three Supreme Court decisions.

The first of these Supreme Court decisions is *H v Lord Advocate* [2012] UKSC 24, in which the Supreme Court considered an apparent contradiction between the Extradition Act 2003 and the Scotland Act 1998. The Supreme Court decided that there was no contradiction between the Acts. Nonetheless, Lord Hope, *obiter*, went on to consider what the position would have been had there been a contradiction between the two Acts.

Under the doctrine of implied repeal, the Extradition Act would have prevailed over the Scotland Act. However, Lord Hope rejected this possibility, stating:

> It would perhaps have been open to Parliament to override the [relevant] provisions of [the Scotland Act] ... But in my opinion only an express provision to that effect could be held to lead to such a result. This is because of the fundamental constitutional nature of the settlement that was achieved by the Scotland Act. This in itself must be held to render it incapable of being altered otherwise than by an express enactment. Its provisions cannot be regarded as vulnerable to alteration by implication from some other enactment in which an intention to alter the Scotland Act is not set forth expressly on the face of the statute.

Whilst Lord Hope was referring to the Scotland Act, there seems no reason to confine his reasoning to that Act. The Scotland Act could not be impliedly repealed because of its 'fundamental constitutional nature'; logically other statutes of a fundamental constitutional nature, ie those described by Laws LJ as 'constitutional statutes', should also be immune to implied repeal.

The issue of implied repeal was also raised in *R (HS2 Action Alliance Ltd) v Secretary of State for Transport* [2014] UKSC 3. The case concerned a challenge to 'HS2', the proposed high speed rail link between London and northern cities. Opponents of HS2 argued the parliamentary process procedure did not comply with EU Directive 2011/92, which requires public participation in major infrastructure decisions affecting the environment. They argued that the parliamentary process did not provide for effective public participation.

The Supreme Court decided that the Directive did not apply, but nonetheless went on to consider in some very interesting *obiter dicta* what the position would have been had it done so. If it had, the Supreme Court would have been obliged to consider whether the parliamentary procedure complied with the requirements of the Directive. According to Lord Reed, this could have impinged 'upon long-established constitutional principles governing the relationship between Parliament and the courts, as reflected for example in article 9 of the Bill of Rights 1689'. This raised the possibility of conflict between parliamentary privilege as set out in article 9 of the Bill of Rights and EU law, a conflict that Lord Reed affirmed would have to be 'resolved by our courts as an issue arising under the constitutional law of the United Kingdom'.

As this case took place during the UK's membership of the EU, the House of Lords accepted the primacy of EU law over national law on the grounds that the ECA 1972 required UK courts to give effect to that principle. However, it is also clear that the Supreme Court thought that there were fundamental principles contained in Acts of Parliament or recognised at common law that will not be overridden even by subsequent constitutional statutes unless there is unequivocal evidence of parliamentary intention to amend or repeal them.

On the facts, the Supreme Court held the Directive did not require it to investigate parliamentary procedure. However, if it had done so, the clear tenor of the judgments of the justices is that the Supreme Court would have refused to carry out such an investigation on the basis of article 9 of the Bill of Rights, which prohibits the courts from enquiring into parliamentary procedure. Article 9 of the Bill of Rights would therefore not have been impliedly repealed by the ECA 1972, which would have required such an investigation.

In *Miller (No 1)* the Supreme Court referred to the 'informative discussion' by Laws LJ in Thoburn and concluded that '[t]he 1972 Act accordingly has a constitutional character'.

6.5.1.5 The 'manner and form' debate

The doctrines of express and implied repeal prevent an earlier Parliament from binding a future Parliament as to the content of legislation which that future Parliament might enact. But is it possible for an earlier Parliament to bind a future Parliament as to the procedure which that future Parliament must follow to enact legislation?

This is known as the 'manner and form' or entrenchment theory – can a Parliament bind its successors as to the procedure to be adopted when repealing legislation enacted by that earlier Parliament?

Arguments in favour of the 'manner and form' theory

The next activity will enable you to consider the significance of the Parliament Acts of 1911 and 1949 in relation to these arguments concerning the 'manner and form' debate.

Activity 1 The Parliament Acts of 1911 and 1949

You have already considered the contents of these Acts at **6.3.4** above.

The Parliament Acts made it 'easier' for legislation to be passed because, in certain circumstances, the Acts removed the requirement for legislation to have been approved by the House of Lords. Why do you think those who support the 'manner and form' theory use the Parliament Acts to support their case?

Comment

The Parliament Acts of 1911 and 1949 made it 'easier' for legislation to be enacted by removing the power of the House of Lords to block legislation which had passed the House of Commons, instead permitting the Lords only to delay the passage of such legislation.

Supporters of the manner and form theory argue that if Parliament (in enacting the Parliament Acts) could make it 'easier' to legislate, there is no reason why Parliament could not make it 'harder' for a future Parliament to legislate. For example, an earlier Parliament could pass an Act and, within that Act, specify that the Act could be repealed only by a specified majority in Parliament (rather than a simple majority), or that, in addition to a Parliamentary vote, repeal could take place only if this was also supported in a referendum. In other words, the Act could be entrenched.

Another argument sometimes raised in support of the manner and form theory is that the rules for identifying an Act of Parliament derive from the common law (ie such rules are 'judge-made'). As an Act of Parliament can override the common law, it is suggested that Parliament can alter the legal rules on which the validity of an Act of Parliament rests.

There are some Commonwealth authorities that suggest that entrenchment of legislation is possible. The case most often cited is *Attorney General for New South Wales v Trethowan* [1932] AC 526. This case concerned an attempt by the Parliament of the Australian state of New South Wales to entrench certain provisions in an Act of Parliament by providing that these provisions could not be repealed unless they were approved in a popular referendum in addition to being approved by the Parliament. When a later Parliament passed a bill repealing the provisions, no referendum was held. The Privy Council held that the repeal of the Act was invalid because a referendum should have taken place.

Arguments against the 'manner and form' theory

Those who take issue with the 'manner and form' theory dispute the importance of the *Trethowan* case. First, they argue that, as a Privy Council case, *Trethowan* is persuasive only and not binding on domestic courts. Secondly, they argue that the position of the legislature of New South Wales cannot be seen as analogous to that of the UK Parliament. This is because the UK Parliament is truly 'supreme' (because it was not created by another body), whereas the Parliament of New South Wales is a subordinate legislature in that it was created by an Act of the UK Parliament (the Colonial Laws Validity Act 1865). Indeed, it has been suggested that *Trethowan* supports the argument that parliamentary sovereignty cannot be limited, because the case is an example of a subordinate legislature (ie the Parliament of New South Wales) being kept within the powers granted to it by the supreme UK Parliament.

Some academics who oppose the 'manner and form' theory have argued that the meaning of Parliament was 'fixed' following the constitutional restructuring in 1688 and the enactment of the Bill of Rights in 1689 (see **6.4.2** above). They argue that the meaning of 'Parliament' cannot be altered by an ordinary Act of Parliament, and so no Parliament has the power to redefine this meaning or to place limitations on the way in which a future Parliament may act.

Conclusion on the 'manner and form' theory

In conclusion, the position on manner and form is unclear and, to form your own conclusion, you will need to critically evaluate the arguments on both sides. There are divergent views at the highest level, as illustrated by the opposing views of two members of the House of Lords in *R (Jackson) v Attorney General* [2005] UKHL 56.

In support of the manner and form theory, Lord Steyn said:

> Parliament could for specific purposes provide for a two-thirds majority in the House of Commons and the House of Lords. This would involve a redefinition of Parliament for a specific purpose. Such redefinition could not be disregarded.

In contrast, Lord Hope said:

> it is a fundamental aspect of the rule of sovereignty that no Parliament can bind its successors. There are no means whereby ... it can entrench an Act of Parliament.

Some provisions in the Scotland Act 2016, the Wales Act 2017 and the Northern Ireland Act 1998 arguably attempt to impose manner and form requirements, in that they require a positive vote in a referendum in addition to an Act of Parliament in some circumstances. The Scotland Act 2016 requires a referendum before either the Scottish Parliament or Scottish Government is abolished (similar provisions are contained in the Wales Act 2017). The Northern Ireland Act 1998 provides that Northern Ireland shall not cease to be part of the UK unless the people vote for this in a poll. It is questionable as to whether domestic courts would uphold legislation that purported to achieve these objectives if approval was not also obtained in a referendum.

6.5.1.6 Henry VIII powers

Legislation that has been introduced by the Government will often contain 'Henry VIII' powers. These powers permit the relevant government minister to amend or even repeal the relevant statute by delegated legislation, ie they permit ministers to make changes to Acts of Parliament by delegated legislation. This is said to be contrary to the fundamental principle of the sovereignty of Parliament because it enables ministers - rather than Parliament - to make or change the law.

In 2010, the Lord Chief Justice, Lord Judge, expressed concerns relating to Henry VIII powers, cautioning that by 'allowing [such powers] to become a habit, we are [risking] the inevitable consequence of yet further damaging the sovereignty of Parliament'.

A recent example is the extensive powers that the Coronavirus Act 2020 gave to ministers to combat the Covid-19 pandemic. Whilst there was widespread acceptance that such powers were necessary due to the unprecedented emergency, there has been criticism that the

Government adopted legislation that had a huge impact on society without there being adequate parliamentary scrutiny.

The Retained EU Law (Revocation and Reform) Act 2023, enacted under the previous Conservative Government, gives ministers and devolved authorities substantial Henry VIII powers in relation to retained EU law/assimilated law, ie the law accumulated during the UK's membership of the EU. There are concerns that these powers could be used to make far-reaching changes without adequate parliamentary scrutiny, but the current Labour Government, which hopes to reset relations with the EU, is probably less likely to make extensive use of these powers than its Conservative predecessor. See **Chapter 9** below for further analysis of this Act.

6.5.1.7 The rule of law

In *R (Jackson) v Attorney General* [2005] UKHL 56 Lord Steyn considered *obiter* that parliamentary sovereignty was not absolute and could be limited by the courts in extreme circumstances. Lord Steyn said that the doctrine of parliamentary sovereignty was a 'construct of the common law' (ie principle created by the judges). The judges could therefore qualify the principle in exceptional circumstances to prevent Parliament from legislating in a manner that was contrary to the rule of law. Lord Steyn cited as an example if Parliament enacted legislation to abolish judicial review of executive action or, more generally, if Parliament abolished the role of the courts. In such circumstances he speculated that the courts might be willing to strike down such legislation.

In contrast, Lord Bingham took a more cautious approach, stating:

> The bedrock of the British constitution is, and in 1911 was, the supremacy of the Crown in Parliament ... Then, as now, the Crown in Parliament was unconstrained by any entrenched or codified constitution. It could make or unmake any law it wished. Statutes, formally enacted as Acts of Parliament, properly interpreted, enjoyed the highest legal authority.'

Other judges have lent support to the view that the rule of law may trump parliamentary sovereignty in certain circumstances. In *Moohan v Lord Advocate* [2014] UKSC 67, Lord Hodge stated, *obiter*:

> I do not exclude the possibility that in the very unlikely event that a parliamentary majority abusively sought to entrench its power by a curtailment of the franchise or similar device, the common law, informed by principles of democracy and the rule of law and international norms, would be able to declare such legislation unlawful.

However, he went on to state that 'the existence and extent of such a power is a matter of debate, at least in the context of the doctrine of the sovereignty of the United Kingdom Parliament'.

6.5.2 European limitations

The European Union treaties and the ECHR are all international treaties that, according to the UK's dualist system, required incorporation into domestic law by an Act of the UK Parliament. Incorporation of both EU law and key ECHR rights into domestic law was undoubtedly significant as providing individuals with remedies under the EU treaties and the ECHR in the domestic courts. However, the method of incorporation adopted for each was rather different. We shall now examine each in turn.

6.5.3 Membership of the European Union

6.5.3.1 The doctrine of supremacy of European Union law

The legal order of the European Union is based on a number of treaties, the key treaties now being known as the Treaty on European Union ([2008] OJ C115/13) (TEU), the Treaty on the Functioning of the European Union ([2012] OJ C326/01) (TFEU) and the Charter of Fundamental Rights of the European Union ([2000] OJ C364/1). During the UK's membership of the EU, the UK was required to give supremacy to EU law. This led to considerable debate about whether parliamentary sovereignty was compatible with the supremacy of EU law.

Although the UK left the EU on 31 January 2020, some understanding of how the UK legal system accommodated the supremacy of EU law is essential to comprehend provisions in the EUWA 2018 regarding retained EU law. Additionally, the UK and EU negotiated a Withdrawal Agreement setting out the terms of the UK's exit from the EU. As well as the Northern Ireland Protocol (**6.4.4** above), the Withdrawal Agreement sets out the financial settlement agreed between the UK and EU and contains citizens' rights provisions which govern the rights of EU and UK citizens who had exercised their rights of free movement before the end of the transition period lasting from the date of the UK's withdrawal until 31 December 2020. See **Chapter 9** for further information.

The EUWA 2018 gives supremacy to the Withdrawal Agreement in a very similar manner to which the ECA 1972 gave supremacy to the EU treaties. The wording of s 7A(1) and (2) (added to the EUWA 2018 by the European Union (Withdrawal Agreement) Act 2020) is based on that used in the ECA 1972, and so provisions of the Withdrawal Agreement that meet the criteria for direct effect will override conflicting national law. The scope of the Withdrawal Agreement, though, is far less extensive than that of the EU Treaties. Moreover, s 38(1) of the 2020 Act, entitled 'Parliamentary sovereignty', recognises that Parliament is sovereign, whilst s 38(2) states that this sovereignty persists notwithstanding any provisions in the 2020 Act giving direct effect to the provisions of the Withdrawal Agreement. Indeed, in June 2022 the Government published the Northern Ireland Protocol Bill which would have overriden many aspects of the Northern Ireland Protocol if it had become law. The Bill expressly provided that key parts of s 7A would not have applied to those aspects of the Northern Ireland Protocol that the Government had wanted to override. However, once the UK and EU reached agreement over the Windsor Framework (see **6.4.4 (b)**) above, the Government withdrew the Bill.

It should also be noted that the Withdrawal Agreement provided for the continued supremacy of EU law during the transition period.

6.5.3.2 Types of EU legislation

The EU treaties comprise the primary source of EU law. They lay down the legal framework of the EU and set out the EU's institutional framework and confer on the EU a wide range of powers in a large number of areas. They also give the EU the power to legislate in a wide range of areas by adopting secondary legislation.

There are four types of EU secondary legislation:

- Regulations: Regulations issued by the EU are directly applicable and automatically binding in all Member States without the need for any further legislation in the Member States.
- Directives: Directives set out objectives to be achieved and oblige Member States to pass domestic legislation themselves to implement those objectives. Directives set a date by which Member States must implement them.
- Decisions: Decisions are directly binding in the same way as Regulations, but only on those to whom they are addressed, which may be Member States, companies or individuals.
- Recommendations and opinions: Recommendations and opinions are not binding.

6.5.3.3 Other sources of EU law

(a) Jurisprudence of the CJEU

As EU Law was originally based on civil law legal systems, it does not have a formal system of precedent. Nonetheless, the CJEU's case law has become a significant source of EU Law. Judgments of the CJEU are binding on the national courts of Member States, and so national courts have applied the CJEU's case law when dealing with questions of EU Law that have arisen in cases that they have been hearing. It is through the CJEU's case law, in particular judgments of the ECJ (the higher of the two courts), that principles such as direct effect and state liability, discussed at **6.5.3.4** and **6.5.3.9** below respectively, have been developed.

Moreover, while the CJEU is not bound by its own previous decisions, it adheres to the principle of legal certainty and so will not lightly depart from its previous decisions. Accordingly, even in the absence of a formal system of precedent, the CJEU's case law has become a prominent feature of EU Law.

(b) General principles of EU Law

The CJEU (mainly through judgments of the ECJ) has in its case law developed general principles of EU Law. Originally, these principles did not explicitly feature in the founding treaties of the original European Economic Community, but the ECJ derived them from the common constitutional traditions of Member States and international treaties to which the Member States were parties, for example the ECHR. Many of these general principles have now found concrete expression in the European Charter of Fundamental Rights.

Examples of general principles include:

- Proportionality: This means that measures taken by Union institutions and Member States when implementing EU Law should be appropriate and necessary for achieving a given aim, and should not go further than is necessary to achieve that aim.
- Equality: This means that when dealing with persons in similar situations, Union institutions and Member States should not treat them differently, unless there is an objective justification for the difference in treatment.
- Fundamental rights, ie internationally recognised human rights.
- Legitimate expectation/legal certainty: This means that, in the absence of overriding concerns of public interest, persons are entitled to assume that EU Law will not be suddenly changed to their disadvantage.

General principles have formed an important source of EU Law, and the CJEU has struck down EU legislation and decisions of the Union institutions for breaching them. Furthermore, national courts have also disapplied national legislation for infringing them.

6.5.3.4 Direct effect

A key principle that gave supremacy to EU law is 'direct effect', which the ECJ first developed in the landmark case of *Van Gend en Loos v Nederlandse Administratie der Belastingen* (Case 26/ 62) [1963] ECR 1. The claimants had imported a product into the Netherlands from Germany and had been charged a customs duty contrary to what is now Article 30 TFEU. They challenged the duty in the Dutch courts, which referred the case to the ECJ. The ECJ ruled that Article 30 had direct effect and so the claimants could rely on it in the Dutch courts to claim back the customs duty. This was an example of 'vertical' direct effect; ie EU law being enforced against the state or a state body.

Subsequently in *Defrenne v SABENA* (Case 43/75) ECLI:EU:C:1976:56, [1976] ECR 455, the ECJ ruled that Treaty articles could also have horizontal direct effect and be enforced against private bodies. The Belgian airline, SABENA, paid its female cabin crew less than its male cabin crew. Although this was permissible under Belgian law, this breached what is now Article 157 TFEU, which provides that men and women should receive equal pay for equal work or work of equal value. The ECJ held that individuals could rely on the direct effect of Article 157 against private bodies before their national courts; accordingly, a female member of SABENA's cabin crew was able to claim equal pay.

The ECJ has also ruled that Regulations and decisions are capable of both vertical and horizontal direct effect. In contrast, Directives can only have vertical direct effect; ie they can only be enforced against the state or emanations of the state. However, in order for a provision of EU law to have direct effect it must be sufficiently clear, precise and unconditional and must not require additional measures, either at national or EU level (the 'Van Gend criteria'). Furthermore, for a Directive to have direct effect, there is an additional requirement that the time limit for implementation by Member States has expired (*Pubblico Ministero v Ratti* (Case 148/78) EU:C:1979:110, [1979] ECR 1629).

One of the leading cases on the vertical direct effect of Directives is *Marshall v Southampton & SW Hampshire Area Health Authority (No 1)* (Case 152/84) [1986] ECR 723. Miss Marshall had been forced to retire at the age of 62, whereas men were able to continue working until 65. She could not rely on the UK's Sex Discrimination Act 1975 as it contained an express provision excluding discrimination in relation to retirement from its scope. She therefore brought a claim against her employer, part of the NHS, based on Article 5 of Directive 76/207 (Equal Treatment Directive) which provided that men and women should be guaranteed the same working conditions.

The ECJ accepted that Directives do not have horizontal direct effect, but could have vertical direct effect against a Member State regardless of the capacity in which it was acting. Thus it was irrelevant whether it was acting as an employer or exercising a public function. This was necessary to prevent Member States from benefiting from their breaches of EU Law by failing to implement Directives properly. Miss Marshall therefore succeeded in her sex discrimination claim as her employer was a public body.

It is therefore particularly important to be able to identify a 'public body', since a claim based on a Directive can only be taken against such a body. The meaning of 'public body' (sometimes also known as an 'emanation of the State') was considered in *Foster v British Gas* (Case C-188/89) [1990] ECR I-3313.

The facts were very similar to those in *Marshall (No 1)*; British Gas had forced female employees to retire at an earlier age than their male colleagues. At the time British Gas was still a nationalised body. The issue was whether British Gas was an emanation of the State; if so, the employees could rely on Article 5 of Directive 76/207 against it. The House of Lords referred the meaning of 'emanation of the State' to the ECJ under what is now Article 267 TFEU.

The ECJ stated in its judgment that a Directive could be enforced against a body, 'whatever its legal form':

- which has been made responsible, pursuant to a measure adopted by the State, for providing a public service ('public service condition');
- under the control of the State ('State control condition'); and
- which has for that purpose special powers beyond those which result from the normal rules applicable in relations between individuals ('special powers condition').

However, the judgment in *Foster* failed to clarify if all three criteria had to be satisfied for a body to be an emanation of the State, or whether it was sufficient if two were satisfied. Ultimately the ECJ ruled on the issue in *Farrell v Whitty and Others* (Case C-413/15) [2017] EUECJ C-413/15. In *Farrell*, the issue was whether the Motor Insurers' Bureau of Ireland (MIBI) was an emanation of the State. The function of the MIBI is to compensate victims of accidents caused by uninsured drivers. Under Irish legislation, the MIBI was not obliged to compensate the victim of an accident in the circumstances that had arisen, but the Irish legislation breached the relevant Directives on the topic; accordingly, if the MIBI was an emanation of the State, it would be obliged to compensate the victim.

The ECJ stated that it was not necessary for a body to meet all three *Foster* criteria to be an emanation of the State, although the ECJ stopped short of saying that one would suffice, as in the operative part of its judgment it merely ruled that a body may still be an emanation of the State even if it did not display all the three characteristics listed in the *Foster* judgment. Nonetheless, it is possible to conclude from *Farrell* that a body will be an emanation of the State if:

- the state has delegated to it a public interest task (a variant of the public service condition); and
- it satisfies either the second (State control) or third (special powers) condition.

6.5.3.5 The UK's approach

When the UK joined the EU, it signed up to the supremacy of EU law. However, the fact that the UK Government accepts treaty obligations on behalf of the UK does not, in itself, have any effect on parliamentary sovereignty. Treaties are made by the UK Government alone and do not of themselves change the law. Under the 'dualist' system that operates in the UK, if the Government signs a treaty that requires a change in the law, it is for Parliament to authorise such a change by legislation.

The UK Government signed what is now the TFEU on 22 January 1972, but the Treaty was not incorporated into domestic law until later that year when Parliament enacted the ECA 1972 which came into force on the UK's accession on 1 January 1973.

The principal provisions of the ECA 1972 were as follows:

- Section 2(1): This provided that directly effective rights and obligations arising under EU law should be enforceable in the UK courts.
- Section 2(2): This enabled the UK Government to make delegated legislation to implement EU law (eg Directives) within the UK.
- Section 2(4): This required all UK legislation whenever adopted (primary and secondary) to 'be construed and have effect' subject to provisions of EU law.
- Section 3(1): This required UK courts to apply EU law in accordance with principles laid down by the Court of Justice of the European Union (CJEU) (ie decisions of the CJEU are in effect binding).

Accordingly, during the UK's membership of the EU, the ECA 1972 required UK courts to apply EU law in the cases they were hearing. The Article 267 TFEU reference procedure aims to ensure that national courts apply and interpret EU law correctly.

6.5.3.6 Article 267 references

The main forum for individuals, including businesses, to enforce their rights under EU law is national courts. Individuals who want to rely on direct effect, indirect effect and state liability must take action in a national court, not the CJEU. Indeed, individuals have very limited rights of access to the CJEU. They may in strictly defined circumstances bring claims against the Union institutions, but they cannot use the CJEU to sue other individuals or government bodies. Consequently, national courts frequently have to deal with issues of EU Law. The Article 267 reference procedure enables national courts to obtain rulings from the ECJ (the highest of the CJEU's two courts) on questions of EU law.

According to Article 267, any national court or tribunal may refer a question of EU Law to the ECJ if a decision on a question of EU Law is 'necessary' to enable it to give judgment in the case before it. However, the body making a reference must be a court or tribunal, ie a body of a judicial nature. The ECJ has laid down guidelines for deciding whether a ruling is necessary (often known as the 'CILFIT criteria' after the case in which they were laid down: *CILFIT Srl v Ministro della Sanità* (Case 283/81) [1982] ECR 3415).

A decision on a question of EU Law will not be necessary if one of the following situations applies:

(a) Where the question of interpretation of EU Law raised before the national court is not relevant to the conclusion of the case.

(b) Where previous decisions of the ECJ have already dealt with the point of EU Law in question.

(c) Where the correct application of EU Law is so obvious as to leave no scope for any reasonable doubt as to the manner in which the question raised is to be resolved (*acte clair*). However, national courts should bear in mind that EU Law is a specialist area and should not be too quick to decide the meaning is clear.

Once a national court has decided that a decision on a point of EU Law is necessary, the next step is to decide whether the court hearing the case is a court of *mandatory* jurisdiction or of *permissive* jurisdiction. Courts of mandatory jurisdiction are courts against whose judgments there is no right of appeal in the case at hand, while courts of permissive jurisdiction are courts whose judgments are subject to appeal. Courts of mandatory jurisdiction are under an obligation to make a reference to the ECJ subject to the *CILFIT* criteria. In contrast, courts of permissive jurisdiction are not under an obligation to refer questions of EU law to the ECJ, but may decide the issue themselves. However, the ECJ has issued guidelines setting out when such courts should exercise their discretion to refer. These guidelines are contained in an *Information Note on references from national courts for a preliminary ruling* 2011/C 160/1. According to the *Information Note*, references are 'particularly useful' where there is a new question of interpretation of general interest for the uniform application of EU Law, or existing case law is not applicable to a new set of facts.

National courts who make a reference are then obliged to apply the ECJ's ruling to the case they are hearing.

Example

First instance court

The High Court of Ireland is hearing a case where the claimant is relying on the direct effect of an EU Regulation. The High Court is uncertain about the meaning of a key provision in the EU Regulation. Under one possible interpretation, the claimant will succeed in their claim. Under another possible interpretation, the defendant will have a defence. There are no previous judgments by the CJEU on this point.

Applying the CILFIT criteria, the High Court should decide that a decision on a point of EU Law is necessary to enable it to give judgment. However, as its judgments are subject to appeal, it is a court of permissive jurisdiction, so it has a discretion whether to refer the interpretation of the EU Regulation to the ECJ. The Information Note suggests that it should, as the case is likely to involve a new question of interpretation of general interest for the uniform application of EU Law.

Court of final instance

Suppose, though, the High Court does not make a reference, and decides in favour of the defendant. The claimant then appeals to the Supreme Court of Ireland, the country's highest judicial authority.

The Supreme Court of Ireland is a court of mandatory jurisdiction as its judgments are not subject to appeal, so under the CILFIT criteria it must refer the interpretation of the EU Regulation to the ECJ.

The flow diagram below summarises the questions that arise when a body hearing a case is deciding whether to make an Article 267 reference.

Figure 6.1 Article 267 reference

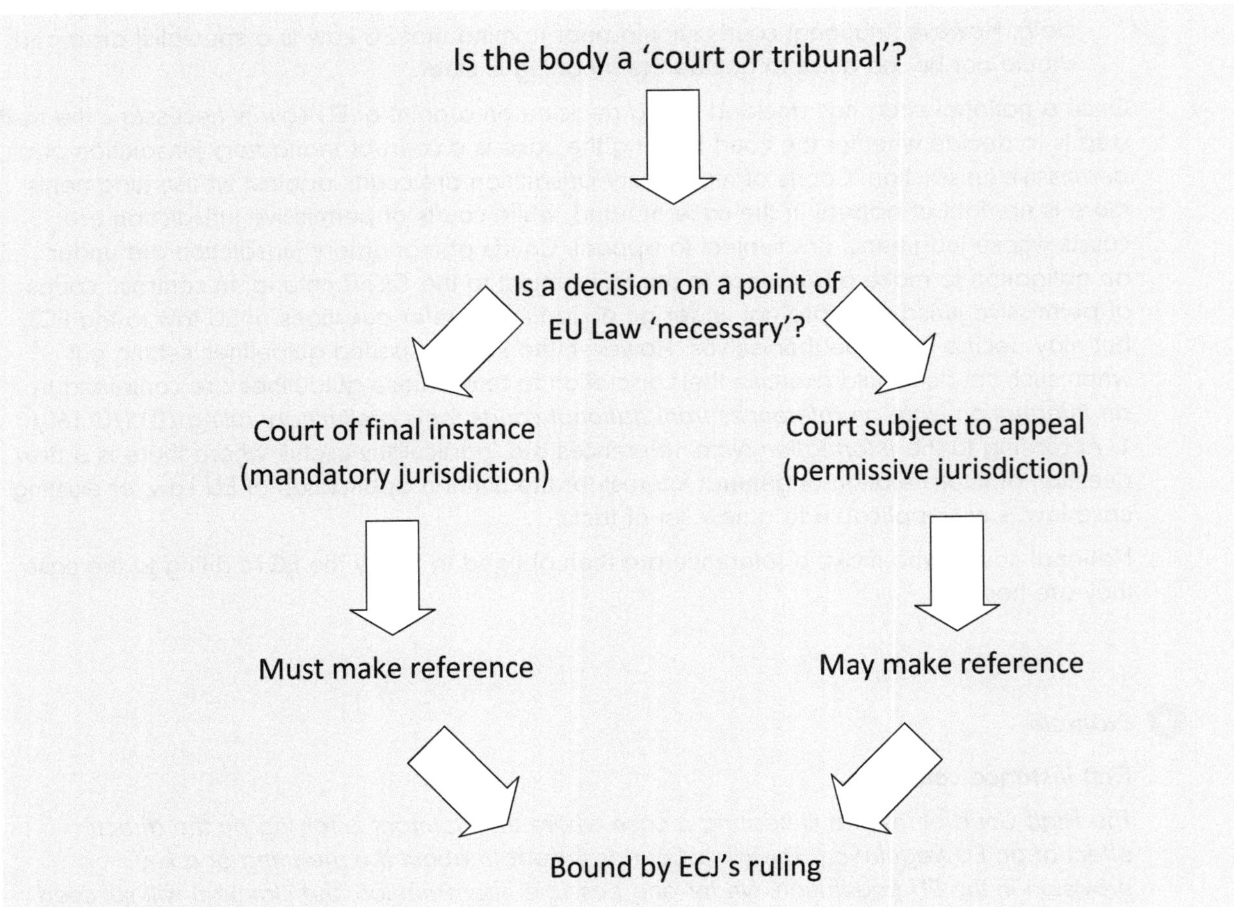

6.5.3.7 The effect of ECA 1972, s 2(4)

It was s 2(4) of the ECA 1972 that had the most significant impact on the doctrine of parliamentary sovereignty. It essentially had two limbs. First, it created a rule of construction, by providing that the courts had to read UK legislation in such a way as to make it compliant with EU law. In EU law, this is known as the doctrine of indirect effect. If, however, it was not possible for the courts to read UK legislation in such a way, the courts had to give precedence to directly effective EU law and set aside inconsistent national legislation.

The House of Lords in the case of *R v Secretary of State, ex p Factortame (No 2)* [1991] 1 AC 603 gave effect to this principle within the UK, holding that, by virtue of s 2(4) of the ECA 1972, directly effective EU law took precedence over conflicting UK law. Lord Bridge stated that:

> [T]he supremacy within the European Community of Community law over the national law of member states was ... well established in the jurisprudence of the European Court of Justice long before the United Kingdom joined the Community. Thus, whatever limitation of its sovereignty Parliament accepted when it enacted the European Communities Act 1972 was entirely voluntary. Under the terms of the Act of 1972 it has always been clear that it was the duty of a United Kingdom court, when delivering final judgment, to override any rule of national law found to be in conflict with any directly enforceable rule of Community law.

The effect of this decision was that the doctrine of implied repeal did not prevent directly effective EU law prevailing over post-1972 Acts of Parliament where there was a conflict between their respective provisions. Where a conflict existed, the provisions of directly effective EU law took precedence.

6.5.3.8 Indirect effect

The leading case on indirect effect is *Marleasing SA v La Comercial Internacional de Alimentacion* SA (Case C-106/89) [1990] ECR I-4135 in which the ECJ stated that 'in applying national law, whether the provisions in question were adopted before or after the directive, the national court called upon to interpret it [ie national law] is required to do so, as far as possible, in the light of the wording and the purpose of the directive in order to achieve the result pursued by the latter [ie the directive] ...'.

An example of indirect effect in the UK can be found in *Pickstone v Freemans plc* [1989] AC 66. Female employees brought an equal pay claim against their employer, the catalogue company Freemans. They worked for Freemans as 'warehouse operatives' but were paid less than a male colleague, who was described as a 'warehouse checker operative'. However, their work was of equal value to Freemans as their male colleague's work. Therefore, they argued, the true reason for the difference in pay was sex discrimination. Such discrimination breached Directive 75/117 – the Equal Pay Directive. However, the UK regulations (supposedly implementing the Directive) only provided for equal pay for the same work done by men and women, not for work of equal value.

The House of Lords held that the purpose of the UK regulations had been to give effect to EU law. A strict reading of them failed to achieve this, and so the House of Lords adopted a 'purposive' interpretation in which it departed from the strict literal interpretation of the UK regulations and implied words into the regulations in order to comply with EU law.

(a) Implementing and non-implementing legislation

The judgment in *Marleasing* makes it clear that the principle of indirect effect applies to both implementing legislation and non-implementing legislation. *Pickstone v Freemans* provides an example of implementing legislation as the UK Government enacted the UK Regulations with the express aim of implementing the Directive. Conversely, the case of *Webb v EMO Air Cargo (UK) Ltd* [1995] 4 All ER 577 involved non-implementing legislation.

In *Webb v EMO* the House of Lords was once again faced with discrepancies between the protection offered by the Equal Treatment Directive 1976 (Directive 76/207) and that offered by the Sex Discrimination Act 1975. The claimant, Pauline Webb, was dismissed by her employer because she was pregnant. She claimed unlawful sex discrimination on the basis that, since only a woman could become pregnant, if she was dismissed for any reason connected with her pregnancy, that was in effect a dismissal on the grounds of her sex contrary to the Sex Discrimination Act 1975. While the Sex Discrimination Act 1975 prohibited direct discrimination on the grounds of sex, it was unclear if it applied to dismissals on the grounds of pregnancy. However, since she was not employed by a public body, she could not rely directly on the Equal Treatment Directive. Instead, she asked the domestic courts to interpret the UK Sex Discrimination Act 1975 in light of Article 5 of the Equal Treatment Directive 1976. Following an Article 267 reference to the ECJ, the ECJ held that dismissal on the grounds of pregnancy was indeed directly discriminatory. After receiving the ruling from the ECJ, the House of Lords interpreted the Sex Discrimination Act 1975 consistently with the Equal Treatment Directive even though the Directive post-dated the 1975 Act. Webb's claim against her employer therefore succeeded.

(b) Limits to indirect effect?

(i) Where national legislation clearly conflicts with the relevant Directive

A good example of this limitation can be found in *Wagner Miret v Fondo de Garantia Salarial* (Case 334/92) [1993] ECR I-6911. Directive 80/987 required Member States to adopt measures to ensure that guarantee institutions should pay employees' arrears of salary in the event of their employer's insolvency. The relevant Spanish law excluded higher management staff from protection. The Directive did not permit this. The claimant could not rely on direct effect; the Directive was not unconditional, as it gave Member States a broad discretion as to the identity of the guarantee institutions. Could the claimant rely on indirect effect instead? The ECJ thought not; there was a clear conflict between the Spanish law and the Directive, and so the national court would be unable to apply indirect effect. The national court would therefore apply national law, even though it breached the Directive.

(ii) Where indirect effect would impose criminal liability

A Member State cannot rely on indirect effect to impose criminal liability on an individual on the basis of a Directive which the State has failed to implement or implement correctly (*Luciano Arcaro* (Case C-168/95) [1996] ECR I-4705). Arcaro was charged with a criminal offence under Italian legislation enacted to implement EU Directives. Had the Italian legislation been correctly drafted, Arcaro would have been guilty; however, the ECJ ruled that the Italian court should not apply indirect effect to a criminal statute.

In other words, sometimes it will not be possible to use indirect effect.

Activity 2 Indirect effect

The EU enacted Directive 2020/877 (fictitious) requiring Member States to take measures to ensure school teachers do not have more than 22 class contact hours (actual teaching) in any one week. The due date for implementation of the Directive was 30 November 2022.

Consider the following scenarios.

1. The Republic of Ireland considered that it was unnecessary to enact new legislation to implement the Directive as an existing statute passed in 2012 provided that teachers could not be required to have more class contact hours than was reasonable.

2. Due to a temporary shortage of teachers, the Cypriot legislation implementing the Directive provided that until the end of next year teachers should not have more than 24 class contact hours in any one week. After that the 22 hours limit would apply.

Could teachers in private schools in Ireland and Cyprus respectively rely on indirect effect to enforce the 22 class contact hours limit? (Teachers at state schools should be able to rely on the vertical direct effect of the Directive.)

Comment

1. The Irish statute from 2012 is non-implementing legislation as it predates the Directive, but *Marleasing* makes it clear that indirect effect applies to non-implementing legislation. The issue for Irish courts is whether they can interpret 'reasonable' in the 2012 statute as meaning 'not more than 22 class contact hours'. As there is not a clear conflict between the 2012 statute and the Directive, it is likely that the Irish courts will consider it possible to interpret 'reasonable' in this way.

2. The Cypriot legislation is implementing legislation. The issue for Cypriot courts is whether they can interpret 'not more than *24* class contact hours' as meaning 'not more than *22* class contact hours'. Applying *Wagner Miret*, there is a clear conflict between the Cypriot legislation and the Directive, so Cypriot courts would apply the limit of 24 hours in the Cypriot legislation, even though it breached the Directive.

6.5.3.9 Conflict between UK law and EU law

Cases such as *Pickstone v Freemans* show that the courts were willing to construe UK legislation in such a way as to make it compliant with EU law, often construing legislation against its strict literal meaning or implying words into statute to achieve the desired result. In some cases, however, it was impossible for the courts to interpret statute in such a way as to comply with EU law because there was a direct conflict between them. This occurred in *Factortame (No 2)*, the seminal case referred to at **6.5.3.7** above.

The UK passed the Merchant Shipping Act 1988 to prevent fishing in British waters by Spanish fishers who had set up a British company (Factortame Ltd) and registered their boats as British under existing merchant shipping legislation. The Act imposed new conditions for registration, and the Secretary of State made regulations under the Act so that vessels had to re-register. The boats owned by Factortame were refused registration. Factortame challenged the Act on the grounds that it breached EU law on free movement and asked for an interim injunction suspending the operation of the Act. This issue was appealed to the House of Lords. The House of Lords refused the interim injunction, but made an Article 267 reference to the ECJ on whether it was correct to do so.

The ECJ held that the House of Lords should have granted an injunction, as this was necessary to protect the rights of Factortame under EU law. Accordingly the House of Lords granted the interim injunction, effectively suspending the operation of an Act of Parliament. The effect of this decision was that the doctrine of implied repeal did not prevent directly effective EU law prevailing over post-1972 Acts of Parliament where there was a conflict between their respective provisions. Where a conflict existed, the provisions of directly effective EU law took precedence by virtue of s 2(4) of the ECA 1972, which had been acknowledged to be a constitutional statute that could not be subject to implied repeal.

The judgment in *Factortame (No 2)* had a profound effect on the doctrine of parliamentary sovereignty. The House of Lords suspended the operation of an Act of Parliament and held that, by virtue of s 2(4), directly effective EU law took precedence over conflicting UK law. However, the reason that the House of Lords did this was because Parliament, by enacting the ECA 1972, had in effect instructed the courts to do so.

Section 18 of the European Union Act 2011 confirmed this approach by clarifying that any 'limits' on sovereignty were imposed only at Parliament's own behest.

6.5.3.10 State liability for breach of EU law

In addition to challenging UK legislation that was incompatible with EU law, an individual who had suffered resulting loss might have been able to obtain damages from the Crown, as a result of the decision in *Francovich v Italian Republic* (Joined Cases C-6/90 and 9/90) ECLI:EU:C:1991:428, [1991] ECR I-5357, as considered and developed in later case law.

In *Francovich*, a case involving a failure by Italy to implement a Directive, the ECJ held that a State which failed to implement a Directive could be liable in damages to those affected provided that:

(1) the Directive was intended to confer rights on individuals;

(2) the content of those rights was clear from the Directive;

(3) there was a causal link between the failure to implement and the injury suffered.

So, under the *Francovich* principle for example, if an individual suffered loss because the UK failed to implement a Directive, they would have had a right of action under *Francovich* even where they would have been unable to use the Directive itself. This might happen where the Directive conferred rights against employers (eg to equal treatment in employment) but the individual was employed by a private employer rather than the state. (Directives only have 'vertical' effect, against state bodies.)

The next significant development came in *Brasserie du Pêcheur v Germany, R v Secretary of State for Transport, ex p Factortame Ltd (Factortame No 4)* (Joined Cases C-46 & 48/93) [1996] ECR I-1029. In *Brasserie du Pêcheur*, the German Government had prevented the importation of French beer contrary to Article 34 TFEU which provides for the free movement of goods; a French brewery sued the German Government for damages to compensate it for the loss suffered. In *Factortame No 4*, the UK Parliament had enacted the Merchant Shipping Act 1988 which prevented Spanish fishermen from catching fish that formed part of the British fishing quota. This breached Article 49 TFEU which permits businesses from one Member State to establish themselves in other Member States; the Spanish fishermen therefore also sued the British Government for damages. As both cases involved the same issues of principle and were referred to the ECJ by the relevant national courts at approximately the same time, the ECJ heard them together.

Francovich involved the complete failure to implement a Directive, and it was unclear whether the principle of state liability extended to other breaches of EU Law, in particular infringement of rights granted by Treaty articles and incorrect implementation of a Directive. In the *Brasserie du Pêcheur/Factortame No 4* case, the ECJ extended the *Francovich* principle beyond failure to implement a Directive, ruling that damages can be obtained when a Member State commits breaches of any type of EU Law.

A Member State will be liable in damages for infringing EU Law if:

(a) the breach infringes a rule of law intended to confer rights on individuals;

(b) the breach is *sufficiently serious*;

(c) there is a direct causal link between the breach and the damage to the claimant.

It accordingly appears that the ECJ introduced an extra criterion – that in situations where Member States have a wide discretion in how to implement EU Law, the breach of EU Law must be 'sufficiently serious'; ie the Member State concerned must have 'manifestly and gravely disregarded the limits on its discretion'. Thus, in situations where a Member State has a wide discretion, it is necessary for a claimant to prove that the Member State's breach of EU Law was 'sufficiently serious'. The factors to take into account in deciding whether a breach is sufficiently serious include:

- the measure of discretion left by the rule that was breached to the national or EU authorities,
- whether the infringement and the damage caused was intentional or involuntary,
- whether any error of law was excusable or inexcusable,
- the fact that the position taken by a Community institution may have contributed towards the omission, and
- the adoption or retention of national measures or practices contrary to EU Law; eg retaining a measure which the ECJ had previously ruled was unlawful.

Subsequently the House of Lords held that the breach by the UK Government was sufficiently serious, while the German courts held that the breach by the German Government was not.

The case of *R v HM Treasury, ex p British Telecommunications* (Case C-392/93) [1996] ECR I-1631 also provides guidance on when a breach is sufficiently serious. The ECJ held that the UK was not liable in damages as its breach was not sufficiently serious; the Directive in question was unclear and other Member States had made the same mistake in implementing it.

Given that the test originally set out in *Francovich* was modified in *Brasserie du Pêcheur/ Factortame No 4*, the question arises whether that original test is still of any importance. This point was addressed in *Dillenkofer and others v Germany* (Joined Cases C-178, 179, 189 and 190/94) [1996] ECR 469. Germany had failed to implement a Directive concerning package holiday travel (in particular, protection for buyers of package holidays). *Dillenkofer*, like *Francovich*, concerned State liability for total failure to implement a Directive. In applying the 'sufficiently serious breach' criterion which it had identified in *Brasserie du Pêcheur/ Factortame No 4*, the ECJ held that where a Member State had little or no discretion when exercising its rule-making powers, mere infringement of EU Law might amount to a sufficiently serious breach. Accordingly, total failure to implement a Directive was automatically a sufficiently serious breach, as Member States had no discretion at all whether or not to implement a Directive.

Claimants therefore do not need to prove a sufficiently serious breach of EU law where their claim involves total non-implementation of EU law, but must prove a sufficiently serious breach for claims based on incorrect implementation of a Directive or other breaches of EU Law.

The significance of the principle of state liability for parliamentary sovereignty was the UK Government might have been liable to pay damages arising from Parliament's failure to pass legislation giving effect to EU law, or the defective implementation of EU law in an Act of Parliament.

6.5.3.11 Express repeal of the ECA 1972

Although the judgment in *Factortame* made it clear that Parliament could not impliedly repeal EU law, legally there was nothing to prevent Parliament passing an Act which expressly repealed the ECA 1972 or any provision of EU law. Following the 2016 referendum when the UK electorate voted to leave the EU, Parliament enacted the EUWA 2018 which repealed the ECA 1972. However, the European Union (Withdrawal Agreement) Act 2020 did keep in force the provisions in ss 2 and 3 of the ECA 1972 providing for the supremacy of EU law until the end of the transition period.

6.5.3.12 Retained EU law/assimilated law

Under the EUWA 2018, all EU law in force at the end of the transition period was converted into domestic law and labelled 'retained EU law'. Section 5(2) of the EUWA 2018 (as originally enacted) provided that the principle of supremacy of EU law would continue to apply to retained EU law, so that if there was a conflict between pre-Brexit domestic law and pre-Brexit directly effective EU law, then the EU law would have taken priority. However, the Retained EU Law (Revocation and Reform) Act 2023 (REULA 2023) ended the supremacy of EU law in the UK from the end of 2023 and made other changes to retained EU law, including relabelling it as assimilated law.

The concepts of retained EU law and assimilated law will be covered in more depth in **Chapter 9**. Briefly retained EU law consisted of:

- EU-derived domestic legislation: This consisted chiefly of secondary legislation adopted pursuant to s 2(2) of the ECA 1972 to implement EU obligations. The secondary legislation would otherwise have fallen away on the repeal of the ECA 1972. It also included Acts of Parliament enacted to implement EU obligations. Although these Acts would not have fallen away on the repeal of the ECA 1972, it was important to define them as retained EU law to ensure they benefited from its special status.

  Whilst the bulk of EU-derived domestic legislation consisted of secondary legislation, it also included some Acts of Parliament.

  Following REULA 2023, EU-derived domestic legislation now forms part of assimilated law.
- Direct EU legislation: This consisted of EU legislation that applied directly in the UK such as regulations and decisions.

  Following REULA 2023, direct EU legislation forms part of assimilated law and is now known as direct assimilated legislation.
- Rights etc arising under s 2(1) of the ECA 1972: This consisted of directly effective EU rights and obligations that did not fall under either of the previous two categories. An example given in the explanatory notes accompanying the EUWA 2018 was Article 157 TFEU – equal pay for male and female workers.

  REULA 2023 has abolished this category of retained EU law, although it gave the Government a limited power to restate provisions that originally fell within this category.

The European Union (Withdrawal Agreement) Act 2020 also gives direct effect to any provisions in the Withdrawal Agreement that meet the criteria for direct effect. **Chapter 9** covers this in more depth.

6.5.4 Incorporation of the ECHR into domestic law

The ECHR was written in 1950 and protects rights such as the right to life (Article 2), the right not to be tortured (Article 3), the right to a fair trial (Article 6), the right to a private and family life (Article 8), and freedom of religion, expression and association (Articles 9–11). The UK became a signatory in 1951, but it was only in 1965 that the UK Government recognised the right of individual citizens to petition the European Court of Human Rights (ECtHR) under the Convention. Further, it was not until the enactment of the Human Rights Act that individual citizens could bring a claim for breach of their rights under the ECHR before our domestic courts. Prior to this, domestic courts would not consider a legal claim based on an alleged breach of an individual's human rights. Individuals in the UK could only enforce their ECHR rights by taking their case to the ECtHR in Strasbourg after exhausting all domestic remedies.

6.5.5 Method of incorporation

In contrast to the 'strong' method of incorporation of EU law into domestic law, the language used in the HRA 1998 suggests a 'weak' method of incorporation of the ECHR.

The key sections of the HRA 1998 regarding parliamentary sovereignty are summarised in the figure below.

Figure 6.2 The HRA 1998 and parliamentary sovereignty: key provisions

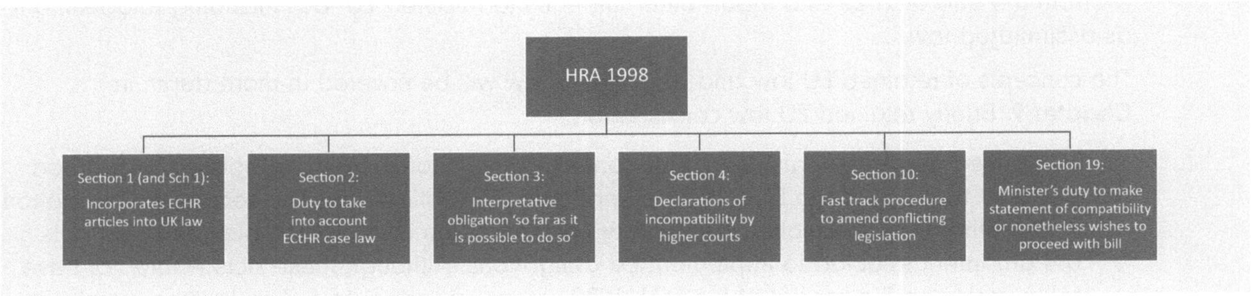

These provisions provide as follows:

(a) Section 1 (and Schedule 1). Section 1 lists the articles of the Convention incorporated into UK law, with the articles themselves set out in Schedule 1.

(b) Section 2. Although domestic courts must 'take into account' judgments of the ECtHR, they are not bound to follow such judgments. However, in practice domestic courts do normally follow them. Lord Bingham provided an authoritative summary of what s 2 entails for UK courts in *R v Special Adjudicator (Respondent), ex p Ullah* [2004] 2 AC 323:

> While ... case law [of the ECtHR] is not strictly binding ... courts should, in the absence of some special circumstances, follow any clear and constant jurisprudence of the Strasbourg court.

Many commentators argue that Lord Bingham was being overly deferential to the ECtHR. There are signs that UK courts are now more willing to depart from ECtHR case law than previously as can be seen, for example, in the comments of the Supreme Court in *R (Hallam) v Secretary of State for Justice* [2019] UKSC 6 where a majority of justices (5:2) decided to follow domestic precedent even though it possibly conflicted with ECtHR case law, although each judge gave different reasoning for doing so.

(c) Section 3. Primary and secondary legislation must be interpreted in accordance with Convention rights 'so far as it is possible to do so'. This applies to legislation passed both before and after the coming into force of the HRA 1998.

(d) Section 4. Where a court cannot interpret legislation in a manner that makes the legislation compliant with Convention rights, the courts may make a declaration of incompatibility. Such a declaration does not invalidate or affect the operation of the offending Act.

(e) Section 10. Where a declaration of incompatibility has been made under s 4 or a judgment of the ECtHR makes it clear that legislation is incompatible with Convention rights, this section creates a 'fast-track' procedure that the Government may use to amend the relevant legislation, if there are 'compelling reasons' to do so; alternatively it can submit a bill to Parliament for this purpose. The Government is not, however, obliged to amend the offending legislation, and if it decides not to, an aggrieved litigant would have to take their case to the ECtHR to obtain redress.

(f) Section 19. A minister who introduces a government bill into Parliament must, before the second reading of the bill, either make a statement that the provisions in the bill are compatible with Convention rights, or alternatively make a statement to the effect that although they are unable to make a statement of compatibility, the Government nevertheless wishes the House of Commons to proceed with the bill.

This has been described as a 'weak' method of incorporation compared to the ECA 1972. The drafting of the HRA 1998 was designed specifically to preserve the supremacy of Parliament. In its White Paper, Rights Brought Home: The Human Rights Bill, the Government said that the Act was 'intended to provide a new basis for judicial interpretation of all legislation, not a basis for striking down any part of it'.

There was a fear that, were a 'strong' method of incorporation chosen, the judiciary would have had the power to strike down Acts of Parliament and deprive such acts of their legal effect.

6.5.6 Impact of the Human Rights Act on parliamentary sovereignty

6.5.6.1 Section 3 of the Human Rights Act 1998: principle of construction

Two House of Lords' cases show that the courts have been willing to use s 3 of the HRA 1998 to stretch the meaning of legislation to make such legislation compatible with Convention rights.

In *R v A (No 2)* [2002] 1 AC 45, s 41 of the Youth Justice and Criminal Evidence Act 1999 imposed restrictions on a defendant charged with rape from being permitted to adduce at his trial evidence of his alleged victim's previous sexual history. The House of Lords considered that a strict reading of this section could contravene a defendant's right to a fair trial under Article 6 of the ECHR, because there were circumstances when such evidence might be relevant to the issue of consent. The House of Lords therefore read this section to mean that evidence of a complainant's previous sexual history could not be adduced, provided this did not infringe the defendant's right to a fair trial.

The House of Lords effectively read extra words into the statute. Lord Steyn conceded that this had required the courts to 'adopt an interpretation which may appear linguistically strained'. He also said that s 3 imposed a duty on the courts to 'strive to find a possible interpretation compatible with Convention rights'.

In *Ghaidan v Godin-Mendoza* [2004] 2 AC 557, under relevant housing legislation, the rights to a tenancy of residential premises could be inherited by the tenant's surviving spouse, or by someone living with the tenant at his or her death as the tenant's wife or husband. The issue on appeal was whether this extended to the survivor of a same-sex couple who had been living together and how, therefore, the relevant provisions should be interpreted in the light of Article 8 of the ECHR (the right to respect for private and family life).

The House of Lords held that, when given its ordinary meaning, the housing legislation treated survivors of homosexual partnerships less favourably than survivors of heterosexual partnerships, without any rational or fair ground for such distinction, and this constituted a breach of the surviving partner's rights under Article 8 of the Convention. Accordingly the House of Lords used its power under s 3 of the HRA 1998 to read the housing legislation as extending to same-sex partners. This took the provisions of the legislation much further than their literal meaning. The lead judgment was again given by Lord Steyn:

> Section 3 requires a broad approach concentrating ... in a purposive way on the importance of the fundamental right involved.

Both cases show that the courts have perhaps gone further than Parliament intended when exercising their powers of interpretation under s 3. The only occasions on which the courts will be unable to use their interpretative powers under s 3 to ensure that a statute is compatible with Convention rights is when to do so would be expressly contrary to the wording of the statute.

6.5.6.2 Disapplying s 3 of the Human Rights Act 1998

It appeared that the previous Conservative Government had an emerging policy of watering down the effect of s 3 by introducing legislation which disapplied its provisions. Examples are the Illegal Migration Act 2023 and the Safety of Rwanda (Asylum and Immigration) 2024 which aimed to deal with challenges facing the UK's asylum process, in particular small boat crossings across the English Channel from France. The aim of these Acts was to facilitate the removal of asylum seekers entering the UK illegally either to their home country or a safe third country such as Rwanda and for their asylum claims to be considered there.

Both Acts disapplied s 3 of the HRA 1998, meaning that courts and public authorities would not be required to interpret the Acts' provisions themselves, nor secondary legislation enacted pursuant to their provisions, compatibly with Convention rights. Additionally, sections in the Victims and Prisoners Act 2024 disapplied s 3 in relation to legislation involving prisoners' release, licences, supervision and recall of offenders.

The aim of disapplying s 3 was to ensure that the courts interpreted and applied specific legislative provisions in the way that Parliament intended, rather than adopting a strained interpretation which departed from the parliamentary intention. In such cases the higher courts would still have the power to issue declarations of incompatibility under s 4.

However, following the change of government after the 2024 general election, the Home Secretary introduced the Border Security, Asylum and Immigration Bill in Parliament on 30 January 2025 which provides for the repeal of the Rwanda Act and much of the Illegal Migration Act. Accordingly, the disapplication provisions in these Acts will be largely of academic interest. Moreover, the provisions in the Victims and Prisoners Act have not yet come into force and, as the Labour Government is more favourably disposed to the HRA 1998 than its Conservative predecessor, they may never do so.

6.5.6.3 Section 4 of the Human Rights Act 1998: declarations of incompatibility

Where the courts are unable to interpret domestic legislation in such a way as to make it compatible with Convention rights, a declaration of incompatibility may be made under s 4 of the HRA 1998. Such a declaration is merely a legal statement that, in the opinion of the court, the relevant legislation contravenes the ECHR. The declaration does not invalidate the legislation, and neither the Government nor Parliament is under any legal obligation to amend it.

However, when the courts have made a declaration of incompatibility there will frequently be considerable political pressure on the Government to amend or repeal the relevant legislation. This occurred following the decision of the House of Lords in *R (Anderson) v Secretary of State for the Home Department* [2002] UKHL 46, [2003] 1 AC 837. This case concerned how long adults convicted of murder should spend in prison for purposes of punishment. At the time of the case, the final decision on this was taken by the Home Secretary in accordance with s 29 of the Crime (Sentences) Act 1997.

It was alleged that the s 29 provision was inconsistent with Article 6 of the ECHR. This was because the imposition of sentence is part of the trial process, and thus should be determined by an independent and impartial tribunal. As a member of the executive, the Home Secretary was not an independent and impartial tribunal. It was not possible to interpret s 29 of the Crime (Sentences) Act 1997 in such a way as to make it compatible with Convention rights, because such an interpretation would have been contrary to the wording of the section:

> Section 3(1) is not available where the suggested interpretation is contrary to express statutory words or is by implication necessarily contradicted by the statute.
>
> (per Lord Steyn)

The House of Lords accordingly made a declaration of incompatibility. The Government subsequently introduced legislation (the Criminal Justice Act 2003) to abolish the Home Secretary's powers to determine the length of sentence in such cases.

The strength of the Government's political obligation to respond to a declaration of incompatibility is illustrated by the Government's response to the decision of the House of Lords in *A and others v Secretary of State for the Home Department* [2005] 2 AC 68 (the 'Belmarsh' case). This involved a challenge to provisions in the Anti-terrorism, Crime and Security Act 2001, which permitted foreign nationals suspected of being involved in terrorist activities (but against whom there was insufficient evidence to bring criminal proceedings) to be detained indefinitely without trial. The House of Lords held that such detention breached the ECHR, and made a declaration of incompatibility in respect of the relevant part of the 2001 Act. Within three months of this decision, the offending legislation was repealed.

The sole example where Parliament has refused to amend incompatible legislation is *Hirst v United Kingdom* (No 2) [2005] ECHR 681, where the ECtHR ruled that a blanket ban on British prisoners exercising the right to vote was contrary to Article 3 of Protocol 1 to the ECHR (the right to free elections). The Scottish Registration Appeal Court in *Smith v Scott* 2007 SC 345 issued a declaration of incompatibility in relation to the ban, but the UK Government and Parliament remained strongly opposed to amending the incompatible UK legislation, and any amendments to UK legislation were highly unlikely. Instead a compromise was reached, with the Government allowing prisoners who are released on temporary licence or on home detention curfew to vote (this did not require a change in legislation). The Council of Europe in December 2018 accepted that this was sufficient to comply with the ECtHR's judgment.

6.5.6.4 Statements of compatibility under s 19 of the Human Rights Act 1998

The requirement for a Minister to make a statement of compatibility does not prevent the Government from proceeding with a Bill that violates Convention rights. The Minister can state that the Government wants to proceed with the Bill even though the Minister cannot state that it is compatible with Convention rights. Accordingly, s 19 does not provide a legal limitation on parliamentary sovereignty.

However, it is very rare for the Government to proceed with a Bill where it has not been possible for the Minister to make a statement of compatibility. The Illegal Migration Bill was only the fourth example. The memorandum accompanying the Bill suggested that government lawyers' main concerns were provisions preventing potential victims of slavery and trafficking from receiving certain legal protections.

The Illegal Migration Act 2023 also contains provisions giving the Home Secretary the power to ignore interim (temporary) injunctions from the ECtHR when making arrangements such as deportation flights for the removal of persons from the UK. The Law Society has stated that ignoring an order from the ECtHR would entail a clear and serious breach of international law. The Government believes the amendments are necessary to secure the UK's borders.

6.5.6.5 Express repeal of the Human Rights Act 1998

Legally there is nothing to prevent Parliament amending or expressly repealing the HRA 1998. For political reasons, however, it had been thought that Parliament was unlikely to take such a step. By incorporating the ECHR into UK law, the 1998 Act has put in place a number of basic rights for citizens of the UK, and to remove such rights would be politically unpopular.

However, there has been considerable criticism of the operation of the 1998 Act and ECHR by some politicians and sections of the media. Consequently the Conservative Party manifesto for the 2019 general election contained a commitment to 'update [the 1998 Act] to ensure that there is a proper balance between the rights of individuals, our vital national security and effective government'. Accordingly, in December 2020, the Government announced an independent review, the Independent Human Rights Act Review (IHRAR), to examine the framework of the HRA 1998, its operation in practice and whether any changes were required.

The IHRAR reported in December 2021 that the HRA 1998 has been a success and made only modest recommendations for change. The Government then announced a consultation on reforms to the HRA 1998, and in the Queen's Speech of May 2022 set out proposals for a British Bill of Rights to replace it. These proposals went considerably beyond the IHRAR's recommendations and, according to the Government, aimed to 'restore the balance of power between the legislature and the courts' and 'end the abuse of the human rights framework and restore some common sense to our justice system'.

The Bill of Rights Bill stated that its aim was to clarify and rebalance the relationship between courts in the United Kingdom, the ECtHR and Parliament. The basic premise was that the HRA 1998 would be repealed in its entirety. However, the Government intended to retain the UK's membership of the ECHR and so under international law would continue to be bound to secure Convention rights in the UK.

Although the Bill proposed to repeal the HRA 1998, there were some similarities between the two:

- The Bill of Rights Bill would have given effect to the same Convention rights as contained in the HRA 1998.
- Public authorities would still have been required to act compatibly with Convention rights.
- Higher courts would have retained the power to issue declarations of incompatibility.

Notwithstanding these similarities, there were also very significant differences, as the Bill would have replaced various provisions of the HRA 1998 with a range of new measures, including:

- introducing a new permission stage, requiring claimants to prove that they had suffered significant disadvantage due to a breach of their rights before they could take their claim to court;
- removing the requirement for courts to interpret legislation compatibly with Convention rights;
- removing the requirement for courts to take into account judgments of the ECtHR;
- requiring courts to adopt a more literal reading of Convention rights;
- making it harder for offenders to rely on their Convention rights;
- requiring courts to give great weight to the views of Parliament when balancing competing factors while carrying out a proportionality assessment;
- removing the requirement for Ministers introducing bills to Parliament to make a statement regarding the bill's compatibility with Convention rights;
- preventing human rights claims arising out of overseas military operations.

Critics of the Bill of Rights Bill argued that it would reduce human rights protection in the UK and result in more cases against the UK Government being taken to the ECtHR, and in June 2023 the Government announced that it was not proceeding with the Bill.

However, the Conservative Party is committed to changing the current system, so critical evaluation of the existing law and proposals for change is likely to remain important.

6.6 Parliamentary privilege

Both Houses of Parliament have a privilege jurisdiction, which is designed to enable them to manage their own proceedings without outside interference. This is part of the law and custom of Parliament. In outline, the main privileges of the House of Commons are as follows:

(a) Freedom of speech

(b) The right to control its own composition and procedures ('exclusive cognisance')

The Committee of Privileges, a Commons select committee, is responsible for considering specific matters relating to privileges referred to it by the House.

6.6.1 Freedom of speech

Freedom of speech is based on article 9 of the Bill of Rights 1689, which provides that freedom of speech and debates or proceedings in Parliament 'ought not to be impeached or questioned in any court or place out of Parliament'. The aim of freedom of speech is to enable parliamentarians to carry out their functions without fear of civil proceedings or criminal prosecutions. However, it also applies to parliamentary officials and non-members such as witnesses before a committee of one of the Houses.

A consequence of this privilege is that MPs and Lords have immunity from legal proceedings, leading to concerns that MPs or Lords may abuse this privilege, for example by libelling individuals with impunity. MPs and Lords also have immunity from contempt of court and have sometimes disclosed in debates facts that could not otherwise be lawfully disclosed. In May 2011 Liberal Democrat MP John Hemming named the former Manchester United footballer Ryan Giggs as being involved in an affair notwithstanding an injunction preventing disclosure of his name. In October 2018 Lord Hain, a former cabinet minister, during a debate in the Lords named Sir Philip Green as the businessman accused of sexual harassment and bullying, even though Sir Philip had obtained an interim injunction preventing disclosure of his identity.

Subsequently, Sir Philip brought proceedings before the ECtHR, claiming that the use of parliamentary privilege to disclose his identity despite the existence of the injunction violated his rights under Article 6 (right to a fair trial) and Article 8 (right to respect for private and family life) of the ECHR. The ECtHR ruled that the UK had not violated the ECHR, finding that it should be left to the UK, and the UK Parliament in particular, to decide on whether and to what extent controls might be needed to prevent parliamentarians from disclosing information subject to injunctions. To rule otherwise would be contrary to the principle of the autonomy of Parliament (*Green v United Kingdom*, App No 22077/19 (ECtHR, 8 April 2025).

This privilege only covers 'proceedings in Parliament'. Whilst the privilege clearly includes core proceedings such as parliamentary debates, questions in Parliament and committee proceedings, defining its exact extent can be problematic. Erskine May (Parliamentary Practice, 25th edn (London, 2019)) states; 'it has been concluded that an exhaustive definition [of proceedings in Parliament] could not be achieved'. As a general rule, however, privilege encompasses ancillary matters such as words spoken or written and actions taken outside the core proceedings themselves, but which are of necessity connected to those proceedings.

Parliament, through its committees, has sometimes attempted to define the scope of privilege. A particularly noteworthy case was that of Duncan Sandys MP. In 1938 he was threatened with prosecution for breaching the Official Secrets Act 1911 when he brought up a matter of national security in a parliamentary question, but refused to disclose his source, namely a leak regarding British military preparedness. The Select Committee of Privileges ruled that an MP should not be threatened with prosecution in this way and that such threats could constitute a breach of privilege.

Although Parliament has asserted its right to define the scope of parliamentary privilege, the Bill of Rights is a statute and so article 9 is subject to interpretation by the courts. In general the courts have interpreted the scope of this privilege widely. In *Church of Scientology v Johnson-Smith* [1972] 1 All ER 37 the claimant was not permitted, in libel proceedings, to prove allegations of malice by relying on statements made by the defendant, an MP, in the House of Commons, as they were absolutely privileged. In contrast, in *Rost v Edwards* [1990] 2 QB 460 the High Court held that the Register of Members' Interests (a record of MPs' financial interests) did not fall within the definition of a proceeding in Parliament, though there has been some debate whether this judgment is correct.

The privilege also extends to official reports of proceedings in Parliament and to committee proceedings. After litigation in the 1830s, Parliament enacted the Parliamentary Papers Act 1840, which makes it clear that papers published by Parliament attract absolute privilege.

There has also been discussion regarding to what extent parliamentary privilege exists for communications between constituents and MPs. In *Rivlin v Bilainkin* (1953) 1 QBD 534 the court held that where there is no connection to proceedings in Parliament, there is no privilege. On the other hand, it is believed that where there is a connection to proceedings in Parliament, privilege will exist.

In addition to the absolute privilege relating to proceedings in Parliament, the courts have held that certain statements and publications are eligible for qualified privilege (ie they are protected from defamations action unless malice can be proved). Accordingly *in Wason v Walter* (1868) LR 4 QB 73 the court held that fair and accurate reports of parliamentary proceedings had qualified privilege.

In *Pepper v Hart* [1993] AC 593 the House of Lords held that where an Act of Parliament is ambiguous or obscure the courts may take into account statements made in Parliament by ministers or other promoters of a bill in construing that legislation. Previously, using Hansard in this way would have been regarded as a breach of parliamentary privilege.

6.6.2 The right to control its own composition and procedures – 'exclusive cognisance'

Parliament has sole control over all aspects of its own affairs: to decide for itself what procedures it should adopt, whether any of its procedures have been breached and, if so, what the consequences will be. This has been largely accepted by the courts who will not question the validity of an Act on the basis that correct procedures were not followed (*Pickin v British Railways Board* [1974] AC 765).

Parliament's right to regulate its own affairs includes disciplinary powers over MPs; eg the right to suspend them for misconduct. It also includes the right to punish anyone, including non-members, for contempt of Parliament – any conduct that might substantially prevent or hinder the work of either House. In theory, Parliament may punish contempt by imprisonment, though this has not occurred since the 19th century. More usually, offenders are given reprimands. In December 2018 MPs voted to hold the Government in contempt of Parliament. The Government had refused to release the legal advice given by the Attorney General Geoffrey Cox to the then Prime Minister, Theresa May, regarding an agreement that the UK had reached with the EU, despite Parliament passing a motion demanding that it be made available. After the contempt motion, the Government published the advice. However, there were no further consequences.

6.6.3 Recent developments

The issue of MPs' expenses and allowances has attracted significant media attention in recent years as a result of a scandal during 2009 particularly focusing on expenses claims by MPs with second homes in London. As a result, criminal prosecutions were started against a few MPs relating to fraudulent expenses claims. One question the courts had to consider was whether parliamentary privilege precluded their jurisdiction to deal with such issues. In December 2010, in *R v Chaytor (David) and others* [2010] UKSC 52, the Supreme Court held that neither article 9 of the Bill of Rights 1689 nor the House of Commons' right to 'exclusive cognisance' of its own affairs affected the Crown Court's jurisdiction to try MPs on charges of false accounting in relation to their parliamentary expenses claims. The Supreme Court regarded article 9 as principally directed at MPs' freedom of speech and debate in the Houses of Parliament and in parliamentary committees. Examination of MPs' expenses claims by the courts would not according to the Supreme Court adversely affect the core or essential business of Parliament.

The Supreme Court also said that Parliament had never claimed an exclusive right to deal with criminal conduct within the precincts of Parliament, even where it relates to or interferes with parliamentary proceedings.

Largely as a response to the expenses scandal, Parliament enacted the Parliamentary Standards Act 2009 setting up the Independent Parliamentary Standards Authority (IPSA) to independently oversee and regulate MPs' expenses.

Summary

Parliament is one of the key actors in the UK constitution. It is the legislative branch of government, but also performs other vital functions such as scrutinising the Government's policies and also providing the personnel of government.

Most Acts of Parliament are passed by both the House of Commons and the House of Lords. However, the Parliament Acts 1911 and 1949 provide a procedure that enables the Commons to bypass the Lords and submit a bill for Royal Assent without the Lords' consent.

Parliamentary sovereignty is one of the fundamental features of the UK constitution. In theory this means Parliament can pass any law it wants to and no one (including the courts) can challenge an Act of Parliament. However, there are limitations on parliamentary sovereignty – domestic and European.

Domestic limitations include:

- The impact of devolution
- The concept of constitutional statutes that cannot be impliedly repealed
- The 'manner and form' debate
- The rule of law

The European limitations arise from the UK's membership of the EU and the incorporation of the ECHR into UK law. Whilst the UK left the EU on 31 January 2020, an understanding of the impact of EU law in the UK remains essential.

You should also check your understanding of parliamentary sovereignty by considering the summary diagram set out in Figure 6.3.

Proceedings in Parliament are absolutely privileged. This is to ensure that parliamentarians can perform their duties without outside interference.

Figure 6.3 Parliamentary sovereignty

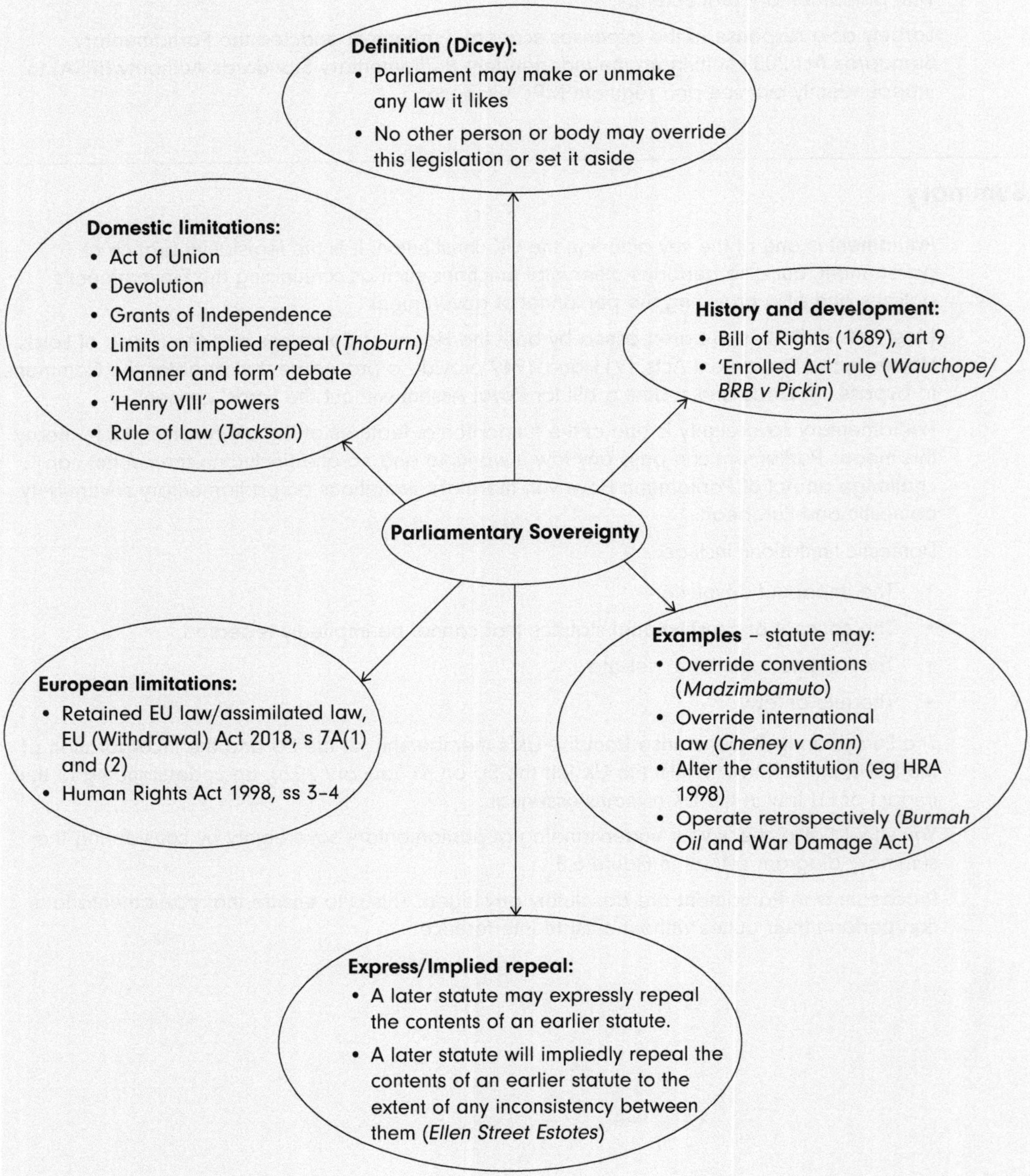

7 The Rule of Law and the Separation of Powers

Learning outcomes

By the end of this chapter you should be able to:

- explain what is meant by the idea of the 'rule of law', evaluating traditional and modern interpretations, and appreciate the importance of this principle;
- appreciate the extent of judicial and statutory recognition of the rule of law;
- describe the doctrine of the separation of powers and explain the reason(s) behind its development;
- understand and analyse the relationship between the executive, legislative and judicial branches of state in the UK; and
- assess the extent to which the UK constitution demonstrates a separation of powers between the different branches of state.

7.1 Legitimacy: the rule of law and separation of powers

The rules that determine whether a particular law has been legally enacted require justification. Individuals need to know why they should obey the law of the land, even if at times it may be inconvenient and on occasion disadvantageous to do so. Political power must be derived from a valid source of authority in terms of shared beliefs on the part of society as a whole to command the respect of citizens. In addition, the rules of power must ensure that the people who wield power have the appropriate qualities to do so and that they govern in the general interest. There need to be constraints on the rulers to ensure that they do not abuse their power. To protect society, the rulers should not have untrammelled powers which they can exercise arbitrarily; their conduct should be subject to adjudication by the courts to ensure that they act lawfully.

Events in South Africa during the apartheid era show that it is not enough for correct procedures to be followed in order for laws to be legitimate. The racially discriminatory laws that deprived black South Africans of voting rights, denied them the right to own property in most of the country and enforced rigid segregation were all validly enacted under the South African constitution, which could be traced back to an Act of the Westminster Parliament, the South Africa Act 1909. However, the apartheid system blatantly lacked legitimacy as it resulted in the gross oppression of the black majority by a white minority government.

The rule of law and separation of powers are two key constitutional principles that buttress the legitimacy of the UK's constitution and prevent the arbitrary exercise of power. They help to ensure the legitimacy of the laws to which British citizens and residents are subject.

7.2 The rule of law

You briefly considered what is meant by the 'rule of law' in **Chapter 1**. It has a long history going back at least to Magna Carta in 1215, which enshrined the principle that not even the King was above the law. A further noteworthy historical development was the creation of the writ of habeas corpus, an order by the court that a prisoner be brought before it so that it can decide whether their detention is lawful and consequently whether they should be released. The Habeas Corpus Acts 1640 and 1679 codified the procedure to counter the King's practice of detaining prisoners and simply asserting his command was sufficient justification for their detention.

7.2.1 The 'traditional' definition of the rule of law

AV Dicey, in his seminal work *An Introduction to the Study of the Law of the Constitution* (1885), said that the rule of law in the context of the UK constitution meant the following three things:

1. 'No man is punishable or can be lawfully made to suffer in body or goods except for a distinct breach of the law established in the ordinary legal manner before the ordinary courts of the land ... It means ... the absolute supremacy ... of regular law as opposed to the influence of arbitrary power'
2. '... no man is above the law ... every man and woman, whatever be his rank or condition, is subject to the ordinary law of the realm and amenable to the jurisdiction of the ordinary tribunals'
3. '... the general principles of the constitution (for example, the right to personal liberty, or the right of public meeting) are with us as a result of judicial decisions ... in particular cases brought before the courts.'

Today, Dicey's account of the rule of law can be seen as dated, particularly because it failed to anticipate modern developments in administrative law (ie the law relating to the control of the exercise of powers by public officials and public bodies - see ***Administrative Law and Human Rights***). However, it is important to consider Dicey's approach because, however dated his interpretation, it has substantially influenced the development of English law. Accordingly, to give Dicey's formulation a more modern slant, the table below attempts to 'translate' his formulation into contemporary language

Dicey's formulation	Present-day values/constitutional requirements
1. 'No man is punishable or can be lawfully made to suffer in body or goods except for a distinct breach of the law established in the ordinary legal manner before the ordinary courts of the land ... It means... the absolute supremacy ... of regular law as opposed to the influence of arbitrary power'	This element has a number of connotations: • Legal certainty Citizens should be able to rely on laws that are both made and set out clearly. There should be no arbitrary exercise of power, where the Government disregards the law and acts in any manner it sees fit. • Personal liberty Citizens should be detained and subject to punishment only if they have broken the law. • Due process of law Citizens have a right to fair procedures for determining civil or criminal liability.

Dicey's formulation	Present-day values/constitutional requirements
2. '... no man is above the law...every man and woman, whatever be his rank or condition, is subject to the ordinary law of the realm and amenable to the jurisdiction of the ordinary tribunals'	This element is concerned with equality before the law. This means not only equality between citizens, but also between public officials and citizens. Thus: • Like cases should be treated in like ways; there should be no unjustified discrimination (for example, on the grounds of race or gender). • State officials have no exemption from legal control or accountability as a result of their position, and are subject to the 'ordinary' law of the land (*see Entick v Carrington in* Chapter 1). • Members of the executive should not legislate or adjudicate in court cases (this links to the principle of the separation of powers).
3. '... the general principles of the constitution (for example, the right to personal liberty, or the right of public meeting) are with us as a result of judicial decisions ... in particular cases brought before the courts.'	Dicey sees the courts as protectors of individual liberty, thereby developing constitutional principles through 'ordinary' judicial decisions (this links to case law being an important source of constitutional law - see **Chapter 5**).

7.2.2 The importance of the rule of law

Now that we have given a more up-to-date meaning to Dicey's view of the rule of law, you also need to understand why upholding the rule of law is such an important principle of the UK constitution.

Activity 1 Why the rule of law is important

Why do you think that it is important that the UK constitution is founded upon the rule of law? Make a list of your reasons.

Comment

Observing the rule of law should ensure that:

1. the Government is prevented from exercising arbitrary power (because 'regular' law is supreme);
2. the Government can be held to account for its actions (through the process of judicial review, in which the courts ensure that the Government does not exceed or abuse the powers that it has been granted);
3. the law is set out clearly for all citizens and is made properly following a set procedure;
4. the law does not operate retrospectively (ie someone should not be punished for an act that was not a crime at the time they carried out that act, if that act subsequently becomes a crime);
5. there is equality before the law for all citizens;
6. there is equal access to the law and the Government or state has no special exemptions or 'get-outs';
7. citizens have a means of legal redress for their grievances; and
8. the independence of the judiciary is maintained, thereby preserving the separation of powers and preventing the Government from exercising its powers in an arbitrary way.

7.2.3 Modern interpretations of the rule of law

Joseph Raz's work, *The Authority of the Law* (1979), has been very influential in contemporary thinking regarding the rule of law. His core argument is that the principal function of the rule of law is to ensure that 'the law should conform to standards designed to enable it effectively to guide action'. This means in practice that the law should:

- be openly and clearly stated, ie be readily accessible to the public;
- not have retrospective effect, ie operate prospectively only;
- be made by proper procedures;
- be relatively stable, ie not change frequently;
- provide for open and fair hearings; and
- be administered by an independent judiciary.

If the law observes these qualities, people will be able to decide whether their actions conform with the law or not; they will know what the consequences of their actions will be and where they stand if they conduct themselves in a given way.

Another of the most authoritative modern definitions of the rule of law was provided by Lord Bingham of Cornhill, an eminent British judge who was successively Master of the Rolls, Lord Chief Justice and Senior Law Lord. He lectured frequently on the topic and also wrote the very influential book, *The Rule of Law* (2010).

Lord Bingham said that the core of the existing principle of the rule of law was as follows: 'all persons and authorities within the state, whether public or private, should be bound by and entitled to the benefit of laws publicly and prospectively promulgated and publicly administered by the courts.'

Lord Bingham broke this definition down into eight sub-rules:

1. The law must be accessible, intelligible, clear and predictable.
2. Questions of legal right and liability should ordinarily be resolved by application of the law and not the exercise of discretion.
3. The laws of the land should apply equally to all, save to the extent that objective differences justify differentiation.
4. The law must afford adequate protection of human rights.
5. Means must be provided for resolving, without excessive cost or delay, civil disputes that the parties cannot resolve themselves.
6. Ministers and public officers must exercise the powers conferred on them reasonably, in good faith, for the purpose for which the powers were conferred and without exceeding the limits of such powers.
7. The adjudicative procedures provided by the state should be fair.
8. The state must comply with its obligations in international law.

In some areas Lord Bingham's definition overlaps with that of Dicey's and Raz's (for example, the idea that laws must be certain and there should be fair and accessible court processes), whilst in other areas Lord Bingham goes a little further (for example, the importance of the protection of human rights and compliance with international law).

One area of debate is the extent to which the rule of law is merely a formal concept, or whether it includes a substantive element as well. Formal concepts of the rule of law state that the rule of law should focus on the form of law and the procedures for making law. Raz thought the rule of law should be morally neutral and would lose its functional importance if it included concepts such as justice, democratic values and non-discrimination. According to him, the aim of the rule of law should not be to promote a particular social philosophy; instead it should merely seek to ensure that laws are made according to proper procedures, and that they are accessible to the public, clear and stable. He considered that it was possible for an undemocratic regime to comply with the rule of law provided it enacted oppressive measures according to the correct procedures. Dicey's view of the rule of law was also largely formal.

In contrast, Lord Bingham's conception of the rule of law is substantive; according to him, the rule of law is not confined to procedural elements, though they are important, but extends to the protection of fundamental rights. Thus, the racially discriminatory legislation that the apartheid regime enacted violated the rule of law, even though the regime followed the correct constitutional procedures.

Critically evaluating the various definitions and conceptions of the rule of law is an important exercise, as you will see at **7.2.4** below that the principle plays a very significant role in the UK constitution.

7.2.4 The contemporary relevance of the rule of law

Although, as we have seen so far in this chapter, the rule of law is a concept open to varying interpretations, it remains fundamental to an understanding of the UK constitution.

7.2.4.1 Judicial and statutory recognition

In recent years, there has been an explicit recognition in both statute and case law of the continuing significance of the rule of law. For example:

- Section 1 of the Constitutional Reform Act (CRA) 2005 (a statute that you will look at later in this chapter) acknowledges the importance of 'the constitutional principle of the rule of law' although, perhaps because of the difficulties of definition, does not seek to define it.
- In *R (Jackson) v Attorney General* [2005] UKHL 56, Lord Hope spoke of the rule of law enforced by the courts as 'the ultimate controlling factor on which our constitution is based'.

Whilst these examples may seem academic, the courts have also been willing to use the rule of law to justify their judgments.

7.2.4.2 The right to liberty

The case of *A and others v Secretary of State for the Home Department* [2005] 2 AC 68 (often referred to as the 'Belmarsh case') is a significant case in showing the importance that the judiciary attaches to the rule of law. The case involved a challenge to, amongst other things, provisions in the Anti-terrorism, Crime and Security Act 2001 enacted in the aftermath of the 9/11 terrorist attacks in the USA. The 2001 Act permitted foreign nationals suspected of being involved in terrorist activities (but against whom there was insufficient evidence to bring criminal proceedings) to be detained indefinitely without trial.

The House of Lords held that such provisions breached Article 5 (right to liberty and security) and Article 14 (protection from discrimination) of the ECHR in so far as it permitted the detention of suspected terrorists in a way that discriminated against them on the ground of nationality, since there were British suspected terrorists who could not be detained under the 2001 Act. The House of Lords issued a declaration of incompatibility pursuant to s 4 of the HRA 1998 regarding the offending provisions in the 2001 Act.

This case emphasises the significance of the rule of law, Lord Nicholls stating that 'indefinite imprisonment without charge or trial is anathema in any country which observes the rule of law .... Wholly exceptional circumstances must exist before this extreme step can be justified.'

The burden on the Government to justify imprisonment without charge was therefore a very heavy one, which it could not discharge.

7.2.4.3 The right to a fair hearing

The right to a fair trial is a fundamental aspect of the rule of law and the courts have been keen to uphold the principle, as shown by the decision of the House of Lords in *R (Anderson) v Secretary of State for the Home Department* [2002] UKHL 46, [2003] 1 AC 837. This case involved an offender who had been convicted of murder and had been given a mandatory life sentence. A mandatory life sentence is accompanied by a tariff, a minimum term that the prisoner must serve before they may be considered for release on licence. At the time of the case, although the trial judge recommended the tariff, s 29 of the Crime (Sentences) Act 1997 gave the Home Secretary the power to set it. In *Anderson* the Home Secretary increased the tariff beyond that recommended by the trial judge. The claimant challenged the increase in tariff, arguing the Home Secretary's power was a breach of Article 6(1) (the right to a fair trial) of the ECHR via the HRA 1998.

In his speech, Lord Steyn stated that 'the proposition that a decision to punish an offender by ordering him to serve a period of imprisonment may only be made by a court of law ... is a principal feature of the rule of law on which our unwritten constitution is based'. Parliament had overridden this principle by enacting s 29 of the 1997 Act but had also, through enacting the Human Rights Act 1998, given the courts the power to decide upon the compatibility of s 29 with Article 6(1) of the ECHR. Accordingly, the House of Lords issued a declaration of incompatibility regarding s 29. Parliament subsequently removed the power to set the tariff from the Home Secretary.

As well as illustrating the significance of the rule of law, this case also shows how the Human Rights Act enables the courts to uphold the principle.

7.2.4.4 Access to justice

The Supreme Court's decision in *R (UNISON) v Lord Chancellor* [2017] UKSC 51 also shows the continuing significance of the rule of law in its jurisprudence. The Lord Chancellor had adopted the Employment Tribunals and the Employment Appeal Tribunal Fees Order 2013, SI 2013/1893 ('the Fees Order') relating to proceedings in employment tribunals and the Employment Appeal Tribunal. Prior to the Fees Order, claimants were able to bring proceedings in an employment tribunal and appeal to the Employment Appeal Tribunal without paying any fees. The trade union, UNISON, challenged the Fees Order by way of judicial review on various grounds, including their effect on access to justice. The Supreme Court held that the Fees Order was unlawful.

Lord Reed emphasised the link between access to justice and the rule of law, stating that the constitutional right of access to the courts is inherent in the rule of law: it is needed to ensure that the courts are able to apply and enforce the laws created by Parliament and also the common law created by the courts themselves. To enable the courts to perform that role, people must in principle have unimpeded access to them.

The Supreme Court held that in order for the fees to be lawful, they had to be set at a level that everyone can afford, taking into account the availability of full or partial remission. Even if the fees were affordable, they might still prevent access to justice if they rendered it futile or irrational to bring a claim. This might include situations where the fee was excessive in comparison to the amount at stake or the remedy sought was not financial (such as the right to written particulars of employment), which had the effect of preventing a sensible person, with no guarantee of fee reimbursement and success, from pursuing a claim. Accordingly, the Fees Order was unlawful as it effectively prevented access to justice.

7.2.4.5 Equality before the law

The case of *M v Home Office* [1993] UKHL 5 also illustrates the fundamental nature of the rule of law. M, a citizen of Zaire, had applied for political asylum in the UK, but his application was refused and he was informed that he would be deported. He applied to the High Court for judicial review of the refusal and the High Court judge asked for M's deportation to be delayed while he considered the case. However, M was already on a plane from London to Paris on his way to Zaire. When the judge was told about the situation, he made an interim order for M's return to the UK. Home Office officials arranged for M's return, but the Home Secretary cancelled those arrangements, believing he had acted legally in ordering M's deportation and that the judge did not have the legal power to make an interim order against a minister of the Crown.

In subsequent contempt proceedings lodged on behalf of M, the judge held that the Crown Proceedings Act 1947 preserved the Crown's immunity from injunction. On appeal, the Court of Appeal held that the Home Secretary was in contempt. On his appeal, the House of Lords held that injunctions were available against officers of the Crown and that the Home Secretary was in contempt of court in ignoring them, rejecting his argument that contempt and injunctions did not apply to the Crown. However, there had been a genuine misunderstanding on the Home Secretary's part and, although he was in contempt of court, no penalty other than the finding of contempt was imposed.

In his speech Lord Templeman criticised 'the argument that there is no power to enforce the law by injunction or contempt proceedings against a minister in his official capacity' as it would 'establish the proposition that the executive obey the law as a matter of grace and not as a matter of necessity, a proposition which would reverse the result of the Civil War'.

Lord Woolf stated in his speech that 'the object of the exercise is not so much to punish an individual as to vindicate the rule of law by a finding of contempt'.

The notion of equality before the law and the rule of law were clearly central to the judgment of the House of Lords. The UK constitution does not grant special privileges or immunities to officers of the state.

7.2.4.6 The limits of the rule of law

There is a potential tension between parliamentary sovereignty and the rule of law. In theory Parliament can pass any Act it chooses, no matter how arbitrary or oppressive. Indeed, there have been *obiter* comments by prominent judges suggesting that that the courts might strike down legislation that is contrary to the rule of law, such as abolishing judicial review; see **6.5.1.7** above. The examples given in these *obiter* comments have been extreme, and the courts have generally acknowledged parliamentary sovereignty by following the 'principle of legality', which Lord Steyn expounded authoritatively in *R v Secretary of State for the Home Dept, ex p Simms* [1999] UKHL 33. Lord Steyn affirmed parliamentary sovereignty by stating that Parliament can, if it chooses to do so, legislate contrary to fundamental principles of human rights. However, he continued that the principle of legality requires Parliament to squarely confront what it is doing and accept the political cost. Fundamental rights cannot be overridden by general or ambiguous words. This assumption can be displaced only by 'clear and specific provision to the contrary'.

Some of the provisions of the Illegal Migration Bill, discussed at **6.5.6.2** above, have been criticised for breaching the rule of law. For example, the Bar Council has stated that it is unlikely to be compliant with the UK's obligations under the ECHR and runs counter to the rule of law.

However, there are limits to the extent to which the courts will uphold the rule of law. In *R (Corner House Research and Another) v Director of Serious Fraud Office* [2008] UKHL 60, the Director of the Serious Fraud Office decided to halt an investigation into the alleged corruption of a company engaged in arms trading with Saudi Arabia following a threat by Saudi Arabia to end co-operation in counter-terrorism initiatives if the investigation continued. Ministers advised the Director that, if the investigation continued, those threats would be carried out with grave consequences both for the arms trade and for the safety of British citizens and service personnel. The Court of Appeal held the decision was unlawful, constituting a breach of the rule of law. On appeal, the House of Lords accepted that the Director's decision had been taken with extreme reluctance, and that he had acted lawfully in deciding that the public interest in pursuing an important investigation into alleged bribery was outweighed by the public interest in protecting the lives of British citizens.

Nonetheless, it is clear that the rule of law is a doctrine that forms a key element or part of the UK constitution. There is near universal acceptance that laws should be enacted properly and that they should be clear. Laws should not be applied arbitrarily, no one is above the law and that no one may be punished other than in accordance with the law. Some definitions of the rule of law also have regard to the content of the law, including the extent to which the law upholds human rights; accordingly any analysis of the extent to which a state complies with the rule of law should not be limited to formal aspects. Although there may be some debate at the margins, it is evident that the rule of law is integral to the UK constitution.

7.3 The separation of powers

The separation of powers is closely linked to the rule of law. An independent judiciary is an essential element of the rule of law and the separation of powers helps to secure judicial independence. Similarly, checks on the Government's actions help to prevent the arbitrary exercise of power.

7.3.1 Development of the doctrine

Although there is no formal separation of powers within the UK, this doctrine is acknowledged as one of the principles that underpin the constitution of the UK. You may remember from **Chapter 1** that the doctrine of the separation of powers identifies three branches of state:

- the legislature (or parliament), which makes the law;
- the executive (or government), which implements or administers the law; and
- the judiciary (or courts), which resolves disputes about the law.

The doctrine holds that, as each branch of state has a different role to play within the constitution, there should be no overlap between the branches, either in terms of their functions or in terms of their personnel. If such an overlap were to exist, this would represent an unhealthy concentration of power, which could lead to arbitrary or oppressive government.

The doctrine also holds that, as each branch of state cannot in reality operate in isolation from the other branches, there should be a system of 'checks and balances' in place so that one branch can be kept 'in check' by the other branches, resulting in a 'balance of power' between the different branches.

Hilaire Barnett has summed up the doctrine as follows:

> The essence of the doctrine is that there should be, ideally, a clear demarcation of personnel and functions between the legislature, executive and judiciary in order that none should have excessive power, and that there should be in place a system of checks and balances between institutions. (*Constitutional and Administrative Law*, 15th edn, Routledge, 2023)

7.3.2 The United States of America – the 'Model'

The constitution of the United States of America is based firmly on preserving a separation of powers between the different branches of state. One of the aims of the framers of the US constitution was to avoid the dominance of the executive, which they perceived to be one of the problems with the UK constitution.

In the next activity, you will examine the way in which the US constitution embodies the principle of the separation of powers.

Activity 2 The US Constitution and the separation of powers

Using the Internet, identify which persons or bodies make up the three branches of state in the United States of America. How does the US constitution ensure that the separation of powers between the three branches is maintained?

Comment

The constitution of the United States of America is based firmly on the doctrine of the separation of powers. It also ensures that no one branch may exercise too much power by creating a system of 'checks and balances'.

The executive branch

The executive branch of state in the USA is made up of the President, the Vice President, the members of the President's Cabinet, and the various government departments and agencies.

The executive is under a constitutional duty to ensure that 'the laws be faithfully executed'. Members of the executive cannot also be members of Congress, which means that there is no overlap in personnel between the executive and legislative branches of state. Neither the President nor his advisers may sit in Congress, or take part in Congressional votes and debates. There is one minor exception to this rule. The Vice President is also President of the Senate and is allowed to vote when needed to break a tie. This proved to be very significant following the November 2020 Senate elections which resulted in a tie in the Senate with Democrats and Republicans each having 50 senators. The then Vice President Kamala Harris's casting vote gave the Democrats control of the Senate.

Although the President cannot sit in Congress or vote on legislation, as the head of the federal Government the President sets the legislative agenda. The President does this each January in the 'State of the Union' address, outlining the areas in which the President hopes Congress will legislate. The President has the right to veto legislation passed by Congress, although Congress may override this with a specified majority vote (see below).

The President is commander-in-chief of the armed forces (although cannot make a declaration of war), and nominates judges to become members of the Supreme Court. The President may serve for a maximum of two four-year terms of office. The President may be impeached (ie removed from office) by Congress for acts of 'treason, bribery or other high crimes and misdemeanors'.

The legislative branch

Congress consists of the Senate and the House of Representatives. The Senate is made up of two members from each state. Senators are subject to election every six years, although Senatorial elections occur every two years, with one-third of senators being elected in every two-year cycle. There are 435 members of the House of Representatives. The number of members of the House from each state is determined by the population of the state. All members of the House of Representatives are subject to election every two years.

Congress controls the federal budget and is responsible for enacting legislation. If the President vetoes legislation which has been passed by Congress, Congress may override this with a two-thirds majority. Congress may impeach (ie remove from office) the President, the Vice President and judges of the Supreme Court for 'treason, bribery or other high crimes and misdemeanors'. In 1974, President Richard Nixon was served with 'articles of impeachment' over his role in the Watergate scandal, but resigned the Presidency before his trial could take place. Two attempts were made to impeach President Trump, the first during and the second after the end of his first term (2017–2021), but it proved impossible to obtain the two-thirds majority in the Senate required for a conviction.

Congress may amend the constitution with a two-thirds majority (together with the support of three-quarters of the individual states). Congress, rather than the President, has the power to make a declaration of war. The Senate must ratify the President's nominations for members of the Cabinet, for Supreme Court judges and for all other federal judges. Any international treaties signed by the President must also be ratified by the Senate.

The judicial branch

The judicial branch of state is made up of the various federal courts, but particularly the Supreme Court.

The Supreme Court's function is to settle disputes arising under the law and constitution of the USA. Judges in the Supreme Court are nominated by the President, but must be approved by the Senate. Supreme Court judges hold office 'during good behavior' (ie until they die or retire), subject to Congress having the power to impeach them upon the same grounds as it may impeach the President. The Supreme Court may strike down either actions of the executive or legislation enacted by Congress if such actions or legislation are unconstitutional. In the case of *Marbury v Madison* 5 US (1 Cranch) 137 (1803), the Supreme Court affirmed the doctrine of judicial review, establishing the courts' authority to declare unconstitutional acts of the legislative or executive branches of state. This means that the US Supreme Court, unlike UK courts, has the power to strike down statutes.

The Supreme Court has played a pivotal role in the development and interpretation of the US constitution. For example, in the 1954 case *of Brown v Board of Education of Topeka* 347 US 483 (1954), the Supreme Court outlawed segregated schools in a landmark decision that gave rise to the civil rights movement.

The three branches of government – legislative, executive and judicial – are co-equal and so are intended to act as a check and balance on each other. However, critics of President Trump have accused him of executive overreach and of usurping the powers of the other branches in the early months of his second term as President.

7.3.3 Separation of powers in the UK constitution?

Unlike in the USA, there is no formal separation of powers under the UK constitution. The standard rationale for this is that, unlike in the USA, there has been no formal 'break' in the constitutional history of the UK. In the USA, the constitution was written in 1787, shortly after the end of the War of Independence from Great Britain. One of the key objectives of the 'founding fathers' who prepared the constitution was to write a document that would ensure the separation of powers between the executive, legislative and judicial branches of state, thereby preventing the exercise of tyrannical and arbitrary government by the executive (which they saw as the weakness of the British constitution).

The absence of a 'break' in the constitutional history of the UK means that our constitution has developed on an ad hoc basis and remains unwritten or uncodified. As a result of having an unwritten constitution, no formal system or arrangement has been put in place to ensure that the separation of powers is maintained. Instead, a partial separation of powers between the three branches of state exists, together with a largely informal system of checks and balances.

Although there is no formal separation of powers within the UK constitution, you saw in **Chapter 5** that it is possible to identify the persons or bodies that make up the branches of state in the UK, as illustrated in the figure below.

Figure 7.1 Branches of central government

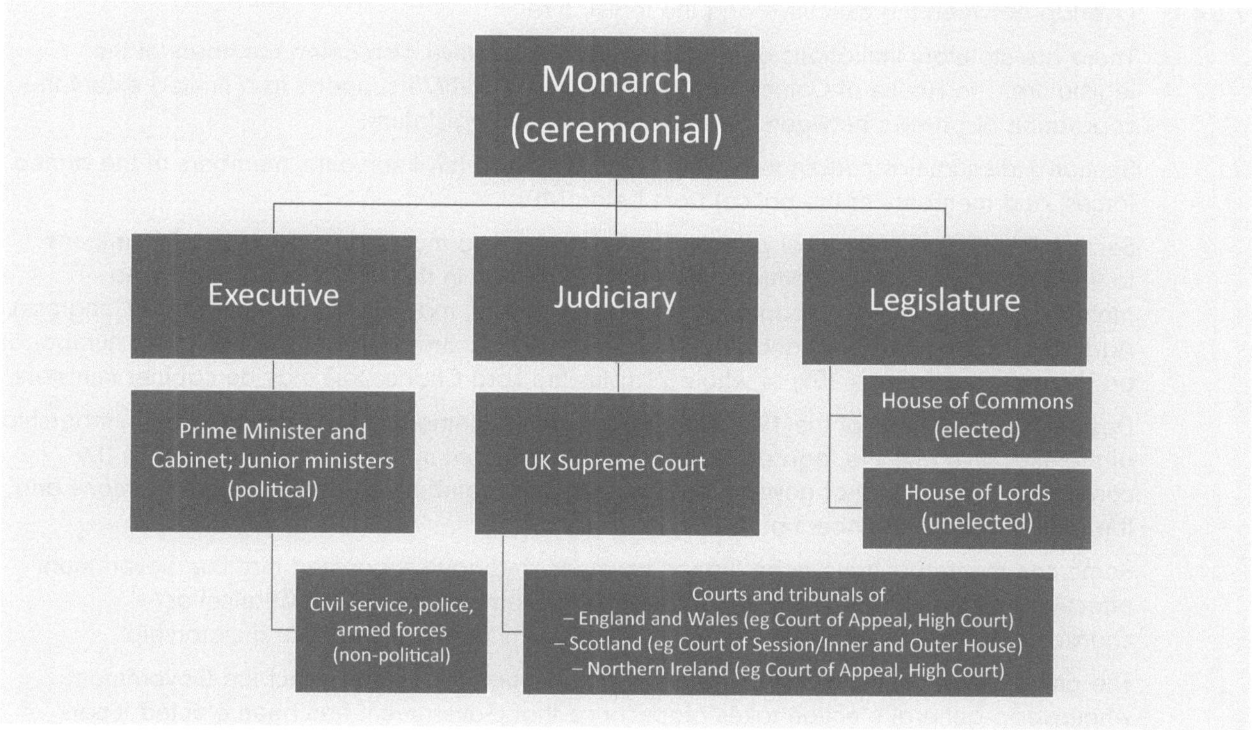

The executive branch of state is made up of the Monarch, the Prime Minister and other government ministers, the civil service, and the members of the police and armed forces. You may come across the terms 'central government' and 'the Crown' in connection with the executive. Central government comprises the Monarch, government ministers and members of the civil service. The Crown is the central government plus members of the police and the armed forces.

The legislative branch of state is made up of the Monarch, the House of Lords and the House of Commons.

The judicial branch of state is made up of the Monarch, all legally qualified judges, and magistrates.

Although the Monarch is part of all three branches of state, his role is largely ceremonial. The Government is legally 'His Majesty's Government', although in reality government ministers are appointed by the Prime Minister and, by convention, most of the Monarch's legal powers are exercised by the Government on their behalf. You considered some examples of this in **Chapter 5**.

The Monarch is part of the legislature because they must give Royal Assent before a bill that has passed through Parliament becomes an Act of Parliament. Although legally the Monarch may refuse to give Royal Assent to a bill, by convention they will always give this (see **Chapter 5**).

The Monarch is also head of the judiciary. Judges are the 'King's judges' and the courts are the 'King's courts'. That is why criminal cases are always cited: 'R v ...' – 'R' stands for 'Rex' (or 'Regina') or the Crown. The Monarch does not, however, exercise any judicial power.

In the rest of this chapter you will consider the degree of separation and overlap between the branches of state in the UK.

7.3.4 The relationship between the executive and the legislature

7.3.4.1 Overlap between the executive and the legislature

There are statutory limitations on members of the executive also being members of the legislature. The House of Commons Disqualification Act 1975 supports to a limited extent the separation of powers between the executive and the legislature.

Section 1 disqualifies certain members of the executive (civil servants, members of the armed forces, and members of the police) from being MPs.

Section 2 limits the number of government ministers who may sit in the House of Commons to 95 (although you might contrast this with the position in the USA, where virtually no member of the executive, apart from the Vice President, may also be a member of Congress). Additionally, the Ministerial and other Salaries Act 1975 provides that the maximum number of paid ministerial posts is 109, of whom 21 (plus the Lord Chancellor) may be cabinet ministers.

Despite the provisions of the 1975 Act, there is clearly some overlap between the membership of the executive and the legislature, because government ministers can also be MPs (by convention the majority of government ministers are members of the House of Commons and the remainder are members of the House of Lords).

Some commentators have gone further, however, and have suggested that the Government effectively controls Parliament. In 1976, Lord Hailsham, a former Lord Chancellor, characterised the system of government in the UK as being an 'elective dictatorship'.

The phrase 'elective dictatorship' means that, although the people elect the Government whenever a general election takes place, once that Government has been elected it can generally act as it pleases and get Parliament to enact its legislative programme in full. The only limitation on the Government is that it must submit itself for re-election at the next general election. Lord Hailsham was suggesting that Parliament does not really play a role in debating or considering legislation proposed by the Government, but merely 'rubber stamps' the Government's legislative plans.

Lord Hailsham described the UK system of government as operating in this way because:

1. Our current 'first past the post' electoral system means that normally most MPs in the House of Commons will be members of the political party that forms the Government. (Although this is the usual position and now pertains following the December 2019 general election, following the general election in May 2010 no single party obtained sufficient seats to form an overall majority. As a result, the UK had a coalition government comprising the Conservative and Liberal Democrat parties between 2010 and May 2015. Similarly, no party gained an overall majority in the June 2017 general election. The Conservative Party obtained the largest number of seats and entered a confidence and supply agreement with the Democratic Unionist Party. This gave it a slim overall majority, but it only applied to votes on the Queen's Speech; the budget; legislation relating to Brexit and national security.)
2. The Government therefore has an in-built majority in the House of Commons, particularly given that most members of the Government (including the Prime Minister and other cabinet ministers) are also MPs.
3. The Government has significant control over the parliamentary timetable, and most of Parliament's time is devoted to the Government's legislative programme.
4. Most of the bills considered by Parliament are introduced by government ministers, and the overwhelming majority of these bills will be passed by Parliament because the majority of MPs represent the governing party.
5. The constitutional convention that the Government will resign if defeated in the House of Commons on a confidence vote or a major part of its legislative programme means that governments are able to persuade their backbench MPs to support government legislation, even if those MPs are reluctant to do so. While the Fixed-term Parliaments Act

2011 was in force, its provisions governed the effect of votes of confidence but, following its repeal, the pre-2011 convention applies once again. The Prime Minister is also expected to resign if they no longer have the confidence of the House and an alternative Government does have the confidence.

6. Huge pressure is placed on MPs from the governing party to support bills introduced by the Government through the government whips.
7. Although Parliament enacts primary legislation, many laws take the form of delegated or subordinate legislation. This is legislation made by government ministers under powers delegated by Parliament and there are only limited opportunities for Parliament to scrutinise such legislation.
8. Acts of Parliament will often contain what are referred to as 'Henry VIII' powers (so called after the 1539 Statute of Proclamations, in which King Henry VIII gave his own declarations the same force as legislation enacted by Parliament). Such powers enable the Government to amend or repeal primary legislation by way of delegated legislation, without reference back to Parliament. The Retained EU Law (Reform and Revocation) Act 2023 has given the Government extensive Henry VIII powers to amend or repeal retained EU law/assimilated law.
9. Although the Government will not necessarily have a majority of the peers in the House of Lords, the House of Lords is weak in comparison to the House of Commons and is unable to keep the Government 'in check'. There is a constitutional convention, the Salisbury Convention, that the House of Lords will not reject a bill giving effect to a significant manifesto commitment of the democratically elected Government. In addition, the Parliament Acts of 1911 and 1949 limit the power of the House of Lords to reject a bill that has been passed by the House of Commons (see **6.3.4** above).

There have been rule of law and separation of powers concerns regarding the Coronavirus Act 2020 and secondary legislation enforcing the lockdown to prevent the spread of the Covid-19 virus. Whilst most commentators have accepted the need for emergency legislation to deal with the pandemic, some have thought that there has been inadequate parliamentary scrutiny of the measures that the Government has taken.

7.3.4.2 Parliamentary scrutiny of the executive

As the previous section shows, there is a significant degree of overlap between the executive and the legislature in the UK. Further, although it is Parliament that enacts legislation, Parliament is effectively legitimising legislative proposals that have been put forward by the Government. Nevertheless, Parliament still has a role to play in scrutinising the Government and holding it to account for its actions. The following are examples of some checks and balances that enable Parliament to fulfil this role.

- Questions. Time is set aside each day for MPs to put oral questions to ministers, and MPs may also ask written questions. The Prime Minister answers questions for 30 minutes each Wednesday.
- Debates. The 'standing orders' of the House of Commons provide for 'emergency debates' on matters that need urgent consideration. The Speaker decides whether the matter should be debated. 'Standing orders' also allocate time to the official Opposition in which it may initiate debates. All government bills are debated by Parliament at their second reading (see **Chapter 6**). The 'standing orders' also allow for brief debates to take place on topical issues of regional, national or international importance.
- General committees (including public bill committees). All government bills are referred to a public bill committee of MPs after the main principles of the bill have been debated. The purpose of the committee is to review the detailed clauses of the bill and make such amendments as are necessary. Additional general committees exist

to discuss matters in specific areas, for example the Scottish Grand Committee, the Welsh Grand Committee, the Northern Ireland Grand Committee and committees on delegated legislation.

- Select committees. These committees are appointed for the life of a Parliament to examine the 'expenditure, administration and policy' of the main government departments. There are select committees for both Houses of Parliament. There is a Commons select committee for each government department, and also some that cross departmental boundaries, eg the Public Accounts and Environmental Audit Committees. Only backbench MPs serve on the Commons Committees. The Government has a majority on each, but the chairman may be a member of the Opposition. The Commons committees report to the House of Commons and it is for the House to consider any necessary action. Select committees will often question government ministers (including the Prime Minister).

  The House of Lords Select Committees do not shadow the work of government departments, but investigate specialist subjects, benefiting from the Lords' expertise. 'Permanent' House of Lords Select Committees include the Communications and Digital Committee, the Constitution Committee and the Environment and Climate Change Committee.

- Parliamentary and Health Service Ombudsman ('the Ombudsman'). The Ombudsman combines two functions, the Parliamentary Commissioner for Administration (PCA) and Health Service Commissioner for England. The Ombudsman is appointed by the Crown, and in their capacity as PCA their main function is to investigate the complaints of persons who have suffered injustice in consequence of 'maladministration' by government departments in exercise of their administrative functions. However, the Ombudsman's decisions are not binding on government ministers.

- MPs may reject government bills. In normal times it is rare for a government bill to suffer a defeat in the House of Commons. Nevertheless, this does occasionally happen, for example in March 2016 when the Government was defeated in its plan to extend Sunday opening hours.

  The period between the June 2017 and December 2019 general elections during which there was a Conservative Party minority government was, however, highly unusual. The Government suffered a large number of defeats during this period, in particular relating to its Brexit policies. Indeed, Parliament passed two Acts, the European Union (Withdrawal) Act 2019 and the European Union (Withdrawal) (No 2) Act 2019 despite government opposition. MPs opposed to the Government's policies on the UK's withdrawal from the EU voted to suspend the normal standing orders giving priority to government business. These Acts required the Government in certain circumstances to seek limited extensions to the UK's membership of the EU to prevent the UK from leaving without a withdrawal agreement in place.

In addition to the formal mechanisms by which Parliament holds the Government to account for its actions, the constitutional conventions of individual ministerial responsibility and collective cabinet responsibility (which you considered in **Chapter 6**) also play an important role here. Legally, government ministers are not accountable to Parliament for their decisions or actions. However, through the operation of these conventions, accountability exists.

Under the convention of individual ministerial responsibility, ministers are responsible to Parliament both for the running and proper administration of their respective departments and also for their personal conduct. There must be no conflict of interest between a minister's public duties and his or her private interests. A minister who breaches this convention should resign. Examples of ministers resigning following a breach of this convention include:

- In 1982, the Foreign Secretary and two junior ministers resigned over allegations that the Foreign Office should have foreseen the Argentine invasion of the Falklands Islands and planned accordingly.
- In 2004, David Blunkett resigned as Home Secretary after he had an affair with a married woman and then had her nanny's visa application fast-tracked. In 2005 he resigned as Work and Pensions Secretary, following allegations concerning financial interests about which he had failed to make proper disclosure.
- In 2017 Priti Patel resigned as Secretary for State for International Development following unauthorised meetings with Israeli government officials about which she had misled the Foreign Secretary and Prime Minister.
- In 2018 Amber Rudd resigned as Home Secretary in connection with the Windrush deportation scandal. She had misled MPs over whether the Home Office had immigration removal targets.
- In 2024 Louise Haigh stepped down as Transport Secretary after it transpired that in 2013 she had pleaded guilty to a criminal offence regarding incorrectly reporting a work mobile phone as stolen.

As discussed at **5.5.4.5** above, there has also been considerable debate regarding whether the former Prime Minister, Boris Johnson, breached this convention in his conduct regarding the 'Partygate' affair.

The convention of collective cabinet responsibility provides that the cabinet is collectively responsible to Parliament for the actions of the Government as a whole, and the Government must retain the confidence of the House of Commons.

This convention also holds that ministers must resign if they wish to speak out in public against government policy. An example of this occurred in 2003, when both Robin Cook and Clare Short resigned as cabinet ministers in order to voice in public their opposition to the war in Iraq. Further examples are the resignation of Baroness Warsi as Foreign Office Minister in 2014 in protest at government policy on Gaza, Iain Duncan Smith's resignation as the Secretary of State for Work and Pensions in 2016 in protest at the Government's proposed cuts to disability benefits and Anneliese Dodds' resignation in 2025 as International Development Minister over cuts to overseas aid to fund an increase in defence spending. There were 36 ministerial resignations between June 2018 and May 2019, most relating to Theresa May's Brexit policies. They included David Davis and Dominic Raab, who had both been Secretaries of State for Exiting the EU, and Boris Johnson who was the Foreign Secretary at the time.

Five cabinet ministers and 25 junior ministers resigned from the Government in July 2022 as they could no longer support Mr Johnson continuing as Prime Minister, a major factor in precipitating his resignation.

Note that it is open to the Prime Minister to suspend the operation of the convention of collective cabinet responsibility, as David Cameron did in the run up to the EU referendum in June 2016.

7.3.4.3 Parliament and the royal prerogative

There are some areas of government activity over which Parliament has historically been unable to exercise effective scrutiny. These are predominantly powers that the Government exercises under the royal prerogative, and include matters of national security, the defence of the realm and the deployment of the armed forces (there is, for example, no legal requirement for the Government to obtain parliamentary approval before sending troops into action). You will see later in this chapter that these are also areas where the powers of the courts to review actions taken by the Government are limited, because the courts consider such areas to be 'non-justiciable' (ie not areas in which the courts should properly become involved).

However, there are indications that Parliament is taking on a greater role in these areas. For example, in 2003 the Government obtained parliamentary approval before sending troops to Iraq. Also in 2013 the Government recalled Parliament to vote and debate possible military action in Syria. Following a 'No' vote in the Commons, the Prime Minister acknowledged that the Government would not become involved in military action in Syria. Subsequently, in September 2014, the Government sought and obtained parliamentary approval for air strikes against Isis targets in Iraq, but not in Syria.

In contrast, in 2011 the Government only sought approval for the deployment of forces in Libya retrospectively, three days after the start of British participation, whilst the deployment of British military personnel in Mali in 2013 was not the subject of a parliamentary debate or vote.

Overall, though, it appears that there is a new convention that, before the Government commits troops to military operations, the House of Commons should have an opportunity to debate the issue. Indeed, the Cabinet Manual states:

> In 2011, the Government acknowledged that a convention had developed in Parliament that before troops were committed the House of Commons should have an opportunity to debate the matter and said that it proposed to observe that Convention except where there was an emergency and such action would not be appropriate.

The (then) Prime Minister repeated this commitment in relation to Libya in Parliament in March 2016.

Like many constitutional conventions, however, the exact scope of this new convention is unclear. In April 2018 the Prime Minister, Theresa May, authorised a military airstrike against Syria without seeking prior parliamentary approval. She stated that this was due to the situation being an emergency. However, the decision not to seek prior approval was controversial, and some argued that the Prime Minister had acted in breach of the convention.

There are also legislative restrictions on the exercise of the royal prerogative. In particular the Constitutional Reform and Governance Act 2010 put parliamentary scrutiny of treaty ratification by the Government on a statutory basis, giving legal effect to any resolution of the House of Commons or Lords that a treaty should not be ratified. According to the explanatory notes to the Act:

> should the House of Commons take the view that the Government should not proceed to ratify a treaty, it can resolve against ratification and thus make it unlawful for the Government to ratify the treaty. The House of Lords will not be able to prevent the Government from ratifying a treaty, but if they resolve against ratification the Government will have to produce a further explanatory statement explaining its belief that the agreement should be ratified.

Whilst treaty ratification remains a prerogative power, the House of Commons can prevent the Government from exercising it. However, treaties are subject to the 'negative resolution procedure', which means that no debate or vote is required prior to ratification. Indeed, no debates have taken place in the House of Commons under the provisions in the 2010 Act since it was passed.

7.4 The relationship between the executive and the judiciary

7.4.1 The importance of judicial independence

The importance of judicial independence from the executive is recognised in s 3 of the CRA 2005, which provides that the Government is under a duty to uphold the independence of the judiciary and that individual ministers should not seek to influence particular decisions through any special access to the judiciary. In 2017 the Lord Chief Justice criticised the Lord Chancellor for failing in her duty under s 3 following the criticism of the judiciary in the press after the High Court's decision in *R (Miller) v Secretary of State for Exiting the European Union* [2017] UKSC 5 (*Miller (No 1)*). Various sections of the press had decried the judges, the Daily Mail claiming that they were the 'enemies of the people'.

7.4.2 Judicial independence from the executive

In the UK, judicial independence from the executive is secured in a number of ways.

(a) Appointment. Judicial appointments are now dealt with by the Judicial Appointments Commission, which is politically impartial and free from executive control.

(b) Tenure. Security of tenure (ie job security) was given to judges of the senior courts historically by the Act of Settlement 1701, although the modern basis of the law is the Senior Courts Act 1981 and, in the case of the Justices of the Supreme Court, the CRA 2005. Senior judges hold office 'during good behaviour', and may be dismissed by the Monarch only following a vote of both Houses of Parliament. Judges cannot be dismissed merely because they give a judgment with which the Government disagrees.

(c) Salary. Judicial salaries are determined by an independent body (the Senior Salaries Review Board) and are paid from the Consolidated Fund. Under the Consolidated Fund legislation, certain expenditure is authorised in permanent form and does not therefore require annual approval. This means that payment of judicial salaries is insulated from executive and parliamentary control (the salaries of judges appointed to the Supreme Court are determined by the Lord Chancellor but will be charged on the Consolidated Fund, making them effectively immune from political interference).

(d) Immunity from civil action. Judges, particularly in the higher courts, have wide-ranging immunity from claims in tort in respect of their judicial actions. In other words, an unsuccessful litigant cannot sue a judge for making an error when carrying out their duties.

(e) Constitutional conventions. By convention, members of the executive do not criticise judicial decisions, and members of the judiciary do not engage in party political activity.

(f) The 'sub-judice' rule. Under this rule, Parliament (and therefore government ministers) refrains from discussing matters currently being heard or waiting to be heard by the courts.

(g) Contempt of court laws. Common law contempt of court and statutory contempt under the Contempt of Court Act 1981 ensure that there is no outside interference with the administration of justice. This prevents government ministers commenting prejudicially outside proceedings in Parliament on cases before the courts, while the sub-judice rule applies to proceedings in Parliament.

7.4.3 The Constitutional Reform Act 2005

One of the reasons for passing the CRA 2005 was the perception that there was too much of an overlap between the executive and the judicial branches of state, particularly in relation to the office of the Lord Chancellor and some of the quasi-judicial functions that government ministers undertook. Hence in 2005 Parliament took steps to remedy the position.

7.4.3.1 Role of the Lord Chancellor

Prior to 2005, the Lord Chancellor was a member of both the executive and the judiciary. As a government minister, the Lord Chancellor was a political appointee with a seat in the cabinet. However, they were also the head of the judiciary of England and Wales, with responsibility for the appointment of senior members of the judiciary. The Lord Chancellor was also entitled to sit as a Law Lord. It was considered that this dual role of the Lord Chancellor created the impression that the executive had too much influence over the judiciary.

There were also concerns about the lack of transparency in the appointment of the judiciary. Judicial appointments depended on a consultation process, or so-called 'secret soundings', following which the Lord Chancellor approached prospective judges regarding their appointment. Critics of the system pointed out that this led to a judiciary that was comprised predominantly of white men who were privately and Oxbridge educated.

To address these concerns, the CRA 2005 introduced the following reforms:

(a) Role of Lord Chancellor. The Lord Chancellor's role as head of the judiciary was transferred to the Lord Chief Justice (now also known as the 'President of the Courts of England and Wales'). The Lord Chief Justice has overall responsibility for the training, guidance and deployment of judges, and for representing the views of the judiciary to Parliament, the Lord Chancellor and other ministers. The Lord Chief Justice has the right to make written representations to Parliament on important matters relating to the judiciary or the administration of justice.

    The Lord Chancellor remains a member of the cabinet, although this role has now been combined with that of Secretary of State for Justice. There has been some criticism regarding the merger of the two roles in a single individual. Before the CRA 2005, the Lord Chancellor had usually been a senior lawyer as well as a politician. However, due to their seniority, Lord Chancellors usually had little interest in advancing their political career. They were therefore better able, according to critics, to stand up for the rule of law and the effective administration of justice. The current holders of the role are now usually politicians with political ambitions of their own, and so are more likely to pursue their political aims at the expense of the interests of justice.

(b) Creation of the Judicial Appointments Commission. The Judicial Appointments Commission (JAC) is an independent body that has been created to ensure that the appointment of judges in England and Wales occurs solely on merit and is not influenced by political considerations. Prior to the Act being passed, the appointment of the judiciary was solely in the hands of the executive and was conducted on the basis of 'secret soundings'. Similar bodies exist in Scotland and Northern Ireland.

The system for appointing judges operates as follows:

(a) The Prime Minister (after receiving a recommendation from the Lord Chancellor) must advise the Monarch on filling any vacancy for the Lord Chief Justice, the Master of the Rolls, Lord Justices of Appeal, the President of the Family Division and of the King's Bench Division, and High Court judges. The Lord Chancellor must consult the Lord Chief Justice before making his or her recommendation, and will normally ask the JAC to convene a 'selection panel' to select a candidate for such recommendation. Similar procedures apply to appointments as circuit judges, recorders, district judges and magistrates.

(b) Appointments to fill vacancies in the Supreme Court are made by the Monarch on the advice of the Prime Minister, who will in turn have received a recommendation from the Lord Chancellor. A 'selection commission' consisting of the President of the Supreme Court, a senior UK judge nominated by the President of the Supreme Court, and one member from each of the three judicial appointments bodies will select candidates for such recommendation.

(c) The system that has been introduced places primary responsibility for judicial appointments on independent bodies, thus minimising any perception of improper political involvement in the appointment of judges.

(d) The Act also requires that selection be based solely on merit. Nonetheless, where there are two or more candidates of equal merit, a candidate may be selected for a post in order to increase judicial diversity.

The CRA 2005 also created the Supreme Court to replace the Judicial Committee of the House of Lords. You will consider this below when you examine the relationship between the legislature and the judiciary.

7.4.3.2 The judicial functions of the executive

One of the reasons behind the enactment of the CRA 2005 was to enhance the separation of powers between the executive and judiciary. Nonetheless, it remains the case that members of the executive sometimes perform quasi-judicial functions. The impact of Article 6 of the ECHR has been to reduce these functions in some areas (eg the removal of the Home Secretary's power to determine the length of tariff for prisoners given a life sentence following the *Anderson* case). Members of the executive do, however, continue to perform quasi-judicial functions in some areas. Compulsory purchase orders (CPOs) provide an example of this. It is sometimes necessary for land to be made the subject of a CPO if it is required for a particular purpose (eg the building of a new motorway). The decision as to which land is to be purchased is a quasi-judicial decision, but will be taken by the relevant government minister.

Nonetheless, although members of the executive are acting in a quasi-judicial capacity, any decisions they make will be susceptible to judicial review (see below). If such decisions are unlawful, irrational or breach any relevant procedural requirements, the courts can quash them.

7.4.3.3 How the judiciary holds the executive to account

One consequence of the UK having an unwritten constitution is that the judiciary does not have the power to declare actions of the executive (or legislation enacted by Parliament) to be unconstitutional. There is no 'higher law' against which all other actions or pieces of legislation may be judged. However, through the process of judicial review, the judiciary is able to ensure that the executive does not exceed or abuse the powers it has been granted, and that any decisions the executive is required to make are made using the correct procedure.

The executive derives its power from two sources: statute and the royal prerogative. If Parliament has granted statutory powers to the executive (for example, giving a particular power to a government minister), through the mechanism of judicial review the courts can ensure that those powers are exercised in accordance with the purpose of the statute and are not exceeded or abused. Again through the mechanism of judicial review, the courts can determine the extent of the royal prerogative and, in most cases, can review the exercise of prerogative powers (see below) to ensure that they have been exercised in an appropriate manner.

When the courts judicially review the actions of the executive, they are examining only the legality of a decision or action, not its merits. The courts' function is to ensure that the executive has acted within its powers and has acted using the correct procedures. This is important in preserving the separation of powers between the executive and judiciary. Were the judiciary to examine the merits of a decision, it would usurp the role of the executive.

7.4.3.4 Judicial control of the exercise of royal prerogative powers

You may remember from **Chapter 5** that the royal prerogative is what remains of the absolute powers that at one time were exercised by the Monarch, which have not been removed by Parliament. By convention, such powers are today exercised by the Government on the Monarch's behalf.

Historically, the courts have been willing to adjudicate upon the extent of the royal prerogative, but only fairly recently have they been prepared to consider how it is exercised.

Extent of the royal prerogative

The judiciary is responsible for deciding the extent of the royal prerogative (in other words, whether a prerogative power exists or not). Through case law, the courts have established that new prerogative powers cannot be created or the scope of existing powers extended. See, for example, the *Case of Proclamations* (1611) 12 Co Rep 74, 77 ER 1352. The King had the power to make royal proclamations that had the force of statute. The powers were intended for use in times of emergency and were subject to a number of qualifications, but the King used them, amongst other things, to prohibit the construction of new houses in London. The Commons sought the opinion of Chief Justice Coke and four fellow judges as to the legality of the proclamations. In his judgment, Chief Justice Coke held that 'the King hath no power but that which the law of the land allows him' (ie the King could not create new prerogative powers for himself).

In the more recent case of *BBC v Johns* [1965] Ch 3, the BBC claimed that the Crown had a prerogative power to regulate broadcasting, which manifested itself in the BBC's Royal Charter. As such, it argued that it was entitled to rely upon the Crown's exemption from income tax (ie a widening of the Crown exemption). This argument was rejected, the court holding that the Crown could not extend the scope of the existing prerogative.

The Supreme Court's judgment in *R (Miller) v The Prime Minister, Cherry v Advocate General for Scotland* [2019] UKSC 41 (*Miller (No 2)/Cherry*) shows that the courts are willing to take a wide approach in analysing the extent of prerogative powers. The case concerned the legality of the Prime Minister's advice to the Queen to prorogue Parliament for five weeks from 10 September 2019 to 14 October 2019, a period that would occupy a large portion of the time available ahead of the UK's withdrawal from the EU, which was then scheduled for 31 October 2019, an event that would bring about a fundamental change to the UK constitution.

The Supreme Court classified the case as being about the extent of the prerogative power rather than the manner of its exercise, stating that the power to prorogue was limited by the constitutional principles with which it would otherwise conflict. The relevant constitutional principles in this case were parliamentary sovereignty and parliamentary accountability. The exercise of the power was unlawful as, without reasonable justification, it frustrated or prevented Parliament's ability to carry out its constitutional functions. The prorogation took place in exceptional circumstances and prevented Parliament from exercising its constitutional functions for five out of the eight weeks leading up to the date on which the UK was due to leave the EU; Parliament would have no voice in the withdrawal process at a very critical period. The Government failed to put forward any justification for taking action with such extreme consequences. The advice to the Queen was therefore unlawful and hence the prorogation was void.

Exercise of the royal prerogative

Although the courts can decide the extent of the royal prerogative, their power to review the exercise of prerogative powers is more limited.

In *Blackburn v Attorney General* [1971] 2 All ER 1380, Blackburn sought a declaration that the Government, by signing the Treaty of Rome (now the Treaty on the Functioning of the European Union), would unlawfully surrender part of Parliament's sovereignty. The court held that it had the power to determine whether a prerogative power existed but, once it had determined the existence of the power, it had no right to review the exercise of the power. The power to sign an international treaty was part of the royal prerogative and the exercise of that power was immune from judicial review.

In *CCSU v Minister for Civil Service* [1984] UKHL 9, the Council of Civil Service Unions asked the courts to review the decision of the Minister for the Civil Service to prohibit staff at GCHQ from being members of a trade union without first consulting with the relevant trade union. On the particular facts of the case, the House of Lords held that the minister's decision had been prompted by concerns about national security and the minister had been entitled to act as she did; the Government was better placed to judge what was in the interests of national security than the courts.

The case is more important, however, for what it said generally about the power of the courts to review the exercise of royal prerogative powers by the executive. Retreating from the decision in *Blackburn*, their Lordships held that the exercise of prerogative powers was not automatically immune from the judicial review process. In his speech, Lord Roskill said that any power exercised by the executive, whether the source of that power was from statute or the royal prerogative, was capable of being judicially reviewed. The only exception to this was if the power being exercised was not 'justiciable' (ie not an appropriate area for the involvement of the courts).

Lord Roskill identified the following royal prerogative powers as being 'non-justiciable':

- making international treaties
- control of the armed forces
- defence of the realm
- the dissolution of Parliament (following the repeal of Fixed-term Parliaments Act 2011, the power to dissolve Parliament is once again a prerogative power (see **Chapter 6**))
- the prerogative of mercy
- granting public honours.

The courts have subsequently reduced Lord Roskill's list by judicially reviewing the exercise of some of those prerogative powers that Lord Roskill considered to be non-justiciable. The courts have, for example, reviewed the exercise of the prerogative of mercy by the Home Secretary (*R v Secretary of State for the Home Department, ex p Bentley* [1993] 4 All ER 442). Nonetheless, there are still some royal prerogative powers that remain non-justiciable and therefore beyond the scope of the courts.

These are areas of 'high politics' (such as the conduct of foreign relations), and the areas of national security and defence of the realm. An example is the prerogative power to make international treaties, the exercise of which the Supreme Court confirmed in *R (Miller) v Secretary of State for Exiting the European Union* [2017] UKSC 5 (*Miller (No 1)*) is not subject to judicial review.

The courts are reluctant to become involved in these areas for two reasons. First, these are areas that are often highly political in nature, and members of the judiciary are concerned that reviewing the actions of the executive in these areas will lead to their becoming politicised and potentially losing their independence. The accountability of the executive in these areas is better secured through the electorate at a general election than through the courts. Secondly, these are areas where the executive is deemed to have greater technical knowledge and expertise than the judiciary.

One consequence of the courts' refusal to review the exercise of prerogative powers in certain areas is that this leaves some of the executive's powers effectively beyond the scrutiny of both the legislature and the judiciary. Some of the areas that the courts deem to be non-justiciable (particularly matters of defence and national security) are the same areas in which Parliament's ability to hold the executive to account is limited (see **7.3.4.3** above).

The example below illustrates this:

Example

The UK and South Africa are proposing to enter a treaty relating to the safeguarding of intellectual property rights and data protection. The UK Government proposes to ratify it using the royal prerogative. Some British businesses, relying on expert economic analysis, believe the treaty will be highly damaging to their interests and will give an unfair advantage to South African businesses. They would therefore like to know whether they can challenge the treaty in the courts or whether Parliament can take any action.

The making of treaties is a prerogative power and historically UK courts have been reluctant to review the exercise of prerogative powers, even though they have been willing to review whether a prerogative power exists. However, their approach shifted in the CCSU case and they are now willing to review the exercise of some prerogative powers. The courts, though, regard treaty making as a political issue for the Government to decide upon (Blackburn v Attorney General) and so it is not subject to review by the courts. The courts will not interfere even if the treaty is unreasonable.

Under the Constitutional Reform and Governance Act 2010, the Government must lay this treaty before Parliament for 21 sitting days before it can ratify it, and the Commons can vote against ratification. However, the negative resolution procedure applies, and there is no statutory requirement for a debate or vote so the Government can ratify it unless the Commons takes active steps against it (see ***7.3.4.3*** *above). Moreover, Parliament has no power to amend treaties.*

7.4.4 The relationship between the legislature and the judiciary

7.4.4.1 Keeping the legislature and judiciary separate

You have already seen that various statutory and other methods are in place to ensure that the executive and judiciary are kept apart. Similarly, there are statutory and other methods for ensuring some degree of separation between the legislature and judiciary. These include:

(a) House of Commons (Disqualification) Act 1975. Under s 1 of this Act, holders of judicial office are disqualified from membership of the House of Commons.

(b) Impact of convention. There is a constitutional convention that Members of Parliament will not make a criticism of a particular judge, and a further convention that members of the judiciary will not become involved in political activities.

(c) The 'sub-judice' rule. Under this rule, Parliament will refrain from discussing details of cases before the courts or waiting to come before the courts.

(d) Bill of Rights 1689, article 9. This article guaranteed freedom of speech in Parliament by stating that Members of Parliament cannot be made subject to legal sanction by the courts for comments made in Parliament. Comments made by members of either House of Parliament are protected by 'parliamentary privilege'. This means that Lords and MPs enjoy immunity from any criminal or civil proceedings arising out of any statements made by them within Parliament.

7.7.4.2 Areas of overlap between the legislature and judiciary

Prior to the enactment of the CRA 2005, there were two significant areas of overlap between the legislature and the judiciary.

First, the Appellate Committee of the House of Lords (the highest court in the country) was part of Parliament. The 'Law Lords' were physically based in the Houses of Parliament and, as peers, were entitled to take part in votes and debates in the chamber of the House of Lords.

Secondly, the Lord Chancellor was the Speaker of the House of Lords, in addition to being both the head of the judiciary and a Law Lord (and also a member of the Government).

The CRA 2005 removed these areas of overlap. The Act created a new Supreme Court for the United Kingdom, consisting of 12 Justices of the Supreme Court. The Supreme Court replaced the 'Law Lords', whose official title was the Appellate Committee of the House of Lords and who heard cases at the Palace of Westminster where Parliament is located.

The Supreme Court opened in 2009 and has its own building away from Parliament. The existing Law Lords at the time of the opening became the first Justices of the Supreme Court. These Lords retained their peerages but did not sit in the House of Lords. However, new Justices of the Supreme Court do not receive a peerage (although in December 2010 the Queen signed a warrant that every Supreme Court Justice should be styled as Lord or Lady).

In addition to the creation of the Supreme Court, the Lord Chancellor is no longer Speaker of the House of Lords. The Lord Speaker is now directly elected by members of the House of Lords.

7.7.4.3 The judiciary's legislative function

Many constitutional commentators have suggested that, in interpreting statute and developing the common law, the judiciary performs a legislative function.

Various theories exist concerning the 'legislative function' of the judiciary. An early theory that developed (the 'declaratory theory') held that judges do not in any sense make the law. All judges do in deciding cases that come before them is to declare what the law - as enacted by Parliament - actually is. This theory is today unrealistic.

Many commentators have argued the opposite, claiming that judges play a significant role in making the law (the 'legislative theory'). Those who support this theory argue that a significant amount of our law is judge-made (ie the common law) and that, in addition to developing the common law, judges also play an important role when interpreting statute.

Although the legislative theory is more persuasive, there are limits on judicial law-making. The theory of 'judicial restraint' holds that the judges should be reluctant to develop the common law either in areas that Parliament intends to consider, or in areas where Parliament has already decided not to legislate because it is satisfied with the current state of the law.

The common law doctrine of the sovereignty of Parliament represents a self-imposed limitation by the judiciary on its powers, with the judiciary accepting that statute takes precedence over the common law. Thus if the courts develop the law in a direction that Parliament dislikes, Parliament may legislate to overturn the common law.

An example of this occurred in 1965. In *Burmah Oil Company v Lord Advocate* [1965] AC 75, the House of Lords awarded compensation to Burmah Oil for financial losses sustained during World War II. Fearing that this would lead to a flood of similar claims, Parliament enacted the War Damage Act 1965, which overruled the House of Lords' decision and provided that compensation was not payable.

7.7.4.4 Judicial powers in relation to primary legislation

The judiciary is unable to prevent Parliament from legislating in any given area. As you have already seen, as a result of the UK having an unwritten constitution (and also the development of the doctrine of the supremacy of Parliament), the judiciary does not have the power to declare an Act of Parliament to be unconstitutional or to strike down such an Act. The UK has no written constitution to provide a 'higher' authority against which all other legislation can be judged.

However, as you saw in **Chapter 6**, during the UK's membership of the EU and also until the end of the transition period following the UK's exit, the courts had the power to suspend legislation that was incompatible with EU law. Following the end of the transition period, a limited form of supremacy of EU law remains. The courts probably have the power to suspend legislation enacted before the end of the transition period that conflicts with retained EU law. Additionally, the European Union (Withdrawal Agreement) Act 2020 also appears to give the Withdrawal Agreement supremacy over UK law. The most likely outcome of this is that if, in future, Parliament passed a statute inconsistent with the Withdrawal Agreement, the courts would disapply the statute in favour of the agreement unless Parliament explicitly instructed them to give priority to the UK Act of Parliament; indeed, as explained at **6.4.4** above, it is possible that the Government will ask Parliament to enact legislation overriding the Northern Ireland Protocol. See **Chapter 9** for further details of retained EU law and the Withdrawal Agreement.

The courts also have the powers under s 4 of the HRA 1998 to declare that an Act of Parliament is incompatible with the ECHR (see **Chapter 6**). Whilst this does not invalidate the relevant statute, it does impose enormous pressure on the Government to amend the offending piece of legislation.

In addition, in *R (Jackson and others) v HM Attorney General* [2005] UKHL 56, *obiter* comments from the House of Lords suggested that some of their Lordships would be prepared to strike down legislation that infringed the rule of law.

7.7.4.5 The politicisation of the judiciary

(a) Controversial issues

As you have seen, a number of statutory and other provisions are in place to ensure that the independence and political neutrality of the judiciary is maintained. In recent years, however, concerns have been expressed over the danger that the judiciary is at risk of becoming politicised.

In recent years, senior members of the judiciary have been appointed to chair public inquiries. These inquiries have often involved issues that are politically sensitive. An example was Lord Hutton's inquiry in 2003 into the death of the government weapons inspector Dr David Kelly. Lord Hutton's subsequent exoneration of the Government from any blame led to allegations that his report was a 'whitewash' and that he had been biased in favour of the Government. Such allegations damage the independence and impartiality of the judiciary.

More recently the Leveson Inquiry, a public inquiry chaired by Leveson LJ into the culture, practices and ethics of the British press, has caused considerable controversy. Its final report, published in November 2012, contained recommendations for press regulation that many newspapers vehemently opposed. The current Grenfell Tower Inquiry – the public inquiry into the fire at Grenfell Tower on the night of 14 June 2017, which caused 72 deaths – has also proved controversial. It is chaired by Sir Martin Moore-Bick, a retired Lord Justice of Appeal.

The implementation of the HRA 1998 and the incorporation of the ECHR into our legal system has, on occasion, resulted in the courts having to decide cases with a significant 'political' element, particularly when the courts are attempting to balance civil liberties and the rights of the individual against the Government's concern about national security and the ongoing terrorist threat. By making such judgments, judges have been drawn into controversial political issues.

There have also been a number of occasions on which both government ministers and backbench MPs have breached the constitutional convention that politicians should not engage in criticism of individual members of the judiciary. Such criticisms have been particularly common in relation to perceived leniency in the sentencing of criminal offenders, and also in relation to a number of judgments in which the courts have declared that some aspects of anti-terror legislation contravene the provisions of the HRA 1998.

More recently, there have been several judgments concerning the rights of individuals, which have brought criticism from politicians. Examples include a ruling from the European Court of Human Rights that the blanket ban on prisoners being entitled to vote was in breach of the ECHR, and a Supreme Court ruling that convicted sex offenders should be permitted (in certain circumstances) to challenge their names being entered for life on the 'Sex Offenders Register'.

The judgments relating to the UK's exit from the EU, *Miller (No 1)* and *Miller (No 2)/Cherry* discussed at **7.4.1** and **7.4.3.4** above respectively, also caused intense controversy. Following the High Court judgment in *Miller (No 1)*, the tabloid press attacked the judges in the case with the Daily Mail denouncing them as 'enemies of the people'. Lord Neuberger, then President of the Supreme Court, criticised as inadequate the responses of politicians, including the Lord Chancellor, to these virulent attacks. He said that 'some of what was said was undermining the rule of law'.

In February 2025, the Lady Chief Justice, Baroness Carr criticised the Prime Minister, Sir Keir Starmer, and the Leader of the Opposition, Kemi Badenoch, over comments made the previous week at Prime Minister's Questions. Both Sir Keir and Mrs Badenoch attacked a tribunal's decision purportedly allowing a Palestinian family to come to Britain via the Ukrainian refugee programme, although an analysis of the judgment shows its decision was not based on the Ukrainian scheme. Sir Keir stated that the decision was 'completely wrong' and that the Home Secretary was working to close the 'loophole' in the scheme.

In response Baroness Carr expressed that she had been 'deeply troubled' by the comments which were 'unacceptable'. She added: 'It is for the government visibly to respect and protect the independence of the judiciary. Where parties, including the government, disagree with their findings, they should do so through the appellate process.'

A Government spokesperson replied: 'The Prime Minister has made clear that it is for Parliament to make the laws and for the Government to decide policy.'

There does seem to be some disagreement between the Government and judiciary regarding the precise scope of this convention.

In the Queen's Speech of May 2022, the previous Conservative Government stated that it wanted to 'restore the balance of power between the legislature and the courts by introducing a Bill of Rights'. Although the Conservative Government subsequently dropped its proposals for a British Bill of Rights, this suggests that the Conservative Government was deeply unhappy about court decisions such as those in *Miller (No 1)* and *Miller (No 2)/Cherry*. Critics of these decisions argue that the courts are trespassing into political realms and usurping the functions of government, thereby damaging settled constitutional arrangements. Conversely, supporters of these decisions argue that they uphold the core principles of parliamentary sovereignty and government accountability to Parliament, and that the problematic relationship is the one between the executive and legislature; the main causes for concern are the executive's growing arbitrary power and Parliament's diminishing capacity to hold ministers to account.

Vigorous debates regarding the relationships between the branches of state are going to continue. Critically evaluating the opposing arguments will help you to develop your own views concerning the robustness of the UK's constitution in upholding democratic values.

(b) Parliament and the judiciary

(i) The Safety of Rwanda (Asylum and Immigration) Act 2024

The Safety of Rwanda (Asylum and Immigration) Act 2024 ('the Rwanda Act') was a very controversial Act enacted under the previous Conservative Government to facilitate the removal of certain asylum seekers to Rwanda. In *R (AAA) (Syria) v Secretary of State for the Home Department* [2023] UKSC 42, the Supreme Court ruled that Government policy to remove asylum seekers to Rwanda was unlawful due to serious concerns regarding the country's safety. Sending asylum seekers there would have breached their rights under international treaties, including the ECHR; accordingly, the Government would have been unable to send people to Rwanda without breaching its duty in s 6 of the HRA 1998 not to act incompatibly with Convention rights.

As part of the UK Government's response to address the Supreme Court's concerns regarding Rwanda's safety, Parliament enacted the Rwanda Act to make the removal arrangements lawful. A key purpose of the Act was to give effect to 'the judgement of Parliament that the Republic of Rwanda is a safe country'.

Significant provisions in the Rwanda Act included:

- Designation of Rwanda as a safe country: All decision-makers, including immigration officers and courts, were required conclusively to treat Rwanda as a safe country for asylum and immigration purposes. This designation aimed to prevent legal challenges using the argument that Rwanda was unsafe.
- Disapplication of HRA 1998: Specific provisions of the HRA 1998, including s 3, were disapplied in relation to decisions concerning the removal of individuals to Rwanda. The intention was to ensure that Convention rights could not be invoked to prevent the Government from sending people to Rwanda.
- Limitations on legal challenges: A limited scope of review existed where there was 'compelling evidence' that the individual circumstances of a person meant there was a real risk of harm to that person in Rwanda, but there was an express prohibition of review on the grounds that Rwanda was unsafe in general.

Bodies such as the Law Society, the Bar Council and the Bingham Centre for Human Rights criticised the Rwanda Act on separation of powers and rule of law grounds. While it was perfectly acceptable for the Government to respond to a Supreme Court judgment by asking Parliament to pass legislation changing the law, the Rwanda Act required courts to treat as a fact something that might not be a fact, namely that Rwanda was a safe country even if there were overwhelming evidence to the contrary. The way the Rwanda Act sought to preclude judicial scrutiny of decisions to remove people to Rwanda contravened the separation of powers, as judicial scrutiny of government decisions is a vital check and balance. The Rwanda Act also risked breaching the Government's obligations under international law.

Conversely, supporters of the Act such as Policy Exchange argued that Parliament was entitled to legislate based on its own understanding of the relevant facts and its evaluation of their significance. Assessing Rwanda's safety was a political, not judicial, issue and so not a matter for the courts.

The Border Security, Asylum and Immigration Bill will repeal the Rwanda Act, but it remains an interesting example of the interaction between the three branches of government in the UK.

(ii) The Post Office (Horizon System) Offences Act 2024

The Post Office (Horizon System) Offences Act 2024 has also raised rule of law and separation of powers concerns. It was enacted to address the wrongful convictions of over 900 sub-postmasters for crimes such as theft and false accounting due to faults in the Post Office's Horizon IT system. The Act provided for the automatic quashing of these convictions.

Some commentators argued that the Post Office Act infringed upon the separation of powers because Parliament was usurping the proper role of the courts by enacting legislation to overturn criminal convictions. Instead, the Government should have introduced a fast-track scheme enabling the courts to overturn the convictions. However, while the Government acknowledged that using legislation was an unprecedented and wholly exceptional legal solution to a miscarriage of justice of unparalleled scale and impact, it argued that it did not set a constitutional precedent.

Summary

In this chapter, you have looked at what is meant by the idea of the rule of law by examining first Dicey's views on this subject and then Raz's and Lord Bingham's more modern versions. You have considered whether the rule of law is merely a formal concept or whether it also embraces substantive elements such as the protection of human rights.

You have also considered the meaning and historical development of the theory of the separation of powers. You have also analysed the relationship between the different branches of state in the UK by considering the degree of overlap and separation between these branches. You have done this in the context of the following relationships:

- Executive/legislature
- Executive/judiciary
- Legislature/judiciary

You have observed that in the UK separation of powers is achieved by a combination of constitutional conventions and statute, in particular the Constitutional Reform Act 2005.

You have begun to assess the extent to which the UK constitution demonstrates an effective separation of powers. There is considerable overlap between the executive and legislature, but a substantial degree of separation between the judiciary and the other branches of government. There is also considerable debate about the appropriateness of the current structures arising from judgments of the Supreme Court in cases such as *Miller (No 1)* and *Miller (No 2)/Cherry* and the extent to which the courts should intervene in political issues.

You should also check your understanding by considering the summary diagram in **Figure 7.2**.

Figure 7.2 Separation of powers in the UK

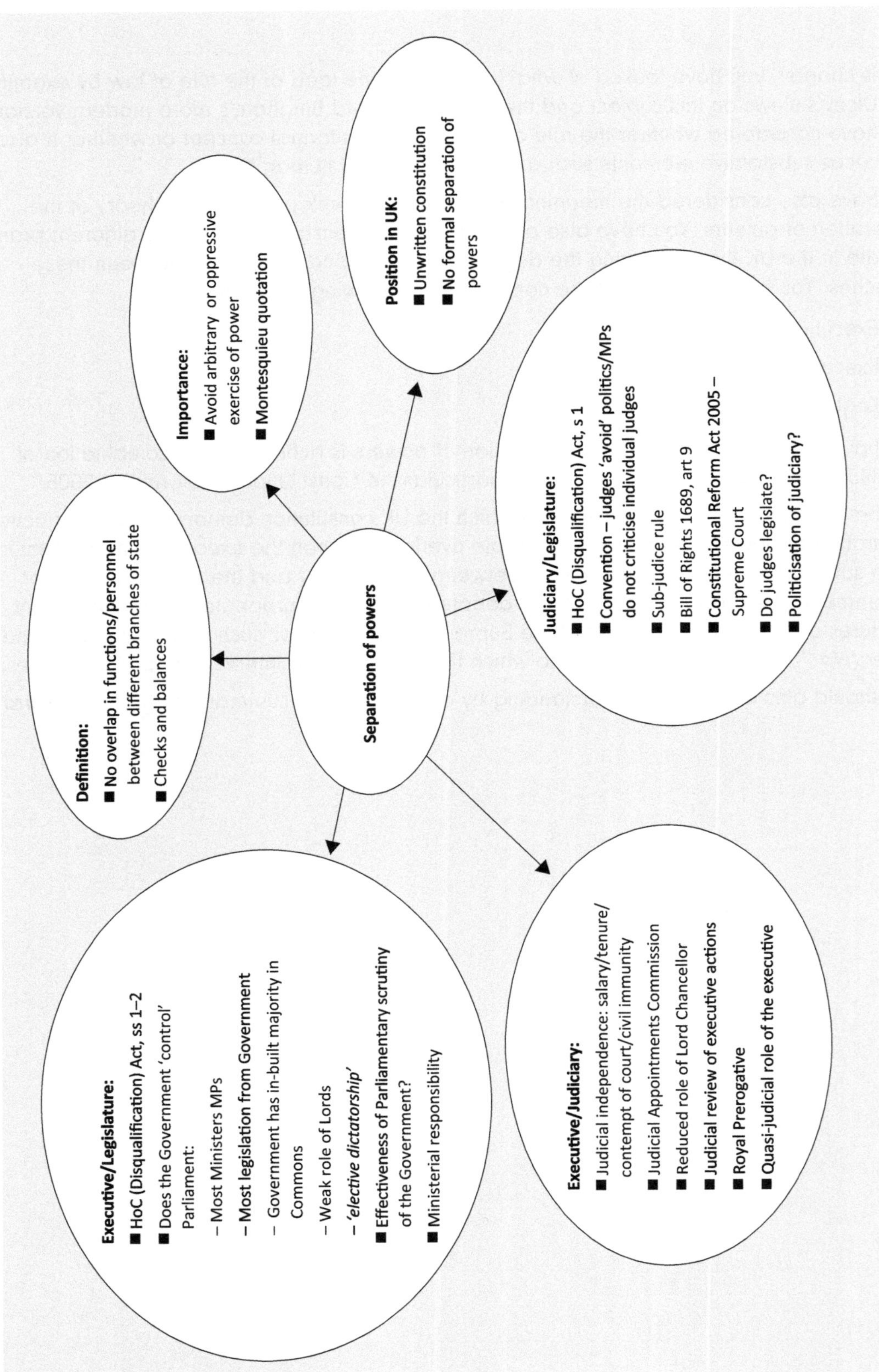

8 Devolution

Learning outcomes

By the end of this chapter you should be able to:

- describe the creation of the Scottish Parliament, the Senedd Cymru of Wales (the Welsh Parliament) and the Northern Ireland Assembly;
- describe the composition of the devolved institutions (legislative and executive);
- understand and analyse the powers of the devolved legislatures;
- analyse the relationship between the devolved institutions and the UK Government and Parliament; and
- understand the role of the courts regarding devolution issues.

8.1 The United Kingdom

The United Kingdom of Great Britain and Northern Ireland consists of four countries: England, Wales, Scotland and Northern Ireland. The union evolved over several centuries in stages.

8.1.1 Scotland

Scotland was a separate country with a separate legal system and constitution until the Act of Union 1707. From the accession of James I (VI of Scotland) in 1603 Scotland had shared the same monarch as England and Wales. The effect of the Act of Union (and similar Scottish legislation) was to abolish the separate Parliaments of England and Wales, and Scotland, and to create a single Parliament of Great Britain, with authority over all three countries. In certain key areas, for example the legal system, education and local government, Scotland has remained distinct from England.

8.1.2 Wales

Wales was militarily conquered by Edward I, the English King, in 1283 and after that English influence steadily grew. Under Henry VIII, the English Parliament passed the Laws in Wales Acts 1535–1542 (subsequently labelled the Acts of Union) under which Wales was effectively incorporated into England. The Welsh were granted the same rights as the King's subjects in England, and Welsh constituencies were added to the House of Commons. English was declared to be the official language of the law.

Over the centuries that followed there was only limited constitutional recognition of the distinctiveness of Wales, and it was not until 1964 that the UK Government created the cabinet post of Secretary of State for Wales. The Welsh Language Act 1967 permitted the use of the Welsh language in legal proceedings in Wales.

8.1.3 Northern Ireland

Although the Crown claimed authority over the whole of Ireland from 1541, Ireland retained its own Parliament until 1800. Before 1800, the Parliament of Great Britain claimed a disputed authority to legislate for Ireland. The issue was resolved by the Act of Union 1800, which united the Kingdoms of Great Britain and Ireland, abolished the Irish Parliament and established the legislative supremacy of the Parliament of Great Britain and Ireland, which had (protestant) Irish representation.

As a result of armed conflict in Ireland the Government of Ireland Act 1920 divided Ireland between six of the counties of Ulster in the north, and the rest of Ireland, the south. The 1920 Act provided for the creation of separate Parliaments for Northern and Southern Ireland with the power to legislate for their respective territories, subject to the exclusion of certain matters that were reserved to the Westminster Parliament.

However, the Southern Ireland Parliament never came into being as in 1922, following the signing of the Anglo-Irish Treaty, the southern counties were given Dominion status (similar to that of Canada for example) making them in effect self-governing as a 'Free State' (the Irish Free State (Constitution) Act 1922). The UK Parliament retained ultimate authority until 1937 when the Irish Government unilaterally adopted an independent constitution. It was not until 1949 that the UK Parliament accepted this loss of supremacy (in the Ireland Act 1949).

From 1922 until 1972 Northern Ireland had its own legislature (the 'Stormont Parliament'). Northern Ireland continued to be represented by MPs in the House of Commons, and Parliament retained supremacy over Northern Ireland. Due to the sectarian violence in Northern Ireland, known as 'the Troubles', the UK Government suspended the Stormont Parliament in 1972 and introduced direct rule pursuant to the Northern Ireland (Temporary Provisions) Act 1972. The Northern Ireland Constitution Act 1973 subsequently abolished the Stormont Parliament and replaced it with a Northern Ireland Assembly in an attempt to restore devolved government. However, the Assembly collapsed in 1974 and the Northern Ireland Act 1974 then made provision for the Government of Northern Ireland. The 1974 Act authorised the dissolution of the Northern Ireland Assembly and transferred its legislative powers to the Queen in Council, ie the UK Government.

In April 1998 the UK Government agreed proposals for constitutional change with the Irish Government and various political parties in Northern Ireland, culminating in the Belfast or Good Friday Agreement which brought an end to the Troubles. The proposals were submitted to the electorate in both Northern Ireland and the Republic of Ireland in May 1998, and approved by referendum. As a result, Parliament passed the Northern Ireland Act (NIA) 1998, which devolved legislative powers to a new Northern Ireland Assembly and created a 'power-sharing executive'. Further details are at **8.5.3** below.

However, in January 2017 the Northern Ireland executive collapsed and was not reconstituted until January 2020. Following the Assembly elections in May 2022, it has not been possible to form a new executive; the executive ministers who held office before the elections remain in post, but only on a caretaker basis.

8.2 Devolution

The United Kingdom is a unitary state. Although it comprises four countries, the Westminster Parliament is sovereign and can, in theory at least, pass whatever legislation it likes for all four countries. It is the one principal source of legal power in the UK and has the competence to legislate for the whole of the UK at all levels. This is in contrast to a federal state where the constitution gives powers to different levels of government, the federal government and state governments, as in the USA and Germany. In a federal state the constitution will allocate certain powers to the federal government, usually those relating to foreign policy, defence, immigration, tariffs and responsibility for the country's currency. There will be certain powers that can be exercised concurrently by the federal and state governments, whilst the constitution will allocate other powers such as education and ownership of property exclusively to the states.

In a modern state the division of powers between federal and state governments can raise highly complex legal issues, but in simple terms if the federal government passes legislation on a matter exclusively allocated to the states, then the courts can strike that legislation down.

The UK remains a unitary state despite devolution. The UK Parliament has devolved legislative powers in many fields to the Scottish and Welsh Parliaments and Northern Ireland Assembly. However, the crucial difference between the UK and a federal state is that the UK Parliament has delegated certain powers to the devolved legislatures and legally could revoke those powers. The UK Parliament remains supreme, and so retains the power to legislate on all devolved matters and to override the devolved legislatures. Whilst overriding the devolved legislatures could have very significant political consequences, it is legally possible for the UK Parliament to do so. Unlike in a federal state, power is not divided between the different levels of government. Instead, the UK Parliament has delegated some of its powers to the devolved legislatures without giving up those powers.

The political and legal impact of devolution has nonetheless been significant. The UK has moved from being a very centralised state with power concentrated in London to one where, in some areas at least, power is dispersed across the four countries.

There have been suggestions that the UK should move towards a federal structure, and the next activity considers this issue.

Activity 1 A federal UK?

Do you think it would be problematic incorporating England in a federal structure?

Comment

The position of England in a federation would indeed be one of the main problems in setting up a federal UK. About 85% of the UK's population lives in England, but there is little appetite for setting up an English parliament distinct from the UK Parliament. There is also little support for setting up regional assembles in England. While there has been some devolution of powers to elected mayors in England and the Labour Government has plans for further devolution, a fully-fledged federal UK seems a remote prospect in the immediate future.

8.3 Scotland

The first attempt at devolution in Scotland occurred in the late 1970s. The Scotland Act 1978 provided for the creation of a devolved assembly, subject to confirmation in a referendum. The Act also required 40% of the eligible electorate to vote in favour of devolution. However, although a majority of those voting supported the creation of the assembly, they represented only 32.9% of the eligible electorate.

Following the election of a new Labour Government in May 1997, the Referendums (Scotland and Wales) Act 1997 paved the way for referendums on devolution in Wales and Scotland, and a substantial majority of Scottish voters supported the creation of a Scottish Parliament.

According to s 63A of the Scotland Act 1998 (added by the Scotland Act 2016), the Scottish Parliament and Scottish Government are a permanent part of the constitutional arrangements of the UK; accordingly, neither institution may be abolished unless the people of Scotland vote for this in a referendum.

8.3.1 The Scottish Parliament

The Scotland Act 1998 established the Scottish Parliament and Scottish Executive (now Scottish Government). The Scottish Parliament has 129 members, known as Members of the Scottish Parliament (MSPs). Of these, 73 are constituency members and 56 are regional members. Originally the Scottish Parliament's constituencies were the same as those for the Westminster Parliament, but following devolution the number of Scottish Westminster constituencies was reduced to reflect the population of Scotland more accurately. The constituency MSPs are elected using the first past the post system, whilst seven regional members are elected from each of eight Scottish regions. The Scottish Parliament has a Presiding Officer (equivalent to the Speaker) assisted by two or more deputies. In Scottish parliamentary elections 16- and 17-year-olds are able to vote.

Initially elections for the Scottish Parliament took place every four years, but the Scottish Elections (Reform) Act 2020, an Act of the Scottish Parliament, extended this to five years. An early (extraordinary) election will take place if two-thirds of MSPs vote in favour of it or Parliament does not nominate a First Minister within 28 days of an election due to:

- the First Minister resigning or otherwise ceasing to be First Minister; or
- the First Minister ceasing to be an MSP otherwise than by dissolution of Parliament.

The First Minister must resign if the Government loses a vote of no confidence.

The last election took place on 6 May 2021 and the next one is scheduled for 7 May 2026. If an extraordinary general election takes place, it is in addition to any scheduled ordinary general elections unless taking place less than six months before the due date of an ordinary general election, in which case the ordinary election would be cancelled.

The 1998 Act gave the Scottish Parliament the power to pass primary legislation. Once the Scottish Parliament has passed a bill and it has received Royal Assent, it is known as an Act of the Scottish Parliament.

8.3.2 Devolved matters

The 1998 Act devolved to the Scottish Parliament all matters other than reserved matters. This is known as the 'reserved powers' model, in that the Scottish Parliament has the power to legislate on all matters that are not expressly reserved to Westminster. Thus, the Scottish Parliament has the power to legislate over a wide range of matters, including health, education, much of civil and criminal law, and local government. Other functions (including responsibility for the constitution, foreign policy and defence) are retained by the UK Parliament.

Following the election of a Scottish National Party Government in Scotland, a referendum took place in 2014 on whether Scotland should become an independent state and leave the UK. During the campaign, the UK Government promised to devolve further powers to Scotland should Scottish voters decide against independence. As Scottish voters voted against independence, the UK Parliament then devolved further powers on the Scottish Parliament. The Scottish Parliament therefore now has significant tax-raising powers. Since 2015, it has had the power to levy its own Scottish Landfill Tax (a tax on the disposal of waste to landfill) in place of the UK Landfill Tax and a Land and Buildings Transaction Tax in place of the UK's Stamp Duty Land Tax (SDLT). It also intends to levy Air Departure Tax (ADT) to replace Air Passenger Duty, a tax levied on passengers departing from UK airports, but ADT has not, at the time of writing, yet come into force.

Originally, the Scottish Parliament also had the power to raise or cut income tax by 3p in the pound, a power it never used. Since April 2016 the Scottish Parliament has had the power to set a different rate of income tax in Scotland, known as the Scottish Rate of Income Tax (SRIT). Since April 2017 it has had the power to set the tax band thresholds (excluding the personal allowance) as well as the rates. This applies to all non-savings and non-dividend income of Scottish taxpayers. Accordingly, while outside Scotland the additional rate of income tax for income over £125,140 is 45%, the rate in Scotland is 48%.

8.3.2.1 Legislative competence

The Scotland Act 1998 provides that an Act of the Scottish Parliament is not law so far as any of its provisions are outside the legislative competence of the Parliament, and expressly specifies which areas are outside its competence. Provisions outside its legislative competence are those that:

- would form part of the law of any territory other than Scotland;
- relate to reserved matters;
- modify certain enactments, including specified provisions of the Union with Scotland Act 1706 and the Union with England Act 1707 so far as they relate to the freedom of trade, certain specified provisions of the European Communities Act 1972 (until the transition period ended), the European Union (Withdrawal) Act (EUWA) 2018 and the Human Rights Act 1998;
- are incompatible with the ECHR and, until the transition period ended, with European Union law; or
- would remove the Lord Advocate from their position as head of the systems of criminal prosecution and investigation of deaths.

The Scottish Parliament has the power to amend or repeal Acts of the UK Parliament provided the subject-matter falls within its legislative competence. Any such amendment or repeal would, however, only be effective in relation to Scotland.

The minister in charge of a bill must make a statement that, in their view, the provisions of the bill are within the Scottish Parliament's legislative competence. The Presiding Officer must also make a statement on legislative competence, but this differs from that of the minister in charge. Whilst the minister's statement must assert the Parliament's legislative competence, the Presiding Officer's statement may, with reasons, indicate that in their opinion the bill is outside its competence. A statement by the Presiding Officer in such terms does not preclude the bill from proceeding. Neither opinion is, however, conclusive on the Parliament's legislative competence. Therefore, the Advocate General (the UK Government's chief adviser legal adviser on Scots law), the Lord Advocate (see **8.3.3** below) or the Attorney General may refer to the Supreme Court the question whether a bill or any of its provisions are within the Parliament's legislative competence.

The Scotland Act 1998 also provides that where a provision in an Act of the Scottish Parliament could be read as being outside its legislative competence, such a provision is to be read as narrowly as is required for it to be within competence, if such a reading is possible (s 101(2)).

The next example illustrates some points regarding legislative competence.

Example

The minister in charge of two bills being presented to the Scottish Parliament has asked for advice on whether they can make a statement that the bills are within the Parliament's legislative competence. The minister's main concern is that both bills amend Acts of the UK Parliament. One of the bills relates to public health, while the other amends the EUWA 2018. Can the minister make a statement that the bills are within the Parliament's legislative competence?

The Scottish Parliament has power to amend Acts of the UK Parliament unless the subject-matter of the bill is outside its legislative competence.

Acts of the UK Parliament are not in themselves reserved matters. The subject matter of some Acts are reserved matters, but for an Act to be a reserved matter it must be specifically listed in the devolution legislation. There are some protected statutes, including the EUWA 2018, which the Scottish Parliament cannot amend.

Accordingly, the minister can make a statement that the bill relating to public health is within the Scottish Parliament's legislative competence. However, the bill amending the EUWA 2018 is outwith the Scottish Parliament's legislative competence.

8.3.3 The Scottish Government

The Scottish Government is headed by the First Minister, currently John Swinney, who is appointed by the Monarch. The First Minister will normally be the leader of the largest party in the Scottish Parliament, currently the Scottish National Party. The Scottish Government also includes:

- ministers and junior ministers appointed by the First Minister with Parliament's agreement and the approval of the Monarch; and
- the Lord Advocate and the Solicitor-General for Scotland (equivalent to the Attorney General and Solicitor-General in the UK Government) recommended by the First Minister with Parliament's agreement but appointed by the Monarch.

The cabinet consists of 10 Scottish Ministers, including the First Minister. There are also 18 Junior Scottish Ministers.

8.3.4 The Sewel Convention

In July 1998, during the passage of the Scotland Act 1998 through the UK Parliament, the UK Government announced that a convention would be established that Westminster would not normally legislate on devolved matters in Scotland without the consent of the Scottish Parliament. This convention has been labelled 'the Sewel Convention' after Lord Sewel, the minister who first announced the policy. The convention was also extended to Wales and Northern Ireland, and was incorporated in a series of memorandums of understanding between the UK Government and the devolved administrations.

There is now statutory recognition of the Sewel Convention, as the Scotland Act 2016 added a provision to the 1998 Act providing that the UK Parliament 'will not normally legislate with regard to devolved matters without the consent of the Scottish Parliament' (s 28(8)). However, this does not affect s 28(7) of the 1998 Act, which provides that the creation of the Scottish Parliament does not affect the power of the UK Parliament to make laws for Scotland. The Sewel Convention does not affect parliamentary sovereignty. The Supreme Court affirmed this in R *(Miller) v Secretary of State for Exiting the European Union* [2017] UKSC 5 (*Miller (No 1)*) by holding that the Sewel Convention, despite its recognition in statute, created no legal obligation on the UK Parliament to seek the consent of the Scottish Parliament before passing legislation to leave the European Union. Whilst the Sewel Convention provides a political constraint on the Westminster Parliament, it is not the role of the courts to police it.

When the UK Parliament wants to legislate on a matter devolved to the Scottish Parliament, it will, pursuant to the Sewel Convention, seek the Scottish Parliament's consent before enacting the legislation in question. The Scottish Parliament will give its consent through Legislative Consent Motions (LCMs). LCMs are often uncontroversial. For example, suppose the UK Parliament is considering legislation extending to Scotland that pertains to both devolved and reserved matters, for example because it deals with technical issues that are sensibly handled on a UK-wide basis. If the Scottish Parliament supports the legislation, it is more convenient for the UK Parliament to deal with it. This avoids the need for two pieces of legislation, an Act of the UK Parliament and an Act of the Scottish Parliament.

Whilst the Scottish Parliament has often been willing to pass LCMs, it has refused to do so regarding much of the legislation regarding the UK's withdrawal from the European Union. For example, it refused consent to the EUWA 2018 and the European Union (Withdrawal Agreement) Act 2020. Indeed, all three devolved legislatures refused consent to the 2020 Act. Nonetheless, the UK Parliament proceeded with their enactment.

8.4 Wales

As with Scotland, there was also an abortive attempt at devolution in the late 1970s. Under the then Labour Government, Parliament passed the Wales Act 1978, which provided for the creation of a devolved assembly in Wales if Welsh voters supported it in a referendum. However, in the ensuing Welsh referendum, 80% of the electorate voted against devolution.

Following the election of the new Labour Government in May 1997, in the referendum triggered by the Referendums (Scotland and Wales) Act 1997, there was a very narrow majority in favour of devolution. Parliament then enacted the Government of Wales Act 1998, which established the National Assembly of Wales. The 1998 Act granted the National Assembly the power to pass delegated legislation in certain specified fields. In contrast to the reserved powers model, this was termed a 'conferred powers' model as it limited the competence of the National Assembly to those powers specifically granted to it.

Initially there was no distinction between the legislative and executive branches of the National Assembly, but the Government of Wales Act (GWA) 2006 split it into two parts, the National Assembly (the legislature – now the Senedd Cymru) and the Welsh Assembly Government, now simply called the Welsh Government (the executive). Section A1 of the GWA 2006 declares these institutions to be a permanent part of the UK's constitutional arrangements in the same way as their Scottish counterparts. Accordingly, they can only be abolished following a referendum.

8.4.1 Senedd Cymru/Welsh Parliament

The Senedd and Elections (Wales) Act 2020, an Act of the National Assembly, provided for the National Assembly to be renamed as Senedd Cymru or the Welsh Parliament, commonly known as the Senedd. Acts of the Assembly are now known as Acts of the Senedd, whilst Assembly Members (AMs) are now known as Members of the Senedd (MSs).

The Senedd has 60 MSs, of which 40 are elected to represent the same Welsh constituencies as are used in elections for the UK Parliament whilst a further 20 are elected to represent the five electoral regions of Wales, based on a system of proportional representation. Those aged 16 and 17 years are now able to vote in Senedd elections. The Senedd Cymru (Members and Elections) Act 2024 increases the number of MSs to 96 with effect from the May 2026 elections due to the increase in the Senedd's responsibilities. It also changes the Senedd's electoral system so that all MSs are elected via closed list proportional representation.

Originally, elections were to be held every four years, but they currently take place every five years with the next election scheduled for 7 May 2026. However, after the 2026 election the Senedd Cymru (Members and Elections) Act 2024 provides that elections will once again take place every four years. An early (extraordinary) election will be triggered in similar circumstances to those in which one would be triggered in Scotland (see **8.3.1** above). The

Labour Party won 30 of the 60 seats in the May 2021 elections and governed Wales with the aid of a co-operation agreement with Plaid Cymru, the Welsh nationalist party until May 2024 when Plaid Cymru withdrew from the agreement. The Labour Party continues in office even though it is one seat short of an overall majority.

The GWA 2006 also paved the way for the extension of the National Assembly's legislative powers, as it conferred the power on the National Assembly to pass primary legislation, known as Acts of the Assembly (now Acts of the Senedd). The procedure for passing an Act of the Senedd is similar to passing an Act of the UK Parliament, as the Senedd must pass a bill, which becomes an Act when it receives Royal Assent. However, the provisions extending the National Assembly's powers had to be approved by a referendum before they could come into force. A referendum took place in 2011 and the electorate voted in favour of them. The 2011 Act gave the Assembly the power to pass legislation in 21 broad subject areas such as agriculture, education, health, the environment, housing, local government and tourism. There were some exceptions; for example, on health the National Assembly could not legislate on health and human embryology.

Subsequently the Wales Act 2017 changed the devolution settlement by moving to a reserved powers model (see **8.3.2** above). This means that the Senedd has the power to pass legislation on all matters that are not explicitly reserved to the Westminster Parliament, such as defence, foreign affairs and immigration. This is the same model that is used for Scotland and Northern Ireland. Whilst some reserved matters are common to all three devolved legislatures, such as constitutional matters, immigration, defence and foreign affairs, others are not. For example, criminal justice is largely a devolved matter in Scotland and Northern Ireland, but a reserved matter in Wales (though there are discussions under way about devolving criminal justice to the Senedd). The Senedd also has some powers regarding taxation, as in April 2018 two taxes, the Land Transaction Tax (LTT) and Landfill Disposals Tax (LDT) were devolved. The LTT, a tax on property transactions, replaced SDLT in Wales whilst LDT replaced the UK Landfill Tax.

Like the Scottish Parliament, an Act outside the Senedd's legislative competence is not law (GWA 2006, s 108A(1)). Very similar restrictions apply to the Senedd's legislative competence as apply to the Scottish Parliament (GoWA 2006, s 108A; also see **8.3.2.1** above). Thus, the minister introducing a bill to the Senedd and the Presiding Officer (the Senedd's equivalent of the Speaker) must make statements regarding whether the provisions of the bill are within the Senedd's legislative competence. Similarly, the Counsel General (see **8.4.2** below) or the Attorney General may refer the question whether a bill, or any provision of a bill, is within the Senedd's legislative competence to the Supreme Court. Where any provision of an Act of the Senedd could be read in such a way as to be outside or inside the Senedd's legislative competence, it should be interpreted as being inside its competence (s 154(2)).

As a result of these changes, a significant body of law pertaining only to Wales is coming into being. Although England and Wales remain a single jurisdiction, there are now some calls for Wales to become a separate jurisdiction in its own right, as are Scotland and Northern Ireland. Indeed, s A2 of the GWA 2006 (added by the Wales Act) recognises the existence of Welsh law, although the provisions fall short of recognising Wales as a separate jurisdiction, as Welsh law is described as being part of the law of England and Wales

8.4.2 The Welsh Government

The Welsh Government is headed by the First Minister, currently Eluned Morgan, appointed by the Monarch after having been nominated by the Senedd. The First Minister recommends for appointment, by the Monarch, the Counsel General to the Welsh Government (equivalent to the Attorney General in the UK Government) and appoints up to 12 Welsh ministers and deputy ministers (with the approval of the Monarch) to serve in the cabinet. The Senedd Cymru (Members and Elections) Act 2024 increases with effect from the May 2026 election the legislative limit on the size of the Welsh Government to 17 (plus the First Minister and Counsel General), with power to further increase the limit to 18 or 19.

8.4.3 The Sewel Convention

The Sewel Convention discussed at **8.3.3** above also applies to Wales. The Wales Act 2017 added to the GWA 2006 provisions giving statutory recognition to the Sewel Convention; see now s 107(5) and (6). These are identical to those applying in Scotland.

The next example illustrates the limits of the Sewel Convention.

Example

The UK Parliament has passed an Act (fictitious) creating a new criminal offence in England and Wales. The criminal offence relates to a matter that has not been reserved to the UK Parliament. The Senedd Cymru has not passed a legislative consent motion in relation to the Act as it opposed the legislation. A man has been prosecuted for committing the new criminal offence in Wales. The man claims that he has not committed a criminal offence as the Act creating it is unenforceable in Wales.

The Westminster Parliament remains sovereign notwithstanding devolution. It can therefore pass Acts for the whole of the UK pertaining to devolved matters even in the face of opposition from the devolved legislatures. Although the Sewel Convention provides that the UK Parliament will not normally legislate on a devolved matter without the devolved legislature's consent, it has the competence to do so as the Sewel Convention is not legally enforceable. The courts will accordingly reject the man's claim.

8.5 Northern Ireland

8.5.1 The Good Friday Agreement

Following often violent conflict starting in the late 1960s (often described as 'the Troubles'), multi-party negotiations between the British and Irish governments and the main Northern Irish political parties culminated in the 'Good Friday Agreement' (or 'Belfast Agreement') of April 1998. As part of the constitutional settlement for Northern Ireland, the Irish Government agreed to amend the Irish Constitution to recognise that a united Ireland shall be brought about only by peaceful means with the consent of a majority of the people in both Northern Ireland and the Irish Republic. Section 1 of the NIA 1998, which the UK Parliament enacted following the Good Friday Agreement, provides that Northern Ireland shall not cease to be part of the UK without the consent of a majority of the people of Northern Ireland voting in a referendum.

There are three strands to the Good Friday Agreement:

(a) The first strand provides for a democratically elected assembly with a power-sharing executive;

(b) The second is the North/South Ministerial Council, comprising ministers from Northern Ireland and the Irish Republic. It co-operates and develops policies on matters of mutual interest within the island of Ireland in fields such as agriculture, education and the environment.

(c) The third is the British–Irish Council, comprising representatives from the British and Irish governments, the devolved administrations (Northern Ireland, Scotland and Wales), the Isle of Man, Guernsey and Jersey. Its purpose is to promote harmonious and mutually beneficial relationships between the peoples represented in the Council.

8.5.2 The Northern Ireland Assembly

The NIA 1998 established the Northern Ireland Assembly, granting it the power to enact primary legislation, known as Acts of the Northern Ireland Assembly. A bill becomes an Act once the Assembly has passed it and it has received Royal Assent. The 1998 Act in essence followed the reserved powers model, although it uses different terminology. It grants the Assembly the competence to legislate over 'transferred matters', but defines transferred matters as all matters except for 'reserved matters' and 'excepted matters'. As with the other devolved legislatures, an Act outside the Assembly's legislative competence is not law (NIA 2018, s 6(1)).

Excepted matters will remain with the UK Government indefinitely and include international relations, defence and immigration. Reserved matters are areas where the Northern Ireland Assembly can legislate with the consent of the Secretary of State and may be devolved in the future. These include firearms and explosives, financial services and pensions regulation, broadcasting, disqualification from Assembly membership, consumer safety and intellectual property. Policing and criminal justice were originally reserved matters but in April 2010 they were devolved and so became transferred matters.

The minister in charge of a bill must make a statement on or before its introduction that in their opinion the bill is within the legislative competence of the Assembly. The Presiding Officer (the Assembly's equivalent to the Speaker) must refer to the Secretary of State any bill that the Presiding Officer considers relates to an excepted or reserved matter.

There is also some entrenched legislation that the Assembly cannot amend, the most significant including the Human Rights Act 1998, many provisions in the NIA 1998 itself, the EUWA 2018 and, until the transition period ended, the European Communities Act 1972 (NIA 1998, s 7).

Legislation that discriminates against any person or class of person on the ground of religious belief or political opinion is also outside the Assembly's competence (NIA 1998, s 6(2)(e)). Also, where primary legislation is capable of being interpreted as within the Assembly's legislative competence or outside a competence, then it should be interpreted as being within a competence (NIA 1998, s 83(2)).

The Sewel Convention applies to Northern Ireland but, unlike the position in Scotland and Wales, it does not have express statutory recognition.

The Assembly comprises 90 members known as Members of the Legislative Assembly ('MLAs'). Members are elected under the single transferable vote form of proportional representation. Originally, elections were to be held every four years, but they now take place every five years. An early (extraordinary) election will take place if two-thirds of MLAs vote in favour of it or ministerial offices are not filled within the requisite time limit. The next election must take place on or before 6 May 2027.

8.5.3 Northern Ireland Executive

Unlike most executives, the Northern Ireland Executive does not consist chiefly of members of the ruling party or parties. Due to the legacy of the Troubles, the Northern Ireland Act 1998 provides for power-sharing between the different communities in Northern Ireland. To ensure balanced community representation, there are three political designations - 'Nationalist', 'Unionist' and 'Other'. Following an Assembly election, the Assembly must appoint a First Minister ('FM'), deputy First Minister ('DFM') and Northern Ireland ministers within 14 days after the first meeting of the Assembly following an election. If it does not appoint them, the Secretary of State must propose a date for another (extraordinary) election, though to stop this happening after the 2017 election the Westminster Parliament passed legislation providing for extensions of the deadline.

The FM is the nominee of the largest political party of the largest political designation, whilst the DFM is the nominee of the largest political party of the next largest political designation. The FM and DFM hold office jointly, so that if one resigns the other ceases to hold office. Despite the different titles, the FM and DFM also have equal status.

Ongoing difficulties with the peace process in Northern Ireland have hindered the practical achievement of devolution. Northern Ireland reverted to the direct control of the relevant Secretary of State for a time during 2000 and 2001, and in fact remained under such control from late 2002 for over four years. However, following a breakthrough in negotiations between the main political parties, the power-sharing executive was restored in 2007. Subsequently, in January 2017 Martin McGuinness of Sinn Féin resigned as DFM in a protest over what has been called the 'Renewable Heat Incentive scandal' and this led to the collapse of the Northern Ireland Executive. It was not until January 2020 that the Northern Irish political parties were able to agree on a new FM and DFM. However, the Democratic Unionist Party (DUP) withdrew from the executive in February 2022 as a protest against the Northern Ireland Protocol; consequently the executive ceased to function.

Elections took place in May 2022 with Sinn Féin emerging as the largest party. This is the first time a Nationalist rather than Unionist party has been the largest. However, the DUP refused to nominate a DFM due to its concerns regarding the Northern Ireland Protocol, and it was only in February 2024 that the DUP agreed to re-enter the executive. Accordingly, Sinn Féin's Michelle O'Neill became Northern Ireland's first nationalist FM, while the DUP's Emma Little-Pengelly became DFM.

The FM and DFM decide the number of ministerial offices, though these cannot exceed 10 without the Secretary of State's consent. Ministers are appointed by the Assembly based on the share of seats held by the political parties, save for the Minister of Justice who is appointed through a cross-community Assembly vote.

8.6 The role of the Supreme Court

As explained above, the devolved legislatures only have the competence to pass legislation on devolved matters; they cannot pass legislation on reserved matters. Both the Scotland Act 1998 and the GWA 2006 provide that whether a provision 'relates to a reserved matter' is to be determined by reference to the purpose of the provision, having regard (amongst other things) to its effect in all the circumstances. There are also other limitations on their competence; for example they cannot pass legislation infringing the ECHR. Although ministers introducing bills in the devolved legislatures and their Presiding Officers have the duty to make statements whether the provisions in bills are within their legislature's competence, it is the courts that actually decide on issues of legislative competence. The Supreme Court plays a particularly significant role in this regard.

There are three ways in which the question whether legislation passed by a devolved legislature is outside its legislative competence can come before the Supreme Court:

- through a reference by a devolved or UK law officer (including the Attorney General for England and Wales) to the Supreme Court. The law officers have the power to refer a bill that the devolved legislature has passed but has not yet received Royal Assent to the Supreme Court for a ruling on whether the bill is within the legislature's competence;
- through an appeal from certain higher courts in England and Wales, Scotland and Northern Ireland; and
- through a reference from certain appellate courts.

8.6.1 Referring a bill to the Supreme Court

References to the Supreme Court of a Bill that is before a devolved legislature to determine whether the Bill is within the legislature's legislative competence are a key aspect of devolution, as they help to determine how far the powers of the devolved legislatures extend. Both the UK Law officer (the Attorney General) and the chief law officers of each of the devolved governments (eg the Lord Advocate in Scotland) have the power to make a reference.

Section 33 of the Scotland Act 1998 gives the law officers the power to refer to the Supreme Court Bills that the Scottish Parliament has passed for a ruling on the Bill's legislative competence. Section 12 of the GWA 2006 and s 11 of the Northern Ireland Act 1998 contain equivalent procedures.

The case of *Agricultural Sector (Wales) Bill, Reference by the Attorney General for England and Wales* [2014] UKSC 43 provides an example of a reference to the Supreme Court. The bill, which the National Assembly of Wales had passed, aimed to establish a scheme regulating the wages of agricultural workers in Wales. The Attorney General disagreed with the Assembly's view that the bill was within the Assembly's competence, arguing that the bill did not relate to agriculture but to employment and industrial relations, which had not been devolved. The Supreme Court held that the bill's provisions regulating the wages of agricultural workers did 'relate to' agriculture, which was a devolved matter and thus within the Assembly's legislative competence. The Supreme Court stated that the bill's purpose was to regulate agricultural wages so that the agricultural industry in Wales would be supported and protected. It did not matter whether the bill might also be capable of being classified as relating to a matter that had not been devolved, such as employment and industrial relations. The devolution legislation did not require that a provision should only be capable of being characterised as relating to a devolved matter.

The case of *UK Withdrawal from the European Union (Legal Continuity) (Scotland) Bill 2018 – Reference by the Attorney General and Advocate General for Scotland* [2018] UKSC 64 was particularly controversial. The Scottish Parliament passed the UK Withdrawal from the European Union (Legal Continuity) (Scotland) Bill 2018 (the Continuity Bill), aimed at ensuring legal continuity in Scottish law after the UK's exit from the EU. The UK Government's law officers referred the Continuity Bill to the Supreme Court, arguing that its provisions were outside the Scottish Parliament's competence.

The Supreme Court stated that, at the time of the Continuity Bill's passage, most of its provisions were within the Scottish Parliament's legislative competence. However, the UK Parliament subsequently enacted the EUWA 2018, which provided that some of the matters covered by the Continuity Bill should become reserved matters. This resulted in many more provisions of the Continuity Bill being outside the Scottish Parliament's competence.

The case of *Reference by the Attorney General and the Advocate General for Scotland – United Nations Convention on the Rights of the Child (Incorporation) (Scotland) Bill, Reference by the Attorney General and the Advocate General for Scotland – European Charter of Local Self-Government (Incorporation) (Scotland) Bill* [2021] UKSC 42 provides a further insight into the Supreme Court's approach.

The Scottish Parliament had passed two bills, the United Nations Convention on the Rights of the Child (Incorporation) (Scotland) Bill ('the UNCRC Bill') and the European Charter of Local Self-Government (Incorporation) (Scotland) Bill ('the ECLSG Bill'). The UNCRC Bill and the ECLSG Bill each aimed to give effect in Scots law to two international treaties, the United Nations Convention on the Rights of the Child ('the UNCRC') and the European Charter of Local Self-Government ('the ECLSG') respectively. Although the UK Government has ratified them both, they have not been incorporated into domestic UK law. Accordingly, both Bills aimed to incorporate the treaties concerned into domestic Scots law.

The UK Government's law officers referred to the Supreme Court whether certain provisions of the Bills were within the legislative competence of the Scottish Parliament. The UK law officers accepted that the Scottish Parliament could incorporate these treaties into domestic law in some manner; however, they claimed the Bills as drafted would modify s 28(7) of the Scotland

Act 1998, which provides that the power of the Scottish Parliament to make laws does not affect the power of the UK Parliament to make laws for Scotland. According to the UK law officers, the Bills did affect the UK Parliament's power to make laws for Scotland and so was outside the Scottish Parliament's legislative competence.

The Supreme Court examined the following provisions in the UNCRC Bill:

(i) provisions empowering the courts to strike down provisions in Acts of the UK Parliament which were incompatible with the UNCRC where those Acts were passed before the coming into force of the UNCRC Bill; and

(ii) provisions empowering the courts to make declarators (the Scottish equivalent of declarations) of incompatibility of Acts of the UK Parliament which were incompatible with the UNCRC where those Acts were passed after the coming into force of the UNCRC Bill.

The Supreme Court agreed with the UK law officers and held that these provisions would affect the power of the UK Parliament to make laws for Scotland. Allowing existing legislation to remain in force unamended is one of the ways in which the UK Parliament exercises its power to make laws for Scotland, so making the continuation in force of an Act conditional on a court deciding it complied with the UNCRC would affect the UK's Parliament to make laws for Scotland. The making of a declarator of incompatibility would impose pressure on the UK Parliament to amend or repeal the offending Act to remove the incompatibility, thereby also affecting its power to make laws for Scotland.

The Supreme Court also examined provisions in the ECLSG Bill empowering the courts to make declarators of incompatibility of Acts of the UK Parliament which were incompatible with the ECLSG. The Supreme Court applied the same approach as it did to similar provisions in the UNCRC Bill and held that they affected the UK Parliament's power to make laws for Scotland.

The Supreme Court also considered, in the case of the UNCRC Bill, a provision making it unlawful for any public authority to act incompatibly with the UNCRC. The Lord Advocate accepted that this provision was plainly outside legislative competence as there was no attempt to confine its scope to matters falling within the legislative competence of the Scottish Parliament, eg it would apply to UK Ministers applying Acts of Parliament relating to reserved matters.

The Lord Advocate argued that it should, pursuant to s 101(2) of the Scotland Act 1998, be interpreted narrowly as complying with the UNCRC. However, the Supreme Court rejected this argument as it would be inconsistent with the rule of law (which requires laws to be intelligible and accessible) to use s 101(2) in this way; it would also be going beyond interpretation as ordinarily understood.

There has been some criticism of the Supreme Court's judgment. Given that the Scottish Parliament has the power to repeal Acts of the UK Parliament in relation to Scotland, it is unclear why giving Scottish courts the power to strike down UK Acts or issue declarators of incompatibility should affect the UK's Parliament power to make laws for Scotland

The Scottish Government remained committed to both Bills, and the Scottish Parliament enacted the UNCRC Act 2024 after the original Bill had been redrafted to comply with the Supreme Court's judgment.

The cases discussed in this paragraph relate to references of Bills that had already been passed by the devolved legislatures. In contrast, the case concerning the Scottish Independence Referendum Bill, *Reference by the Lord Advocate of devolution issues under paragraph 34 of Schedule 6 to the Scotland Act 1998* [2022] UKSC 31, involved a draft bill.

The Scottish Government wanted to introduce a bill to the Scottish Parliament providing for a referendum on whether Scotland should be an independent country. Unlike the referendum held in 2014, the UK Government refused its consent to the second proposed referendum. The Lord Advocate was unsure whether the Bill was within the Scottish Parliament's legislative competence, so could not clear the required ministerial statement that it was; see **8.3.2.1** above. The Lord Advocate therefore wanted to refer the question of whether the Bill was within the Scottish Parliament's legislative competence to the Supreme Court.

The UK Government argued:

(i) that the Lord Advocate did not have the power to refer a draft Bill to the Supreme Court as the question was purely hypothetical; and

(ii) in any event, the draft Bill was outside the Scottish Parliament's legislative competence.

Judgment

(1) The Supreme Court held that the Lord Advocate did have the requisite power. Paragraph 34 of Sch 6 to the Scotland Act 1998 gave the law officers the power to refer 'devolution issues' to the Supreme Court, and whether the Scottish Parliament had legislative competence to the pass the Bill in question was a devolution issue as it related to the powers of the Scottish Parliament. Moreover, the issue was not hypothetical as the Scottish Government would submit the Bill to the Scottish Parliament should it transpire that the Bill fell within its legislative competence.

(2) However, the Supreme Court held that Bill was outside the Scottish Parliament's legislative competence as it related to reserved matters, namely the Union of the Kingdoms of Scotland and England and/or the Parliament of the United Kingdom. The Scottish Government argued that it did not relate to reserved matters as the result of the referendum would not have been legally binding. However, the Supreme Court stated that, even if a referendum had 'no immediate legal consequences', it would still be 'a political event with important political consequences', and concluded:

> It is therefore clear that the proposed Bill has more than a loose or consequential connection with the reserved matters of the Union of Scotland and England and the sovereignty of the United Kingdom Parliament.

In the absence of the UK Government's consent, the Scottish Government has been unable to proceed with the proposed referendum.

8.6.2 Appeals/references from higher/appellate courts

Significant cases involving devolution issues have also reached the Supreme Court by way of appeals from the superior courts of England and Wales, Scotland and Northern Ireland. Some of these appeals take place under the specific provisions of the Scotland Act 1998 relating to devolution issues, while others take place in the normal course of legal proceedings. Certain appellate courts can also refer devolution issues to the Supreme Court.

A case involving an appeal was *Imperial Tobacco Ltd v Lord Advocate (Scotland)* [2012] UKSC 61 regarding ss 1 and 9 of the Tobacco and Primary Medical Services (Scotland) Act 2010. Section 1 prohibited the display of tobacco products in a place where tobacco products were offered for sale, whilst s 9 prohibited vending machines for the sale of tobacco products. Imperial Tobacco applied for judicial review of these provisions, arguing that the sections in the 2010 Act related to 'the sale and supply of goods to consumers', which were reserved matters. Imperial Tobacco failed at first instance in the Court of Session and on appeal in the Inner House of the Court of Session, so appealed to the Supreme Court.

The Supreme Court stated that the rules in the Scotland Act 1998 regarding legislative competence must be interpreted in the same way as other rules found in a UK statute. Also, although the 1998 Act was a 'constitutional statute', that could not, in itself, be taken as a guide to its interpretation; it must be interpreted like any other statute. The Supreme Court then went on to reject the appeal after examining the purpose of the 2010 Act. The purpose of s 1 was to render tobacco products less visible to potential consumers and thereby achieve a reduction in sales and thus in smoking. The purpose of s 9 was to make cigarettes less readily available, particularly (but not only) to children and young people, with the aim of reducing smoking. This had no connection with any reserved matter, and so the 2010 Act was within the Scottish Parliament's legislative competence.

One question that the courts have considered is whether Acts of the devolved legislatures are subject to judicial review in the way that delegated legislation is. The next activity examines this issue.

Activity 2 Challenges to the Acts of the devolved legislatures

To what extent do you think Acts of the devolved legislatures should be judicially reviewable?

Comment

The Supreme Court has made it clear that Acts of the devolved legislatures can normally only be challenged on the grounds that they exceed the legislative competence of the legislature, for example by covering a reserved matter or violating the ECHR (*AXA General Insurance v Lord Advocate* [2011] UKSC 46). They cannot be challenged on common law grounds such as irrationality, as it would be inappropriate for the judges to substitute their opinions for the considered views of a democratically elected legislature.

Challenges to legislative competence have also arisen in the context of criminal prosecutions, as in *HM Lord Advocate v Martin* [2010] UKSC 10. The Road Traffic Offenders Act 1988 provided that the maximum sentence that a Scottish sheriff (similar to a magistrate) sitting summarily could impose for the offence of driving while disqualified under the Road Traffic Act (RTA) 1988 was six months' imprisonment or the statutory maximum fine or both. If the offence was prosecuted on indictment (triable before a jury), the maximum sentence was 12 months' imprisonment or a fine or both.

The Scottish Parliament enacted the Criminal Proceedings etc (Reform) (Scotland) Act 2007 increasing the maximum sentence that sheriffs sitting summarily could impose for the offence of driving while disqualified. The aim of the 2007 Act was to reduce pressure on the higher courts.

Two individuals were each sentenced by sheriffs to terms of more than six months' imprisonment for driving while disqualified contrary to the RTA 1988. They both challenged their sentences, claiming that the relevant provisions of the 2007 Act were outside the legislative competence of the Scottish Parliament. After the High Court of Justiciary dismissed their appeals, they appealed to the Supreme Court. The basis of their appeal was that the Scotland Act 1998 defined, under the heading 'Road Transport', the following as reserved matters: 'the Road Traffic Act 1988 and the Road Traffic Offenders Act 1988'.

The Supreme Court by a 3–2 majority rejected the appeal. The change was within the competence of the Scottish Parliament. The purpose of the provisions was to reform summary justice by reducing pressure on the higher courts by reallocating business within the Scottish court system; the jurisdiction of a sheriff was a matter of Scots criminal law, and so did not relate to a reserved matter. It was a simply a change in procedure.

8.6.3 Section 35 orders

Section 35 of the Scotland Act 1998 grants the Secretary of State for Scotland the power, in specified circumstances, to prevent legislation enacted by the Scottish Parliament being submitted for royal assent, even if it covers a devolved matter.

In December 2022, the Scottish Parliament passed the Gender Recognition Reform (Scotland) Bill, modifying the Gender Recognition Act 2004 (a UK Act) making it easier for residents of Scotland to obtain a Gender Recognition Certificate (GRC), a document which changes a person's legal sex on their birth certificate. While gender recognition is devolved in Scotland, equal opportunities is a 'reserved matter'. A GRC changes someone's legal sex for the purpose of the Equality Act 2010, and the UK Government argued that the Bill would adversely affect the Equality Act's application to reserved matters. According to the UK Government, having a different system in Scotland compared to England and Wales could cause confusion, for example in relation to the use of single-sex spaces which the Equality Act permits in certain circumstances. It could also result in an increase in fraudulent applications. The Secretary of State for Scotland therefore issued a s 35 order, effectively vetoing the Bill.

In *Scottish Ministers v Advocate General for Scotland* [2023] CSOH 89 the Outer House of the Court of Session rejected the Scottish Government's petition for judicial review of the s 35 order. However, the case could well reach the Supreme Court.

8.7 Relationships between the UK Government and the devolved administrations

The UK Government and the devolved governments agreed a memorandum of understanding in 1999 aimed at co-ordinating the overall relationship between them. The memorandum of understanding created the Joint Ministerial Committee ('JMC') that consisted of ministers from the UK and the devolved governments, including in certain circumstances the Prime Minister and the First Ministers. Despite updates to the memorandum of understanding, relations between the UK Government and devolved governments became increasingly strained, as Brexit and the Covid-19 pandemic raised questions about the operation of devolution. Accordingly, a new three-tier intergovernmental relations ('IGR') structure was introduced in January 2022 aimed at improving relations and inter-government cooperation.

The IGR structure now governs the relationship between the UK Government and the devolved governments, and aims to facilitate cooperation and coordination on matters of shared interest.

8.7.1 Committee structure

A three-tier committee structure provides for formal multilateral engagement between ministers, which is supplemented by informal interaction at both political and official levels.

8.7.1.1 The Prime Minister and Heads of Devolved Government Council

The Prime Minister and Heads of Devolved Government Council ('the Council') is the top tier of the new structure. Chaired by the Prime Minister, its membership includes the First Ministers of Scotland and Wales, as well as the First and Deputy First Ministers of Northern Ireland. Other ministers are invited as necessary.

The Council considers strategic issues affecting the UK as a whole and provides direction to the wider IGR structure.

8.7.1.2 Interministerial Standing Committee and Finance Interministerial Standing Committee

The middle tier comprises the Interministerial Standing Committee ('IMSC') and the Finance Interministerial Standing Committee ('F:ISC'), with additional time-limited committees possible for specific issues.

IMSC addresses strategic matters beyond individual portfolios and reviews portfolio-level engagement. Its membership varies but always includes ministers responsible for IGR.

F:ISC has a similar strategic role but focuses on fiscal issues, including funding and financial disputes, with finance ministers from the UK and devolved governments as members.

8.7.1.3 Interministerial Groups

Interministerial Groups (IMGs) are the lowest tier. These are intended to facilitate regular portfolio-level discussion between departmental ministers and cover devolved areas (eg culture) as well as reserved areas that have an impact on devolved matters (eg trade).

8.7.2 Other bodies/initiatives

8.7.2.1 The Intergovernmental Secretariat

The Secretariat Provides administrative support for intergovernmental meetings and drafts annual reports on IGR for scrutiny by the four legislatures. Despite being hosted in the Cabinet Office, it is accountable to the Council as a whole, rather than any single government.

8.7.2.2 Common frameworks

Operating in parallel with the IGR structures discussed above, a set of 'common frameworks' have been agreed to facilitate coordination and manage divergence in devolved policy areas that EU law previously covered, eg motor insurance, blood safety, and chemicals and pesticides.

8.7.2.3 The Council of Nations and Regions

The Council of Nations and Regions ('CNR') was set up in 2024 by the Labour Government independently from the IGR framework. Chaired by the Prime Minister, it includes the First Ministers of Scotland and Wales, as well as the First and Deputy First Ministers of Northern Ireland, the Mayor of London, and English metro mayors. Its purpose is to promote collaboration and share best practices on shared challenges. The first meeting, held in Edinburgh in October 2024, focused on attracting inward investment to support economic growth.

8.7.3 Dispute Resolution Mechanism

A formal dispute resolution system exists to prevent escalation and to encourage cooperation between governments. Disagreements should be resolved at the portfolio level if possible, with mediation sought before the start of formal procedures. An impartial body must chair the process.

While no disputes have yet been officially resolved through this system, the previous JMC protocol was invoked four times – three over funding allocations and one concerning fishing quotas.

8.7.4 United Kingdom Internal Market Act 2020

During the UK's membership of the EU, the devolved legislatures had competence over areas such as agriculture and the environment. The significance of this was minimal as the bulk of the legislation that applied in these areas emanated from the EU. Common standards therefore applied across the UK and so there were no internal trade barriers in the UK. Following the UK's exit from the EU, the devolved legislatures have the competence to legislate in these areas so it is possible, say, for Scotland to have different standards for agricultural products than the rest of the UK. This could result in a producer of English products being unable to sell their goods in Scotland if they did not comply with Scottish standards.

The UK Parliament therefore passed the United Kingdom Internal Market Act 2020 to ensure that no internal trade barriers came into being in the UK. This Act is based on the twin principles of mutual recognition and non-discrimination. While the Act in theory permits devolved governments to set their own regulations, the mutual recognition principle provides that goods and services which can be legally sold in one part of the UK can also legally be sold in all other parts. So the Scottish Government could not exclude goods that are lawfully produced to the English standards, even if the English standards are lower than the Scottish. The principle of non-discrimination prohibits devolved governments from enacting regulations that discriminate directly or indirectly between goods produced in, and services provided from, other parts of the UK.

The Scottish and Welsh Governments were very critical of the Act, arguing that it could lead to 'a race to the bottom' in regulatory standards. For example, the Scottish Government has expressed concern that the UK might agree a trade deal with the USA permitting the importation of products such as chlorinated chicken into the UK. The Act would force the Scottish Government to accept such products even if their production were banned in Scotland. However, it is possible to apply for exclusions from the Act under the common frameworks discussed at **8.7.2.2** above. Thus in 2022 the Scottish Government obtained approval from the UK Government to Scottish legislation banning the use of single use plastics, even though no such ban applies in the rest of the UK.

The UK government did not ask the devolved legislatures for their consent. Nonetheless, the Scottish Parliament held a consent vote in which it refused consent. The Welsh Government applied for a judicial review of the Act, seeking a declaration that it impliedly limited the Senedd's legislative competence. However, the Court of Appeal upheld the conclusion of the Divisional Court that it was premature to consider the issue in the absence of any specific Act of the Senedd affected by the UK Internal Market Act. Moreover, the correct procedure for determining questions of legislative competence was to refer the question to the Supreme Court (see **8.6.1** above) (*R (Counsel General for Wales) v Secretary of State for Business, Energy and Industrial Strategy* [2022] EWCA Civ 118).

Where different parties are in power in Westminster and the devolved administrations, disagreements between the Westminster Government and the devolved governments are more likely. Brexit added to the tensions, but the IGR structure outlined at **8.7** above has helped to improve relationships.

Summary

The process of devolution in its modern form began in 1998 with the enactment by the UK Parliament of legislation providing for the creation of devolved legislatures and governments in Scotland, Wales and Northern Ireland. Since 1998, the UK Parliament has granted increasing powers to the devolved legislatures - the Scottish Parliament, the Senedd Cymru or Welsh Parliament, and the Northern Ireland Assembly.

Figure 8.1 Devolution models

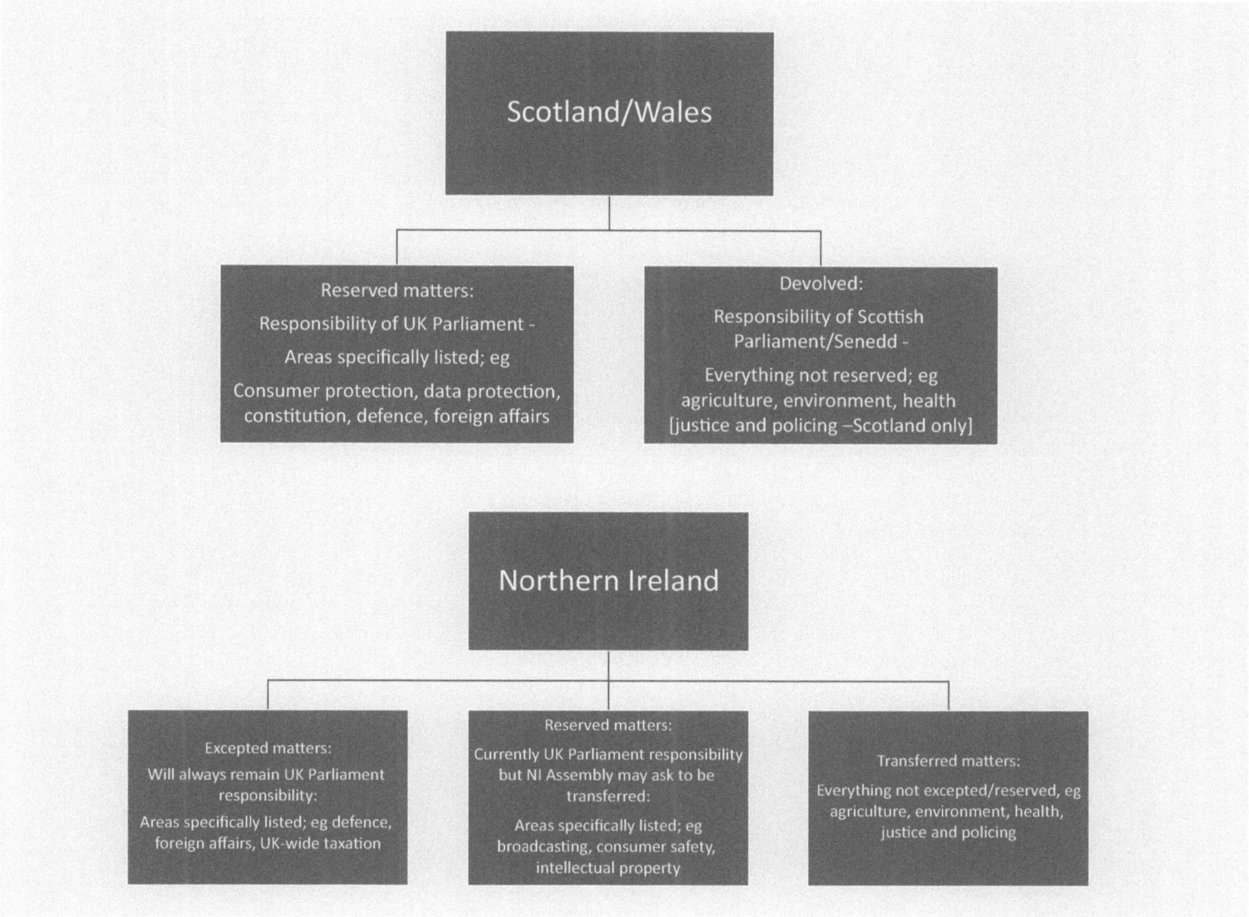

Those three legislatures can only pass Acts on devolved matters (or 'transferred' areas in the case of Northern Ireland), with reserved matters (or reserved and excepted in Northern Ireland) remaining with the UK Parliament. The UK Parliament can still legislate in devolved areas, but under the Sewel Convention does 'not normally' do so without the consent of the relevant devolved legislature. The figure above summarises the devolution settlement for each legislature.

In each of the devolved legislatures the minister introducing a bill and the Presiding Officer must make statements regarding whether the provisions of the bill are within the legislature's legislative competence. However, the courts are the final arbiter of whether legislation passed by the devolved legislatures are within their competence.

9 Retained EU Law/ Assimilated Law and the Withdrawal Agreement

Learning outcomes

By the end of this chapter you should be able to:

- explain the meaning of retained EU law/assimilated law and its sources;
- understand and analyse the different categories of EU law;
- understand how retained EU law/assimilated law may be amended or repealed;
- apply retained EU law/assimilated law in practice;
- understand basic provisions of EU law relating to the free movement of workers; and
- explain key provisions of the Withdrawal Agreement agreed between the UK and EU and analyse how it may give rise to enforceable rights, particularly in the context of citizens' rights.

9.1 Introduction to retained EU law/assimilated law

The UK joined the European Communities on 1 January 1973. Over time the European Communities became the European Union (EU) and EU law became an ever more pervasive part of the UK legal system. Substantial parts of English law are based on or are profoundly influenced by EU law, in particular large swathes of commercial law, employment law (including laws prohibiting discrimination), environmental law, mergers and acquisitions and trade law. EU and English law are also very much intertwined in fields such as agriculture, consumer protection, public health and tourism. As you saw in **Chapter 6**, in many instances EU law had supremacy over UK law should there have been a conflict between the two. This was in accordance with the provisions of the European Communities Act (ECA) 1972, which was repealed by the European Union (Withdrawal) Act 2018 (EUWA 2018).

In a referendum held on 23 June 2016 the UK voted by 52% to 48% to leave the EU and subsequently the UK's exit took place on 31 January 2020 pursuant to a Withdrawal Agreement agreed between the UK and EU in October 2019, which entered into force on 1 February 2020. The Withdrawal Agreement provided for a transition period lasting until 31 December 2020 during which for many purposes the UK was treated as a Member State. During the transition period EU law remained in full force in the UK, and so there was little change in the UK legal system until 31 December 2020. However, the end of the transition period signalled a profound change in the UK legal system.

9.1.1 Retained EU law and the Withdrawal Agreement

If on the UK's exit from the EU all EU law had ceased to apply, there would have been massive gaps in the UK's statute book and regulatory systems. The UK Parliament therefore enacted the EUWA 2018, which aimed to provide legal continuity by creating the concept of 'retained EU law'. EU law as it existed at the date of the UK's exit from the EU would be preserved as a new category of English law with its own distinctive features. The original version of the EUWA 2018 was designed to cater for the possibility of the UK leaving the EU without agreement (a 'no-deal Brexit'); however, the UK did ultimately leave the EU on the basis of the Withdrawal Agreement. As the Withdrawal Agreement is an international treaty, the UK Government needed to ensure that its provisions were implemented into UK domestic law. Parliament therefore enacted the European Union (Withdrawal Agreement) Act 2020 (the Withdrawal Agreement Act 2020) in order to do this.

The Withdrawal Agreement Act 2020 gave effect to the Withdrawal Agreement in part by amending the EUWA 2018 and in part through its own self-standing provisions. Accordingly, to understand how the Withdrawal Agreement has been implemented into UK law, it is necessary to consider the EUWA 2018 as amended and the free-standing provisions of the Withdrawal Agreement Act 2020.

9.1.2 The Retained EU Law (Revocation and Reform Act) 2023

The previous Conservative Government believed that a gradualist approach towards the review, amendment or repeal of retained EU law was insufficient to allow the UK to take advantage of the benefits of Brexit. Parliament therefore passed the Retained EU Law (Revocation and Reform) Act 2023 (REULA 2023) which received royal assent on 29 June 2023 and made significant changes to the status, interpretation and application of retained EU law with effect from 1 January 2024. According to the Conservative Government, the aim of REULA 2023 was to enable it to amend retained EU law more easily and to remove its special features from the UK legal system. The Conservative Government believed REULA 2023 put the UK statute book on a more sustainable footing. By ending the special status of retained EU law, REULA 2023 reclaimed the sovereignty of Parliament and restored primacy to Acts of Parliament. It also enabled the Government to update outmoded legislation in response to various reviews it conducted.

The original Bill provided for the revocation of all retained EU law with effect from 31 December 2023, unless specifically retained or preserved, or contained in EU derived primary legislation.

Following widespread criticism highlighting the risk of inadvertent omission, namely that some instruments of retained EU law might lapse on 31 December 2023 without anyone's knowledge because government departments had failed to identify them, these extensive sun-setting provisions were dropped from the Bill. Instead, REULA 2023 provided for a more limited sunset.

Section 1 of REULA 2023 provided for the revocation at the end of 31 December 2023 ('the sunset') of 587 instruments of retained EU law listed in Sch 1 to the REULA 2023. However, this list was not completely reliable, as subsequently the Government removed a few of these instruments of retained EU law from the sunset by way of statutory instrument. Conversely, other legislation also contained sunsetting provisions. For example, the Procurement Act 2023 revoked some instruments of retained EU law relating to public procurement – that is the process by which public bodies acquire goods, services and construction works from external providers.

Notwithstanding REULA 2023, retained EU law (renamed assimilated law by REULA 2023) remains a significant source of law. As of March 2025, the dashboard maintained by the UK Government held a total of 6,901 individual pieces of retained EU law/assimilated law, covering around 400 policy areas. 4,417 pieces of this law remain unchanged, 806 amended, 1,484 repealed, 43 replaced and 62 expired, with the status of 89 to be confirmed.

REULA 2023 gives considerable powers to both UK ministers and the devolved administrations, but in this context the powers of the devolved administration are outside the scope of this book. While the previous Conservative Government was keen to eliminate all vestiges of EU law from the UK legal system as quickly as reasonably possible, the current Labour Government does not share this aim and hopes to reset relations with the EU. The rate of change in this area of law is therefore likely to slow down.

Since 1 January 2024 it is accordingly assimilated law that applies in the UK. However, to understand the concept of assimilated law, it is vital to grasp what retained EU law was, as all assimilated law was previously retained EU law.

9.1.3 Other instruments

It is also essential in considering the continuing impact of EU law in the UK to take account of

- the Trade and Cooperation Agreement between the UK and EU (TCA) (Trade and Cooperation Agreement between the European Union and the European Atomic Energy Community, of the one part, and the United Kingdom of Great Britain and Northern Ireland, of the other part [2020] OJ L444/14);
- the European Union (Future Relationship) Act 2020 (EU(FR)A 2020);
- the Product Regulation and Metrology Bill.

The TCA governs the relationship between the UK and EU following the UK's exit from the EU and covers a wide range of issues. The TCA is a free trade agreement and provides for quota and tariff free trade in goods between the UK and EU. It also covers areas such as the movement of services, competition, state subsidies, air and road transport, energy and sustainability, fisheries, data protection, and social security. However, it falls considerably short of the arrangements that the UK had as a Member State and there are more barriers to trade than previously existed.

The EU(FR)A 2020 implements the TCA into domestic UK law. While it and other legislation expressly amends or repeals some domestic law, s 29 of the EU(FR)A 2020 is an extremely unusual provision which has an impact on the application of retained EU law/assimilated law. It is a 'sweeping-up' mechanism and provides that any modification (eg amendment) that is required to be made in existing UK domestic law (statute or common law) in order to implement the provisions of the TCA is deemed by s 29 to have been made. It only applies to provisions of the TCA which are not implemented by another mechanism and aims to ensure that all aspects of the TCA are implemented to the extent necessary to comply with the UK's international obligations.

The Product Regulation and Metrology Bill aims to ensure product safety and quality before products reach consumers. It sets requirements for product design, manufacturing and distribution to protect consumers from harm.

When enacted, the Bill will grant UK ministers the authority to align domestic regulations with EU product standards, particularly for the purpose of environmental impact mitigation. Clause 1(2) in particular allows the Secretary of State to implement domestic provisions resembling relevant EU laws. The Labour Government supports this alignment to reduce business costs and maintain regulatory stability, with decisions being made case by case in the UK's sovereign interest.

9.2 What is retained EU law/assimilated law?

Originally, retained EU law was intended to come into force on the day the UK left the EU (exit day). However, in order to give effect to the transitional arrangements provided for in the Withdrawal Agreement, the Withdrawal Agreement Act 2020 amended the EUWA 2018 so that retained EU law came into effect at the end of the transition period. Somewhat confusingly, the EUWA 2018 as amended refers to the end of the transition period as 'IP completion day', with 'IP' standing for 'implementation period', the UK Government's preferred description of the transition period. The Withdrawal Agreement Act 2020 defines IP completion day as 11.00pm on 31 December 2020. Retained EU law was therefore effectively a snapshot of EU law that was in force in the UK immediately before IP completion day, and that law continues in force despite the UK's exit from the EU. However, some key aspects of EU law were repealed with effect from IP completion day. For example, as the UK Government decided that the UK should leave the customs union and single market, UK legislation repealed the bulk of EU law on free movement, which was therefore not retained. Nonetheless, there remained a huge body of retained EU law, which the UK and devolved governments could decide over time whether to keep or replace with their own laws.

It is important to understand the different types of EU legislation that can be converted into retained EU law, and **6.5.3.2** above provides a summary of this. Please ensure in particular that you understand the following types of EU legislation:

- Treaty articles
- Regulations
- Directives
- Decisions.

Section **6.5.3.12** also gives a summary of the three main categories of retained EU law, and whether REULA 2023 converted it into assimilated law, namely:

- EU-derived domestic legislation
- direct EU legislation
- rights etc arising under s 2(1) of the ECA 1972.

However, the following paragraphs cover these in more depth.

9.2.1 EU-derived domestic legislation

Section 2 of the EUWA 2018 preserved certain 'EU-derived domestic legislation' made under the ECA 1972. It includes secondary legislation enacted by the UK Government, often in the form of regulations (not to be confused with EU Regulations), to implement EU obligations, for example those contained in EU Directives. Under s 2(2) of the ECA 1972, ministers had the power to implement EU Directives into UK law through secondary legislation. For example, the EU adopted Council Directive 93/104/EC ([2003] OJ L299/9) concerning working time, which, subject to certain exemptions, provides for a maximum average working week of 48 hours. The UK Government then enacted the Working Time Regulations 1998/1833 to implement the Working Time Directive.

If secondary legislation implementing EU obligations had not been converted into retained EU law, it would have fallen away at the end of transition period, leaving huge gaps in UK law. However, secondary legislation such as the Working Time Regulations is preserved to ensure continuity.

Whilst the bulk of EU-derived domestic legislation consists of secondary legislation, it also includes some Acts of Parliament. For example, parts of the Equality Act 2010 were enacted to implement EU anti-discrimination Directives, so will fall within the scope of EU-derived domestic legislation. Whilst these Acts would have remained in force despite the end of the transition period, their status as retained EU law was significant, as it was subject to ministers' powers to correct deficiencies (**9.8** below) and benefited from a limited degree of supremacy (**9.9** below). REULA 2023 converted EU-derived domestic legislation into assimilated law and so has changed its status within the UK legal system. However, the impact of REULA 2013 is not as great on this category of retained EU law as on the other categories.

9.2.2 Direct EU legislation

Section 3 of the EUWA 2018 converted certain 'direct EU legislation' into UK law so far as 'operative' immediately before 'IP completion day'.

During the UK's membership of the EU, some EU legislation applied directly in the UK legal system without the need for any implementing UK legislation, in particular EU Regulations and certain decisions of the EU. EU Regulations are directly applicable and fully binding in all Member States. Decisions are binding on those to whom they are addressed (eg an EU Member State or an individual company) and are directly applicable. UK courts gave effect to rights and obligations arising under Regulations and decisions under s 2(1) of the ECA 1972.

Following the end of the transition period, EU legislation could no longer directly apply in the UK. Section 3 of the EUWA 2018 ensured that, where appropriate, EU legislation continued to have effect in the UK legal system by converting 'direct EU legislation' into domestic legislation at IP completion day. Where legislation was converted under this section, it was the English language text that existed on IP completion day that was converted.

EU decisions that were addressed only to a Member State other than the UK were not converted into domestic law. Additionally, if EU-derived domestic legislation under s 2 reproduced the effect of an EU Regulation or decision, then it was not converted under s 3. This was to avoid unnecessary duplication.

An example of an EU Regulation that became direct EU legislation is Regulation (EC) 261/2004 ([2004] OJ L46/1) protecting air passenger rights. This Regulation requires airlines to pay compensation to passengers (eg €250 for a flight of less than 1,500 km) if a flight is significantly delayed or cancelled unless due to circumstances beyond the airline's control and in any event to provide assistance (meals, accommodation and phone calls). Passengers in the UK, backed up by judgments in English courts, have claimed millions of pounds in compensation from airlines under this Regulation. Section 3 ensured that airline passengers in the UK continued to benefit from it after IP completion day, though as explained at **9.8** below it was amended slightly.

REULA 2023 converted direct EU legislation into direct assimilated legislation. However, as explained at **9.9** below, it made significant changes to its status.

9.2.3 Rights etc arising under s 2(1) of the ECA 1972

Section 4(1) preserved certain rights, powers, liabilities, obligations, restrictions, remedies and procedures recognised and available in UK law immediately before IP completion day under the ECA 1972. It aimed to ensure that any remaining EU rights and obligations that did not fall within the scope of ss 2 and 3 become part of retained EU law.

One of the main types of rights covered by s 4 was directly effective rights contained within EU treaties, ie those provisions of EU treaties that are sufficiently clear, precise and unconditional to confer rights directly on individuals, which they can enforce before national courts without the need for national implementing measures. It is, however, the right that was retained, not the text of the article itself.

The most important directly effective treaty right that became retained EU law in this way was the right for men and women to receive equal pay under Article 157 of the Treaty on the Functioning of the European Union (TFEU). The Equality Act 2010 prohibits sex discrimination in the workplace, so in practice most victims of discrimination would have relied on the Equality Act 2010 rather than the retained rights granted by Article 157. However, should for any reason the right to equal pay under the Equality Act 2010 have fallen short of the rights conferred by Article 157, then a victim of discrimination could have relied on their retained Article 157 rights against their employer to the extent of the shortfall.

Whilst many other treaty articles have direct effect, for example those relating to the free movement of goods, people and services, they did not form part of retained EU law as the UK repealed them due to the Government's decision to leave the single market and customs union.

Directives themselves were as a general rule excluded from the scope of retained EU law (EUWA 2018, s 4(1)) as they were implemented into national law by domestic legislation, which is preserved as EU-derived domestic legislation. However, they are also capable of having direct effect if they have not been implemented or have been implemented incorrectly, although only vertically against the state or state bodies. Where rights arising under directly effective provisions of Directives were of a kind that had been recognised by a UK or EU court or tribunal before IP completion day, rights of that kind became retained EU law. If, however, the right was of a kind that had not been recognised by a court, then it was excluded from retained EU law (EUWA 2018, s 4(2)).

EU Directives did not themselves become part of retained EU law, so any retention of rights and obligations in them depended on their implementation through EU-derived domestic legislation and/or s 4 of the EUWA 2018.

However, s 2 of the REULA 2023 repealed s 4 of the EUWA 2018 with effect from the end of 2023, so that no rights retained as a result of that section are enforceable in UK law from that date. This means that individuals (including businesses) can no longer rely on directly effective rights arising under Treaty articles or directives before UK courts. Nevertheless, under powers discussed at **9.9** below, it is possible for the Government to enact statutory instruments to codify rights that had been retained on IP completion day pursuant to s 4. The Government has done this with Article 157 TFEU which provides that men and women should receive equal pay for equal work or work of equal value. The rights granted by Article 157 go beyond those granted by the Equality Act 2010, and so the Government has issued a statutory instrument preserving the directly effective rights granted by Article 157 and codifying case law of the Court of Justice of the European Union (CJEU) to ensure that employees do not lose those rights.

The Finance Act 2024 also provides that s 4 of the EUWA 2018 continues to have effect for the purpose of interpreting VAT and excise law. This means that the principle of consistent interpretation (the *Marleasing* principle (discussed at **6.5.3.6**)) continues to apply to VAT and excise law. However, the principle of direct effect has been abolished, so it is no longer possible for any UK VAT or excise legislation to be quashed or disapplied on the grounds that it is incompatible with EU law.

The next example illustrates the position regarding Directives.

Example

An EU Directive (fictitious) adopted in 2017 provides that Member States must ensure that the use of latex gloves is prohibited in restaurants, cafeterias and other places that serve hot food for consumption on the premises. The Directive was adopted due to medical evidence that latex gloves were causing an allergic reaction. The Directive further provides that Member States should implement it by 30 November 2019. The UK Government took no steps to implement it. In May 2020 the CJEU ruled that the provisions of the Directive have direct effect.

On 20 December 2023 a woman working in a cafeteria operated by a government department suffered an allergic reaction as a result of wearing latex gloves. Last month a man suffered identical harm.

Can the woman and man make claims against the government department based on the Directive?

Directives are capable of having direct effect if they have not been implemented or implemented incorrectly, although only vertically against the state or state bodies. As the rights granted by the Directive in this question were of a kind that had been recognised by a UK or EU court or tribunal before IP completion day, the rights it became retained EU law. Note that it is the rights granted by the Directive that became retained EU law rather than the Directive.

The woman can therefore bring a claim against the government department, as the harm she suffered occurred before the end of 2023. In contrast the man cannot do so, as REULA 2023 abolished the directly effective rights that had originally become part of retained EU law.

9.3 Status of retained EU law/assimilated law

Section 7 of the EUWA 2018 (as amended by REULA 2023) defines the status of assimilated law. Section 7(1) provides that EU law assimilated under s 2 of the EUWA 2018 (EU-derived domestic legislation) has the same status as it had pre-IP completion day either as primary or secondary legislation.

EU law assimilated under s 3 of the EUWA 2018 (as amended by REULA 2023), however, does not fall into the existing categories as it is neither primary nor secondary legislation; instead it constitutes a new category of domestic law – assimilated direct legislation (previously retained direct EU legislation). Section 7 of the EUWA 2018 subdivides assimilated direct legislation (ie legislation retained under s 3) into two categories:

- assimilated direct 'principal' legislation; and
- assimilated direct 'minor' legislation.

The distinction is very technical. However, assimilated direct principal legislation includes most EU Regulations such as Regulation (EC) 261/2004 governing compensation for flight delays and cancellations. Assimilated direct minor legislation is defined as any assimilated direct legislation that is not assimilated direct principal legislation. This broadly covers EU tertiary legislation (acts adopted by the EU institutions pursuant to powers granted to them by a Regulation or Directive) and EU decisions.

The key difference between 'minor' and 'principal' assimilated direct legislation is that the EUWA 2018 treats the latter as if it were 'primary' legislation for the purposes of the Human Rights Act (HRA) 1998. This prevents it from being declared invalid for incompatibility with the Convention rights. A declaration of incompatibility pursuant to s 4 of the 1998 Act is possible, but this would not invalidate the legislation.

Before REULA 2023 came into force on 1 January 2024, it was easier to amend minor legislation than principal legislation, but both can now be amended in the same way.

9.4 Interpretation of retained EU law/assimilated law

Section 6(3) of the EUWA 2018 (as amended by REULA 2023) provides that questions on the meaning of assimilated law that remains 'unmodified' on or after IP completion day by UK law will be determined by UK courts in accordance with relevant 'retained case law'; see **9.5** below for an explanation of this concept.

Section 6(6) provides that questions on the meaning of assimilated law that has been modified, eg amended, on or after IP completion day by UK law can be determined in accordance with relevant retained case law if doing so is consistent with the intention of the modifications.

9.5 Retained EU case law/assimilated case law

As stated at **9.4** above, assimilated law is normally to be interpreted in line with assimilated case law. Assimilated case law consists of retained domestic case law and retained EU case law.

Assimilated domestic case law means the principles and decisions laid down by UK courts and tribunals before the end of IP completion day in relation to assimilated law (subject to certain exceptions).

Assimilated EU case law means the principles and decisions laid down by the Court of Justice of the European Union (CJEU) before IP completion day in relation to assimilated law (subject to certain exceptions).

Accordingly, although it is no longer be possible for UK courts to make references to the CJEU pursuant to Article 267 TFEU on questions of EU law, its judgments remain binding on all UK courts below the level of the Court of Appeal (or equivalent courts such as the Court Martial Appeal Court).

9.6 Retained general principles of EU law

General principles of EU law are an important source of EU Law, as explained at **6.5.3.3(b)** above. The EUWA 2018 as originally enacted provided for the retention of those general principles of EU law that had been recognised as such by EU case law before IP completion day. However, retained general principles could only be used to interpret retained EU law. Unlike the position before IP completion day, failure to comply with a general principle could not give rise to a right of action. This meant that UK courts could not disapply national legislation that breached a general principle.

However, s 4 of REULA 2023 abolished retained general principles of EU law from the end of 2023. Accordingly, they have not become assimilated law.

The consequence of abolishing them is illustrated by analysing *Kücükdeveci v Swedex GmbH & Co KG* (Case C-555/07) EU:C:2010:21, [2010] ECR I-00365, in which the CJEU stated that national courts had to set aside any provision of national law that breached the general principle of equality. In this case, an employee was suing his employer for age discrimination before a German court. The employer relied on German legislation that permitted employers to discriminate against employees aged under 25 years on the grounds of age. However, as the German law breached the principle of equality, the German court had to disapply the offending German law, enabling the employee to succeed in his claim.

During the UK's membership of the EU, UK courts would have been required to adopt the same approach and to disapply legislation, including primary legislation, that breached the principle of equality. However, after IP completion day this was no longer the case, although until the end of 2023 UK courts would have used the principle of equality to interpret retained EU law in the field of discrimination. Now they are not even an aid to interpretation of assimilated law, though remain relevant to the application of the Withdrawal Agreement between the EU and UK.

9.7 Exclusion of state liability

In addition to the exclusions referred to in **9.6** above, the EUWA 2018 also excluded the principle of state liability ('Francovich damages'). In certain circumstances, EU law gives individuals the right to claim damages from a Member State for its failure to implement a Directive at all or properly, or for other breaches of EU law. This was first recognised in the CJEU case of *Francovich v Italian Republic* (Joined Cases C-6/90 and 9/90) ECLI:EU:C:1991:428, [1991] ECR I-5357 so the principle of state liability has also been labelled the right to 'Francovich damages'.

There is a saving for claims for Francovich damages begun within the period of two years beginning with IP completion day so far as the proceedings relate to anything that occurred before IP completion day.

9.8 Correcting 'deficiencies' in retained EU law

Section 8 of the EUWA 2018 granted temporary powers for UK Government ministers, and devolved administrations in relation to domestic legislation within areas of devolved competence, to make secondary legislation that corrected 'deficiencies' in retained EU law.

Deficiencies were defined to include:

- provisions that have no practical application after the UK has left the EU;
- provisions on functions that during the UK's membership of the EU were carried out in the EU on the UK's behalf, for example by an EU agency;
- provisions on reciprocal arrangements or rights between the UK and other EU Member States that are no longer in place or are no longer appropriate;
- any other arrangements or rights, including through EU treaties, that are no longer in place or no longer appropriate; and
- EU references that are no longer appropriate.

Deficiencies not on the list but which were 'of a similar kind' to those listed also fell within the scope of the correcting power.

As this list indicates, deficiencies could have arisen for a number of reasons. For example, EU legislation would sometimes require governments of Member States to consult with the European Commission before taking certain action. Following IP completion day, it was no longer appropriate to require the UK Government to consult with the Commission. EU legislation might also contain references to the UK being a Member State. Where such legislation was converted into retained EU law, it would have contained inaccurate references or provided for arrangements that were no longer appropriate. Accordingly, it was possible to correct these deficiencies through secondary legislation.

The power could only be used to correct deficiencies arising from the UK's withdrawal from the EU; it was not a power to make changes of substance to retained EU law.

Activity 1 Correcting deficiencies in retained EU law

Regulation 261/2004 states that it applies to passengers departing from, or arriving at, an airport in a Member State. What deficiency might the UK Government have wanted to correct?

Comment

Regulation 261/2004 provided a good example of where the UK Government has corrected a deficiency. The UK adopted a statutory instrument providing that the retained version of the Regulation applied to passengers departing from, or arriving at, an airport in the UK to ensure it made sense after the UK had ceased to be a Member State. Regulation 261/2004 as corrected now forms part of assimilated law.

The power granted to correct deficiencies expired two years from IP completion day, ie on 31 December 2022. However, REULA 2023 gives the Government extensive powers to amend and revoke retained EU law; see **9.11** below.

9.9 Supremacy of retained EU law/assimilated law

9.9.1 Position pre-REULA 2023

As explained at **6.5.3.12**, retained EU law kept a limited form of supremacy until the end of 2023 when REULA 2023 ended it. Although following IP completion day EU law itself no longer had supremacy over UK law, retained EU law would have had supremacy in limited circumstances. For this purpose there were three categories of law:

- retained EU law;
- UK legislation enacted pre-IP completion day that was not retained EU law; and
- all UK legislation enacted after IP completion day.

The following example illustrates how this limited form of supremacy applied until the end of December 2023.

Example

An EU Regulation adopted in 2010 conflicts with an Act of Parliament of 2018. Which piece of legislation would have prevailed?

Should a conflict have occurred between a provision of retained EU law and a piece of pre-IP completion day legislation that was not retained EU law, then the former would have prevailed over the latter.

As the EU Regulation became retained EU law under s 3 of the EUWA 2018, the Regulation of 2010 would have had supremacy over the Act of 2018.

However, REULA 2023 ended the limited supremacy of retained EU law.

9.9.2 REULA 2023: abolition of supremacy

Section 3 of REULA 2023 provided for the abolition in the UK of the supremacy of retained EU law from 31 December 2023. Specifically, it ended the supremacy of EU law in relation to any enactment or rule of law whenever passed or made. It also explicitly sets out a new priority rule for assimilated direct legislation (previously retained direct EU legislation) which:

(a) must, so far as possible, be read and given effect in a way which is compatible with all domestic enactments, and

(b) is subject to all domestic enactments, so far as it is incompatible with them.

As explained in the Example at **9.9.1** above, if there were a conflict between an EU regulation adopted in 2010 which had become retained EU law and an Act of Parliament enacted in 2018, the EU regulation would have prevailed until 31 December 2023. Now it appears the Act of 2018 will have priority. REULA 2023 has accordingly reversed the priorities that had previously applied in relation to direct legislation.

The Bar Council has criticised abolishing supremacy on the grounds that it creates legal uncertainty. For example, it would retrospectively alter the effect of domestic legislation in a way that the domestic legislator could not have foreseen at the time. The Example above illustrates this. When Parliament passed the Act in 2018, the Act would not have overridden the EU Regulation adopted in 2010. Altering the effect of the Act of 2018 several years after it was passed to override the EU Regulation could lead to unpredictable and unforeseen consequences. Moreover, when Parliament passed the Act of 2018, it did so in the knowledge that it would take effect subject to any previously enacted EU legislation. To change the effect of the Act is arguably to contradict Parliament's intention.

REULA 2023 also removed the principle of consistent interpretation (the *Marleasing* principle) in relation to all domestic legislation. This means that UK courts are no longer required to interpret UK regulations enacted to implement an EU Directive consistently with that Directive. This does not necessarily mean that UK courts will disregard the existence of the relevant Directive. Under national principles of statutory interpretation, UK courts are likely to take the Directive into account as an extrinsic aid to interpretation.

Although the principle of supremacy and general principles have been abolished, ministers may by statutory instrument 'recreate' their effect, albeit in a limited form. Thus, a minister can specify that a provision of direct assimilated legislation will prevail over another specific enactment, but not all enactments in general. So, in the above Example, a minister could specify that the EU Regulation of 2010 should have priority over the Act of 2018 or any other piece of domestic legislation, though not over domestic legislation in general.

Moreover, the Finance Act 2024 referred to at **9.2** above provides that the supremacy principle will be retained for certain purposes in relation to VAT and excise law, and, likewise, retained general principles will remain relevant to the interpretation of VAT and excise law.

Table 9.1 below traces how the main categories of EU law were converted into retained EU law and then into assimilated law, and summarises the effect of REULA 2023 on the principle of supremacy.

Table 9.1 REULA 2023 and the principle of supremacy

During EU membership	IP completion day	1 January 2024	Status under REULA 2023
Directive implemented by UK statutory instrument or Act	EU-derived domestic legislation (s 2 EUWA)	EU-derived domestic legislation (label unchanged)	Supremacy removed*
EU Regulation	Direct EU legislation (s 3 EUWA)	Direct assimilated legislation	Priorities reversed*
Directly effective rights under Treaty articles and directives	Saving for rights etc under s 2(1) of the ECA (s 4 EUWA)	Sun-setted unless specifically retained	Supremacy removed*

*subject to power to grant effect similar to supremacy over specified enactments (**9.12.1** below)

The previous Conservative Government did not analyse the actual impact of ending the principle of supremacy of retained EU law so that it does not apply to assimilated law. Accordingly, the extent to which ending supremacy affects the rights of individuals and businesses in particular cases is unclear. Assimilated law remains an important source of the rules governing consumer rights, data protection, employment law and health and safety, so it was risky to make a change when the impact of that change was unknown. Time will tell whether there will be adverse consequences to the ending of supremacy.

9.9.3 Incompatibility orders

If a court finds that there is a conflict between a piece of retained direct EU legislation and domestic legislation, then it must issue an incompatibility order (s 8). The Act gives the courts considerable discretion in setting out the legal consequences of the incompatibility in the incompatibility order. The incompatibility order may:

- set out the effect in the case concerned of one provision taking priority over another;
- delay the order coming into force; or
- remove or limit the effect of the operation of the relevant provision in any other way before the coming into force of the order, eg where this might give rise to unfairness to individuals or other effects contrary to the public interest.

However, courts cannot change the order of priority of the conflicting pieces of law. Incompatibility orders are a novelty in the UK's legal system, and it remains to be seen how the courts will use them in practice.

9.10 Challenges to retained EU law/assimilated law

As explained at **9.3** above, domestic law that has become assimilated law by virtue of s 2 of the EUWA 2018, as amended by REULA 2023 (EU-derived domestic legislation) continues to be classed as primary or secondary legislation as applicable. EU-derived domestic legislation that is primary legislation will be treated in the same way as any other Act of Parliament.

Secondary legislation that falls within s 2 of the EUWA 2018 can be challenged on the same public law grounds that apply to any other secondary legislation, as covered in ***Administrative Law and Human Rights***.

The EUWA 2018 also provides that no provision of assimilated EU law can be challenged on or after IP completion day on the basis that an EU instrument, such as an EU regulation or decision, was invalid. For example, if an EU regulation had become retained EU law and subsequently assimilated law under s 3 of the EUWA 2018, it is not possible to challenge the validity of the assimilated regulation on the grounds that the original EU regulation was invalid. However, this exclusion does not apply where the CJEU has found the EU instrument to be invalid prior to IP completion day, or where regulations made by a UK minister permit the challenge. The Challenges to Validity of EU Instruments (EU Exit) Regulations 2019 (SI 2019/673) do, in fact, permit such a challenge as they allow the courts to decide challenges to the validity of EU instruments that started before IP completion day but concluded after it.

As explained at **9.3** above, assimilated direct principal legislation is treated as primary legislation for the purposes of challenges under the HRA 1998, ie it can be subject to a declaration of incompatibility, but that finding does not affect its continued validity. Conversely, assimilated direct minor legislation is treated as subordinate legislation for HRA 1998 purposes, so it can be declared invalid if held to be incompatible.

It is likely that a significant number of challenges will be in relation to modifications made to retained EU law by ministers using the powers to correct deficiencies. Although the EUWA 2018 defines deficiencies widely, challenges are probable on the basis that ministers have used them to make substantive policy changes rather than simply to correct deficiencies. There are also likely to be challenges to secondary legislation made by the Government to revoke retained EU law/assimilated law discussed further at **9.12** below.

9.11 UK courts and retained EU law/assimilated law

9.11.1 Applying retained EU law/assimilated law

The Court of Appeal judgment in *Lipton & Anor v BA City Flyer Ltd* [2021] EWCA Civ 454 provides helpful guidance in applying retained EU law. The case involved Regulation 261/2004 (discussed at **9.2.2** above); the claimants were relying on it to sue the defendant airline for compensation following the cancellation of their flight.

As the Court of Appeal was hearing the claim after IP completion day, it applied the retained version of Regulation 261/2004 even though the events leading to the case took place before IP completion day. However, the Supreme Court, when hearing the appeal from the Court of Appeal's judgment, ruled that the EU text of Regulation 261/2004 as it existed at the date of the claim should apply and not the retained version ([2024] UKSC 24). Although this did not change the outcome of the case, it was therefore unnecessary for the Supreme Court to analyse the retained version. Accordingly, subject to certain modifications discussed below, Green LJ's analysis remains the most authoritative.

In applying retained EU law, Green LJ set out the following approach:

- It was necessary to determine the status of any relevant EU regulation and whether it had become retained EU law.

Green LJ found that Regulation 261/2004 was operative prior to IP completion day (11pm on 31 December 2020) and so continued in force as direct EU legislation, a category of retained EU law (EUWA 2018, s 3(1) and (2)).

The principle of supremacy, albeit limited, applied to Regulation 261/04. It therefore took precedence over any other domestic law that pre-dated IP completion day which might be inconsistent with it (EUWA 2018, s 5(2)).

- It was then necessary to consider whether any domestic UK legislation had amended it.

  As explained at **9.8** above, the UK version of Regulation 261/2004 was amended to ensure that it applies to flights departing from or arriving at UK airports.

- Retained EU law should be given a purposive construction.
- UK courts should take into account pre-IP completion day case law of the CJEU.

  While the Court of Appeal had the power to depart from CJEU, Green LJ did not consider it necessary to do so (see further **9.11.2** below).

- UK courts should take into account general principles of EU law that had been recognised in case law before IP completion day.

  However, in *Lipton* there did not appear to be any relevant general principles.

- Finally, it is necessary to analyse whether retained EU law has been amended or superseded by the TCA and the EU(FR)A 2020.

  The TCA provides that the EU and UK must ensure there are effective remedies in the pursuit of consumer protection to protect air passengers whose flights are cancelled or delayed. As Regulation 261/2004 already provided effective procedures, there was no need to use s 29 of the EU(FR)A 2020 to amend it.

Green LJ thought that s 29 of the EU(FR)A 2020 automatically repealed or rewrote any laws (statute or case law) existing on IP completion day that were inconsistent with the TCA. However, on appeal, the Supreme Court took the position that s 29 does not have the effect Green LJ suggested regarding provisions of the TCA 'which are expressed in ... general and aspirational terms', though it acknowledged that, if a future party were to submit an argument that the effect of s 29 is to modify the wording of some existing domestic law, then the court should consider the effect of s 29 afresh without regard to Green LJ's views.

There are as yet no reported judgments on how the courts will approach assimilated law. It is likely that they will adopt a similar approach to that in *Lipton* subject to the following:

- They will no longer consider if there are any relevant general principles of EU law following their abolition by REULA 2023.
- While it is probable that they will continue to adopt a purposive approach, they will no longer use the *Marleasing* principle of consistent interpretation.
- They will also need to consider any arguments based on s 29 of the EU(FR)A 2020 having regard to the Supreme Court's views of its effect.

9.11.2 Departing from retained/assimilated EU case law

Retained case law comprises both judgments of the CJEU handed down before IP completion day - retained/assimilated EU case law - and judgments handed down by domestic courts before IP completion day - retained/assimilated domestic case law. Both have precedential value, but there are differences between the two.

9.11.2.1 Retained/assimilated EU case law

Originally, the EUWA 2018 only gave the power to depart from retained EU case law to the UK Supreme Court and the High Court of Justiciary as the final criminal court of appeal in Scotland in cases where there is no appeal to the UK Supreme Court. Section 6(6) provided that in deciding whether to depart from any retained EU case law, the Supreme Court or the High Court of Justiciary had to apply the same test as it would apply in deciding whether to depart from its own case law. Thus, the Supreme Court had to apply the principles contained in the *Practice Statement (Judicial Precedent)* [1966] 1 WLR 1234.

However, s 6(5A)–(5D) of the EUWA 2018 (inserted by the Withdrawal Agreement Act 2020) gave the Government the power to make regulations by extending the ability to depart from retained EU case law to additional courts and tribunals. The Government accordingly adopted the European Union (Withdrawal) Act 2018 (Relevant Court) (Retained EU Case Law) Regulations 2020 (SI 2020/155) extending the power to depart from retained EU case law to the Court of Appeal and courts of equivalent status.

In deciding whether to depart from retained EU case law, these courts had to apply the same test as the Supreme Court would apply in deciding whether to depart its own case law (2020 Regulations, reg 5). Thus, they also had to apply the principles in the *Practice Statement*. REULA 2023 has renamed retained EU case law as 'assimilated EU case law' (s 5). REULA 2023 introduces a new test discussed at **9.11.4** below which courts should apply in deciding to depart from assimilated EU case law, but these provisions are not yet in force and indeed may never come into force. Accordingly, the *Practice Statement* remains relevant.

Chapter 4, in particular **4.7.3**, covers the *Practice Statement*, but there is little guidance on how the courts will exercise their power to depart from assimilated EU case law. However, it is likely that the courts will exercise their power sparingly, as a court will not overturn an earlier decision merely because it believes that decision is wrong. For example, if an earlier albeit wrong decision has been relied on by many people and businesses in arranging their affairs, it is unlikely that it will be overturned. Overturning the earlier decision could cause considerable difficulties for everyone who had relied on it in good faith, as judicial decisions apply retrospectively. The courts are likely to leave it to the legislature to make any changes, as statutes normally apply prospectively only and would not upset existing arrangements. The Court of Appeal judgment in *TuneIn Inc v Warner Music UK Ltd* [2021] EWCA Civ 441 confirms that the courts are likely to take a cautious approach.

TuneIn is an internet radio app which provided hyperlinks to various radio stations around the world. Some of these stations played music without obtaining the consent of the holders of the copyright in the works played. The holders of the copyright sued TuneIn for copyright infringement under the Copyright, Designs and Patents Act 1988. Section 20 of the 1988 Act prohibits a 'communication to the public' of a work protected by copyright without the requisite consents, and CJEU case law had held that providing hyperlinks was a communication to the public. TuneIn asked the Court of Appeal to depart from the CJEU's case law. The Court of Appeal declined to do so for various reasons, including the following:

- There had been no change in the domestic legislation (ie retained EU law). Parliament could amend it, but for the time being it was Parliament's will that the legislation should remain in its current form. It would therefore be inappropriate for the courts to change the law when Parliament had not yet chosen to do so.
- There had been no change in the international legislative framework, which was relevant in circumstances where the EU law in question gave effect to other international law obligations. Where an issue is regulated by international treaties, courts in the states that have signed the relevant treaty should seek consistency of interpretation, rather than unilaterally adopting their own interpretations.
- The interpretation of the relevant provision (whether hyperlinking amounted to 'communication to the public') was 'a difficult task' as the legislation contained no guidance and there was a conflict between copyrights which are exploited on a territorial basis and the global nature of the internet. According to Arnold LJ, the CJEU 'has unrivalled experience in confronting this issue in a variety of factual scenarios. Moreover, it has developed and refined its jurisprudence over time.'
- Although there was distinguished academic commentary criticising the CJEU's view, there was also considerable support for it. (This seems to imply that overwhelming academic criticism of a judgment might be grounds for departing from it.)

- Jurisprudence from other courts in countries such as Australia, Canada and the USA was materially irrelevant as the statutory framework differed in those countries and their case law did not offer helpful and settled guidance.
- Departing from the CJEU's case law would result in returning to the drawing board and starting all over again, creating considerable legal uncertainty for little purpose as it would not provide TuneIn with a clear defence to the infringement proceedings in any case.

While the judgment in *TuneIn* concerned retained EU law rather than assimilated law, it is unlikely that UK courts will change their approach unless the new test provided for by REULA 2023 comes into force. However, in *Industrial Cleaning v Intelligent Cleaning Equipment* [2023] EWCA Civ 1451, the Court of Appeal did depart from the CJEU's decision in *Budejovicky Budvararodni Podnik v Anheuser-Busch Inc* (Case C-482/09) EU:C:2011:605, a case involving trade marks.

The reason for doing so was that the CJEU's judgment in *Budvar* was simply a bald statement of its conclusions and did not contain any analysis of the issues. It was also an 'isolated judgment', not entirely consistent with other CJEU cases. In contrast the CJEU cases considered in *TuneIn* constituted well-reasoned and settled jurisprudence. While courts should be slow to depart from settled case law in the interests of legal certainty, that was not a factor in *Industrial Cleaning* as few trade mark owners would have based their strategies on the *Budvar* judgment.

9.11.3 Departing from retained/assimilated domestic case law

During the UK's membership of the EU, UK courts would sometimes interpret provisions of EU law without referring the question to the CJEU. Generally, these judgments have the same precedential value as any other judgment by a UK court. The approach of the Court of Appeal in *Merck Serono v Comptroller-General of Patents* [2025] EWCA Civ 45 illustrates this. A key issue considered by the Court of Appeal was whether it could depart from assimilated domestic case law. It decided that the usual domestic rules of precedent applied. This meant that the court could only depart from one of its previous decisions that formed part of assimilated case law if one of the exceptions in *Young v Bristol Aeroplane Co Ltd* applied; see **4.7.4** above. In accordance with the usual rules of precedent, it remains bound by judgments of the Supreme Court, but can depart from judgments of lower courts.

9.11.4 REULA 2023: departing from assimilated case law

(a) Assimilated EU case law

Section 6 of REULA 2023 sets out a new test for the Supreme Court and Court of Appeal to apply once its provisions come into force. It lists the following non-exhaustive factors they must take into account in deciding whether to depart from assimilated EU case law:

(a) the fact that decisions of a foreign court are not usually binding;

(b) any changes of circumstances which are relevant to the assimilated EU case law; and

(c) the extent to which the assimilated EU case law restricts the proper development of domestic law.

The intention may be to make it more likely for the courts to depart from assimilated EU case law, as the previous Conservative Government was keen for the UK's legal system and regulatory framework to develop according to common law principles which it believed were better suited to the UK than civil law principles. However, while the previous Government had issued a commencement order providing that the new test should come into force on 1 October 2024, the Labour Government revoked the commencement order. As the Labour Government hopes to reset relations with the EU, it is possible that the new test will never come into force.

While lower courts will not be able to depart from assimilated EU case law, REULA 2023 establishes a reference system whereby a lower court may refer a point of law to a higher court for its decision. The point of law must be relevant to the case the lower court is hearing and, if so, it may exercise its discretion to refer if it is bound by the assimilated case law and the issue is one of general public importance. The introduction of the reference system is, however, dependent on s 6 coming into force.

The law officers of the UK Government and devolved administrations are also given the power to make references regarding points of assimilated EU case law which arise in legal proceedings.

(b) Assimilated domestic case law

The higher courts will, if s 6 ever comes into force, apply a similar test in deciding whether to depart from assimilated domestic case law, only differing on the first factor which instead reads 'the extent to which the assimilated domestic case law is determined or influenced by assimilated EU case law from which the court has departed or would depart'.

9.11.5 Post IP-completion day

Section 6(1) of the EUWA 2018 provides that UK courts and tribunals cease to be bound by principles laid down by the CJEU, or any decisions made by that court, after IP completion day, though such judgments may have persuasive effect (s 6(2)). This means that assimilated EU case law comprises only those judgments of the CJEU that were handed down pre-IP completion day. UK courts may therefore have regard to post-IP completion day judgments of the CJEU, but will not be bound by them.

9.12 REULA 2023: ministerial powers

As part of the Government's wider ambitions for regulatory reform and to reduce the impact of EU law in the UK's legal system, REULA 2023 gives ministers extensive powers.

9.12.1 Power to restate or reproduce

These powers are set out in ss 11–16 of REULA 2023.

9.12.1.1 Restating retained EU law

Ministers had the power to restate retained secondary EU law (all retained EU law that was not contained in primary legislation) up till 31 December 2023. The reason this power ended then is that retained EU law became assimilated law on 1 January 2024, and ministers have continuing equivalent powers regarding assimilated law.

9.12.1.2 Power to restate assimilated law or reproduce retained EU rights, powers, liabilities etc

Ministers also have the power to restate secondary assimilated law.

Ministers may also reproduce directly effective rights that became retained EU law by virtue of s 4 of the EUWA 2018. See **9.2.3** above for an example of this in relation to Article 157 TFEU.

As part of any restatement, ministers cannot reproduce into domestic legislation the principle of supremacy or general principles, but ministers may reproduce an effect that is equivalent to them. This enables ministers to achieve the same policy outcome as the retained EU law/assimilated law being restated, where they consider it appropriate. In restating retained EU law/assimilated law, ministers may:

- resolve ambiguities;
- remove doubts or anomalies;
- facilitate improvement in the clarity or accessibility of the law.

The Aviation (Consumers) (Amendment) Regulations 2023 (SI 2023/1370) ('the Aviation Regulations 2023') provide an example of a restatement of retained EU law. EU Regulation 261/2004 provides that airlines must compensate passengers for flight cancellations and delays in certain circumstances. Regulation 261/2004 subsequently became retained EU law and is now assimilated law. There has been a considerable amount of litigation concerning the interpretation of Regulation 261/2004 leading to judgments by the CJEU clarifying ambiguities and uncertainties in the text. However, under REULA 2023, the supremacy of retained EU law ceased to have effect at the end of 2023 and assimilated law is now interpreted differently from retained EU law. The Aviation Regulations 2023 accordingly restate and codify certain key principles derived from CJEU case law by inserting them into Regulation 261/2004 to ensure that the changes to the status of retained EU law made by REULA 2023 do not create uncertainty regarding the interpretation and application of Regulation 261/2004.

9.12.1.3 Power to revoke etc

Ministers also have the power as regard retained EU law/assimilated law to:

- revoke it without replacement;
- revoke and restate it, and
- revoke or replace it with an 'appropriate' provision that 'achieve[s] the same or similar objectives' as the provisions being revoked. In replacing retained EU law, ministers may not impose new regulatory burdens.

The powers listed at **9.12.1.2** and **9.12.1.3** expire on 23 June 2026.

9.12.1.4 Status of restated or replaced retained EU law/assimilated law

Where ministers have used their powers to restate or replace retained EU law or assimilated law, the effect of the restatement or replacement is that the relevant law will be contained in a domestic statutory instrument and will not form part of retained EU law or assimilated law. Accordingly, the statutory instrument carrying out the restatement or replacement is domestic law and is subject to normal domestic principles of statutory interpretation and precedent, and not to the provisions governing assimilated law. This means that even where a piece of retained EU law has been restated verbatim, assimilated EU case law will merely be persuasive. Overall, there is the risk that issues that have been settled by judgments of the CJEU will be relitigated, causing uncertainty, expense and delay. However, as illustrated by the Aviation Regulations 2023 above, the restatement or replacement may codify relevant CJEU judgments.

9.12.1.5 Extent of powers

The Secondary Legislation Scrutiny Committee of the House of Lords believes that the powers given to ministers are too wide-ranging due to the absence of consultation on the changes to retained EU law and the lack of effective parliamentary scrutiny. While Parliament will need to pass an Act to change primary assimilated law, much secondary assimilated law is of considerable importance.

For its part the Government claims that the Act will make it easier to amend or remove outdated retained EU law and to get rid of burdensome 'red tape'. Many EU laws which were retained were originally agreed as a messy compromise between 28 different EU Member States and often did not reflect the UK's own priorities or objectives, nor did many receive sufficient scrutiny in the UK's democratic institutions.

9.13 EU law/retained EU law and assimilated law

Despite the UK's exit from the EU and the changes to retained EU law wrought by REULA 2023, EU law through the medium of assimilated law remains a significant source of UK law and is likely to remain so for the foreseeable future. **Table 9.2** below summarises how REULA 2023 has relabelled retained EU law. Despite the abolition of supremacy and the general principles of EU law, assimilated law retains significant characteristics derived from EU law.

Table 9.2 Retained EU law and assimilated law

Name until 31 December 2023	*Name since 1 January 2024*
Retained EU law	Assimilated law
Retained case law	Assimilated case law
Retained direct EU legislation	Assimilated direct legislation
Retained direct minor EU legislation	Assimilated direct minor legislation
Retained direct principal EU legislation	Assimilated direct principal legilation
Retained domestic case law	Assimilated domestic case law
Retained EU case law	Assimilated EU case law

9.14 The Withdrawal Agreement

9.14.1 Main provisions

In October 2019 the UK Government and the EU reached agreement on a Withdrawal Agreement, which set out the terms for the UK's exit from the EU. It entered into force on 1 February 2020 together with the Political Declaration setting out the framework of the future EU-UK partnership. The Withdrawal Agreement is legally binding in international law, whereas the Political Declaration is not legally binding but aimed to set out the parameters of the negotiations for the future relationship between the UK and EU.

The Withdrawal Agreement covers a number of issues, including the following:

- *Citizens' rights:* The Withdrawal Agreement protects the rights of UK citizens living in the EU and EU citizens living in the UK at the end of the transition period, as well as their family members. They will have the right to continue to live and work in their host state. This also applies to citizens who moved to the UK or the EU during the transition period, ie after the UK's exit from the EU but before IP completion day.

  The Withdrawal Agreement states that citizens may need to apply for a residence status in their host state in accordance with the host state's law. EU citizens resident in the UK must apply using the EU Settlement Scheme. Citizens who have been living in the host state for five years continuously will be eligible for permanent residence (termed 'settled status' in the UK).
- *Financial settlement:* The UK agreed to abide by the financial commitments it made as a Member State, including its contributions to the EU budget.
- *The Northern Ireland Protocol:* This aims to avoid the introduction of a hard border on the island of Ireland between Northern Ireland and the Republic of Ireland unless the UK and EU were to agree other arrangements that deal satisfactorily with the border issues.
- *Governance and dispute resolution:* A joint committee oversees the Withdrawal Agreement. It comprises representatives from – and is co-chaired by – the EU and the UK. The UK and EU will first seek to resolve disputes through the joint committee where they will try to find a solution. If the committee cannot agree, then either the EU or the UK can request that the dispute be referred to an arbitration panel.

The provisions of the Withdrawal Agreement that lawyers practising in England and Wales are most likely to come across relate to citizens' rights. These are likely to remain relevant for many decades as not only EU citizens born in the UK before IP completion day will be able to rely on them, but also their children.

9.14.2 Application of the Withdrawal Agreement in the UK

Article 4 of the Withdrawal Agreement states that the provisions of the Withdrawal Agreement itself and the provisions of EU law that it incorporates shall have the same effect in UK law as they produce within the EU and EU Member States. This includes the ability of individuals (including businesses) to rely directly on provisions contained or referred to in the Agreement that meet the criteria for direct effect under EU law. One of the main practical effects of this is that EU citizens living in the UK at the end of the transition period should be able to rely on the direct effect of the citizens' rights provisions in the Withdrawal Agreement.

Section 7A of the EUWA 2018 (inserted by the Withdrawal Agreement Act 2020) provides for the enforcement of rights arising under the Withdrawal Agreement in very similar terms to those contained in the ECA 1972 regarding the EU Treaties. This gives supremacy to the Withdrawal Agreement in much the same way that the ECA 1972 gave supremacy to the EU Treaties. Direct effect will continue to play a role in UK law, albeit in a more limited field.

9.14.3 Citizens' rights

Even though most of the EU legislation regarding free movement of persons does not form part of retained EU law as the UK has repealed it, much of that legislation remains relevant after the UK's withdrawal from the EU under the Withdrawal Agreement, as the next activity illustrates.

Activity 2 EU law and the Withdrawal Agreement

You will find below a short extract from the Withdrawal Agreement. The Union citizens and United Kingdom nationals referred to are those who were respectively resident in the UK or EU on IP completion day.

> Article 13
>
> Residence rights
>
> 1. Union citizens and United Kingdom nationals shall have the right to reside in the host State under the limitations and conditions as set out in Articles 21, 45 or 49 TFEU and in Article 6(1), points (a), (b) or (c) of Article 7(1), Article 7(3), Article 14, Article 16(1) or Article 17(1) of Directive 2004/38/EC.

An EU national who was living in the UK on IP completion day claims that they have the right to reside in the UK. To decide whether they have the right, what laws would you examine?

Comment

You would look at the articles of the TFEU and of Directive 2004/38/EC referred to in Article 13(1) of the Withdrawal Agreement, provisions of EU law which the EUWA 2018 (as amended) has incorporated into UK law. In other words, the EU citizen's right to live in the UK very much depends on EU law. Similar provisions apply to family members of EU citizens. Directive 2004/38 EC on the right of citizens of the Union and their family members to move and reside freely within the territory of the Member States (often known as 'the Citizenship Directive') is a very important piece of legislation in this area.

Under the Withdrawal Agreement, whether UK citizens, EU27 citizens and their respective family members are eligible for permanent residence depends largely on whether they satisfy the criteria set in relevant EU legislation.

Additionally, UK courts are still able to make Article 267 references concerning the citizens' rights provisions in the Withdrawal Agreement for a period of up to eight years after the end of the transition period. However, this is a discretionary power in that UK courts are not obliged to make a reference, unlike the position during the UK's membership of the EU when references were in certain circumstances mandatory. Nevertheless, if a UK court does make a reference, it will be bound by the CJEU's ruling.

As indicated above, the wording of the Withdrawal Agreement also suggests that the citizens' rights provisions have direct effect, so UK and EU27 citizens and their respective family members are able to rely on them even if national legislation implementing those provisions is defective. For example, suppose UK immigration legislation denies an EU citizen some rights granted to them by the Withdrawal Agreement. The EU citizen will be able to enforce those rights in a UK court and possibly also claim damages under the Francovich principle for any loss suffered. See further the discussion at **9.16** of *R (Independent Monitoring Authority for the Citizens' Rights Agreements) v Secretary of State for the Home Department* [2022] EWHC 3274 (Admin) in which the Administrative Court applied the direct effect of the Withdrawal Agreement.

To understand and apply the rights of EU citizens covered by the Withdrawal Agreement, knowledge of the core elements of EU law on free movement is essential. The following sections therefore provide an overview of the basic principles. They concentrate on the rights of workers, but self-employed persons, students and persons with sufficient resources to support themselves have similar rights.

9.15 EU law: free movement of persons

The EC Treaty gave (and the TFEU now gives) the right of free movement within the Union to people who wished to take up offers of employment made from outside their home State. This fundamental Treaty right has been buttressed by a considerable amount of secondary legislation. Further, EU law has developed to the stage where the rights of individuals to move within the EU are not necessarily dependent on the desire to take up employment. Indeed, as a consequence of the Single European Act, from 1 January 1993, internal barriers to movement within the EU should have been removed. Further, Article 20 TFEU now states that every EU national shall be a citizen of the European Union. Under Article 21 TFEU, the Union citizen has the right to move and reside freely within the territory of the Member States, subject to the limitations and conditions in the Treaty and in other legislation.

9.15.1 What does the TFEU provide?

Free movement of workers is guaranteed by Article 45 TFEU, which gives the EU worker the right of entry and residence for the purpose of taking up employment. According to Article 45(2) TFEU, Member States must abolish:

> any discrimination based on nationality between workers of the Member States as regards employment, remuneration and other conditions of work and employment.

'Work and employment' has been interpreted very widely to include sportspeople. Hence, in *Union Royale Belge des Sociétés de Football Association ASBL v Bosman* (Case C-415/93) [1995] ECR I-4921, the ECJ made it plain that restrictions on the number of EU nationals in football teams imposed by UEFA and requirements for large transfer fees in cross-border transfers were both illegal.

9.15.1.1 Directive 2004/38: Union citizens

Union citizens (ie nationals of a Member State) moving from one Member State to another also benefit from Directive 2004/38. The following provisions are particularly relevant.

- Article 5(1): This grants Union citizens moving from their home State the right to enter another Member State (the host State) simply on production of their passport or national identity card.
- Article 6(1): This grants Union citizens a right of residence of up to three months in the host State. During this period, the Union citizen does not have to satisfy any conditions to

qualify for the right of residence, save that they must not become an unreasonable burden on the social assistance system of the host Member State.

- Article 7(1): This provides the following with a right of residence for more three months:
  - o workers and self-employed (Article 7(1)(a));
  - o persons with sufficient resources to support themselves and their family members who have comprehensive sickness insurance (CSI) (Article 7(1)(b));
  - o students who declare that they have sufficient resources to support themselves and their family members and have CSI (Article 7(1)(c));
  - o family members of the Union citizens referred to in Articles 7(1)(a)–(c) (Article 7(1)(d)). This would include children of migrant Union citizens.
- Article 16(1): a right of permanent residence after five years.
- Article 23: the right to take up employment or self-employment in the host State.

Workers therefore have the rights that Article 45 TFEU grants them, and also benefit from Directive 2004/38. In particular, Directive 2004/38 confirms that they may bring their family members with them when they move, even if the family members are not Union citizens.

9.15.1.2 Directive 2004/38: Family members of Union citizens

Family members of Union citizens who themselves are not Union citizens also benefit from Directive 2004/38. Article 2(2) of Directive 2004/38 provides that the following are family members:

- Article 2(2)(a): spouse;
- Article 2(2)(b): the Union citizen's registered partner if the legislation of the host Member State treats registered partnerships as equivalent to marriage;
- Article 2(2)(c): the direct descendants who are under the age of 21 or are dependants and those of the spouse or registered partner (eg children);
- Article 2(2)(d): the dependent direct relatives in the ascending line and those of the spouse or registered partner (eg parents).

Family members have the right to accompany the migrant Union citizens and have the following rights:

- Article 5(1): the right to enter the host State on production of their passport. The host State may require a visa, but this should be a formality (Article 5(2));
- Article 6(2): a right of residence of up to three months in the host State when accompanying or joining a Union citizen;
- Articles 7(2): a right of residence for more three months when accompanying or joining a Union citizen covered by Article 7(1)(a)–(c);
- Article 16(2): a right of permanent residence after five years.
- Article 23: the right to take up employment or self-employment in the host State.

The Union citizen has a primary right of residence, while the rights of family members are contingent on the Union citizen's rights.

Other family members, eg non-dependent children over 21 and parents, may benefit from Article 3(2) which provides that the host State must facilitate their entry and residence in accordance with its national legislation (Article 3(2)(b)). However, the rights granted by Article 3(2) are not as extensive as those granted to the family members that come within the scope of Article 2(2).

A partner of a Union citizen does not qualify as a family member. In *Netherlands State v Reed* (Case 59/ 85) [1986] ECR 1283, the ECJ ruled that the term 'spouse' did not cover non-marital relationships; thus the cohabitee of a migrant worker was not a 'family member' with rights of entry and residence. However, Article 3(2)(b) of Directive 2004/38 covers 'the partner with whom the Union citizen has a durable relationship, duly attested'. Although cohabitees are not 'family members' as defined in Article 2(2)(b), they do benefit from the lesser rights granted by Article 3(2).

9.15.1.3 Spouse: breakdown of relationship

Separation

In *Diatta v Land Berlin* (Case 267/83) [1985] ECR 567, a Senegalese national married to a French national working in Germany left him with the intention of obtaining a divorce. The German authorities sought to deport her, claiming she was no longer a true 'spouse' as she no longer lived with her husband. However, the ECJ ruled that the rights of a spouse are not dependent on their residing with the worker, and thus can terminate only if the worker leaves the host State.

If the worker leaves the host State, if the spouse is a Union citizen, they may be able to activate their own primary right of residence under Directive 2004/38, eg by finding a job. However, the situation of a spouse who is not a Union citizen is more precarious. Article 12(3) of Directive 2004/38 gives a spouse (or registered partner) who has custody of minor children in education a right to remain following the Union citizen's departure, but it is silent about the position where no children are involved. By implication, the spouse (or registered partner) therefore has no right to remain

Divorce

Prior to Directive 2004/38 there was no clear European authority as to whether deportation could follow divorce, but in *Baumbast v Secretary of State for the Home Department* (Case C-413/99) [2002] ECR I-7091 the mother of children was entitled to remain having been awarded custody. Directive 2004/38 provides for the spouse (or registered partner) to remain in the country if they have resided for three years, or if they have been awarded custody or access to children, or alternatively if the court considers that allowing them to remain is warranted in the circumstances.

9.15.2 How is nationality interpreted?

Nationality is entirely a matter for the domestic law of each Member State, which means that, inevitably, rules vary. In particular, not all Member States permit their nationals to hold dual nationality. One result of this was seen in *Micheletti v Delegacion del Gobierno en Cantabria* (Case C-369/90) [1992] ECR I-4238. The case concerned a dual national of Argentina and Italy who sought entry into Spain. Entry was refused because under Spanish law only the nationality of the State in which the person had last been habitually resident was recognised, and in this case that was Argentina. The ECJ found, however, that as he was an Italian national under Italian law, he was an EC (now EU) migrant worker protected by Article 48 of the EC Treaty (now Article 45 TFEU), so that entry into Spain could not be denied.

9.15.3 What rights of residence does the worker obtain under Article 45 TFEU?

The EU national worker has an absolute right of residence so long as they remain in work. If the worker becomes involuntarily unemployed, Directive 2004/38 will continue to guarantee them a right to reside in the host State. However, if they become voluntarily unemployed, their position is changed as (in accordance with most social security systems) they would be disqualified from social security benefits. Under Directive 2004/38, the worker has a right of residence simply by being a citizen of another Member State as long as they have sufficient resources not to be a burden on the host State, though they may need CSI. If a worker becomes permanently disabled or reaches retirement age, their right of residence continues under this Directive as well.

An individual can claim the rights of a worker as long as they are genuinely employed, even if their work is part time and obtained so that EU rights can be asserted, and even if the salary paid is below a minimum wage limit (*Levin v Staatssecretaris van Justitie* (Case 53/81) [1982] ECR 1035).

A period of five years' residence gives the worker and their family a right of permanent residence (see **9.15.1.1** and **9.15.1.2** above).

9.15.4 What terms of employment is an EU national entitled to expect?

An EU national can claim the same terms as those offered to a national of the host State. Article 45(2) TFEU expressly refers to the right not to be discriminated against as regards conditions of work. So, in the case *of Allué (Pilar) and Coonan (Mary Carmel) v Università degli Studi di Venezia* (Cases C-259/91, C-331/91 and C-332/91) [1993] ECR I-4309, an Italian law which provided that non-Italians who accepted jobs in Italy to teach a language could only enter into fixed-term contracts for one year was contrary to Article 48(2) of the EC Treaty (now Article 45(2) TFEU).

In addition, Article 7 of Regulation 492/2011 and Article 24 of Directive 2004/38 prohibit discrimination in relation to conditions of employment, dismissal, social and tax advantages, training and union membership.

9.15.5 What about their social security rights?

Social security rights are governed by Regulation 883/2004, which basically guarantees to EU nationals the social security benefits of the host State.

However, where the benefits are dependent on contributions, a worker's entitlement will take into account contributions to the equivalent benefit in their home State or other Member States in which they have worked. The Regulation does not provide for harmonisation of benefits or of levels of benefits throughout the Union.

9.15.6 Does an EU national have a right of entry to look for work?

Article 45 TFEU (or its predecessors) has been interpreted to mean that an EU national has a right of entry to look for work and a reasonable period of residence to find it. This is confirmed in Directive 2004/38, which grants a three month right of residence without qualifying as a worker. In the UK, the immigration rules used to allow such a person to be deported if they did not succeed in finding work after six months. The ECJ held this rule to be consistent with EU law in *R v Immigration Appeals Tribunal, ex p Antonissen* (Case C-292/89) [1991] ECR I-745, although it stressed that the job seeker might still have a right of residence if they had reasonable prospects of finding work. An EU national has a right to remain in the host State as an ordinary citizen if their resources are sufficient and they have CSI (Directive 2004/38).

9.15.7 When does the TFEU allow Member States to derogate?

9.15.7.1 Exclusion/expulsion

Article 45(3) TFEU permits derogations on grounds of public policy, public security and public health. Because these are derogations from one of the fundamental freedoms of the EU, the ECJ has interpreted them strictly. Further, Directive 2004/38 has made it clear that only personal conduct can be taken into account. Even prior criminal convictions will not necessarily entitle the Member State to deny entry. They will do so only where they indicate that the individual represents a current threat to public security. For example, in *Astrid Proll v Entry Clearance Officer* [1988] 2 CMLR 387, the former Baader Meinhoff terrorist was allowed entry into the UK because she did not represent a present threat.

The host State can refuse entry to family members only in those circumstances which allow it to refuse entry to the worker they are accompanying or joining.

9.15.7.2 Employment restrictions

Article 45(4) TFEU provides that the rights granted earlier in the Article do not apply to employment in the public service. This has been interpreted strictly by the ECJ in *Commission of European Communities v Belgium; Re Public Employees (No 1)* (Case 149/79) [1980] ECR 3881 to mean only 'posts involving the exercise of official authority and functions related to safeguarding the general interests of the State'.

9.15.8 Enforcement of rights

If an EU national or a family member is refused entry or residence rights by a Member State's immigration authorities, they will be allowed to invoke their EU rights before the appropriate immigration authority or court, or as a defence in criminal proceedings where deportation is being considered.

If an EU national believes that they have been discriminated against in relation to employment, they should follow the appropriate national procedure in the host State to obtain a suitable remedy, eg by suing their employer before an employment court or tribunal. It is important to remember that, to comply with EU law, such national procedure must not discriminate, even indirectly, against the EU national and must give an effective remedy for breach of EU law.

The following example illustrates the application of free movement rights.

Example

Agus has dual Dutch and Indonesian nationality. He has recently moved from the Netherlands to start a job in France. However, his French employer is unsure whether he has the right to work in France due to his Indonesian nationality.

Agus's daughter, Fleur, aged 18, is an Indonesian national and would like to join him and work in France. However, she has been informed by a friend that she needs CSI.

*As the Netherlands recognises that Agus is a Dutch citizen, he is a Union citizen notwithstanding his Indonesian nationality (*Micheletti*) and so he can rely on Article 45 TFEU to work in France. As a Union citizen, Agus has a right of residence in France for up to three months pursuant to Article 6(1) of Directive 2004/38. As he is a worker, he has a right of residence for more than three months pursuant to Article 7(1)(a). The French employer's concerns are therefore groundless.*

Fleur is a family member of Agus pursuant to Article 2(2)(c) of Directive 2004/38 – direct descendant under the age of 21. She has the right to join him for up to three months pursuant to Article 6(2) of Directive 2004/38. Additionally, Article 7(2) grants her a right of residence of more than three months as she is a family member of a migrant Union citizen working in France. She does not need CSI; the requirement for CSI only applies to students and persons of sufficient resources.

9.16 Citizens' rights in the UK

Under the terms of the Withdrawal Agreement, the UK Government has adopted the EU Settlement Scheme, requiring EU citizens resident in the UK to obtain pre-settled or settled status to retain their right to live in the UK. Failure to apply for pre-settled or settled status by the deadline results in the loss of the right to reside in the UK. The deadline was 30 June 2021, though may be extended if the applicant has a good reason.

Settled status is available to EU citizens who have been continuously resident in the UK for five years or more and very much equates to permanent residence.

Pre-settled status is available to EU citizens who have been resident in the UK for fewer than five years. It does not grant permanent residence, but allows the applicant to stay in the UK for a further five years from the date they obtained pre-settled status. EU citizens who have been granted pre-settled status may apply for settled status once they have been in the UK for five years, and initially the UK Government required them to do so before their pre-settled status expired; otherwise they would lose their right to reside in the UK. However, in *R (Independent Monitoring Authority for the Citizens' Rights Agreements) v Secretary of State for the Home Department*, the Administrative Court issued a declaration that the requirement to apply before the expiry of pre-settled status was unlawful, as it breached the Withdrawal Agreement. The High Court applied the direct effect of the Withdrawal Agreement in reaching this conclusion. Subsequently, in *AT v Secretary of State for Work and Pensions* [2023] EWCA Civ 1307, the Court of Appeal held that the Charter of Fundamental Rights applied to EU citizens with pre-settled status. EU citizens who fall within the scope of the Withdrawal Agreement are therefore able to rely on its provisions. Accordingly, the Secretary of State was required to take into account the claimant's fundamental rights (and the rights of her child) when making his decision whether to refuse her universal credit.

The judgment of the Northern Ireland Court of Appeal in *Re Dillon (Northern Ireland Troubles (Legacy and Reconciliation) Act 2023)* [2024] NICA 59 is also significant. The Northern Ireland Troubles (Legacy and Reconciliation Act) 2023 ('the Legacy Act') provided that criminal and civil investigations and inquests into events arising out of the Troubles should cease and be replaced with investigations carried out by a new body, the Independent Commission for Reconciliation and Information Recovery ('ICRIC'), which was given the power to grant conditional immunity for perpetrators who cooperate with it.

Re Dillon involved numerous grounds of challenge to the Legacy Act, but one of the grounds was that it breached the Victims' Directive (Directive 2012/29/EU of the European Parliament and of the Council of 25 October 2012 establishing minimum standards on the rights, support and protection of victims of crime, and replacing Council Framework Decision 2001/220/JHA). The Victims' Directive had been implemented into UK law, and hence Northern Ireland law. One of its key provisions is that victims must be able to review a decision not to prosecute, a right which would be infringed where the ICRIC granted immunity from prosecution under the Legacy Act. The Belfast/Good Friday Agreement of 1998 which ended the Troubles includes provisions protecting the rights of victims; the Victims' Directive gave effect to those provisions. The Northern Ireland Protocol (now known as the Windsor Framework), part of the Withdrawal Agreement agreed between the UK and EU, provides that there will be no diminution of such protections as a result of Brexit. The Northern Ireland Court of Appeal, invoking s 7A of the EUWA 2018, accordingly disapplied those parts of the Legacy Act that breached the Victims' Directive.

As well as a right of residence, settled and pre-settled status secures other rights such as the right to work, to access public services and not to be discriminated against on grounds of nationality. Whether the UK Government can expel a Union citizen with pre-settled or settled status depends on UK immigration law. Before IP completion day, the expulsion of Union citizens by UK authorities was covered by the EU rules outlined at **9.15.7.1**, but the Withdrawal Agreement makes it clear that national legislation now applies.

The issue of CSI has led to some debate as it was believed, on a strict interpretation of the Withdrawal Agreement, that students and persons of sufficient resources needed it to acquire settled or pre-settled status. The reason for this is that the right to reside granted by the Withdrawal Agreement depends on the applicant satisfying the conditions in Directive 2004/38 which requires students and persons of sufficient resources to have CSI.

This could have been particularly problematic for EU students as during the UK's membership of the EU they had access to the UK National Health Service in the same way as British citizens resident in the UK; hence they did not need to obtain CSI to access medical treatment. However, the UK Government waived the requirement for applicants under the EU Settlement Scheme to have CSI. Moreover, in March 2022 the ECJ ruled in *VI v Her Majesty's Revenue and Customs* (Case C-247/20) ECLI:EU:C:2022:177 that access to the NHS satisfied the requirement for CSI.

The following example considers the Withdrawal Agreement and citizens' rights.

Example

Lukasz, who is a Polish citizen, has been resident in the UK for over five years and applies for settled status. Under the terms of the Withdrawal Agreement governing the UK's exit from the EU, he is entitled to permanent residence in the UK. The Home Office rejects his application on the grounds that a section in an Act (fictitious) of the UK Parliament excludes a person in his position from settled status. The Act does not, however, attempt to override the Withdrawal Agreement.

Can Lars challenge the Home Office's refusal to grant him settled status?

Yes, he can. The EUWA 2018 provides for the Withdrawal Agreement, including the citizens' rights provisions, to have direct effect, so its provisions will override the conflicting UK statute. If the UK statute had expressly and unequivocally overridden the relevant provisions of the Withdrawal Agreement, then UK courts would have applied the statute. Parliament can legislate contrary to international treaties even though such legislation would breach international law, as Parliament is sovereign. However, the question indicates that is not the case.

Summary

In this chapter you have examined the concept of retained EU law/assimilated law. EU law pervaded into large parts of the UK legal system and repealing and replacing it prior to the UK's exit from the EU would have been impossible. The EUWA 2018 aimed to ensure legal continuity and a functioning statute post-exit by taking a snapshot of EU law as it existed in the UK at the end of the transition period (defined as IP completion day) and converting it into 'retained EU law', a novel type of law with its own characteristics.

REULA 2023 made some significant changes that came into effect on 1 January 2024. REULA 2023 renamed retained EU law as 'assimilated law' and made changes to its status.

Assimilated law

The two main categories of assimilated law are:

- EU-derived domestic legislation (secondary legislation and primary legislation enacted to implement the UK's EU obligations)
- Direct assimilated legislation (primarily EU Regulations and decisions)

Retained EU law kept a limited form of supremacy in that it prevailed over other legislation enacted pre-IP completion day. Conversely, legislation enacted after IP completion day prevailed over retained EU law. However, REULA 2023 ended the principle of supremacy from 1 January 2024.

Legislative powers

REULA 2023 gives relevant national authorities such as the UK Government and the devolved governments the power to reform secondary retained EU law and assimilated law by introducing secondary legislation to amend, revoke, restate and/or replace retained EU law and assimilated law. Ministers can reproduce the legal effects associated with retained EU law/assimilated law in restated EU law or assimilated law, including the effect of supremacy in relation to specific enactments. The restated law may include relevant case law from the CJEU.

The Withdrawal Agreement

Although the Withdrawal Agreement covers a range of issues relating to the UK's exit from the EU, it is the citizens' rights provisions that practising lawyers are most likely to encounter. The key point is that these provisions appear to have direct effect, and that means that EU citizens are able to rely on them in national courts should domestic UK legislation fail to protect their rights adequately.

Index

Note: Page numbers in *italics* and **bold** denote figures and tables, respectively.

J

L

M

N

O

P

T

U

W